WITHDRAWN

The Birth of Saudi Arabia

THE BIRTH OF SAUDI ARABIA

Britain and the Rise of the House of Sa'ud

GARY TROELLER
Senior Analyst, Batelle Institute, Frankfurt

FRANK CASS : LONDON

First published 1976 in Great Britain by
FRANK CASS AND COMPANY LIMITED
11 Gainsborough Road, London E11 1RS, England

and in United States of America by
FRANK CASS AND COMPANY LIMITED
c/o International Scholarly Book Services, Inc.
P.O. Box 555, Forest Grove, Oregon 97116

Copyright © 1976 G. TROELLER

ISBN 0 7146 3062 4

All Rights Reserved. No part of this publication may be reproduced in any form or by any means, electronic, mechanical, photocopying, recording or otherwise, without the prior permission of Frank Cass and Company Limited in writing.

DS
244
T73
1976

Made and printed in Great Britain by
The Garden City Press Limited
Letchworth, Hertfordshire SG6 1JS

For
*My Parents and Charles Crawley
and Professors Hinsley and Malone*

Contents

Preface	ix
Notes on Documentation and Transliteration	xiii
Abbreviations	xiv
Introduction	xv

Chapter I: **Perspective**   1
Anglo-Wahhabi relations in the nineteenth century and the rise of ibn Sa'ud

Chapter II: **The Pre-War Era: 1910 to 1914**   34
The first encounter—The seizure of Hasa: ibn Sa'ud reaches the coast

Chapter III: **Anglo-Sa'udi Relations during the First World War**   73
Ibn Sa'ud and Husain: a comparison in importance—The Anglo-Sa'udi Treaty—Summary—The Sa'udi wartime role: 1916 to 1918—The Great *Durbar* at Kuwait—The mission to ibn Sa'ud

Chapter IV: **The Khurma and Turaba Dispute**   127
The *Ikhwan*—Khurma—Turaba

Chapter V: **British Policy 1920 to 1922: Subsidies and Frontiers**   159
A question of subsidies—The end of Rashidi rule—The Najdi-Kuwaiti border dispute—The Najdi-Iraqi dispute

Chapter VI: **Conflict in the Wadi Sirhan and the Kuwait Conference: 1922 to 1924**   189
Jauf, Qaf and the Wadi Sirhan—Channel of communication—The Kuwait Conference

Chapter VII: **The Wahhabi Capture of the Hedjaz and the Conclusion of the Hadda and Bahra Agreements** 216
    The Invasion of the Hedjaz—Clayton's mission—The Wahhabi victory

    Postscript 236

    Conclusion 243

Appendices
I   Abbreviated Genealogy of the Al Sa'ud 247
II   The Turko-Sa'udi Treaty of 1914 248
III (Part 1) A Comparison of the Drafts of the Anglo-Sa'udi Treaty of 1915 250
    (Part 2) Anglo-Sa'udi Treaty of 1915 254
    Bibliography 257
    Index 271

Maps

1 Map of Arabia *circa* 1925 268
2 Tribal Map of Arabia 269

Preface

Today the name Sa'udi Arabia evokes images of desert wastes, limitless reservoirs of oil and economic might. When one thinks of the predominant foreign power concerned with the desert kingdom, one thinks of the United States. Forty years ago, oil had yet to be discovered, ibn Sa'ud had just unified the greater part of the Arabian Peninsula and Great Britain exercised paramount influence at the Sa'udi Court. This book deals with the drama of the immediate pre-oil era and sets the stage for the Sa'udi Arabia of today.

The following pages examine in detail the unification of Arabia and British policy towards ibn Sa'ud during the early twentieth century when he laid the foundations of present-day Sa'udi Arabia. It would be impossible to tell the story of the rise of ibn Sa'ud and exclude British dealings with him. During the period under consideration, and indeed throughout the nineteenth century owing to her predominant position in the Persian Gulf, Britain was the only Great Power to have regular dealings with the House of Sa'ud. The British have left behind an extensive record of Sa'udi history. The Sa'udis have not. There can be little doubt that British archival material is, and most probably will remain, the most important source for this period. Although dealing with ibn Sa'ud from the British vantage point, the writer hopes that his five years' residence in the Middle East, which almost equals the period of time spent in England preparing this book has enabled him to write with some degree of imaginative understanding about ibn Sa'ud. It should be noted in passing that H. St J. B. Philby, who has written exhaustively on the history of the Sa'udis using indigenous historical material, has pointed out the dearth of such sources, or even other reputable Arabic sources dealing with the Al Sa'ud in the twentieth century. Dr Derek Hopwood of St Antony's College, Oxford has expressed the same opinion in the introduction to his recent book, *The Arabian Peninsula*. As to general books in Arabic dealing with Arabia in this century, Professor Albert Hourani, Chairman of the Oriental Studies Faculty at Oxford, suggested to me a half dozen sources. However, as he predicted, a careful reading of these works revealed very little of real importance.

This book is based upon a doctoral dissertation which the writer completed at Cambridge University. If it therefore suffers from a somewhat Germanically exhaustive approach, it has at least benefited—as most dissertations do—from the careful scrutiny and guidance of various scholars.

Of those who have helped with advice and criticism over the years my first thanks go to my supervisor C. W. Crawley M.A., Emeritus Fellow and former Vice Master of Trinity Hall, Cambridge for his guidance, patience and kindness. F. H. Hinsley O.B.E., M.A., Professor in the History of International Relations at Cambridge, read several earlier drafts of this work and has been a continuous source of inspiration and encouragement. While editor of the *Historical Journal*, Professor Hinsley was kind enough to publish a section of my third chapter.

I should also like to thank Dr J. B. Kelly, formerly of the University of Wisconsin, who read and twice commented on an earlier version of this typescript. Professor B. C. Busch of Colgate University offered me advice when my research was at an embarrassingly early stage of development.

While at Cambridge I was fortunate to be given an Associate Membership of St Antony's College, Oxford from 1968 to 1970. For this opportunity to carry out research at Oxford one of my greatest debts goes to Professor Hourani, who read much of my typescript twice and saved me from many errors. Also at St Antony's I should like to thank Elizabeth Monroe as our convergent research interests proved beneficial to both of us.

Dr J. J. Malone, Adjunct Professor of History at the University of Pittsburgh, originally kindled my interest in British history while I was an undergraduate at the American University of Beirut. As hackneyed as it may sound I owe him more than I could ever repay. Also at the AUB my thanks go to Professors Zeine N. Zeine, Samir Seikaly and Malcolm Kerr (presently Chairman of the Political Science Department at UCLA) through whose courses I was introduced to modern Arab history and politics.

Of the many Arab friends who have helped in various ways I should especially like to acknowledge the profitable discussions I have had with Mr Assad al Faqieh, the former Sa'udi Ambassador in Washington and a personal friend of the late ibn Sa'ud.

Others who have helped along the way, and to them also, my thanks: Professor E. T. Stokes of St Catharine's College, Cambridge; Mr J. P. T. Bury, Corpus Christi College, Cambridge; Sir Reader Bullard; Professor P. M. Holt of London University; Dr and Mrs J. Israelaschvili (and Josephin) and Mr Bogdan Szykowski of the National University of Canberra; Hermann Hauser, M.A., and John Crawford, M.A. of Cambridge.

For the thankless task of typing and editing I should like to thank Rosemary Graham, Cila Tenenbaum and Lynne Swift. My thanks also go to Professor Dr Meinholf Dierkes, Director of the Division of applied Social and Behavioural Sciences at the Battelle Institute, Frankfurt, for encouragement and assistance in the final revisions of this work.

It goes without saying that thanking those who have helped is in no way to implicate them in the result.

My final thanks go to the following institutions for permission to quote: George Allen and Unwin Ltd from H. R. P. Dickson's *Kuwait and Her Neighbours*; The University of California Press from B. C. Busch's *Britain and the Persian Gulf, 1898–1914* and *Britain, India and the Arabs 1914–1921*; Faber and Faber from J. B. Kelly's *Eastern Arabian Frontiers*; and the Controller of Her Majesty's Stationery Office for permission to quote from Crown Copyright Records in the Public Records Office and from India Office Records. I should also like to thank the Middle East Centres at St Antony's College, Oxford and the University of Durham for access to their Private Papers Collections.

Notes on Documentation and Transliteration

For the sake of simplicity, Arabic words have been spelled without any diacritical marks. Throughout the book the Arabic letter *ain* has been represented by '. In general I have followed the spellings used by H. St J. B. Philby in *Sa'udi Arabia*. However, in certain instances I have chosen, with reference to well-known place-names, the more common renderings: for example, Hedjaz and Jedda instead of Philby's Hijaz and Jidda. Moreover, although Philby wrote 'Abdul-'Aziz ibn Sa'ud shortened to the popular version Ibn Sa'ud, I have used the more correct modern spelling of 'Abd al-'Aziz shortened to ibn Sa'ud.

In those few instances Turkish and Persian words are referred to I have used the spellings favoured at the time, e.g. Abdul Hamid for Abdülhamid.

Scholars of the Middle East are painfully aware of the plethora of variant spellings for the same Arabic word. As I have used a modern and simplified system of transliteration, the reader might encounter, for example, in a passage containing several direct quotations, the following spellings for the same word, viz., ibn Sa'ud, Ibn Sa'ud and Bin Saud. Obviously today's transliteration systems differ greatly from the many, not to say haphazard, systems employed by the British fifty to sixty years ago.

As regards documentation, although a despatch originating, for example, from Kuwait and coming to rest in the Foreign Office could easily suffer errors in transmission as it made its way via Bushire, Simla and the Indian Office, London, the chances are that such discrepancies would come to light during the course of the despatch's circulation. Many telegrams were also paraphrased to protect the code before being circulated and/or printed. In my experience, going through the Foreign, India and Colonial Office files—although encountering a welter of duplication—I have usually been able to locate those few instances when copies differed substantially from originals. In the interests of thoroughness I have usually used, or at least checked, the original hand-written drafts.

Abbreviations

LFI	Letters from India series (India Office Records)
HC	Home Correspondence series (India Office Records)
L/P & S/10	Political and Secret Department Subject Files (India Office Records)
IO	India Office
FO	Foreign Office
SSI	Secretary of State for India
GI	Government of India
CO	Colonial Office
SSC	Secretary of State for the Colonies
HCB	High Commissioner Baghdad
CCB	Civil Commissioner Baghdad
CPO	Chief Political Officer
Pol Res	Political Resident in the Persian Gulf
Pol Bagh. (or Pol/B.)	Political Department in Baghdad
BD	*British Documents on the Origins of the War, 1898–1914*, ed. by G. P. Gooch and Harold Temperley (London, 1926–1938)
T	Telegram
L	Letter
WO	War Office
CAB	Great Britain Public Record Office Cabinet Files

Introduction

In the brief space of sixteen years, from 1910 to 1926, 'Abd al-'Aziz ibn 'Abd al-Rahman Al Sa'ud rose from the position of an obscure tribal chief of a vanquished dynasty to become the acknowledged leader of most of the Arabian peninsula. At the head of Wahhabism, a militant, fundamentalist Islamic reform movement, he imposed his will on the majority of the traditionally individualistic and warlike shaikhs of Arabia, thus unifying the greater part of the peninsula. The last period in Islamic history which saw the unification of Arabia had been during the time of the great Arab conquests in the century following the death of Muhammad.

The period of concentration of this work is from 1910 to 1926, or from ibn Sa'ud's first contact with a British official until he captured the Hedjaz from the Hashimites, thus eliminating his chief rivals in Arabia. In the following year, the Sa'udi leader was recognised by Britain, the chief Great Power concerned with Arabia, as King of the Hedjaz, Najd and its Dependencies. These years witnessed the laying of the foundation for the present-day state of Sa'udi Arabia.

During the period under consideration, and indeed throughout the nineteenth century owing to her predominant position in the Persian Gulf, the British were the only European Power, aside from the Turks, to have contact with the House of Sa'ud. As will be seen in the following chapter, Britain first came into contact with the Sa'udis in the early nineteenth century when, fired by religious fervour, the Wahhabis [1] burst out of the inner fastnesses of central Arabia wreaking havoc on, among other places, the Arabian littoral of the Gulf. Consequent to the invasions, increased outbreaks of piracy in the Gulf prompted Britain to take stern measures to establish order on the Arabian coast of the Persian Gulf. After several punitive expeditions and the conclusion of many agreements, by mid-century the 'Pirate Coast' came to be known as the Trucial Coast. The latter owed its name to the truces arranged by the British between the various petty shaikhs of the littoral.

As the century progressed, British contacts with the Sa'udis were few, far between and largely indirect. This was due to several factors. First, after 1818, with the exception of several instances in Faisal's reign (1834–1838, 1843–1865), the Wahhabis did not constitute a threat to British interests. Secondly, owing to the economic unimportance of central Arabia, its inaccessibility and the reluctance of the British to get involved militarily in the forbidding interior, Britain pursued a policy of avoiding entanglement in central Arabian affairs. It was only in the twentieth century with the resurgence of Sa'udi power that Britain was forced, especially after the outbreak of World War I, to become directly involved with the Sa'udis.

Sa'udi history and British dealings with the Al Sa'ud in the first quarter of the twentieth century have received scant attention compared to other areas of the Middle East. Although many writers have devoted a section or a chapter or two to the rise of ibn Sa'ud and British relations with him, only H. St J. B. Philby has written extensively on this subject. It is indeed primarily through Philby's works that we know of ibn Sa'ud, his life and times. His many books, of which for our purposes the most significant are *Sa'udi Arabia, Arabian Jubilee, Arabia, Forty Years in the Wilderness, The Heart of Arabia*, and *Arabia of the Wahhabis*, are invaluable for first-hand accounts of the period dealt with here. It should be borne in mind, however, that with the exception of the two last-named works, Philby covers a much broader period than that presently under consideration. He, therefore, understandably skims the surface of events treated in the main body of this work. Moreover, although Philby has provided an important account of British relations with ibn Sa'ud, it will be seen that some of his judgements—and those of other writers basing their accounts largely upon his works—are greatly overdrawn.

Few would dispute Philby's importance as an explorer and an Arabist. Equally, few would ascribe to him the virtues of objectivity and the disinterested presentation of historical events. That Philby was captivated by ibn Sa'ud is obvious, even from the most cursory perusal of any of his many works. It should be noted, however, that Philby was not alone in his admiration for ibn Sa'ud. As will become evident in the following pages, ibn

Sa'ud's imposing character and stature as a leader were to impress virtually all who met him. Few, however, carried their admiration, as did Philby, nearly to the point of apotheosis. Indeed he makes no effort to conceal this admiration. That he was equally prejudiced against the British government's handling of ibn Sa'ud in particular and Arab affairs in general is also obvious from his writings and his subsequent career. Despite these qualifications, however, Philby's works will continue to be invaluable for a contemporary account of the sequence of events in Sa'udi Arabia.

It must be remembered that ibn Sa'ud's rise to power occurred during one of the most difficult periods in British history. Faced, prior to 1914, with the ever-growing threat of war, then with the holocaust itself, followed by the post-war period with its many problems both at home and abroad, British policy-makers naturally had far more pressing questions to consider than the fortunes of a distant desert shaikh. As our story unfolds, a recurrent theme will be the subordination of Anglo–Sa'udi relations first to the larger issue of Anglo–Ottoman relations and later to the question of Anglo–Hashimite relations.

The complications of British dealings with ibn Sa'ud are many and varied. It needs no great imagination to perceive the difficulties inherent in relations between, on the one hand, the most powerful empire in the world and, on the other, a desert ruler, albeit of genius, who had no personal experience of the world outside the confines of Arabia. And it should be emphasised that the Arabia of this period had changed little since the days of Muhammad. The society was tribal in structure, patriarchal in government and the economy was mainly a subsistence one. In the severe climate of central Arabia, the nomadic pastoral tribe and the oasis dweller lived in much the same way as they had for millennia. There were no fixed boundaries in the western sense. Almost every tribe claimed supremacy in a certain grazing area (*dirah*) which was marked primarily by the ownership of wells or, in some cases, of date palms. One tribe's area, however, often shaded into that claimed by another tribe and disputes were frequent.

In this traditional Islamic setting there was no separation betwen the realm of God and the realm of Caesar, or the realm of law and the realm of ethics. They were theocratically one. In Arabian society the most important community was the kinship group. The focus of power in this community was the shaikh who, within the limits prescribed by tribal custom and Islamic law (*shariʿa*) exercised considerable power. And in Arabia in the early part of the twentieth century this community was suffused with and reinforced by the spiritual force of the most conservative school of Islam. Under the leadership of a great shaikh such as ibn Saʿud, this Saʿudi–Wahhabi theocracy constituted a powerful means for expansion.

In view of the contrast between the world as Great Britain knew it and the traditional world of ibn Saʿud, the opportunities for misunderstandings on both sides and especially for affronts to Arab dignity were many. In addition there was also the factor of the physical distance and remoteness of Arabia from the centres of British policy-making. And if these centres were remote, so too, were the policy-makers. Officials in Delhi (and Simla) and London dealt with a country which almost none of them had ever seen and with issues which they had intellectually assessed from memoranda and despatches. Of course their decisions were determined by their view of Saʿudi developments as one part—and a marginal one at that—of the broader spectrum of international affairs and Middle Eastern developments. If any of these officials in London or India had more than a nodding acquaintance with Saʿudi issues their perspective was coloured, if not distorted, by seeing ibn Saʿud's rise against the background of Wahhabi excesses in the previous century. If 'men on the spot' sometimes exaggerated ibn Saʿud's importance and the threat he posed to British interests if he were not taken seriously, the higher officials, especially in London, tended to underestimate him. Moreover, owing to the elongated chain of command between London and eastern Arabia, by the time a decision had been reached on a particular issue or policy, its efficacy in action had often passed.[2]

In addition to the above-mentioned factors, Anglo–Saʿudi relations were complicated by the overlapping administrative jurisdiction of several British authorities concerned with Arabia. Until 1921 when the necessity for a co-ordinated Middle Eastern policy became so pressing that the Colonial Office took responsibility for Middle Eastern affairs, the Government of India, which could and did make foreign policy in its own right, had been traditionally responsible for Anglo–Saʿudi relations. In this century, however, with the resurgence of the Saʿudis in the context of Great Power interests in the Gulf and of Anglo–Ottoman relations, the Foreign Office became interested in ibn Sa'ud. The link between London and India was the Secretary of State for India and the India Office in Whitehall. It was the responsibility of the Secretary for India and his staff to interpret the Viceroy's views to the various departments of the Imperial government. Each of the three authorities directly concerned with Arabia, the Foreign and India Offices and the Government of India understandably viewed Sa'udi issues from the standpoint of its interests in the Gulf while in London the Foreign and India Offices, especially the former, emphasised the international aspect.

Although the Foreign Office came increasingly to call the tune in Anglo–Sa'udi relations, the power of the Secretary of State for India and the Viceroy in India should not be overlooked. As the Mesopotamia Commission reported in 1917: 'The powers of the Secretary of State for India are immense, greatly exceeding those exercised by any ordinary Secretary of State. So far as finance and expenditure are concerned, the Council [Council of India through which the Secretary for India acted in consultation] stands to the Secretary of State For India in much the same relation as that in which Parliament stands to the other Secretaries of State.'[3] As a Cabinet Minister he was responsible to Parliament, however, ' he was neither in theory or practice responsible to parliament for the day-to-day administration of the Indian Empire '.[4] This was the responsibility of the Viceroy, and administration also meant making foreign policy.[5] The Viceroy was chiefly responsible for defending the interests of India and it was not unusual for him to oppose strongly the home government. ' It was almost inevitable that the Government of India's views should differ from those entertained at home. Its first responsibility was the defence and security of India, and it naturally regarded these as the first claim on British resources and as the prior consideration in the formation of British policy.'[6] In view of the foregoing it is not difficult to see why the increasing dominance of the Foreign Office in Anglo–Sa'udi relations was resented by both the India Office and, especially, the Government of India.

Although British policy towards ibn Sa'ud came increasingly to be made in Whitehall, the ' Sa'udi issue ' was largely a departmental concern. Anglo–Sa'udi relations, save on a few occasions, were not important enough to be discussed by the Cabinet. Nor were they affected by changes of government. In the formation of British policy towards ibn Sa'ud, the role of the permanent under-secretary and senior clerk is much in evidence.[7] Officials such as Alwyn Parker at the Foreign Office and Arthur Hirtzel at the India Office will be seen to have played an important part in Anglo–Sa'udi relations. On more than one occasion, however, while the higher authorities were fighting over the proper policy to be pursued, the Indian government's Political Resident and Agents in the Persian Gulf were forced to deal with the exigencies of ibn Sa'ud's increasing power. And owing to Arabia's remoteness and the extended chain of command there was ample opportunity for powerful personalities such as Sir Percy Cox, Sir Arnold Wilson, and Philby to make their presence felt.

As the twentieth century progressed, British relations with ibn Sa'ud became inextricably blended with the higher issues of international diplomacy. The first instance of this merging of the particular with the general problems of British diplomacy occurred when from 1911 to 1913 Britain sought to settle the outstanding questions between herself and Turkey. These questions centred primarily on the German-backed Baghdad Railway and its possible extension to the head of the Persian Gulf. The Government of India emphasised the potential danger of ibn Sa'ud's impact on the Hasa, Qatar and Trucial Coasts should his constant requests for an agreement with the British be ignored. The Foreign Office chose to view ibn Sa'ud as a rebel against his rightful suzerain, the Ottoman government, if not as an irritant to Anglo–Turkish relations. The Foreign Office naturally discounted the Sa'udi issue when compared with the vital importance of settling questions which could lead to a general conflagration. In this case, as during the War, and in some respects even until 1926, London conflicted with New Delhi. The former attached primary importance to the Hashimites while the latter stressed the ramifications of Sa'udi power and militancy on the maritime peace in the Gulf and the effect on Indian Moslems if the Wahhabis were to overrun Mecca and Medina.

In addition to the usual factors involved in the formation of policy—economic, political, strategic, and local, and international considerations, not to mention the less tangible but important factors of personality and public opinion—inter-office rivalry played a major role in Anglo–Sa'udi relations. Indeed for much of the period, owing to divided control of the Middle East, British policy was inconsistent, confused and hotly contested within. In the following pages, wherever possible, the particular responsibility for a line of policy will be assigned to the proper individuals or authority concerned.

Before turning to the main themes of this work, several limitations must be outlined. First, it is not intended to give accounts of either the internal developments or the history of Arabia proper or it neighbours, although reference will be made to both factors when it serves to elucidate British policy. Secondly, during this period the question of oil did not really arise.

Detailed consideration, then, has been devoted to an account of the rise of ibn Sa'ud and to British policy and the factors which determined that policy primarily from 1910 to 1926. The period has been divided generally into sections dealing with the pre-war years, British war-time policy, the Khurma and Turaba dispute, Sa'udi expansionism and territorial disputes, British attempts to solve the problems between their protégés, and, lastly, the siege of Jedda culminating in the conquest of the Hedjaz.

Before any of these issues can be dealt with, however, it is necessary to give a brief account of the kind of world in which Britain began her negotiations with ibn Sa'ud. Anglo–Sa'udi relations will thus be placed in their proper context, and the range and nature of British interests in the Persian Gulf where the Sa'udi resurgence first made its presence felt will emerge. Also, a brief summary of Anglo–Wahhabi relations in the nineteenth century may enable the reader better to appreciate the historical experience which conditioned Anglo–Sa'udi relations in the twentieth century.

Notes

1. During the nineteenth century the Sa'udis and their followers were referred to as Wahhabis.
2. Communications concerning ibn Sa'ud made their way to the Foreign Office via Bahrain, Bushire, New Delhi and the India Office, and back again the same way. As there was no British representative in eastern Arabia the Indian government's Political Agent in Bahrain was the official who was in the most immediate contact with ibn Sa'ud.
3. *Report of the Mesopotamia Commission* (Cmd. 8610), p. 101. Quoted in M. Beloff, *Imperial Sunset, Britain's Liberal Empire, 1897–1921*, Vol. 1 (London, 1969), p. 35. Hereafter *Beloff*.
4. *Beloff*, p. 34.

5. As Beloff notes (p. 37) 'the British presence in the Far East had come about through a process of expansion dictated largely by Indian interests'. The same can be said about the British position in the Persian Gulf, again the work and responsibility of the Government of India.
6. *Ibid.*, pp. 35, 36.
7. Dr Z. Steiner in her *The Foreign Office and Foreign Policy 1898–1914* (Cambridge, 1969) has indicated the increasing importance, especially after 1905, of the permanent under-secretary and senior clerk as advisors as well as administrators. The role of similar officials in the India Office was of equal importance.

CHAPTER I

Perspective

Throughout the greater part of the nineteenth century, Britain enjoyed in the Persian Gulf a position of unchallenged political paramountcy. Although in theory the Gulf was an international waterway, in practice it was a 'British Lake'.[1] In an area and a period where a great seapower could exercise a predominant role, Britain reigned supreme. As will be seen, it was not until the last decade of the nineteenth century that her position in the Persian Gulf came to be contested. In the 1890s Britain suffered successive challenges from France, Russia and Germany. These intrusions by the Great Powers were complemented by Turkish efforts, which were a manifestation of a general policy of consolidation in the Ottoman Empire, to assert their shadowy authority in Kuwait and along the northern part of the Arabian littoral.[2]

Just before the Persian Gulf became the scene of international rivalry at the close of the nineteenth century, this British sphere of influence was comparatively peaceful. During the previous ninety years the British 'Raj' had imposed a maritime truce on the Arabian coast through the suppression of piracy. The British authorities in India had also suppressed slave-trade and arms traffic in the Gulf. In addition they had surveyed the shores, sounded the channels and, above all, acquired a near monopoly in the Gulf's commerce.[3]

To those acquainted with British imperial history it will be obvious that it was primarily with regard to India that the Persian Gulf was of vital importance. Throughout the nineteenth century, British policy in the Persian Gulf had been motivated by two considerations: (1) to protect the flank of the route to India and (2) to maintain peace in the Gulf, promoting her trade there and denying other Powers access to this British preserve.

Strategically, the Gulf's importance to India is self-evident. Moreover British telegraphic communications with India ran through the Gulf. And as Lord Curzon, Viceroy of India from 1898 to 1905, and one of the most eloquent and consistent exponents of the importance of Persia and the Persian Gulf to Indian defence [4] pointed out, 30% of the traffic on these lines was Australasian; thus these cables—and for that matter the Gulf itself—were of imperial and not only Indian importance.[5]

Commercially, the Persian Gulf was also of significance to Great Britain. By the late nineteenth century her earlier near-monopoly in the Gulf trade had become even more complete. In the triennial period 1895–6–7 over 80% of the area's entire export trade was with British possessions. Moreover in the same period ' out of a total of 2,161 steamers which entered and cleared from the Gulf ports, 2,039 were British, and their tonnage represented 84 per cent of the total tonnage '.[6] At the head of the Gulf the carrying trade between Basra and Baghdad was monopolised by the British Lynch Company.

In addition to strategic and commercial considerations it is important to note the legal and historical basis of the British Gulf position.[7] In the first half of the nineteenth century, the British, in the course of imposing the maritime peace on what had been known as the Pirate Coast, had extracted treaties from the Arab tribes of the coast which stipulated that all disputes had to be referred to the chief British officer in the Gulf, the Political Resident stationed in the Persian port of Bushire. By 1892, primarily in response to Turkish pressure, Britain had added non-alienation bonds to her original treaties with the Trucial Shaikhdoms, Bahrain and Muscat. ' The texts of these new assurances were all alike and obliged the respective rulers not to enter into agreement or correspondence with any power other than Britain, not to consent to the residence within their territory of an agent of any other government, except with British permission, and not to cede, sell, or mortgage any part of their territory to anyone but the British Government.' [8]

It is clear, therefore, that in the Persian Gulf Britain had a sphere of influence of multi-faceted dimensions—both in the importance of the area and in the complexities involved. Issues of imperial and Indian defence, Anglo–Ottoman relations, commerce, and local Gulf policy were all inter-related in the area. To complicate matters still further, and perhaps as a reflection of the diversity and complexity of the issues involved, British administrative jurisdiction of Gulf affairs was divided between the Government of India and the Foreign Office.

The principal British official in the Gulf was the Political

Resident. This officer held the title of 'His Britannic Majesty's Political Resident in the Persian Gulf and Consul-General for Fars and Khuzistan'. He was appointed by the Government of India and was a member of the Indian Political Service. In the words of one writer these officers (usually of Colonel's rank) were 'picked men picked from picked men'.[9] As is obvious from his title, this Indian officer had several functions. As Political Resident he was responsible to the Foreign Department of the Government of India and answerable to that authority for dealings with the Arabian side of the Gulf. As Consul-General the Resident was responsible to the British Minister in Teheran who was under the jurisdiction of the Foreign Office. This complicated situation of overlapping administration and confused jurisdictional responsibility also applied to the various Political Agents in the Gulf who were subordinate to the Resident. On the Persian side of the Gulf, Consuls in ports and cities were members of the Indian Political Service and responsible to the Government of India as Political Agents. Of course in their consular capacity they were answerable ultimately to Whitehall. On the Arabian side of the Gulf, Political Agents who by 1910 were stationed at Muscat, Kuwait and Bahrain were members of the Indian Political Service and subordinate to the Resident. With the exception of the British Official in the Sultanate of Muscat and Oman, the officers on the Arabian littoral were not consuls.[10]

The administrative anomalies prevailing in the Gulf were complemented by a similar situation at the head of the Gulf. In Baghdad, another Resident was stationed who enjoyed equal status with the Resident of Bushire. Subordinate to this official was a Consul in Basra. Although the Resident in Baghdad and (until 1898) the Consul in Basra were usually members of the Indian Political Service, they reported to London through the British Ambassador in Constantinople. With so many authorities reporting from the Gulf area, conflicting responsibility and interests were often complemented by conflicting information. Moreover an elongated, and obviously a rather tangled, chain of command influenced the formulation and execution of Gulf policy.[11]

This pattern of divided and overlapping administrative responsibility resulted in an inevitable clash between the two policy-making centres of the British Empire: the Government of India and the Imperial Government in London. Increasingly in the late nineteenth and in the twentieth century, British policy in the Gulf was the source of friction between these two authorities. This inter-office rivalry indeed constitutes one of the predominant themes of the period under consideration. India, of course, viewed the areas as vital to its defence, while London, stressing the broader plane of international relations, viewed the Persian Gulf as just another area requiring attention.

To add further to the complexities in the Gulf already described there was the issue, and many times a rather heated one at that, of financial responsibility in the area. Generally the Government of India bore the burden of expense for the establishments in the Persian Gulf. However, as the area was drawn into the vortex of international rivalries and subsequently became important to London, the Government of India was naturally reluctant 'to provide funds for an area in which control of policy formation was increasingly in the hands of the Home government'.[12]

The development of Great Power rivalries in the Gulf was of course a manifestation of the larger picture of rising colonial antagonisms in Asia, Africa and the Middle East and the growing sense of insecurity which began to pervade the major governments of Europe in the last decade of the nineteenth century. In 1890, the impetuous, sabre-rattling William II replaced the great Bismarck as the chief architect of German foreign policy and set Germany on her new course in quest of a 'place in the sun'. In 1891, marking a turning point in European history, revolutonary France and autocratic Russia failing to find other allies were forced together and agreed to act in concert if the peace were threatened. As one historian ironically described it : 'Both made a sacrifice of their principles and traditions. The autocrat of all the Russias stood to attention for the Marseillaise; and that hymn of revolutionary nationalism was played in honour of the oppressor of the Poles'.[13]

In 1894 this Franco-Russian agreement became a formal alliance. This greatly threatened Britain's position in the Mediterranean. She could not defend Constantinople against a possible Russian attack without concentrating a large proportion of her fleet in the eastern Mediterranean. Such a concentration would risk the escape of the French squadron at Toulon into the English Channel.[14] As has been well said, close co-operation between France and Russia in the Gulf was a 'missed opportunity'.[15]

Nevertheless, intrusions by both these Powers were sufficiently alarming to prompt Britain into tightening her hold over the Gulf. Although the issues of French, Russian, German and Ottoman attempts to increase their power in the Gulf were overlapping, it is convenient to describe first the French and Russian intrusions as these countries ceased to be threats; by 1904 in the case of France, and by 1907 in the case of Russia. The Germans, especially with their Baghdad Railway programme, and the Turks, with their expansionist (or consolidationist) policy, were to discomfit Britain until 1914.

Between 1890 and the conclusion of the Entente Cordiale in 1904, Anglo–French relations clashed over Muscat. The three major confrontations during this period occurred over French attempts to establish a coaling station in 1899; over the practice of granting French flags to Omanis from 1900 to 1905; and over the issue of the arms trade and the French involvement therein.[16] The establishment of a coaling station threatened Britain's strategic position in the Gulf and the Indian Ocean. The question of the flags undermined the British policy of suppressing slavery as the French issued flags to Omani slaving vessels. The French involvement in the arms trade also conflicted with the British Gulf policy. Both Britain and France enjoyed positions of influence in Muscat, but Britain certainly held the predominant one.[17] However while France constituted 'the more overt physical challenge'[18] in the Gulf during this period it was Russia whom the British feared the most. As one writer has emphasised: 'the entire British outlook at this period of Asian affairs was coloured by the Russian menace'.[19]

For much of the nineteenth century, Britain viewed Russia as the chief threat to the Gulf. Russia's eastern expansion, coupled with her pressure on Persia and her traditional quest for a warm-water port, exercised especially the British in India. In 1895 the visit of a Russian surveyor to Hormuz was thought important enough by one leading authority to be described as the first 'attack on the political predominance of Britain in the Persian Gulf'.[20] In December 1897 there were rumours that Russia desired a coaling station in the Kuwait area.[21] And by the middle of 1898 it was learned that the nephew of the Russian Ambassador to Vienna, Count Vladimir Kapnist, was seeking a concession from the Porte to construct a railway from Tripoli in Syria to Kuwait.[22] Although the Kapnist scheme came to nothing, Russian interest in a possible railway continued, especially after the turn of the century when among other advantages such a line would have served to counterbalance Germany's Baghdad Railway.[23]

The Russian threat to the Gulf at this point was all the more important because it coincided with a general deterioration in Britain's diplomatic position in the world. By the turn of the century, Britain's traditional policy of 'splendid isolation' seemed less splendid than ever. In late 1898 she had estranged France over Fashoda and in the following year embarked upon the unpopular Boer War. The conflict in South Africa irritated Anglo–German relations and occupied much of the British army. It also served to illustrate the weakness of the British army as it took three years to suppress the rebellion. Furthermore, through her treatment of the Boers, whom many saw as a valiant little people struggling for their independence, she outraged public opinion in many European capitals. It was in this context that Britain defended her Gulf position.[24]

In February 1900, the Russian ship *Gilyak* visited the Persian port of Bandar Abbas and its commander was reported to have requested a coaling station from the local Persian governor.[25] Although the incident proved to be of no consequence, the British reaction was feverish. Again in 1903 the Russians alarmed the British, this time in the form of a joint Russo–French visit to Kuwait. As will be seen, the Russian consul at Bushire had an interview with ibn Sa'ud in the course of the visit. However, despite British fears of Russia, by 1907 a combination of factors, significant among which were Russia's defeat in the Russo–Japanese War (1904–1905) and near-revolution at home, culminated in the Anglo–Russian Agreement. The importance of this agreement for our purposes was the designation of south Persia and, hence the Persian Gulf, as a British sphere of influence. Three years earlier, Russia's ally France through the Anglo–French Agreement had also ceased to be a threat in the Gulf. But the threat of German and Turkish activities in the Gulf remained and was to occupy British attention until the outbreak of World War I.

After Salisbury's return to power in 1895, it could be said that a significant change took place in the traditional British attitude towards the Ottoman Empire. Against the background of, among other factors, Great Power rivalries, the switch of the British centre of gravity in the eastern Mediterranean from Constantinople to Egypt, the rise of German influence at the Porte and the failure of Turkish reforms,[26] Salisbury suggested the partition of the Ottoman Empire. Ever since the days of Pitt, British policy towards the Ottoman Empire had been governed by the principle of preserving Turkish integrity in order to maintain the balance of power in Europe, safeguard the British position in the eastern Mediterranean and principally to protect the British routes to the East. After throwing out hints at something akin to partition in 1895,[27] in 1898 Salisbury contemplated ' " a division of preponderance " in the Far and Middle East, a division which would give Arabia and the Tigris-Euphrates basin (and the Gulf by implication) to Britain '.[28]

As remarked earlier, Ottoman attempts to assert their power along the northern coast of the Arabian littoral had precipitated Britain's decision to obtain non-alienation bonds from Bahrain and the Trucial Shaikhdoms.[29] But at this point the British were primarily concerned with increased Turkish activity in Kuwait and the Hasa-Qatar area. This is important, as will be seen in the following section, because British relations with the Turks and the Sa'udis before 1910 largely depended upon the maintenance of the maritime peace in the Gulf, especially along the Hasa and Qatar coast.

The Wahhabis first overran Hasa and Qatar in the first decade of the nineteenth centnry. By 1871, Turkish authority under the famous Midhat Pasha had replaced Wahhabi influence in these areas. Although Turkish authority here was less than imposing, the Porte did maintain garrisons in Hasa and Qatar. In the 1890s the Sultan's attempts to activate the Turkish position in Qatar clashed with British interests. The Government of India feared that any development of the Turkish position in Qatar would threaten their position along the Trucial coast. Furthermore, Bahrain had important connections with Qatar and, in turn, British interests in Bahrain were extensive.[30] In 1893 the British notified the Porte that she recognised Turkish sovereignty as extending from Basra to Qatif but that the coast south of this point was ' debatable land '.[31] Events were further complicated by the revolt against Turkey of the ruler of Qatar, Qasim ibn Thani who held the Turkish Office of *Qaimaqam* (district governor).[32] He also applied to the British for dependency status.[33] As will be seen in the following pages his predisposition to the British was not uncommon among the Arab shaikhs on the coast and in the interior of Arabia. British concern for Qatar and repeated Turkish pressure in the peninsula were to continue until the outbreak of war. Much the same was true of the more important area of Kuwait.

Until the mid-1890s the status of Kuwait did not pose any problem for Britain. This Shaikhdom at the head of the Persian Gulf was recognised as being under nominal Turkish jurisdiction. In 1896, however, internal Kuwaiti developments, coupled (especially after 1900) with the growing importance of the area as a possible terminus for the Baghdad Railway, propelled this sleepy Shaikhdom into the maelstrom of international diplomacy. For the purposes of this work the chief significance of Kuwait was in its association with the fortunes of the House of Sa'ud. This story, however, will be dealt with more appropriately at a later stage.

In 1896, the redoubtable Shaikh Mubarak al Sabah came to power in Kuwait after killing his brother.[34] In Constantinople it was reported that the Turkish government was convinced that the British Resident in the Gulf had instigated the murder.[35] Shortly after Mubarak's accession, outbreaks of piracy in the Shatt al-Arab, for which the British Resident in Baghdad believed the shaikh responsible, raised the question of Kuwait's status.[36] The Resident in Baghdad wanted the British Ambassador in Constantinople, Sir Philip Currie, to address the Porte on the issue of retribution. Given the prevailing atmosphere of Anglo–Turkish hostility the Ambassador was hesitant about giving the Turks any pretext to consolidate their hold in the Gulf. He declined to petition the Porte, stating that ' the Shaikh in question is in reality an independent potentate and only nominally subject to the Sultan '.[37]

Of course Mubarak, an exceptionally shrewd and able ruler, was not unaware of the gains to be made by playing off the British against the Turks. He also feared the tightening of Turkish control in Kuwait and vengeful relatives who, with Turkish connivance, had threatened him on more than one occasion. Mubarak accordingly made overtures to the British Consul at Basra ' hinting that some sort of protectorate relationship might prove convenient '.[38] At this point, however, Turkish suspicions coupled with the many indications that Kuwait, despite its *de facto* independence, was *de jure* under Ottoman jurisdiction, prevented Britain from recognising Mubarak's independence.[39]

Over the next few years increased Turkish pressure on Kuwait, taken with Great Power interest in the area in the context of railway schemes moved Britain to enter into closer, if secret, relations with Kuwait.

In 1899, the British obtained a secret bond from the Kuwaiti Shaikh similar to those obtained a decade earlier with Bahrain, the Trucial Shaikhs and Muscat.[40] The impetus for British action was provided by a rumour in Constantinople that the Kapnist railway scheme had received the support of Count Witte, the powerful Russian Finance Minister.[41] The Kapnist scheme, as already noted, came to nothing but it did cause some anxiety to the British at the time. Concurrent with the Russian threat were Turkish attempts to assert their power in Kuwait. In September 1899, the Porte was warned against translating its vague suzerainty into anything more concrete.[42] With few exceptions they ceased to worry the British until 1901. In that year Mubarak's troubles with the Turks stemmed from events in the interior of north-eastern Arabia which involved the fortunes of the House of Sa'ud.[43] But British anxiety over Kuwait was not only concerned with Turkish ambitions; the larger issue of the Baghdad Railway with its projected terminus at Kuwait was far more important.[44]

In January 1900, the German Consul-General in Constantinople, von Stemrich, visited Kuwait. His object was to survey the possibilities of Kuwait as a terminus for the Baghdad Railway. While in Basra, von Stemrich told Wratislaw, the British Consul, ' that the location of the terminus was a problem to be settled directly with the Sultan; should Kuwait be chosen Mubarak—to say nothing of Britain—would be bypassed '.[45] The effect of this visit was not lost on the British in view of its many-faceted implications. Firstly, there was the nebulous status of Kuwait. Scondly, there was the factor of the non-alienation bond. Thirdly, there were the strategic advantages that the line would give to the Porte in enabling it to transport troops rapidly to, among other parts of the Empire, the head of the Persian Gulf. Finally, there were the strategic, commercial and political advantages that this railway would give the Ottoman Empire in the Persian Gulf.

The British, although concerned about the project, held several good cards in their hand. Despite the awkwardness which might have ensued had the secret bond been made an issue, they at least had a strong hold over Mubarak's freedom of action. Furthermore, in order to find money for the Baghdad Railway the Porte, whose financial position was always precarious, needed to increase her customs dues. Since the Sultan could not do this without the consent of the Ottoman Public Debt Administration, Britain, as a member of this authority, held the power to veto the construction of the railway.

At this point the Foreign Office was basically favourable to the railway. It would have provided an alternative route to the East and would have benefited commerce. In fact until 1903 negotiations for possible British participation in the project were carried on. In 1901 the Turks made another effort to assert their authority before the conclusion of the railway agreement with Germany. The Turkish warship *Zuhaff* sailed into Kuwait only to be informed by the commander of HMS *Perseus* that he could not permit the landing of Turkish troops.[46] The Turks and the Germans protested to London. Furthermore the Turks indicated that they knew of the non-alienation bond and that it could have no validity for an Ottoman subject. The end result of this affair was a pledge by Germany, Turkey and Britain to respect the *status quo* in Kuwait and a promise by the Porte not to attack the Shaikhdom.[47] It should be noted that a pledge to defend the *status quo* as unprecisely defined as that of Kuwait was singularly dangerous. What one party considered a defence could be viewed by another party as a violation.[48] After 1902, attempts by the Turks to assert their power in Kuwait took two forms. First they tried to extend their military power over the area between Basra and Kuwait and, second, they exerted legal pressure on Mubarak's substantial date holdings in the Fao area. This pressure continued until 1914.[49]

As mentioned above, British participation in the Baghdad Railway project was a possibility until 1903. In that year, however, as agreement on the extent of the British share of the financing was nearing completion, a massive attack on participation was mounted in the British press.[50] This attack was prompted largely by the growing hostility in England towards Germany. At the same time, British companies with vested interests in the East brought pressure to bear on Downing Street. In the light of this outcry, the British government decided to withdraw its support for participation. Although the Baghdad Railway was never to reach the Gulf, Anglo–Turkish and Anglo–German relations were coloured by this issue until 1914. A. J. Balfour the Prime Minister (1902–1905) and Lansdowne had both favoured British participation. The latter felt that the development of this line without British participation would constitute a ' national misfortune '.⁵¹ He added in a private letter to Curzon that Britain ' might have pulled off a great stroke by achieving internationalization of the line. That would have meant in turn, the end of Gulf questions for years to come.' ⁵²

In view of the collapse of the Baghdad Railway negotiations and continued Russian pressure for a base in the Gulf, the British government finally decided to make a clear declaration of its policy. On May 5, 1903 in the House of Lords Lansdowne made his famous statement on the British position in the Persian Gulf.

> ... I say it without hesitation—we should regard the establishment of a naval base, or a fortified port in the Persian Gulf by any other Power as a very grave menace to British interests, and we should certainly resist it with all means at our disposal.⁵³

To further underline British pre-eminence in this sphere in November 1903 Lord Curzon embarked on a personal visit to the Gulf. In the full panoply of viceregal grandeur—for which his grandiloquent and imperious manner were so eminently suited—Curzon toured the Gulf. Aboard the RIMS *Hardinge* Curzon was escorted by a flotilla that was the largest seen in the Gulf since that of Albuquerque in 1515.⁵⁴ Included among his fleet was the first-class cruiser *Argonaut*, the ' largest ship to visit the Gulf before World War I '.⁵⁵

In one ringing speech during his tour he defended the British position in a style characteristic of the era of the White Man's Burden.

> The history of your states ... is the answer. We were here before any other Power.... We found strife and we have created order.... The great Empire of India, which it is our duty to defend, lies almost at your gate.... We are not going to throw away this century of costly and triumphant enterprise; we shall not wipe out the most unselfish page in history. The peace of these waters must still be maintained; your independence will continue to be upheld; and the British Government must remain supreme.⁵⁶

With Lansdowne's declaration and ' Curzon's prancings in the Persian puddle ' [57]—as the former described the latter's tour—the British dramatically and publicly asserted their intention to retain their paramount position in the Gulf. Russia and Germany specifically, and France and Turkey by implication, had been warned. As one author puts it : ' Now having issued a clear warning in general and made its position on Kuwait known in particular, Britain began a slightly more forward policy (or perhaps a drift away from the *status quo*), which was pushed in the Gulf by Curzon and Gulf subordinates to the limit of Home approval, and sometimes beyond '.[58] As will become evident in the substance of this work the extension of Gulf policy to the limit and sometimes beyond that which the Home government approved was a practice not only characteristic of Curzon's Viceroyalty.

In 1902, Britain ended her traditional policy of isolation and entered into an alliance with Japan. In 1904 and 1907 agreements with France and Russia eliminated these two Powers as serious threats to Britain in the Gulf. From Lord Curzon's resignation as the Viceroy in 1905, until 1910, when our detailed study begins, Britain was not seriously challenged in the Gulf. Although the Turks continually irritated the British by piecemeal attempts to extend their authority in Kuwait, they constituted no real threat. Moreover in 1908 the Young Turk Revolution and the unsuccessful counter-revolution the following year, combined with Bulgaria's proclamation of independence and Austria's annexation of Bosnia–Herzegovina, fully occupied Turkish attention. These events also disturbed Anglo–German negotiations on the Baghdad Railway. After the collapse of the plan for participation in financing the entire line, Britain determined upon controlling the line's southernmost section. British negotiations with Germany on this basis continued until 1914.

It is clear from the preceding pages that any threat to Britain's position in the Gulf produced tremors in Whitehall as well as in India. Among the many problems Britain had to contend with in the Gulf in the first decade of the twentieth century was the rapid rise of the young Sa'ud exile ibn Sa'ud. She could not ignore his growing ascendancy in Najd, or Mubarak's support of him in the context of Anglo–Ottoman relations. Moreover, in view of Wahhabi depredations on the coast of the Arabian littoral at the beginning of the last century there was also the fear that the Sa'udi revival might threaten the maritime peace.

Anglo–Wahhabi Relations in the Nineteenth Century and the Rise of ibn Sa'ud

Before dealing with ibn Sa'ud's early exploits and contacts with the British, we must touch briefly on the rise of Wahhabism and those aspects of nineteenth-century Anglo–Wahhabi relations and Sa'udi history which form an important background for the understanding of events during our period.[59]

The modern history of Sa'udi Arabia began in the mid-eighteenth century with the alliance between Muhammad ibn 'Abd al-Wahhab (1703–1787)[60] and Muhammad ibn Sa'ud (d. 1765).[61] The former was the founder of the Wahhabi or Unitarian movement; the latter was the son of the founder of the Sa'udi dynasty and the ruler of a small district surrounding the town of Dar'iya in central Arabia.

Muhammad ibn 'Abd al-Wahhab (hereafter ibn 'Abd al-Wahhab), born in 'Ayaina in Najd, was a fervent teacher of the Hanbali school of Islamic jurisprudence as interpreted by Taqi al-Din Ahmad ibn Taimiya, the great theologian and jurist of the fourteenth century. In brief, 'Abd al-Wahhab urged Moslems to return to the simple and pure ways of the early period of Islam. He attacked innovation and condemned luxury and the worship of saints.

In 1745, Muhammad ibn Sa'ud, with whom 'Abd al-Wahhab had sought and been granted refuge, formed an alliance with the religious leader. This alliance was cemented by the marriage of 'Abd al-Aziz, Muhammad's son, to a daughter of 'Abd al-Wahhab. This alliance was important in the context of tribal politics. Various tribes paid allegiance to their respective shaikhs, but in general tribal society was war-torn and fragmented. The Bedouin was markedly individualistic, arrogant, fickle and proud. Suffused with a vivid sense of honour and pride, he was proverbially unruly. His pride made him disdainful of others, for instance, of the city-dwelling Arab. Only under a great leader or in the interests of a great religious cause would the dissident tribes band together. The alliance between the Al Sa'ud and 'Abd al-Wahhab provided both elements. Religion and the sword, that fateful combination, were joined.[62]

Muhammad reigned until 1765. During this period the rise

of a united Najd began under the political, military, and religious force of the Sa'udi–Wahhabi theocracy.⁶³ Over the next half century the Sa'udi state grew sufficiently strong to invade neighbouring Iraq in 1801, sacking the Shi'i holy city of Karbela and massacring its inhabitants. Mecca was captured in 1803 and Medina in 1804. By 1812 the Wahhabis controlled most of the peninsula and exerted influence as far north as the vicinity of Aleppo.⁶⁴

Given the extent of the Wahhabi Empire by the end of the first decade of the nineteenth century, the Sa'udis found themselves over-extended and unable to defend their domains. And with their capture of Mecca and Medina they naturally provoked the Sublime Porte. When the Wahhabis plundered Medina in 1810, opening the Prophet's tomb and selling or distributing its relics and jewels, the Porte was finally forced to take action. Sultan Mahmud II (r. 1808–1839) urged Muhammad 'Ali, the rapidly rising viceroy of Egypt, to drive the Wahhabis out of the Holy Cities. Viewing this task as an opportunity to increase his power, Muhammad 'Ali invaded central Arabia in 1811. By 1818, Ibrahim Pasha, Muhammad 'Ali's son and field commander, took Dar'iya from the Wahhabis, razing it to the ground. By the mid-1830s Wahhabi rule had been re-established in central and eastern Arabia. In 1838, Muhammad 'Ali again tried to impose his effective rule in central Arabia, but owing to British pressure he was forced to withdraw.⁶⁵

The first mention of British relations with the Wahhabis occurs with the rise of Wahhabi power in the Arabian peninsula and the increased outbreaks of piracy in the Persian Gulf in the early nineteenth century. The plunder of those beyond the pale was a characteristic of Wahhabism. Indeed the Bedouin's natural tendency towards the raid (*ghazzu*) was galvanised, fuelled and sanctioned by this religious doctrine. Under the aegis of Wahhabism, the coastal shaikhdoms began to prey on British shipping in the Gulf. In the first two decades of the last century, owing to these outbreaks of piracy, Britain found it necessary to take stern measures to establish order on the eastern coast of the Gulf. It will be recalled that British policy in the Persian Gulf throughout the nineteenth century was governed by two principles: the maintenance of the maritime peace in order to promote trade, and the exclusion of other powers from the area for the sake of the security of India. It was this first object which led the British to suppress piracy.

The principal pirates of the Omani coast were the Qawasim [66] who, under the influence of Wahhabism and 'organised to a large extent on the lines of a *jihad*' [67] or holy war, preyed on British and European shipping. In 1809, the Bombay government sent a military expedition against the pirate stronghold in Oman. In 1816 another outbreak of piracy of 'even greater ferocity' [68] prompted the Bombay government to despatch a further expedition in 1819. In 1820, the Omani chiefs were induced to sign a General Treaty of Peace with Great Britain by which the Government of Bombay was granted the right to police the waters in the Gulf. Legally it only granted Bombay the right to act against piracy. Practically the British government applied it to all political relations, thus becoming the dominant power in the Gulf.[69]

In 1835, the Maritime Truce was signed between the shaikhs of the Pirate Coast and the British. The significance of this agreement lay in that its signatories agreed to British arbitration in any disput arising between them.[70] In 1853, the Treaty of Peace in Perpetuity was signed. This treaty was to end hostilities at sea for 'evermore'. By the latter half of the nineteenth century the old Pirate Coast came to be known as the 'Trucial Coast'.[71]

During the long reign of Faisal ibn Turki, known as Faisal the Great (r. 1834–1838, 1843–1865), the British had several contacts with the Al Sa'ud. In 1843, Faisal returned from Cairo where he had been held captive by Muhammad 'Ali since 1838. He promptly set about re-conquering his family's domains. He first sought to occupy Buraimi, an important oasis lying at the junction of what is today known as the Sultanate of Muscat and Oman and the Trucial State of Abu Dhabi. The chiefs of Buraimi subsequently applied to Britain for protection. They were informed by the Bombay government that since the Egyptians no longer posed a threat, the British position was not to be extended. Britain had no intention of interfering in the politics of Arabia 'further than was necessary to maintain peace in the Gulf'.[72]

In 1848, Faisal appealed to the Resident to support his representative in Trucial Oman and 'to restrain the maritime tribes of Trucial Oman from interfering with the passage of supplies to him from Hasa'.[73] From this point until his death in 1866, the Wahhabis endeavoured to assert or reassert their power at various times in Bahrain, Qatar, the Trucial Shaikhdoms and in northern Oman. In 1849, Faisal enlisted the aid of the powerful Sharif of Mecca, Muhammad ibn 'Aun, in an attempt to extend his power along the Trucial Coast.[74] In view of Sa'udi–Sharifian rivalry in the twentieth century, it is interesting to note that the Sharif was described by one authority as both Faisal's ' overlord '[75] and ' His principal rival in Arabia '.[76] Two years earlier Faisal had clashed with the Sharif who, supported by a contingent of Turkish troops, had invaded the important district of Qasim.[77] When an emissary from the Sharif appealed to the British Resident at Bushire on Faisal's behalf, he emphasised that the Sa'udi ruler was a subject of the Ottoman Sultan and that he paid tribute to the Sharif.[78]

In 1851, Faisal once again turned his attention to Bahrain. In an attempt to assert his authority in the principality he applied to the Resident for assistance.

> Here he was handicapped in his plans to invade the island principality by the lack of ships, so he appealed, as was becoming his wont whenever his pretensions to overlordship in eastern Arabia exceeded his ability to realize them, to the Resident in the Gulf for support, saying that all he wanted from Bahrain was the renewed payment of *zakat*. He was told in reply that the British Government did not recognize Wahhabi authority over any of the maritime states of Eastern Arabia, which had been dealt with as independent shaikhdoms for over thirty years.[79]

By demanding *zakat*, alms tax, Faisal was saying in effect that he did not want to subjugate Bahrain directly; however, it was not uncommon in traditional Islam generally and among the Al Sa'ud particularly that the demand of *zakat* implied the assertion of power. Arab shaikhs based the territorial extent of their power on their ability to impose order on neighbouring tribes, to avenge or prevent raids or excesses within the areas claimed, and to enforce the payment of *zakat*.[80]

Faisal's actions and the British responses to Wahhabi intrigues are instructive as to a great extent they prefigure Anglo–Sa'udi relations in the early twentieth century. Like ibn Sa'ud over half a century later, Faisal sought to regain the Sa'udi patrimony. The great Sa'udi chief realised, however, that his ambitions along the

Arabian littoral were limited by the British. He therefore tried to elicit British support. The British of course declined. They had no interests in central Arabia, and in view of recent history could not but view Wahhabism as a disruptive force. The British were also reluctant to get involved in the maelstrom of central Arabian politics with its attendant features of discord and shifting allegiances. Obviously British naval power in the Gulf would have been of little value in controlling Arab relations in the interior.

Failing to gain British support, Faisal fell back to the ploy of attempting to further his ends by asserting his position as an Ottoman dependent. Faisal, like ibn Sa'ud after him, was confronted by the Sharif of Mecca as his chief rival in Arabia. But their clashes were fewer and, even as a means to an end, it would be difficult to imagine ibn Sa'ud calling on the Sharif as did his great ancestor.

In 1865, exploiting dissension in Oman, the Wahhabis once again began to harass the area.[81] In the spring of 1865 Colonel Lewis Pelly, the Political Resident, visited Riyadh. However, Faisal was failing and the royal family was torn by dynastic competition. Pelly left after a few days, having accomplished little.[82] In 1865 the Wahhabis 'plundered the coastal town of Sur and murdered a British Indian subject'.[83] Towards the end of the year a Wahhabis force attacked a town on the Batina coast of Oman. In the course of the attack another British Indian died. Pelly then sent a demand to Riyadh for compensation. Before receiving the reply he carried out an 'ineffectual naval bombardment of Dammam [on the Hasa coast] in January 1866'.[84] Although the bombardment was ineffectual this action indicated the vulnerability of the Sa'udis to pressure on the Hasa coast. This problem was to plague ibn Sa'ud as it did his forebears.

In 1866, an emissary of Faisal's son and successor, 'Abdullah, came to an agreement with Colonel Pelly. Later the Sa'udis were to view this as a treaty with Great Britain; however, this instrument was viewed differently by the British. Technically this agreement was a declaration by the Sa'udi Amir

> containing an undertaking of non-aggression against Muscat and the Trucial Shaikhdoms. This declaration was not, strictly speaking, a treaty. It was a unilateral undertaking given by an envoy from Amir Faisal [sic] to the British Political Resident at Bushire, in the course of an incident in

1865 in which British Indian subjects had been the victims of the Wahhabi raid on Sur.[85]

The period from Faisal's death in 1865 to the exile of ibn Sa'ud and his father in 1891 or 1892 is significant primarily for fratricide and dynastic rivalry which, taken together with the Turkish capture of Hasa in 1871, helped the Rashidi dynasty of Jabal Shammar, the district lying to the north of Najd, to achieve dominance in hitherto Sa'udi territory. The head of the House of Rashid, Muhammad ibn Rashid, one of Arabia's greatest rules, entered into an alliance with the Turks.[86] From the late 1860s until the turn of the century, the Wahhabis were in eclipse while the Rashidi star was ascendant in central Arabia. During these years the British had very few contacts with the Sa'udis.

Although it is beyond our scope to follow the tortuous narrative of Sa'udi internecine strife during this period, it is important to note briefly that Faisal's legitimate heir, 'Abdullah, was challenged by his younger brother, Sa'ud. In 1873 the rivalry between the two brothers ended with the death of Sa'ud by smallpox. However, chaos prevailed. Replacing Sa'ud as a rival for the Amirate were his two sons, as well as the younger son of Amir Faisal and the brother of ' Abdullah, 'Abd al-Rahman ibn Sa'ud, the father of ibn Sa'ud. For our purposes the chief significance of his rivalry was the fact that in later years the descendants of Faisal's elder sons were to challenge ibn Sa'ud's position as Sa'udi Amir.[87]

While the Sa'udis were fighting among themselves the Turks decided to assert their power in eastern Arabia. Prior to 1871 the Sultans of Turkey had never exercised any effective jurisdiction in central Arabia. It has been argued that the appointment of Midhat Pasha to the Governor-generalship of Baghdad in 1868 ' signified the adoption of an active Arabian policy by the Porte '.[88] It will be recalled that in the late nineteenth century the Porte began to pursue a policy of consolidation and expansion in the Arabic-speaking parts of the Empire. This was especially true during the reign of Abdul Hamid (1876–1909).

In 1872 Midhat left Baghdad. The state of affairs he left behind him was, to some extent, important for Turkey. Although the Turks did not effectively penetrate the inner fastness of Arabia, their position in Hasa did afford them the opportunity of exercising a modicum of control over whoever ruled Najd.

They controlled the lines of communications from the Gulf to inner Arabia and posed a constant threat of invasion by sea should any tribe or ruler grow too strong. The Turks could not only worry the British from this position, they could also pursue their policy of playing off one tribe against another. As one authority has rightly commented: ' It is noteworthy that the first decisive act of revived Wahhabism under 'Abd al-Aziz Al Sa'ud [ibn Sa'ud] was the expulsion of Ottoman power from El Hassa, alien control over which rendered Arab "independence" illusionary '.[89]

After ruling briefly in Riyadh from 1889 to 1891, 'Abd al-Rahman was defeated by ibn Rashid's forces and driven into exile in Kuwait. He was accompanied by his family, including ibn Sa'ud who was eleven or twelve at this time. The Porte supplied him with a pension. For the next ten years the Al Sa'ud family had to bide their time in exile while ' The Najd of the Wahhabis... [became] an insignificant province of an alien dynasty '.[90]

It will be recalled that in 1896 Mubarak came to power in Kuwait. The following year a further change in Arabian politics took place when Muhammad ibn Rashid died. He was succeeded by the less gifted 'Abd al-Aziz ibn Rashid. As was so often the case in Arabian politics, with the death of the powerful leader the tribe's fortunes waned and the power base Muhammad ibn Rashid had built up began to crumble.

After Mubarak came to an agreement with England in 1899 regarding the non-alienation of territory the Porte incited the Rashidis to attack.[91] When in 1900 'Abd al-Rahman led an incursion into Najd—with Mubarak's sanction—he found that owing to Muhammad ibn Rashid's death, old loyalties had begun to dissolve and discontent was rife in central Arabia. In 1901 Mubarak, fortified by his alliance with England and supported by the Al Sa'ud, led an expedition against the Al Rashid to forestall the risk of an attack on his own territory. He was thoroughly defeated at Sarif, near Buraida, in February 1901.[92] In the spring of 1901, the British Consul at Basra reported the arrival of Turkish troops headed by General Muhammad Pasha Daghestani, Commander-in-Chief of the VI Army Corps, with the probable intention of marching on Kuwait. Muhsin Pasha, the Vali of Basra, is reported to have dissuaded them from pursuing this course. Muhsin then tried to get Mubarak to accept Turkish protection.[93] In August—after Muhsin had been relieved of his command—a Turkish ship, the *Zuhaff*, sailed into Kuwait harbour. Moreover, Turkish troops were once again massed at Basra. However, the presence of HMS *Perseus* in Kuwait harbour precluded the Turks from invading the principality. It will be remembered that the Germans and the Turks both protested to the Foreign Office about British actions at Kuwait. The result of this uproar was the agreement among the three Powers to respect the *status quo*.

Owing to Mubarak's crushing defeat in 1901 his territorial ambitions were circumscribed. The great Shaikh, however, did continue to support, and probably attempted to further his own ends through the Sa'udi exiles. They were undoubtedly encouraged by Mubarak to regain their patrimony. It was naturally in Mubarak's interest to undermine the Rashidis, who were in league with the Turks. The Al Sa'ud were supplied with arms by Mubarak. Although Britain was staunchly opposed to arms traffic, she could not afford to antagonise Mubarak by cutting off his supply of arms. It has been asserted that even Lord Curzon believed that to preclude the flow of arms to ibn Sa'ud would probably increase the possibilities of Turkish dominance in the hinterland. Obviously this would have impinged on British influence in Kuwait and along the coast.[94] Once again principle bowed to expediency.

In 1900 or 1901 'Abd al-Rahman turned over the effective reins of leadership to ibn Sa'ud who was about twenty-two at this time. The father retained the office of Imam or leader in prayer. This action was significant. The young Amir henceforth guided the fortunes of his family. Moreover, in the father's retention of the office of Imam,[95] it may perhaps be seen that ibn Sa'ud, although religious and able to fan the flames of religion in his tribesmen, was not the Wahhabi zealot that most of his followers were. In fact he rarely let the more extreme aspects of Wahhabism, when he could control them, interfere with his appreciation of *Realpolitik*. In 1902 ibn Sa'ud proved his ability to lead the Sa'udi dynasty, with his dramatic capture of Riyadh. At the head of a force of around forty retainers he set out for the interior late in 1901. By January 15, 1902 he had reconquered Riyadh. He entered the city by night with six followers. The following morning he threw open the main gate of the city and he and his followers defeated the superior forces of the Rashidi garrison.

The story of ibn Saʻud's capture of Riyadh has become a legend in Arabian folklore. By this exploit he proved that he had the requisite qualities for a shaikh: courage, leadership and *hadh* or luck.[96] It should also be noted that the daring of his exploit at Riyadh was bound to capture the imagination of the inhabitants of central Arabia. In addition to the aforementioned attributes few authorities would dispute the charisma he possessed. Standing six feet three or four he was almost a foot taller than the average Najdi. He was broad-shouldered, handsome and the 'very type of Arab masculinity'.[97] Perhaps at this time he also had the charm that so many who met him in later years remarked upon. Fired by ambition and by the awareness of the glory and honour attached by the Bedouin to the exploits of his ancestors (the concept of *hasab*),[98] ibn Saʻud set out to capture the Saʻudi patrimony.

After his capture of Riyadh, ibn Saʻud moved his family back to Riyadh. For the time being ibn Rashid did not challenge him, probably owing to his own tribal difficulties and a reputed lack of support by Constantinople. Ibn Rashid was in difficult straits at this juncture. In the middle of March he sent an emissary to Basra to request the Vali for Turkish aid to subdue the 'revolt'. At about the same time he wrote to the Grand Vizier in Constantinople. He 'attributed to the British Government a design of entering into close relations with Central Arabia through the agency of ibn-Saʻud and the Shaikh of Kuwait'.[99] Although this allegation was untrue, one can emagine the Turkish suspicion given the prevailing atmosphere in Anglo–Turkish relations.

After ibn Saʻud's capture of Riyadh in 1902 and his assumption of the Amirate of Najd, he tried to elicit British support. In 1903 a Wahabi emissary met Captain Prideaux, the Political Agent at Bahrain, and tried to obtain British backing. The emissary mentioned the upsurge of Arab unrest and the Wahhabi aim to drive the Turks out of Hasa.[100] However, this goal could only be reached if Britain supported ibn Saʻud, thus eliminating the possibility of Turkish counter-attack by sea. Prideaux answered evasively but the overture was entertained with some interest in India. Sir Louis Dane, the foreign secretary of the Indian government, declined to grant protection to the Wahhabis but they could not be dismissed. The Najd territory flanked the projected route of the Baghdad Railway and if ibn Saʻud reached full power he could—if unrestrained by treaty relations—menace the coast. Colonel Kemball, Political Resident in the Gulf, was consulted regarding the efficacy of sending a secret mission to Riyadh. He advised against this, maintaining that such a mission would not be kept secret from the Porte or Hail. Also, such a mission would be construed as an overt backing of the Wahhabis and at that time a Rashidi comeback could not be effectively ruled out.[101]

In 1903 while the Sa'udis were making overtures to the British, it will be recalled that ibn Sa'ud is reported to have received an offer of aid from the Russian Consul-General at Bushire. This offer, however, came to nothing and did not particularly concern the British.[102] In 1904 after an important Sa'udi victory at Bukariya, 'Abd al-Rahman asked for British protection in the light of Turkish support of ibn Rashid.[103] He also informed Britain of the Russian offer. The Foreign Department in India requested London to warn the Porte against aiding military intervention in Arabia.[104]

These developments found the Indian government in its usual state of conflict with the Foreign Office. O'Conor maintained that Abdul Hamid could not be dissuaded from trying to prevent a disturbance of the tenuous equilibrium in central Arabia. The British had agreed to support this balance of power in 1901. The Government of India countered these arguments by stating that the 1901 guarantee of the *status quo* worked two ways and the Turks were supporting the Al Rashid. And this intervention could not but eventually affect the littoral. The Indian government went on to point out that '... [the re-establishment of the Sa'udi dynasty] would present no difficulty in respect of the British sphere of influence'. As opposed to this, if ibn Rashid won through Ottoman assistance the situation would become serious.[105] The Government of India stated further that if ibn Rashid grew all-powerful the Turks could become predominant in Najd and Mubarak's position would also be in jeopardy. ' The Foreign Office was led by Indian insistence to instruct O'Connor [sic] to address a remonstrance to the Porte on the lines suggested by the Government of India '.[106]

After his victory at Bukariya, ibn Sa'ud was in need of recognition and support to sustain his gains. Failing to gain British assistance, he was forced to turn to the Porte. Ibn Sa'ud met a senior Turkish official at Safwan and was appointed *Qaimaqam* or district governor of Najd under Ottoman suzerainty.[107]

In the summer of 1905 ibn Sa'ud travelled to the base of the Qatar peninsula. While camped there he was informed by Shaikh Qasim ibn Thani's brother, Ahmad, that any attempt to proceed further would be countered by the combined forces of Qatar and Abu Dhabi.[108] Ibn Sa'ud then wrote letters to the Trucial Shaikhs stating that he planned to visit them the following year. As in the nineteenth century, whenever Wahhabi fortunes were in the ascendant, pressure was being brought to bear on the Arabian littoral. The Ruler of Abu Dhabi ' journeyed to Muscat in November 1905 to consult with the Sultan on what might be done to oppose ibn Sa'ud, and the following month the Sultan paid a visit to Abu Dhabi where the two rulers had a meeting with the Political Resident, Major Cox '. A warning was sent to ibn Sa'ud. He replied in February 1906 to the effect that he meant no harm. Lacking resources and not wanting to overextend himself and alienate the British, he made no moves towards Oman.[109]

Major (later Sir Percy) Cox became Political Resident in the Persian Gulf in 1904. He had previously been assistant Political Resident in British Somaliland from 1892 to 1901 and Consul at Muscat from 1901 to 1904. In view of his importance in Anglo–Sa'udi relations until his retirement in 1923, a few words should be said about him at this point. A tall, thin, taciturn man, Cox had been handpicked by Curzon for his position in the Gulf. A recurrent theme in the accounts of those who worked under him such as Arnold Wilson, Gertrude Bell, and Philby amongst others is one of praise for his abilities. Had he been more colourful, less humble, and left memoirs to shed light on his career, he might have been mentioned in the same breath as Cromer or Curzon or other exemplars of proconsular excellence. He had his faults and, above all, he was a ' government man '. There is little doubt, however, that he was also an exceptional man. One of the greatest testimonies to his abilities is the affection and trust he inspired not only in the British officials who knew him, but in the Arabs with whom he dealt. Later in his career his name almost became a by-word among the Arabs of central and north-eastern Arabia and Mesopotamia.[110]

Cox was quick to see the potential of ibn Sa'ud, and wanted the British to come to terms with him; but his repeated requests foundered on the rock of London's determination not to undermine Anglo–Turkish relations. While Cox, arguably overlooking the larger issues at stake, continued to appeal in vain for British recognition, ibn Sa'ud continued to increase his power in central Arabia.

By 1906 ibn Sa'ud, having vanquished and killed ibn Rashid, had established himself in Najd. It was also reported at this time that the Wahhabi Amir had alienated the Shaikh of Kuwait who was said to have opened correspondence with ibn Rashid and to have received satisfactory responses. In this same year, ibn Sa'ud made three overtures to Great Britain for recognition. He applied through a personal emissary, through the Shaikh of Qatar, and finally through Mubarak. Ibn Sa'ud wanted to subscribe to the Trucial System and accept a British political agent, and would have agreed to trucial provisions regarding piracy, slave trade, maritime warfare, non-alienation of territory, and British control of foreign relations.[111] In September 1906 Cox wrote to the Government of India stating that he thought it advisable to enter into some sort of relationship with ibn Sa'ud on the following grounds, given here in very abbreviated form from the *Home Correspondence* for 1908:

1. Ibn Sa'ud might construe indifference or rejection as hostility.
2. Friendly agreement between ibn Sa'ud and Britain would allay the fears of the Muscati Sultan and Trucial Chiefs.
3. A friendly ibn Sa'ud could help suppress piracy.
4. Such understanding would facilitate Cox's dealing with the Trucial Chiefs and permit occasional tours of Najd.
5. An Arab revival is foreseeable and ibn Sa'ud might turn elsewhere if rebuffed.

Cox's suggestions did not even elicit comment.[112]

On November 9 the Secretary of State for India, John Morley, informed the Government of India by telegram that 'His Majesty's Government maintained the view that their interest and influence should be confined to [the] coast. No steps... should be taken to enter into relations without my previous sanction.' In November 1906, Cox requested an authoritative reply to ibn Sa'ud lest the former's reputation be compromised by the appearance of negligence towards the latter. This request resulted, finally, in a despatch by Morley in May 1907. In brief this despatch maintained that no alteration of the policy laid down by his predecessor in 1904 should be effected. In essence it reiterated that British policy was confined to the coast and followed Sir Nicholas O'Conor's dictum of no entanglement with the Wahhabis. Ibn Sa'ud, if necessary, was to be informed that his 'proposals involve considerations which it is impossible for His Majesty's Government to entertain and that no reply is to be expected'.[113]

The mention of an Arab revival did not carry much weight at the Foreign Office as it was not deemed imminent at the time. Moreover, Whitehall also feared the Wahhabi effect on the coast plus the impact of an agreement with ibn Sa'ud on Russo–British relations, and German ascendancy in Constantinople in the context of Anglo–Turkish relations. Regarding the possibility of ibn Sa'ud turning elsewhere for aid, the British had little to fear as they were supreme in the Gulf. In addition O'Connor argued that:

> The chances are that the present Ottoman regime will ... come to an end and be succeeded by a nationalist and popular government, or that the disintegration of the component parts of the Empire will have begun. In the latter case we cannot escape our responsibility, but I should be sorry to see England enter into relations with a new Turkish regime, having previously agreed to a secret arrangement with ibn Saud for the disruption of the Empire.[114]

O'Connor prevailed and ibn Sa'ud's overtures were rejected.

The pattern emerging from the foregoing pages is one of non-involvement in central Arabia and the subordination of local interests in the Persian Gulf to the wider plane of interests in British international relations. However, it must be added, that although Britain did not directly back ibn Sa'ud, the British relationship with Kuwait taken with the Sa'udi relationship with Shaikh Mubarak did much to contribute to the Wahhabi revival.

Notes

1. For the best introduction to the Gulf see Sir A. T. Wilson, *The Persian Gulf—An Historical Sketch from the Earliest Times to the Beginning of the Twentieth Century* (London, 1928), hereafter *Wilson*. See also J. Marlowe, *The Persian Gulf in the Twentieth Century* (London, 1962), hereafter *Marlowe*; Sir R. Hay, *The Persian Gulf States* (Washington D.C., 1959) and J. J. Berreby, *Le Golfe persique, mer le légende—reservoir de pétrole* (Paris, 1959).
2. The best account of Great Power rivalry in the Gulf in this period is

B. C. Busch, *Britain and the Persian Gulf, 1894–1914* (Berkeley and Los Angeles, 1967), hereafter *Busch*. See also R. Kumar, *India and the Persian Gulf, 1858–1907, A Study of British Imperial Policy* (New York, 1965), hereafter *Kumar*. The author is particularly indebted to Busch for much of the material presented in this section.

3. On the British policy in the Gulf the definitive work is J. B. Kelly, *Britain and the Persian Gulf, 1795–1880* (Oxford, 1968), hereafter Kelly, *Britain and the Persian Gulf*. Also of great importance is J. G. Lorimer, *Gazetteer of the Persian Gulf, Oman, and Central Arabia*, 2 vols. (Calcutta, 1905–1915), hereafter, *Lorimer*. See also Col. S. B. Miles, *Countries and Tribes of the Persian Gulf*, 2 vols. (London, 1919). On piracy see R. Bayly Winder, *Saudi Arabia in the Nineteenth Century* (N.Y., 1965), hereafter *Winder*; Sir C. Belgrave, *The Pirate Coast* (London, 1966), H. Moyse-Bartlett, *The Pirates of Trucial Oman* (London, 1966), hereafter *Moyse-Bartlett*; and *Wilson*.

4. As Curzon put it: 'there are few things in the world upon which I feel more strongly than on the subject of Southern Persia and the Persian Gulf'. Curzon (private) to Hamilton (Secretary of State for India), April 26 and May 3 1899, *Curzon Mss*. Quoted in *Busch*, p. 122.

5. See 'Curzon's Analysis of British Policy and Interests in Persia and the Persian Gulf (1899)' in J. C. Hurewitz, *Diplomacy in the Near and Middle East: A Documentary Record: 1535–1914*, Vol. I (Princeton, 1956), No. 101, p. 222; hereafter, *Hurewitz, I*.

6. *Ibid.*, p. 227.

7. A good, concise article on this subject is J. B. Kelly, 'The Legal and Historical Basis of the British position in the Persian Gulf', *St. Antony's Papers*, No. 4, *Middle Eastern Affairs*, No. 1 (1958).

8. *Busch*, pp. 24, 25.

9. P. Woodruff, *The Men Who Ruled India: The Guardians* (N.Y., 1954), p. 270. As Curzon said aptly, the Resident at Bushire 'is really the uncrowned King of the Gulf'. Curzon (private) to Hamilton, Aug. 12 1903. Curzon Mss. Quoted in *Busch*, p. 258.

10. *Busch*, pp. 6, 7. Other accounts of the Gulf system are found in J. Marlowe, *Late Victorian, The Life of Sir Arnold Talbot Wilson* (London, 1967), p. 40, hereafter Marlowe, *Late Victorian* and his previously cited work on the Persian Gulf, p. 42.

11. *Busch*, p. 7.

12. *Ibid.*, p. 10. For a further account of this financial issue see his p. 240, n. 11.

13. See A. J. P. Taylor, *The Struggle for Mastery in Europe 1848–1918* (Oxford, 1954), p. 336; hereafter *Taylor*. For a general account of international diplomacy in the 90s and after the turn of the century the standard works are *Taylor*, Chaps. XV–XIX; W. L. Langer, *The Franco-Russian Alliance, 1890–1894*, Harvard Historical Studies XXX (Cambridge, Mass., 1929) and *The Diplomacy of Imperialism, 1890–1902* (N.Y., 1951). See also F. H. Hinsley, 'British Foreign Policy and Colonial Questions, 1895–1904' in *The Cambridge History of the British Empire III: The Empire-Commonwealth, 1870–*

1919, ed. E. A. Benians et al. (Cambridge, 1959). See also G. Monger, *The End of Isolation* (London, 1963) and J. A. S. Grenville, *Lord Salisbury and Foreign Policy, The Close of the nineteenth century* (London, 1964).

14. On the naval question in the eastern Mediterranean the best account is of course A. J. Marder, *The Anatomy of British Sea Power: A History of British Naval Policy in the Pre-Dreadnought Era, 1880–1905* (New York, 1940).
15. *Busch*, p. 50.
16. *Ibid.*, p. 52. It should be noted that the question of the arms trade was not to be settled until the eve of the First World War.
17. As Curzon put it in 1892: 'We subsidise its ruler; we dictate its policy; we should tolerate no alien interference'. See G. N. Curzon, *Persia and the Persian Question* (London, 1892), vol. 2, p. 443.
18. *Busch*, p. 50.
19. *Ibid.*, p. 117.
20. *Lorimer*, vol. 1, pt. 1, p. 393.
21. *Busch*, p. 103.
22. *Ibid.*, p. 105, see also *Kumar*, pp. 141–144.
23. For a summary of the economic threat that the Baghdad Railway posed for Russia see *Kumar*, p. 153.
24. 'Historians, British and foreign, concur in noting the existence of these widespread feelings of hostility towards Britain, and there was clear evidence of it in the general sympathy expressed for the Boers...' See *Beloff*, p. 24.
25. Busch adds that 'It is still not clear whether the Russian commander had asked, and been refused, permission to land coal as Russian property', p. 130. See also *Kumar*, p. 224. The importance which Curzon attached to the possibility of the Russians obtaining a coaling station in the Gulf is dramatically reflected in the following statement: 'I should regard the concession of a port upon the Persian Gulf to Russia by any Power as a deliberate insult to Great Britain, as a wanton rupture of the *status quo*, and as an intentional provocation to war; and I should impeach the British Minister, who was guilty of acquiescing in such a surrender, as a traitor to his country'. Quoted in L. Fraser, *India Under Curzon and After* (London, 1911), p. 85; hereafter *Fraser*.
26. As early as 1865 Lord Clarendon had said: 'The only way to improve them, is to improve them off the face of the earth'. Quoted in E. Kedourie, *England and the Middle East: The Destruction of the Ottoman Empire, 1914–1921* (London, 1956), p. 15; hereafter Kedourie, *England*.
27. See *Taylor*, pp. 359, 360. Kedourie points out that Salisbury apparently had thought partition desirable as early as the 1870s. See his pp. 20, 21.
28. Salisbury (Prime Minister and For. Secy.) to O'Conor (Ambassador to St. Petersburg) Jan. 25, 1898, No. 9 in *British Documents on the Origins of the War: 1898–1914*, ed. by Gooch and Temperly, Vol. 1 (London, 1926–1938). Quoted in *Busch*, pp. 103, 104.

29. The Muscat bond was due, of course, to French pressures.
30. In view of her agreements with Bahrain Britain exercised a virtual protectorate over the country. See *Hurewitz*, Vol. 1, p. 194. Moreover Bahrain was the centre of the pearl trade in the Gulf and by the beginning of the twentieth century this trade 'amounted to nearly £500,000 a year'. See P. Graves, *The Life of Sir Percy Cox* (London, 1950), p. 96; hereafter *Graves*.
31. Ford (Constantinople) to Rosebery (Foreign Secy.), April 23, 1893, *F.O.* 78/5109 (Foreign Office files, Series 78 vol. 5109, Public Record Office). Quoted in *Busch*, p. 25.
32. The following are the Turkish administrative units and ranks which were operative until the dissolution of the Ottoman Empire.

administrative unit	official in charge
Vilayet (province)	Vali (governor)
Sanjaq (sub-province)	Mutasarrif (sub-governor)
Qada or Kaza (district)	Qaimaqam (district-governor)
Nahiye (canton or commune)	Mudir (cantonal officer)

33. Busch points out that 'an assertion that Qatar was part of the Trucial System would bring into effect the clause in those treaties requiring submission of disputes to the Resident, which the Turks would certainly challenge. By calling Turkish sovereignty "debatable" Britain had chosen a policy which would leave open the door to direct relations with Qatar chiefs but would not force interference in favour of Qasim', p. 29.
34. Mubarak in old age was characterized by Lovat Fraser as 'sitting in his high chamber, gazing seaward with inscrutable eyes, with the face of Richelieu and something of Richelieu's ambition yet unquenched within him'. Quoted in A. T. Wilson, *Loyalties, Mesopotamia, 1914–1917* (London, 1930), p. 31, hereafter Wilson, *Loyalties* I.
35. *Busch*, p. 97.
36. This question of piracy constituted a dilemma for the British. The Gulf officials wanted it stopped but had little influence in Kuwait. And by applying to the Porte for action they would be underwriting Turkish authority in the Shaikhdom and translating this vague suzerainty into something more tangible.
37. Currie to Salisbury, Nov. 24, 1896, *Home* 930/96. [*Home Corresdonpence* proceeding No. 930 for 1896, India Office Records, London]. Quoted in *Busch*, p. 97.
38. *Busch*, p. 98.
39. Mubarak was also said to have accepted the appointment of Qaimaqam under the jurisdiction of the Vali of Basra. See *Busch*, pp. 97, 98.
40. The India Office authorized Lord Curzon in making this agreement 'to follow the example of the Muscat Bond of 1871'. This was of importance as the Trucial Bonds of 1892 were slightly more comprehensive than the Muscat agreement in that they also prohibited correspondence with other Powers. Much to the consternation of the Foreign and India Offices the Resident in the Gulf who concluded this agreement added, on his own initiative, an additional clause

which stipulated that the Shaikh and his heirs and successors would not receive the representative of any Power without prior consent of the British government. In the end Britain ratified the agreement in order not to compromise the Resident. See *Busch*, pp. 108–112.
41. *Busch*, p. 105.
42. *Ibid.*, p. 188. *Kumar*, pp. 146–148.
43. This will be discussed on pp. 19, 20.
44. The standard works on the Baghdad Railway are E. M. Earle, *Turkey, the Great Powers, and the Baghdad Railway: A study in Imperialism* (New York, 1923), hereafter *Earle*; M. K. Chapman, *Great Britain and the Baghdad Railway, 1888–1917* (Massachusetts, 1948), hereafter *Chapman* and J. B. Wolf, 'The Diplomatic History of the Baghdad Railroad', *University of Missouri Studies*, XI (1936).
45. *Busch*, p. 190.
46. *Ibid.*, p. 205.
47. *Ibid.*, p. 206.
48. *Ibid.*, p. 207.
49. *Ibid.*, pp. 213, 214.
50. See *Busch*, p. 223, *Earle*, pp. 180–195, *Chapman*, pp. 53–71 and *Kumar*, pp. 173–176.
51. Quoted in *Busch*, p. 223.
52. *Busch*, p. 223.
53. *Parl. Deb.* 4th Series, 121 (1903), p. 1348.
54. *Fraser*, p. 110. The flotilla consisted of the HMS and RIMS *Argonaut, Hyacinth Fox, Pomona, Sphinx, Lapwing* and *Lawrence*. See *Busch*, p. 259.
55. *Busch*, p. 259.
56. Speech by Curzon aboard the *Argonaut*, Nov. 21, 1903. Cited in *Lorimer*, Vol. 1, Pt. II, App. P, pp. 2638, 2639. Also quoted in *Kumar*, p. 238.
57. See Lord Newton, *Lord Lansdowne* (London, 1929), p. 287. Quoted in A. P. Thornton, *The Imperial Idea and its Enemies* (New York, 1966), p. 112; hereafter *Thornton*.
58. *Busch*, p. 224.
59. As the rise of Wahhabism and Anglo-Wahhabi relations in the 19th century have received full and competent treatment by others, only a brief outline will be given here. For detailed treatments of these subjects see *Winder*, Kelly's *Britain and the Persian Gulf* and *Eastern Arabian Frontiers* (London, 1964), hereafter *Kelly, Eastern Arabian Frontiers; Lorimer;* and Philby's works, especially *Sa'udi Arabia* (London, 1955), hereafter *Philby, Sa'udi Arabia*. For early contemporary accounts of the Wahhabis see J. L. Burckhardt, *Notes on the Bedouins and the Wahabys*, 2 vols. (London, 1830) and his *Travels in Arabia*, 2 vols. (London, 1829). For a succinct account of the origins of Wahhabism and the rise of the Al Sa'ud, the best treatment is found in the *Shorter Encyclopedia of Islam*, ed. by H. A. R. Gibb and J. H. Kramers (Leiden, 1953), pp. 618–21.
60. Although some authors differ on these dates, the majority accept 1703 to 1787 as 'Abd al-Wahhab's lifetime. For a comprehensive

treatment of 'Abd al-Wahhab see G. S. Rentez, 'Muhammad 'Abd al-Wahhab (1703/4–1792) and the Beginnings of the Unitarian Empire in Arabia' (unpublished Ph.D. dissertation at the University of California, 1948).

61. See Appendix I for genealogy. 'Muhammad-bin-Sa'ud belonged to a family known as the Al Maqram, of the Mishalikh section of the Wald 'Ali division of the Anaizah tribe; and from the name of his fathers was derived the alternate family name of Al Sa'ud, which has been transmitted to his descendants'. See *Lorimer*, Vol. 1, Pt. 1, p. 1053.

62. For an excellent treatment of the Bedouin see M. Freiherr von Oppenheim, *Die Beduinin*, 4 vols. (Wiesbaden, 1952). For an account of the Bedouin of Najd in the early twentieth century the best work is Dickson, *Arab*. For a commentary on this work see G. Rentz, 'Dick-Dickson, *Arab*. For a commentary on this work see G. Rentz, 'Dickson's Arab of the Desert' in *The Muslim World* XLI (1951). Of the many other works one could cite on this subject, C. M. Doughty's *Travels in Arabia Deserta* (Cambridge, 1888), hereafter *Doughty*, is the classic work.

63. It should be noted here that the designation "Wahhabi" was used pejoratively by Westerners when referring to the followers of ibn 'Abd al-Wahhab. His followers actually called themselves *Muwahhidun*, or Unitarians.

64. *United Kingdom Memorial: Arbitration Concerning Buraimi and the Common Frontier Between Abu Dhabi and Sa'udi Arabia*, Vol. 1 (London, 1955), p. 74; hereafter *UK Mem*.

65. For an account of this expedition, see J. B. Kelly, "Mehmet Ali's Expedition to the Persian Gulf, 1837–1840", *Middle Eastern Studies* (hereafter *M.E.S.*), Vol. 1, No. 4, Pt. 1, pp. 350–81 and Vol. 2, No. 1, Pt. 2, pp. 31–65 (1965). After the razing of Dar'iya the Wahhabis moved their capital to Riyadh.

66. 'The term "Qawasim" and its singular "Qasimi", strictly applies to the ruling family of Sharjah and Ras al Khaima [see Map II], but it is used loosely to denote the heterogeneous collection of tribes, sections and individuals that inhabit those two ports'. See J. B. Kelly, 'Mehmet Ali's Expedition to the Persian Gulf, 1837–1840',*MES* Vol. 1, No. 4, Pt. 1, p. 379.

67. S. Searight, *The British in the Middle East* (London, 1969), p. 113; hereafter *Searight*.

68. Kelly, *Eastern Arabian Frontiers*, p. 58.

69. *Kumar*, p. 17. For an authoritative, comprehensive and detailed treatment of the British reaction to Gulf piracy see Kelly, *Britain and the Persian Gulf*, pp. 99–166. For a shorter account, his *Eastern Arabian Frontiers*, chap. II, is also useful.

70. Apparently with the cessation of piracy, the Arabs on the southern coast threatened to annihilate one another through constant tribal wars.

71. *Kumar*, p. 18. For the full text of the treaty, see C. U. Aitchison, *A Collection of Treaties' Engagements and Sanads relating to India and*

small Turkish garrisons in Hufhuf and Qatif in Hasa, a legacy of the invasion of 1871.
108. Kelly, *Eastern Arabian Frontiers*, p. 104.
109. *Ibid.*, pp. 104, 105.
110. A characteristic tribute to Cox is the one paid to him by Curzon on the latter's resignation from the viceroyalty in 1905. Curzon wrote: '... it has been the greatest satisfaction to me to befriend so able, high-minded and devoted an officer as yourself, always to be trusted to do his best and that best of a very high order'. Quoted in *Graves*, p. 103 and *Busch*, p. 269. At this point Cox had been in the Gulf just under five years. He still had eighteen years of service left! He was to hold the position of Political Resident until 1914. He then served briefly as the Foreign Secretary to the Indian government. From Britain's entry into World War I until 1917 when he was appointed Civil Commissioner of Baghdad he was both Chief Political Officer to the Indian Expeditionary Force and Political Resident. From 1918 to 1920 he was Minister to Teheran and from 1920 to his retirement in 1923 he was High Commissioner in Iraq. On his career generally see *Graves*.
111. Busch in his work, *Britain, India an dthe Arabs* (Berkeley, 1971), p. 230 states incorrectly that the Al Sa'ud 'entered into contact with Britain only in 1906 ...' Philby in his *Arabian Jubilee* (London, 1952), p. 34 [hereafter Philby, *Arabian Jubilee*], also gets the date of the first overture wrong. He states that it occurred in 1904.
112. 'The Wahabbees', Memorandum respecting British interest in the Persian Gulf, February 1908, No. 2859; *H.C.*, [*Home Correspendence*, India Office (IO)], Vol. 250.
113. *Ibid*.
114. O'Connor to FO, April 1, 1907, Foreign Dept., Secret and Political (India), No. 448, Sept. 1907 as cited in *Kumar*, p. 210. In 1908 and 1909, ibn Sa'ud made overtures to the British, and they were again rejected.

CHAPTER II

The Pre-War Era: 1910 to 1914

The period from 1909 to 1912 has been aptly called by one eminent diplomatic historian 'the years of Anglo–German hostility'.[1] The Moroccan and Bosnian crises of 1905 and 1908 had served to convince many officials in the British government that Germany was determined to dominate Europe. When in March 1909 it was learned that Germany had stepped up her naval ship-building programme, this conviction was reinforced and British public opinion began to march in step with official policy. Many people believed at this point that the German naval programme indicated a desire to dominate not only Europe but the world. 'The alarm of German "acceleration" stirred the British people as they had not been roused since the annexation of Savoy by Napoleon III in 1860'.[2] With the rallying cry 'we want eight and we won't wait' the British took up the challenge.[3]

In 1911 Anglo–German relations again reached crisis point over Morocco. The following year Haldane's mission to Berlin to effect a conciliation between Germany and England failed. While Britain sought simultaneously to avoid war with Germany and to prepare herself for the dreaded contingency, events in the Ottoman Empire also caused the 'Weary Titan'[4] concern. The Young Turk Revolution of 1908, which had been greeted by many, both in the Ottoman Empire and in European governments, as holding out the prospect of reform and regeneration, did not live up to these hopes. True the 'long night of Hamidian despotism'[5] had come to an end, but the Young Turk dawn did not usher in a new liberal era. If the Young Turks were originally sincere in their liberal intentions, they had little chance to prove it. The new regime in Constantinople was immediately assailed by internal and external difficulties. In 1908 Austria seized Bosnia and Herzegovina, Crete announced her union with Greece, and Bulgaria declared her independence. In 1909 Abdul Hamid led an unsuccessful counter-revolution against the Young Turks. In 1911 Italy invaded Tripoli (Libya) and the following year the first Balkan War broke out. After the conclusion of the second Balkan War in 1913, Turkey stood stripped of her European territories. As one writer has observed: ' With the ending of the Balkan wars, the future of Turkey-in-Asia was becoming the decisive question in international relations '.[6]

With the world outside growing darker and more menacing as the shadow of war lengthened, Britain also faced formidable problems on the home front. ' These were the years of political uproar, the volume of which has not been since repeated: the row over the Education Bill, the Dreadnought scares, the terrorist methods of the suffragettes, the protracted mêlée over the Budget of 1909 and the guerilla warfare between Limehouse and the shires...'[7] Among her domestic problems the crisis over Home Rule for Ireland threatened to plunge the Liberal government into civil war. Many Tory imperialists, still smarting from the sting of electoral defeats in 1906 and 1910 and the circumscription of the power of the House of Lords by the Parliament Act of 1911, viewed Home Rule as the beginning of the end of the British Empire. In the years between 1911 and 1914 the Conservatives, or at least many in their ranks, endeavoured to undermine the constitutional government of England by inciting Ulster to revolt and encouraging mutiny in the British Army. It is widely held that only the coming of the War in 1914 prevented the outbreak of civil war at home.[8]

This then is the domestic and diplomatic framework which conditioned British relations with ibn Sa'ud in the last years before the outbreak of World War I. Naturally the larger issues at home and abroad dominated the attention of the British government. In this context it is not surprising that Sa'udi developments should have been treated as a very marginal issue.

British policy towards ibn Sa'ud from 1910 until the outbreak of war with Turkey in 1914 is characterised on the one hand by ibn Sa'ud's growing power in Arabia and on the other hand by the divided opinion in British governmental circles as to how this power and ibn Sa'ud's repeated requests for recognition should be dealt with. The India Office and the Government of India were usually in accord in wishing to treat with ibn Sa'ud lest he impinge upon their interests in the area. The Foreign Office, primarily concerned in the Middle East with the settlement of the outstanding issues between Britain and Turkey which could lead to war, viewed ibn Sa'ud as a figure of minimal importance in the context of general Anglo–Turkish relations. In the following pages the subordination of the relatively minor issue of increasing Sa'udi power will be seen to be the predominant theme.

The First Encounter

In 1910, ibn Sa'ud had his first meeting with a British official, Captain W. H. I. Shakespear, the Political Agent at Kuwait. William Henry Irwine Shakespear was to become ibn Sa'ud's principal advocate until his untimely death in 1915. According to his contemporaries, Shakespear, who was about ibn Sa'ud's age, was a man of exceptional qualities. Some idea of the character of this representative of the best tradition among servants of the Empire is reflected in the following anecdote related by Sir Arnold Wilson.

> I was once on board the slow mail from Kuwait to Bushire in a stiff *shamal* when we met him in his launch going in the opposite direction, rolling alarmingly. Up ran the signals on his foremast: ' Do you require assistance? ' I thought at first that he had sent the wrong signal, but the Master knew the man he was dealing with and sent an appropriate reply. Such men are the salt of the earth, and of any Service . . .[9]

Shakespear first met ibn Sa'ud when the latter was on a visit to Mubarak. The Political Agent was impressed by the more than usually generous entertainment provided by the Shaikh for the Wahhabi Amir. Ibn Sa'ud struck Shakespear ' as a broad-minded " straight " man, who could probably be trusted further than most Arabs '.[10] According to his report there was between the Englishman and the Amir no political talk of any consequence. Ibn Sa'ud, however, did invite Shakespear to visit him if ever the former were near Riyadh. Shakespear's first positive impression of the Najdi ruler was to grow into a strong admiration which was not unreciprocated. Indeed until his death in 1915 the enthusiastic young Political Agent was to prove a consistent supporter of ibn Sa'ud. However, his repeated suggestions that Britain enter into some agreement with the Amir came to nought. Britain was reluctant to make any moves towards the Arabs which might give the impression to the Porte that she was exploiting Arab unrest.

At this juncture Turkey was highly suspicious of Britain's attitude towards the quest for autonomy in many Arab countries. 'Autonomy' instead of 'nationalism' is used here for several reasons. Firstly, nationalism will be treated more fully in the following chapter. Secondly, although there were definite Arab nationalist movements at this time in Beirut, Damascus and Baghdad, it is debatable whether the same term is applicable to the discontent prevailing generally in Arabia and Mesopotamia. In the case of ibn Sa'ud his drive for independence was based on religion, recapturing his traditional domains, general anti-Turkism and, most probably an understandable element of self-aggrandizement.[11]

In some of the Arabic speaking parts of the Ottoman Empire, especially the great cities, the elation which had followed the accession of the Young Turks to power had turned to despair and alienation when the Constantinople government failed to carry out liberal reforms. Instead of the autonomy which the Arabs had increasingly begun to hope for, they were confronted with a new emphasis on the Turkish element and a continuation of Abdul Hamid's policy of centralization. To make matters worse, whereas Abdul Hamid had at least played on Moslem religiosity through his espousal of Pan-Islamism, the Young Turks were primarily secular rulers. Moreover, the new regime in Constantinople soon adopted Turkish nationalism as its motivating ideological force. Naturally this nationalism 'clashed with the Arabs' pride in their race, religion and language'.[12] As Sir G. Lowther, the British Ambassador to Constantinople (1908–1913) commented: 'That the Committee have given up any idea of Ottomanizing all the non-Turkish elements by sympathetic and constitutional ways has long been manifest. To them " Ottoman " evidently means " Turk " and their present policy of " Ottomanization " is one of pounding the non-Turkish elements in a Turkish mortar'.[13] Lowther had also reported in June 1910 that many of the Arabs who had come into 'contact with or had experience of British methods in Egypt, Aden, India, and the Gulf have begun to develop leanings towards England as opposed to the Turk'.[14] However, while relations between the Arabs and Turks deteriorated, local Arab chieftains, in time-honoured fashion, still waged war against each other.

Early in the summer of 1910 the first confrontation took place between the Sharif of Mecca, Husain ibn 'Ali, and ibn Sa'ud. The enmity and rivalry between the two was not to end until the latter took the Hedjaz sixteen years later. Husain succeeded to his post in 1908 and held great influence in the Moslem world as custodian of Mecca and Medina. He was appointed by imperial *firman* and as a member of the Quraish tribe and the family of Hashim he was generally believed to be a lineal descendant of Muhammad. Since his accession to the Sharifate, Husain, an ambitious man as his subsequent career eloquently reflects, had sought to restore the influence of his office which had dwindled under his predecessor.[15] Having spent fifteen years in Constantinople with his family as an ' honoured guest ' of Abdul Hamid, Husain had been well-schooled in the devious traits required for survival in the corruption and decadence which characterised the twilight period of the Ottoman Empire. Although no friend of the Turks he did have a Turkish veneer.[16] Husain's ambition, coupled with the influence of the Turkish officials in the Hedjaz which had been increasing since the late nineteenth century,[17] naturally antagonised ibn Sa'ud. Moreover, even if ibn Sa'ud, though religious, was too politic to be fettered by the more extreme aspects of Wahhabism, both he and his ardent followers must have been galled by the corruption and moral laxity of the Meccans, not to mention the Turks.

On June 10th the British Consul in Jedda reported that he had received word that Sharif Husain had recently demanded from ibn Sa'ud a yearly sum of TL 900 for the district of Qasim. This due had not been paid for thirty years and Husain was said, moreover, to have exhorted ' the inhabitants of Kassim to throw off their allegiance to ibn Saoud and become his, ... that is, the Ottoman Government's subjects ... ' [18]

The Sharif proceeded to send a punitive expedition to engage ibn Sa'ud with the result that the Amir's favourite brother, Sa'd, was captured at Quai'iya in 'Ataiba territory where he had arrived to collect recruits for a campaign against the *Araif*. As there were two sections of the 'Ataiba tribe, one in eastern and one in western Arabia, the issue was ripe for dispute.[19] Before continuing the account of the first Sa'udi–Sharifian clash it is necessary to consider briefly the significance of the *Araif*, as this tribe was to cause ibn Sa'ud trouble for the next few years.

Around 1910 the *Araif* (Arabic for ' lost camels refound '), the descendants of Sa'ud ibn Faisal,[20] revolted against ibn Sa'ud.

They were, in fact, senior in the Sa'udi line of succession. This collateral branch of the Sa'udi dynasty joined with the rebellious Ajman tribe and harassed ibn Sa'ud's flank. It will be seen that throughout the war years ibn Sa'ud was to be plagued by the Ajman and *al Araif*.

In the late autumn, 1910, ibn Sa'ud wrote to Mubarak explaining the capture of Sa'd. According to Mubarak's information—as related to Shakespear—the Najdi ruler was forced to beg for the release of his brother. Husain's conditions were stiff. Ibn Sa'ud had to pay 6,000 dollars (about 450 pounds) as tribute from the revenues of Qasim to remain ruler of southern Najd and Qasim. Ibn Sa'ud agreed to this but after his brother was returned he broke the agreement stating that as it had been made under compulsion it was not binding.[21]

In the same letter ibn Sa'ud asked Mubarak's advice ' as to complaining of the Sharif's inroad to the Turkish authorities in Basrah and Baghdad '. Mubarak informed the Political Agent ' that he had replied to Abdul Aziz [ibn Sa'ud] strongly deprecating such a course as most unadvisable for neither the Baghdad nor the Basra Vali could do any more than write reports to Constantinople and Abdul Aziz's complaint might open the door to further expeditions into Najd; that at present " the door is shut; and if once opened, no matter how little, God knows when it may again be closed " '.[22] Although he was anti-Turkish ibn Sa'ud, like his forebears, was not adverse to pledging his allegiance to the Porte when it served his purpose.

In March 1911, Capt. Shakespear had his first long meeting with ibn Sa'ud. The Political Agent had been on a tour of the Kuwait hinterland when he was invited to ibn Sa'ud's camp. Shakespear was again favourably impressed by ibn Sa'ud.[23] Ibn Sa'ud explained to the Political Agent that he wanted the Turks driven out of Hasa and Qatif because these constituted part of the traditional Wahhabi domains. Moreover, these districts were also the richest provinces and Turkish control over them made it difficult for him to control the tribes between Riyadh and the sea. Ibn Sa'ud wanted the British to protect him from invasion by sea and would be pleased to accept a British Agent after the Turks had been driven out. Although Shakespear explained to the Wahhabi chief that Great Britain was not in a position to support him, the latter still requested that his views be made known to the Government.

In London, Sir W. Lee Warner, a member of the Council at the India Office, wrote in a minute to this correspondence that the Turkish rail line to Medina might increase Turkish strength in Arabia and should the Turks be turned out of Europe they could become a formidable adversary in Asia.[24] Moreover, if Turkish pressure were to abate, ibn Sa'ud might sweep into Muscat. There was also the spectre of Germany behind Turkey; therefore, Britain would be well advised to steer clear of any involvement in central Arabia.[25]

In another minute on the same correspondence, Arthur Hirtzel, Secretary to the Political Department, speculated that if ibn Sa'ud drove the Turkish garrison out of Hasa and Britain blocked Turkish reinforcements via the Gulf, 'Turkish authority must disappear from the Arabian coast of the Gulf. It is worth thinking of in case they [the Turks] drive us to extremities.'[26] Hirtzel also commented that ibn Sa'ud's suggestion to Shakespear to post a British Agent in 'Uqair or Qatif would not necessarily lead to entanglements in central Arabia.[27] For the next three years Hirtzel, a cynical but incisive judge of affairs, was one of the very few government officials, if not the only one, in London to support consistently the Sa'udi case.

In answer to Shakespear's report, a letter was sent by the India Office to the Foreign Office in June. It outlined the traditional British policy towards central Arabia which was to prevail until Turkey entered the War on Germany's side.

> The objections to a policy of adventure in Central Arabia are not less strong than when the question was under consideration in 1904 ... But in view of the intractable attitude of the Turkish Government in the Persian Gulf it is important that His Majesty's Government should leave none of the weapons at their disposal unexamined, though the question of applying one or more of them at any particular time must require separate consideration and it is evident that one of the most powerful of these is such a response to the overtures now made by Abdul Aziz-bin-Saud as would render the position of the Turks untenable.
>
> Captain Shakespear's letter seems worth consideration from this point of view, but the negative attitude ... he adopted towards the proposal was strictly in accordance with the orders of His Majesty's Government, and if the

Government of India wish to recommend a departure from it they will no doubt submit their recommendation in due course.²⁸

In a long and detailed letter in the latter part of July, Colonel Cox pressed for some form of arrangement with ibn Sa'ud. The Political Resident pointed out that since the case was last reviewed in 1907 the Turks had not made an effort to re-establish a foothold in Najd.²⁹ Conversely, ibn Sa'ud had grown in power and influence and, according to Shakespear, the Wahhabi ruler now

> asserts himself northwards to a point more than halfway between Buraida and Hali [sic], while on the south he collects tribute as far as the Wadi Dawasir. He thus feels no doubt that he is in a stronger position than ever to recover Hasa and Qatif, if only the sea were closed to the Turks.³⁰

Cox went on to state that although Britain's satisfactory diplomatic relations with the Porte precluded any agreement with ibn Sa'ud, he should not be completely rejected. The Wahhabi Amir's offer to Shakespear to receive a British Agent if he reached the coast deserved consideration. It was advisable that Shakespear should be directed to reply promptly and in a friendly manner, however disappointing the purport of the message. Cox proposed that, if it would be consonant with British policy in the Gulf and not inimical to the Turkish position, ibn Sa'ud should enter into a trucial-type agreement with Great Britain.³¹ The British Resident argued further that if ibn Sa'ud did not consent to such an agreement, at least Britain would have answered him and the above terms would be relatively harmless diplomatically. As regards Anglo-Turkish relations, Britain could argue that she had brought pressure to bear on a recalcitrant subject in prohibiting the import of arms and the British government would then have reasonable grounds for protest if the Porte tried to coerce ibn Sa'ud by sea. Moreover if relations became strained with Turkey ' we might usefully remind them that they only retained their control of Hasa and Qatif, thanks to our pacific and deterrent influence over Bin Sa'ud, and that were that influence withdrawn their position in those districts would not be worth a month's purchase '.³²

The Foreign Office was in agreement with the India Office. His Majesty's Government was to continue to follow its original policy of non-involvement in central Arabian affairs. Presumably a polite reply was given to ibn Sa'ud. It is not altogether clear from the documents whether this was done or not.

In March 1911, at the instigation of the Turkish government, discussions were started with Great Britain with a view to settling the outstanding problems existing between the two countries. The road leading to the settlement of these problems had, to a great extent, been cleared four months previously when in November 1910 the Czar and the Kaiser had reached agreement at Potsdam on the Baghdad Railway. Hence, amidst outcries in France and England that Russia was breaking up the Triple Entente, the first and most consistent opponent of the railway was removed. The British, who had formerly insisted on four-way discussions among the Triple Entente and Germany, found this line no longer tenable. 'The first breach had been made in the heretofore solid front presented by the Entente.' [33]

As usual the Turks were in need of financial assistance. After failing to raise loans in Paris and London, the Porte proposed a 4% increase in customs. As will be recalled, this needed the approval of Great Britain who was a member of the Ottoman Public Debt Administration. In the ensuing negotiations, the Porte undoubtedly seized upon Britain's anxiety to settle the Baghdad Railway questions,[34] in order that she might in turn obtain her customs increase.

On July 29 1911, Britain replied to the Turkish overtures.[35] The matters for discussion were grouped in three categories: (1) the respective interests of Britain and Turkey in the Persian Gulf region (2) the Baghdad Railway and (3) an increase in Turkish customs duties. The last matter required assent of the interested foreign governments. All three categories were so intertwined that none could be settled independently. On this basis negotiations were started in 1911.[36] However, owing to the Agadir Crisis when 'war between Great Britain and Germany stood clear on the horizon'[37] and the outbreak of the Tripolitan War on September 29 1911, negotiations were only resumed in earnest in 1913. On July 1913, several conventions relating to the Persian Gulf and the Shatt-al-Arab were signed.

As the Anglo–Turkish Convention has been treated fully in many secondary sources[38] it is important only to note here that under the convention relating to the Persian Gulf an important reference to Najd was made. This matter will be developed later. As to the immediate question of reaching some sort of an agreement with ibn Sa'ud, it will be apparent that the larger issues embodied in the Anglo–Turkish Convention—especially the question of the Baghdad Railway—relegated the rising Amir to a position of marginal importance.

In the autumn of 1911 relations between ibn Sa'ud and Husain deteriorated further. The Acting Consul in Jedda reported that all communication between Najd and the Hedjaz had stopped. Apparently ibn Sa'ud, in consolidating his power, was levying taxes on the 'Ataiba tribe which was reported as being ' the mainstay and backbone of the Sharif's authority in the country...' [39] As the levying of taxes in desert politics was often tantamount to asserting sovereignty over those taxed, Husain was understandably angered. In retaliation, the Sharif served notice that any goods coming from or going to Najd ' will be looted without any responsibility on his part '.[40] However, there was no clash reported in the latter part of 1911.

In late 1911 or early 1912, the Turks are said to have made contact with ibn Sa'ud. Given the Wahhabi's growing stature in desert politics the Turks ' sought to bring him into their counsels as a make-weight against the nationalist movement in the settled lands on his borders '.[41] The Vali of Basra, Sulaiman Shafiq Pasha, contacted ibn Sa'ud to ascertain his views. The Amir suggested that the Porte come to an agreement with the Arabs on a voluntary basis. Ibn Sa'ud proposed that a meeting should be convened at some neutral place where all the Arab chiefs would be represented. He held that the Turks had two alternatives: the Arab countries could continue as they were at present, a group of separate political entities but operating under local administrative independence with one of their own rulers functioning as a Vali in a Turkish province; or a system could be devised whereby a single Arab group would be presided over by an elected leader. In either case the Arabs would still be under Turkish suzerainty. Ibn Sa'ud's proposals were sent on to Constantinople but nothing was done.[42]

The Seizure of Hasa: ibn Sa'ud Reaches the Coast

In May of 1913 ibn Sa'ud, aware of the Turkish preoccupation in the Balkans and her defeat by Italy, asserted himself dramatically and seized Hasa, driving out the Turkish garrisons which had been there since 1872. Apparently with the aid of the inhabitants of Hufhuf, the provincial capital, ibn Sa'ud occupied Hasa with very little fighting. The Turkish troops were taken to Bahrain in the British ship *John O'Scott*. On their arrival in Bahrain command of the Turkish troops was assumed by one, Major Nuri Bey, recently arrived from Basra. He sailed a week later with all available troops for Qatif but reached there too late as ibn Sa'ud had already taken it. The Major and his men returned by the British vessel to Bahrain. On the 26th, a Turkish Colonel, Abdul Jabir Bey, took command and despatched Nuri Bey with a contingent of troops to 'Uqair. They captured a tower but later fled when fresh Arab warriors arrived, leaving sixty men and one officer behind. These troops surrendered to ibn Sa'ud the next day and were despatched to Bahrain. No further attempts were made to retake Hasa or Qatif.[43]

On May 18, the British Consul at Basra reported to Lowther in Constantinople that Sayyid Talib, a prominent Basra Arab, had received a letter from ibn Sa'ud regarding Hasa. Sayyid Talib told the Consul that the letter contained expressions of loyalty to the Porte ' but complained of the mismanagement of Hasa affairs by the Turkish officials and nonpayment of the allowance previously granted him by the Government '.[44] Ibn Sa'ud wrote that as Hasa was composed of Arabs owing him allegiance, his re-taking of the province was a return to the traditional state of affairs. Sayyid Talib also mentioned that there was another letter to the Vali of Basra enclosed in this correspondence. In this letter ibn Sa'ud affirmed his subservience to the Porte.[45] In these protestations of loyalty to the Porte, the Wahhabi Amir was probably endeavouring to prevent the Turks from taking any more punitive measures against him.

As early as 1893 Britain had informed the Porte that she would not permit the trans-shipment of Ottoman troops in Bahrain waters. When Cox relayed this to Grey and requested instructions, Alwyn Parker, of the Foreign Office, wrote in a minute which was later telegraphed to Cox on May 21st : ' You should take no action. The negotiations with Turkey are proceeding satisfactorily, and if necessary we could protest against any trans-shipment *ex post facto* '.[46]

The situation was further complicated by the fact that Shakespear visited ibn Sa'ud shortly before the latter's invasion. This gave the impression to an ever suspicious Turkey that the Amir's manoeuvre was at least condoned by the British government. Shakespear reported that his conversations with ibn Sa'ud during this meeting were in general a repetition of his 1911 encounter. The Wahhabi Amir alluded to treaties between the Turks and the Wahhabis, and between Great Britain and his forebears. He claimed that these treaties recognised his claim to Qatif and Hasa.[47] Ibn Sa'ud went on to point out that the Turks had tried to dominate him by pressing him for men and money. They had tried to get him to show his loyalty by (1) sending his sons to Constantinople for education and military service (2) acknowledging Turkish suzerainty by accepting a Turkish title and appointment to the Government of Najd, and (3) handing over all letters and documents exchanged between himself and the British government. Ibn Sa'ud stressed that all the Arab chiefs were discontented with Turkish attempts to subjugate them and that Arab leaders looked to him for example. The Wahhabi leader saw his chance to assert himself in Hasa and Qatif in the light of Turkish troubles with Italy and more recently in the Balkan Wars. Shakespear cautioned ibn Sa'ud against attacking —but to no avail. At the same time the British Agent viewed ibn Sa'ud as the future leader of Arabia and urged Britain to reconsider Anglo–Wahhabi relations.[48] However, Shakespear's foresight and ardent appeals for an agreement with ibn Sa'ud, which were backed by Cox, ran up against a brick wall of Foreign Office opposition.

In a despatch from Cox suggesting that Britain arrive at a solution to the problem of Turko–Sa'udi relations, Parker wrote in the margin: 'I don't see why we need interfere in any way whatsoever'. Also in the margin of Shakespear's report, where the Political Agent had written that he had spent four days with ibn Sa'ud, Parker wrote: 'a great pity'. Finally, to emphasise his disapproval of Shakespear's advice, he singled out the following statement: 'On the other hand to reject the Amir's overtures will assuredly cause a feeling of resentment *which may react upon our interests along the whole Arabian littoral of the Gulf*'. Parker underlined the foregoing and wrote in the margin: 'nonsense'.[49]

The Anglo–Turkish Draft Convention unfortunately did not provide for ibn Sa'ud's incursions in Qatif and Hasa. Article

II awarded control of Najd to the Turks even though they had never penetrated further than Hufhuf.[50]

Cox thought that, although Britain was committed to recognition of Turkish suzerainty over Najd, she must have relations with the *de facto* ruler of Najd. An arrangement could be effected, with Turkish countenance, whereby ibn Sa'ud would be recognised as autonomous ruler of Najd under Ottoman suzerainty, and Britain would have the right ' to accredit an agent to him as one of the maritime rulers, and make agreements with him, with the knowledge of the Porte, in connection with the suppression of arms traffic, slave trade, and piracy, and our mission in the Gulf generally '.[51] In forwarding Cox's despatch the Viceroy, Lord Hardinge, added a concluding paragraph which reflected a more realistic appreciation of the diplomatic situation at the time and the usual pragmatic approach.

> It seems impossible at this late hour to raise the status of Nejd without running the risk of wrecking the negotiations. In the circumstances we presume that His Majesty's Government will decide, while keeping on friendly terms with Bin Saud, *to await further developments.*[52]

Cox was overruled. The Political Resident was advised to ' refer for instruction any overtures that may be made by ibn Sa'ud. It is the policy of His Majesty's Government to consolidate the Government of Turkey in Asia Minor, and to abstain from intervention in Nejd, whether direct or indirect, as long as possible '.[53]

Grey was in complete concurrence with Parker. He deprecated even broaching the subject of discussion with ibn Sa'ud and was in favour of awaiting developments. ' The general attitude of His Majesty's Government, which in this matter is based on considerations of European policy, is to consolidate the power of the Central Government in Asiatic Turkey; and if His Majesty's Government were to approach the Ottoman Government, as suggested by Sir P. Cox, with a view to concluding direct agreements with ibn Sa'ud as an autonomous ruler, it would give rise to suspicion, and might have far-reaching and regrettable effects '.[54] Grey directed that the Political Agent at Kuwait be instructed to abstain from any communication with ibn Sa'ud and not commit Britain to any line of policy.[55]

The Amir of Najd, naturally unaware of the hardening negative attitude to him in London, contacted the Political Agent in Bahrain. In letters from him carried by an envoy, he once again raised the subject of his long and continued friendship with Great Britain. The correspondence referred to the Wahhabi's 1866 agreement with Pelly and also addressed a remonstrance to the British Agent in Bahrain for assisting the Turkish troops. Ibn Sa'ud was anxious that his long friendship be preserved and pledged protection and good treatment of British subjects. However, he showed his disappointment with the absence of British support when he asked that 'if the situation is now altered and Great Britain is not willing to preserve former friendship, which is his earnest desire, he may be definitely informed, so that he may look to his own interests'.[56]

Hardinge asked for direct instructions to be sent to Cox about the nature of the reply to be given to ibn Sa'ud. The Government of India advised that if the answer were to be non-committal it should be added that Britain did not wish to deviate from her former policy of friendly relations.[57] On July 2, a long and unusually harsh letter was sent from the Foreign Office to the India Office. To a great extent it summed up previous correspondence on ibn Sa'ud through May and June and flatly reiterated British policy:

> ... [Sir Edward Grey] has under careful consideration the despatch, dated the 26th May, 1913, from His Majesty's consul-general at Bushire to the Government of India, and the enclosure, as despatch, dated the 15th May, 1913, from the political agent at Koweit respecting the situation in Nejd.
>
> Sir E. Grey has learnt with regret that Captain Shakespear recently spent four days in the camp of Ibn Saud, a course which does not seem to have been a necessary condition of any mission with which that officer may have been charged in the 'hinterland of Koweit' and one which is obviously calculated to arouse suspicions with regard to British aspirations and intentions.
>
> Captain Shakespear, in paragraph 10 of this report writes: '... on the other hand to reject the Amir's overtures will assuredly cause a feeling of resentment which may react upon our interests along the whole Arabian littoral of the Gulf ...'

Sir E. Grey is not in a position to gauge the accuracy of this forecast, but he is fully convinced that the consequences of any such resentment would be unimportant by comparison with those which might result from the establishment of direct relations between the Amir and His Majesty's Government.

Sir P. Cox, in forwarding Captain Shakespear's report, and commenting upon it after the fall of Hasa and Katif observes:

It is difficult to see how the Porte with an empty exchequer and with trouble brewing simultaneously in the Basra vilayet, can hope for some time to come to undertake punitive operations against Bin Saud. In any case, if any attempt is made to operate by sea, we shall at once be faced with the question as to whether our policy will admit of our acquiescing in such a course, which in all probability would prove abortive and leave us a legacy of bitter resentment on the part of Bin Saud.

I am to state that Sir E. Grey fails to see why His Majesty's Government need interfere in any way whatsoever in such a contingency as that indicated; he considers that their attitude should be one of strict neutrality.

In view of this and recent despatches from British officers in the Persian Gulf Sir E. Grey is of the opinion that further and more stringent telegraphic instructions should be issued to Sir P. Cox enjoining upon him and his subordinates to abstain carefully from any communication whatsoever other than that of a purely formal nature where inevitable, with Ibn Saud or any other Arabian chief with whom His Majesty's Government have no treaty relations.

The cardinal factor of British policy, which is based upon considerations not purely local, is to uphold the integrity of the Turkish dominions in Asia.[58]

The tone of this despatch was thought severe even among some of Grey's subordinates. Louis Mallet commented in the margin of the rough draft of the above letter that in view of recent telegrams he thought these instructions were 'unnecessary'.[59] Sir Arthur Nicolson also commented that he thought 'this stricture too severe—and scarcely justified—Capt. Shakespear himself spoke very plainly and sensibly to Bin Saud'.[60]

In the despatch to be sent to ibn Sa'ud by the India Office it was stated that Britain had not assisted Turkish troops and although they recognised ibn Sa'ud's importance, Great Britain must remain strictly neutral.[61] In a comment on the harsher rewording of the India Office's draft telegram to ibn Sa'ud proposed by the Foreign Office, Crewe underscored the disagreement between the two Offices and the paramount position of the Foreign Office when he wrote: ' I prefer the earlier version but it is largely a FO matter and we must accept their revision '.[62]

Controversy was to rage around Shakespear's visit for several weeks. Parker thought it was in ' contravention of the explicit instructions contained in Mr. Brodrick's telegram of February 8, 1907 '.[63] Hirtzel, in a long and carefully argued minute, attempted to refute this allegation. He held that as Shakespear's first visit to ibn Sa'ud (in 1911) had caused no comment, he therefore had naturally thought nothing of seeing him again. Where he was blameworthy was in his being 150 miles southwest of the farthest point claimed as Kuwait territory when he heard that the Amir was in the neighbourhood.[64]

It was thought at this juncture that the stringent attitude adopted by the Foreign Office would interfere with the duties of the Gulf Agents and Resident. These men were concerned with everyday facts in the Gulf developments. From the tone of the Foreign Office's communications, it would appear that in their understandable emphasis on the preservation of Turkey and the Anglo–Turkish negotiations they chose to turn their backs on the complicating but nevertheless important political changes of scene in the Persian Gulf.

Crewe answered Grey's letter in a polite but firm tone. The Secretary of State stressed that he valued the opinions of his officials and that since the visit had taken place three months previously and followed the precedent of 1911, he did not think Shakespear was indiscreet. In forwarding Shakespear's and Cox's reports Crewe wanted it understood that he did not intend to commit himself to any policy.[65] In a draft despatch to the Government of India, Crewe directed that in future Shakespear was, unless otherwise directed, to confine himself to the limits of the territory ' assigned to Kowait under the Anglo–Turkish Convention '.[66]

The controversy over Shakespear's visit was another manifestation of the inter-office rivalry so characteristic of British dealings with ibn Sa'ud. From the Foreign Office standpoint the question of Sa'udi overtures must have seemed remarkably insignificant when viewed against the overall importance of Anglo–Turkish relations. To understand the reaction of the Foreign Office one must also remember the pressures on Grey and his staff on the eve of the First World War, and also the fact that Grey was one of the least travelled of any Foreign Secretaries. Having little experience of Europe, let alone the East, his attitude towards ibn Sa'ud, especially in the diplomatic climate of the day, is not surprising.[67]

From the India Office's viewpoint Crewe must have felt that not only was the Foreign Office over-reacting but, if its views were carried to their logical conclusion, British interests in the Gulf would surely suffer. In the Gulf itself one can validly argue that despite the larger issues, Cox and Shakespear did have to deal with local realities. However, in this case, it appears that they were unable to raise their field of vision from the restricted horizon of Gulf politics to the broader plane of Anglo–Turkish relations. In essence if the Foreign Office over-reacted, the Gulf officials displayed a certain lack of imagination, a failure to appreciate diplomatic priorities and an inability to grasp the power the British held vis-à-vis ibn Sa'ud The conclusions of one author commenting on Anglo–Sa'udi relations in 1907 hold true for the situation prevailing in 1913. In the final analysis ibn Sa'ud could not have pursued an anti-British policy. Fearing invasion by sea he would ' be dependent upon England [the paramount power in the Gulf] diplomatically and strategically for a considerable time to come '.[68] It is therefore incorrect to hold as did several authors that Britain missed an opportunity to support ibn Sa'ud before 1914.[69]

Cox had specified in his telegram of June 27th that he had to have an answer by July 3rd because the mail left that day. Unfortunately Crewe's telegram of July 3rd outlining the answer to be given by Cox to ibn Sa'ud reached the Political Resident too late. It appears that as a result of this delay the British missed an opportunity to communicate with the Amir. Cox was informed by the Agent in Bahrain that one of ibn Sa'ud's envoys had arrived in Bahrain en route for Basra. The envoy carried telegrams destined for Constantinople. It was explained that ibn Sa'ud's action was forced upon him ' in the public interests and that he entertained the utmost loyalty to the Sublime Porte '.⁷⁰

Sometime in July 1913 ibn Sa'ud was said to have written to the Shaikh of Qatar demanding that the Shaikh expel the Turks from his land. To complicate matters the old Shaikh, Qasim ibn Thani, died and his son 'Abdullah, the new ruler of Qatar, was reported by the Political Agent at Bahrain to have arranged to meet the Wahhabi ruler. It was suggested that ibn Sa'ud might force the new Shaikh to evict the Turks or else he himself would take possession of Qatar.⁷⁴ The Shaikhs of Abu Dhabi and Dubai were also reported to be making ready for a Sa'udi onslaught. The Shaikh of Abu Dhabi was understandably fearful of an attack as he presently controlled Buraimi—which ibn Sa'ud claimed. The Shaikhs threatened to call out their Bedouin followers to meet any Sa'udi incursions.⁷² If this were not enough to tax British policy, ibn Sa'ud could also threaten Trucial Oman, owing to the Muscat Rebellion.⁷³

Hardinge wrote to Crewe that ibn Sa'ud was now in a powerful position to infringe on British interests. Therefore the Wahhabi leader must be ' conciliated or estranged '.⁷⁴ Ibn Sa'ud could be expelled but as he had been friendly the Viceroy proposed the following solution. There was to be an ' amicable exchange of views ' with the British intentions explained to the Porte.⁷⁵ At the same time the Trucial Chiefs would be warned against provocative action.

Predictably Parker disagreed with the above action, maintaining that the Turks should put their house in order. Grey, however, agreed with Louis Mallet's views which were recorded in a minute on the above correspondence. Mallet argued that it would do no good to ask the Turks to communicate with ibn Sa'ud as he was in rebellion against them and would pay no attention. He urged that the situation should be explained to Hakki Pasha, the Turkish Ambassador in London. The Ruler of Najd should be informed that he ' must not interfere with the territory of chiefs with whom we have treaty or other relations in the Gulf littoral '.⁷⁶

The above course was translated into action as Hakki was informed of the British decision and the Government of India was directed to forward the message to ibn Sa'ud. The Porte was to be informed in writing of the British communications to the

Amir when the Foreign Office received the exact terms of the message sent to ibn Sa'ud.⁷⁷

In early September, the Political Resident received a friendly letter from the Sa'udi Amir requesting a clear explanation of Britain's attitude towards him. Cox was authorised to reply as follows:

> Meanwhile I have my Government's authority to assure you that provided you undertake on your part to abstain from all action calculated to disturb the *status quo*, or to create unrest amongst Arab principalities whose rulers are in relations with His Majesty's Government, including the principality of Katar independence of which under the government of the late Sheikh Jasim and his successors of the Bin Thani has been recently recognised, the British Government will continue to maintain friendly relations which have been sustained in the past.⁷⁸

Cox sent this despatch on September 11th. Great Britain was naturally wary of any Sa'udi action in Qatar. Not only would this disturb the status quo, but it would probably necessitate British military involvement. Moreover, by the terms of the Anglo–Turkish Convention, the Turks had agreed to withdraw their garrison from Qatar. Although this convention was signed on July 29th, ratification still awaited the outcome of the Baghdad Railway negotiations.⁷⁹ Britain was afraid that any Gulf developments would exacerbate the negotiations and give the Turks the opportunity to open other questions. Another very important feature of this convention was that in Article II part of central Arabia was designated as the 'Ottoman sanjak of Nejd'. The eastern boundary of Najd was defined by what came to be known as the 'Blue Line'. The short article dealing with Najd deserves to be quoted in full.

> Le sandjak ottoman de Nedjd, dont la limite septentrionale est indiquée par la ligne de démarcation définie à l'article 7 de cette convention, se termine vers le sud au golfe faisant face à l'île de Zannoumie, qui appartient au dit sandjak. Une ligne partant du fond extreme dudit golfe ira directement au sud jusqu'au Ruba'-al-Khali et séparera le Nedjd de la presqu'île d'El-Katr. Les limites du Nedjd sont indiquées par une ligne bleue sur la carte annexée à la presente convention...⁸⁰

With Qatar taken care of and Najd and Hasa awarded to the Turks, the Foreign Office had all the more reason to wish ibn Sa'ud to remain peaceful. He was to be informed that the garrison was not very important and that he should not interfere in Qatar. Great Britain offered to mediate between ibn Sa'ud and the Porte but Hakki declined. He claimed that the Turkish government was already ' en pourparlers avec Ebonsoud '.[81]

Shakespear and Trevor (the Political Agent at Bahrain) met ibn Sa'ud at 'Uqair on December 15th and 16th, 1913. Once again the Amir recounted how the Turks had fomented trouble between him and his followers. When asked specifically what he wanted from Britain, he replied that he desired protection of his honour and preservation of his ancestral right. If this could not be realised he would be forced to come to terms with the Turks. He then proceeded to offer his co-operation with arms and trucial agreements, and asserted his willingness to abstain from incursions into Trucial Oman and Qatar.[82]

The Wahhabi leader pressed for a settlement as he had kept the Turks waiting since August. The Ottoman government had apparently laid down the following stipulations to ibn Sa'ud. He was to have partial autonomy under the Sultan but would have to comply with the following terms, given here in abbreviated form.

1. The Turkish garrisons were to be reinstated in Hasa.
2. *Qadis* and other judicial officials were to be appointed by firman by the Sultan.
3. All agents and merchants of foreign powers were to be excluded from Najd.
4. All communications from foreign powers were to be referred to the Porte.
5. He was to pay an annual revenue of TL 3,000.
6. There were to be no concessions to foreign powers for car or railway services.[83]

Ibn Sa'ud offered to admit and protect British subjects. He informed the two Agents that he had sent instructions to his man in Qatif to allow British subjects to trade and open shop there. They were to be under his protection. The Amir also requested a pass to obtain 4,000 Martini rifles and carbines plus 400 rounds of ammunition per weapon. He assured Trevor that he would not sell the weapons. The Political Agent recommended that ibn Saʻud be given the rifles. If this were not possible at the moment, Trevor advised that the weapons be forwarded to ibn Saʻud when the Anglo–Turkish negotiations were near completion. It was believed that ibn Saʻud's overtures reflected his willingness to co-operate. Hence the Political Agent advised that some arrangements be effected lest ibn Saʻud be driven to obtain the weapons illegally.[84]

The Acting Resident advised that Britain arrange that Qatar and Trucial Oman did not harbour the *Araif*. It was suggested that ibn Saʻud be informed that Britain was ready to mediate between him and the Turks. He was to be told that Great Britain would try to support him. It was also put forward that Cox's suggestion should be implemented. Cox had proposed that Britain obtain an undertaking from the Turks whereby they would not attack the Amir by sea without a previous exchange of views with Britain.[85]

Grey, however, probably thinking that other men were as honourable as himself, was still afraid of too much intercourse with ibn Saʻud. Displaying a rather naive attitude, the Foreign Secretary held that the Porte would meet reasonable requests if treated with frankness. He wanted to avoid the impression that Britain was trying to undermine Turkish authority in Najd.[86]

In London, Parker met Hakki to discuss Anglo–Turkish negotiations and was informed that the Ottoman government was upset about the British Agent's meeting with ibn Saʻud. Basra had reported that Britain had entered into direct relations with the Najdi Amir. Britain, of course, denied this. Parker told Hakki that he should meet Cox, and that Britain was ready to offer to help effect reconciliation. This was declined as Hakki pointed out that matters were nearly completed. Parker stated that his Government was afraid that ibn Saʻud would interfere in Trucial Oman, thus forcing Britain to interfere. Moreover, in the conditions put to the Wahhabi ruler, British merchants had been excluded from Qatif. Hakki professed disbelief on the last point. The Turkish Ambassador held that in view of the concessions made to Britain by Turkey respecting the Turko–Persian frontier, Aden, and Qatar, great emphasis was placed on British recognition of Turkish authority in Najd. Hakki was reassured.[87]

In a second meeting Hakki was urged to allow Britain to mediate before undertaking military operations against ibn Saʻud.

The British also told Hakki that 'military operations were in fact impossible, owing to the nature of the coast, without infringing the neutrality of Bahrain (this he refused to believe), which we ... [could] not allow (this he admitted)'.[88] As the Arabian coast to the north of Bahrain was treacherous owing to an abundance of reefs, it was extremely difficult to stage a landing between Kuwait and the Qatar promontory. Moreover, the coastline of the Qatar promontory itself was a mariner's nightmare of reefs and shoals.[89]

On March 9, 1914, the British government summarised in a memorandum their desiderata with regard to ibn Sa'ud and communicated it to Hakki. Although firm, the tone and content of the memorandum were in harmony with the previous discussions with the Turkish Ambassador. In essence it stated that Britain must have relations with someone *de facto* in power. They recognised that Najd was an Ottoman province, but as ibn Sa'ud had reached the coast, Britain had to deal with him. The British government was aware that several of the Turkish stipulations were directed against it, and accordingly wanted them withdrawn.

The British desired that in addition to abiding by the maritime truce as regards arms, piracy and non-interference on the Trucial Coast or in Qatar, ibn Sa'ud should admit British traders to Qatif, offer them protection and exclude all foreign merchants. The Amir of Najd should be recognised as *Mutasarrif* (deputy governor) of Hasa. Furthermore, the Porte should 'refrain from hostile action by sea against the El Hasa coast without first consulting us, and giving us an opportunity of friendly mediation if such be possible'.[90]

Although after July 29 1913, Britain asserted continually that she recognised Najd as an Ottoman province, practically speaking this protestation was political fiction. It appears that when circumstances would be served by a declaration of loyalty to the Porte, ibn Sa'ud, demonstrating the art of political survival, had no compunction about emphasising his fealty to the Turks. However, as the Turks never substantially penetrated the inner fastnesses of Arabia or exerted any concerted or sustained power over ibn Sa'ud, it would be purely academic to argue at this point that he came under effective Ottoman jurisdiction. These anomalies were to be only partially erased with the advent of the War.

While Britain and Turkey attempted to iron out their difficulties with respect to ibn Sa'ud, discontent continued to grow among the Arabs in the Ottoman Empire. Mallet, now ambassador in Constantinople, had pointed out that a rumour was current which intimated that the great Shaikhs were to hold a congress at Kuwait or elsewhere. According to a despatch received from the Consul General at Basra, ibn Sa'ud, Husain, ibn Rashid, the 'Ajaimi Shaikh of the Muntafiq and Sayyid Talib were to be there. As Mallet indicated in his correspondence, this rumour, even if untrue, showed growing unrest. Finally he cautioned against the break up of the Empire, the inevitable partition, and the effect of the dissolution of the Caliphate on the Indian Moslems.[91]

Ibn Sa'ud wrote to Trevor on February 26th stating that he had heard nothing from the Political Agent since their meeting and he hoped that 'some good cause has kept . . . you [Trevor] from writing'.[92] After the December meeting with ibn Sa'ud, Trevor had requested the Government of India to forward any order for communication with the Wahhabi ruler before he moved north in early spring. Ibn Sa'ud had mentioned that he must receive something soon as he could not keep the Turks off for much longer. Trevor replied that he had failed to answer because he had not received instructions. On March 16 the Government of India directed in a telegram that, as the 'High British Government' was attempting to effect an arrangement with Turkey, it was inadvisable that ibn Sa'ud take any independent action. The Political Agent carried out these instructions.

Around the end of the month the Turks were ready to implement their plans to negotiate with ibn Sa'ud. Sayyid Talib was helping to arrange things through the Shaikh of Kuwait. Mallett warned against offering mediation now as the Grand Vizier, Talaat Pasha, had informed him that the Turks hoped to come to a settlement by themselves. Mallet instructed the Consul at Basra to offer mediation only if desirable.[93]

Grey was still disturbed about the Government of India's telegram of March 16 advising ibn Sa'ud not to negotiate independently of His Majesty's Government. He had 'grave doubts' as to the wisdom of conveying that warning to the Sa'udi Amir.[94] Writing on behalf of Grey, Sir Eyre Crowe elaborated on these 'grave doubts'.

Grey doesn't approve of Great Britain advising a Turkish subject not to negotiate with his Government especially in light of the Anglo–Turkish Convention. If terms inimical to Great Britain in the Gulf have been agreed to between Sa'ud and the Porte the answer lies in direct talks with the Porte... discontinuance of direct communications of a questionable nature with Sa'ud, may possibly, Sir E. Grey holds, cause some minor local inconvenience in the Persian Gulf; but such inconvenience would in all probability be of short duration, and it is desirable to incur it rather than to run the risk of the graver dangers so forcibly portrayed in the Viceroy's telegram of last September.[95]

Grey did not even want mediation offered unless it was emphatically stated in writing that Britain adhered strictly to the treaty of July 29th and had no intention of 'undermining Ottoman authority'.[96] Mallet informed Talaat accordingly.

Hirtzel argued that Grey, through Sir Eyre Crowe, had concurred in the telegram of the 16th. He thought that the Foreign Office, by its latest action, had reverted to its old policy 'of pretending that Saud doesn't exist'.[97] Hirtzel went on to emphasise—what should have been obvious for quite some time now—that it was advisable to have one policy and adhere to it, and carry on the negotiations through one channel.[98] Unfortunately almost a decade was to elapse before this desire was fulfilled.

Crewe still saw nothing inconsistent in effecting an arrangement with the *de facto* ruler of Najd. He held that if ibn Sa'ud negotiated unilaterally and the Porte coerced him, he would naturally rebel and Turkey's integrity would be dealt a blow. Moreover if the Wahhabi ruler thought Britain indifferent he could alternatively throw himself into the arms of the Porte and become hostile to Great Britain. Crewe thought it would be dangerous if ibn Sa'ud negotiated unaware of London developments. It was for this reason that he sent the telegram of March 16th. However, as the London talks had got nowhere, Crewe, if Grey agreed, would advise ibn Sa'ud that there was no objection to his talking alone. But Crewe did not want the Sa'udi Amir to conclude anything until Britain was satisfied that it did not conflict with her interests.[99] Grey relented and the Viceroy was directed to have ibn Sa'ud informed that he was free to negotiate. Sir Edward Grey, however, stipulated that the Porte, and not ibn Saʻud, inform Britain if any terms conflicted with British interests in the Gulf.[100]

The Turks attempted to contact ibn Saʻud through Basra. A Turkish major arrived in Basra and wrote to the Shaikh of Kuwait asking about his relationship with Britain and the Saʻudi Amir. Mubarak gave standard diplomatic replies. The Turkish major asked the Shaikh to arrange an interview between him and ibn Saʻud. Mubarak refused. The Shaikh of Kuwait did not want to be drawn into the negotiations because he feared that the Turks might take this opportunity to increase their influence on Kuwait. It was also true that Mubarak was jealous of ibn Saʻud's rising stature in Arabia and wanted to remain the sole link between the Turks and the Amir. However Mubarak finally did convey to ibn Saʻud the Turkish message suggesting talks. Ibn Saʻud in turn contacted Trevor to ask for a meeting before he would accept the overture.[101]

The Vali of Basra was reported at this time to have written to Mubarak intimating that the Turkish decoration, Order of Osmanlieh, First Class division, was to be bestowed on him and that the Vali wanted to come to Kuwait immediately to bestow this order. The Shaikh declined. He interpreted this as a ploy to draw him into talks with ibn Saʻud. He preferred to go to Fao for the investiture.[102]

On the eve of the Turko–Saʻudi negotiations the position of the British government was summed up in a brief memorandum by T. W. Holderness of the India Office.

> Our view wh. [which] is that of the Viceroy is opposed to that at present held by the FO.
>
> The FO regards Bin Saud as a rebel agst. [against] the Turkish Government, and an Arabian chief towards whom HM's Govt. has no obligations, and no *locus standi*. HM's Govt. is not required to interfere on his behalf, and is indifferent to what may befall him; and should not intervene since interference might be prejudicial to its intercourse with the Turkish Govt.
>
> Our view is that as he is the *de facto* possessor of territory on the Gulf and at the present the strongest power in Arabia, HM's G. cannot view with indifference the attempts of the Turks to crush him, and to wrest from him his

possessions on the Gulf. As he is anxious to be guided by our advice, he should be advised by us in his negotiations with the Turks, and the latter should be made aware of our wish to bring about a settlement; fair to him and to our own position in the Gulf.

Our view is necessarily limited to Indian interests, and may conflict with larger considerations of wh. [which] the FO has to take account.[103]

Crewe agreed with Holderness. ' I am strongly of the opinion that it would be a blunder to let any Arab chief, in particular Bin Saud, gain the impression that we are indifferent to what happens in Arabia '.[104]

Colonel Grey, having replaced Shakespear temporarily as Political Agent at Kuwait, met ibn Saʻud at Malah, the Amir's camping place between Kuwait and Subaihiya. Ibn Saʻud was disappointed at Britain's failure to support him; however, he was pleased when told that Britain had offered to mediate but the Turks had refused. The Political Agent informed ibn Saʻud that Britain did not mind if he negotiated directly with the Turkish government. The Amir asked once again if Britain would protect him against invasion by sea. Grey replied that he could only repeat that information regarding the Bahrain waters.[105]

Colonel Grey also forwarded a copy of a translation of ibn Saʻud's answer to Mubarak's letter which suggested that the Amir meet the Turks. It is an interesting despatch firstly from the point of view of ibn Saʻud's seeming deference to Mubarak, secondly his attitude towards the Turks and thirdly his awareness of his increasing power.

> In agreeing to approach [Kuwait] I have obeyed your instructions as regards obedience and submission to our Government, but you know well with what contempt and disdain the officials of the Government have treated me, and you have seen the patience with which I have submitted to their conduct all these years notwithstanding that I have never experienced anything from them which could console me. And now, heaven be praised, I am in a position to do great things even as far as Iraq were it not that I do not wish to be the cause of [further] decline to the

Government and additional revolt on the part of the Arabs.

Now I have recovered my own country as you are witness, Oh Mubarak ... I ask you is it or is it not correct what I say about all the difficulties which have been brought upon me by the officials and the submission to the Government—I did not disobey you formerly that [sic] I should do so now, so if the matter which will guard my rights is granted and I and my affairs secure protection—then submission will certainly be incumbent upon me.[105]

According to the same despatch, the Shaikh of Kuwait planned to show this to the Turkish deputation. In so doing he would save face as regards trying to arrange a meeting while still asserting ibn Sa'ud's position.

At this juncture the Foreign Office was interested in finding out if the Porte had given Britain assurances respecting their memorandum of March 9th. However, as the Turks were working through a British protégé, Mubarak, Britain refrained from pressing the Ottoman government. Although Shaikh Mubarak refused to help formally, he was made aware of Britain's desiderata for communication to the Sa'udi Amir.[107]

The Turkish deputation arrived in Kuwait at the end of April. They met ibn Sa'ud at Subaihiya on May 2nd, remaining until May 4th.[108] It was first reported by Mubarak that the Turks had failed to come to an agreement with ibn Sa'ud.[109] In late June, however, reports began to come in to the effect that the Amir had come to an agreement with the Porte. The Political Resident telegraphed to the Government of India that the Agent at Bahrain, Keyes, was shown a letter from ibn Sa'ud which stated that the agreement was affirmed by royal *firman*.[110] In early July, Colonel Grey informed Mallet that Hakki Pasha had made the following communication:

An Imperial firman nominates Bin Saud Governor-General and Commander-in-Chief of Najd. He has the powers of a Vali and the right to create a local militia to ensure order and public security in Najd.

Garrisons will be established on the coast, and their strength will be increased if Bin Saud so requests.

Bin Saud will not have the right to conclude treaties or to contract engagements with foreign Powers. He will not have the right to grant concessions. He is bound always to respect the treaties between the Ottoman Empire and other states.

Foreigners in Najd may apply in regard to their interests and business, in accordance with treaty provisions to the local authorities and to Bin Saud in his capacity of Vali.[111]

It was reported that the Turks would station five soldiers at each of the following: Jubail, Qatif and 'Uqair. No troops were to be stationed in Hasa. Ibn Sa'ud was to receive a monthly sum of TL 250 and was to be permitted to collect customs dues, deduct the expenses of administration, and pay the Turks one-tenth of the balance.[112] According to the date on a copy of the original treaty found in 1916 in the Basra archives, the agreement was signed May 15, 1914 by the Vali of Basra and ibn Sa'ud.[113]

The confusion over the initial outcome of the May negotiations was not to be cleared up until January 1915 when Shakespear met ibn Sa'ud again. Part of the text from a report of that meeting deserves reproduction here as it not only set straight the record of the Turko–Sa'udi negotiations but cast light on the disintegrating relations between the rising Amir and his aging one-time mentor. Ibn Sa'ud related the story to Shakespear as follows:

> ... having received frequent letters from Shaikh Sir Mubarak-as-Subah urging him to come north to meet the Turkish officials, holding out strong hope of a satisfactory solution with them, he proceeded to Koweit, feeling sure (as he had kept the Political Agent, Bahrain, fully informed as to his movements) that he would be able to consult the Political Agent, Koweit, before closing with the Turks. On reaching Subhaihiya he was astonished to receive from Shaikh Sir Mubarak-as-Subah a letter advising him to refuse to treat with the Turks and intimating that he himself would not be present at the negotiations as he had previously promised. Added to this *volte face* on Shaikh Mubarak's part he understood from Lieutenant-Colonel Grey that His Majesty's Government were not prepared to support him at all as they had concluded an agreement with the Porte and could not jeopardize their own interests, especially as the Turks refused their friendly offer of mediation. There

were other matters between him and Sir Mubarak-as-Subah which added further to his resentment with the result that he arranged with Sayyid Talib ... that the negotiations should be kept secret from Mubarak. The negotiations culminated eventually in a series of conditions set down in draft for the sanction of the Porte and it was this draft which was sent to Constantinople. Several of the conditions were flatly refused at first by ' Bin Saud ' but later he agreed to their inclusion on the express assurance of the delegates that they were required to save the face of the Turkish Government, which, however, had no intention of insisting on their execution. Subsequently firmans, congratulatory letters and telegrams came to him from the Porte and various ministers.[114]

While the British were still in the dark over the exact outcome of the Turko–Sa'udi negotiations, the Porte accused Great Britain of intriguing with ibn Sa'ud during these talks. The allegation was without foundation. Mallet wrote after the negotiations that the Turks did have cause, however, to feel suspicious of Britain owing to the impression created by His Majesty's government over the past year. The British Ambassador pointed out that before ibn Sa'ud raided Hasa he was visited by a British Agent. Earlier this year he was visited again and Hakki issued a protest. In March an initial effort to negotiate with the Amir proved abortive owing to the coldness of Mubarak, a British protégé. Moreover, the British India Steamship Company let it be known that they wanted to contact ibn Sa'ud for commercial purposes. [115]

Mallet urged that both sides should be left ' severely alone, at any rate in appearance '. The British Ambassador went on to state that he believed that the Turks would try to retake Hasa but would leave ibn Sa'ud independent, and that if Britain recognised the *de facto* position of ibn Sa'ud, other Arab tribes would be encouraged. Mallet finished by stating : ' I do not wish to exaggerate the risk of arousing Turkish suspicions, but it must not be forgotten that there are people here whose interest lies in maintaining an atmosphere of distrust between Great Britain and Turkey which makes it additionally important to avoid any cause of offence '.[116]

Grey wrote in a minute to this correspondence :

An instruction must be drawn up pointing out that by recent agreement we have recognised Bin Saud as being in Turkish territory and subject to Turkey and that he must be treated as such and independent communications with him must not be held. He must be dealt with as a Turkish official or not at all. If the agents who do communicate with him are under our instructions I will send it direct; if not I will ask the IO to see that it is sent direct.[117]

Several days later the British Ambassador shifted his ground.[118] He wrote to Grey that he did not want it inferred from his letter that he was not alive to the necessity of arriving at an understanding with the Porte as to British relations with ibn Sa'ud. Mallet thought it best to defer or temporise until the July 29th agreement came into effect. He reasoned that if negotiations were undertaken sooner, the Turkish government might attempt to reopen other questions already settled by the agreements respecting the Gulf. If a supplementary agreement were negotiated with ibn Sa'ud after ratification, this contingency would not arise. The Ambassador saw nothing inconsistent in the articles dealing with Najd and Qatar and an independent ruler of Najd under Ottoman suzerainty. Moreover, he could not see how those articles, as they stood, could be resented by ibn Sa'ud. There was also the possibility that the Wahhabi Amir's acceptance might not have to be obtained immediately. Mallet finished by mentioning that it would be advisable to go no further than the requirements enumerated in the memorandum of March 9th 'on the unlikely supposition that the situation might, at some future time, change in their [the Porte's] favour'. The despatch ended with the prediction that 'it is impossible that Turkish ascendancy will reassert itself on the shores of the Gulf, the practical development of British relations with the Wahhabi ruler will become natural and inevitable and can be pursued without any prejudice to British interests in the Ottoman Empire'.[119]

Crowe and Grey were surprised at this change in viewpoint. The Secretary of State wrote in a minute to this despatch that it seemed 'to be contemplating future contingencies and not present action, that is the only way in which I can reconcile it with the previous despatch'.[120]

Meanwhile in London informal discussions were carried on

with Hakki. It was urged that he should be authorised to discuss the problem in London with a view to arriving at some arrangement. Grey still advocated a policy of no direct relations with ibn Sa'ud unless unavoidable.[121] This was communicated to the Viceroy on June 5th.[122]

On June 26th Shakespear—on leave in London—wrote to Hirtzel commenting on developments in Arabia. The Political Agent mentioned that some information sent by him from Riyadh to Bushire had apparently never reached London. He reported that he was shown letters from ibn Sa'ud from Sayyid Muhammed al Idrisi, Iman Yahya of Sana, and Nuri al Sha'lan, paramount Shaikh of the western branch of the 'Anaza, plus correspondence from the Turks. Ibn Sa'ud said that a coalition had arisen from shaikhs and himself. He also mentioned that ibn Rashid had recently received 30,000 rifles (Mauser and Mannlicher) via the Hedjaz railway. This latter point could have accounted for the uncompromising attitudes of the Shaikh of Kuwait as regards the recent Turko–Sa'udi negotiations.

Captain Shakespear went on to point out that he was struck by the ubiquity of the Arab disenchantment with Turkey, and by the Amir's rising prominence. The Porte was incapable of reasserting itself, and the Political Agent thought that, if the Turks persisted in their present ways, they would be expelled from Arabia. He did not believe that ibn Sa'ud aimed to become Sultan of Arabia. Shakespear summed up the difficulties in the following terms:

a. Utter inability of the Porte to coerce Arabia at present for years.
b. Strong natural position militarily and geographically of the Arabs.
c. Probable coalition of all tribes if coerced.
d. Desire of Great Britain to promote Turkey-in-Asia with detriment to British interests [in the Gulf].

Shakespear went on to suggest the following remedies:

1. Acceptance by the Porte of the *de facto* independent status of the Great Shaikhs.
2. Frank and more honest attitude by the Porte towards these Shaikhs.
3. Less suspicion by the Porte of Great Britain and recognition of her interests.

4. Frank invitation by the Porte for British co-operation in Arabian affairs.[123]

His proposals, however, were too enthusiastically ideal for application.

Although the Imperial Government in London was aware of the growing unrest among the Arabs, their determined refusal to exploit this is understandable in the context of Anglo–Ottoman relations. This determination, however, was equalled by that of the Indian officials who were resolved not to let their interests be jeopardised. The Foreign Office might have ultimately called the diplomatic tune but the Government of India and the India Office hardly ' jumped to it '. Both authorities fought a spirited action in defence of their interests. If the Foreign Office tended to ride roughshod over local Gulf realities, the Government of India—especially against the background of the gathering storm in Europe—appeared in many respects to be a ' bull in the Foreign Office's china shop '.[124] Rather than criticising any one authority, however, one should criticise the divided jurisdictional responsibility—an imperial legacy from less complicated times before communications improved—which bedevilled British policy in this area. It was only natural that Indian officers defended Indian interests. It was equally natural that the Foreign Office viewed eastern Arabia as a peripheral area where concessions could be made, despite the fact that they militated against local realities. If Neville Chamberlain in 1939 could describe Czechoslovakia as a ' far-away country ' and its inhabitants as a ' people of whom we know nothing ', Grey's reaction to ibn Sa'ud on the eve of World War I is understandable. Perhaps Grey and his subordinates felt towards ibn Sa'ud a little as Salisbury did when confronted at the Congress of Berlin with the demands of small delegations like the Armenians. Salisbury wrote: 'At Potsdam there were mosquitoes—here there are minor powers... I don't know which is worse.' [125]

With the outbreak of World War I the British began to take more seriously the possibility of Turkey joining Germany. It was at this time that Britain was forced to think seriously of a leader for a possible Arab rising. With the declaration of war between Britain and Turkey on November 5, 1914, Britain's policy of avoiding entanglement in central Arabia—and formal ties with ibn Sa'ud—was changed.

Notes

1. *Taylor*, p. 457.
2. *Ibid.*, p. 458. Another author has observed that 'British excitement reached the level of panic in March 1909, when a writer in *The Times* commented, "The people will be quite sane in a fortnight—they always went like this in March"'. See D. Thomson, *Europe Since Napoleon*, 2nd ed. (London, 1962), p. 499. Hereafter *Thomson*.
3. On the issue of how many Dreadnoughts Britain should build Churchill observed wryly: 'The Admiralty had demanded six: the economists offered four: and we finally compromised on eight'. Quoted in Thomson, p. 499.
4. The metaphor is Joseph Chamberlain's.
5. B. Lewis, *The Emergence of Modern Turkey* (London, 1961), p. 206. Hereafter *Lewis*.
6. *Taylor*, p. 504. See also A. Cunningham, 'The Wrong Horse?—A Study of Anglo-Turkish Relations Before the First World War', *St Antony's Papers*, No. 17, *Middle Eastern Affairs*, No. 4 (1965).
7. *Thornton*, p. 132.
8. See, for example, *Thornton*, pp. 133–135; *Thomson*, pp. 385, 386 and *Beloff*, p. 109.
9. Quoted in Wilson, *Loyalties*, I, p. 31.
10. Shakespear to Trevor (Acting Political Resident) March 9, 1910 (L.) No. 621; *LFI* [Letters from India (IO)], Vol. 238.
11. For the history of the Arab nationalist movement the classic work is G. Antonius, *The Arab Awakening* (London, 1955), hereafter *Antonius*. A useful corrective to some of Antonius' theses is Z. N. Zeine, *Arab–Turkish Relations and the Emergence of Arab Nationalism* (Beirut, 1958), hereafter *Zeine*. For an excellent account of Arab nationalism the standard work is S. Haim, *Arab Nationalism: an Anthology* (Los Angeles and London, 1962). See also the following articles by C. E. Dawn: 'The Rise of Arabism in Syria', *The Middle East Journal* XVI (1962) and 'From Ottomanism to Arabism', *Review of Politics* XXIII (1962).
12. *Zeine*, p. 77.
13. *BD*, IX, 1, pp. 207–209. Quoted in *Lewis*, p. 214 and *Zeine*, p. 75. On the Young Turks generally the most recent work is F. Ahmad, *The Young Turks, The Committee of Union and Progress in Turkish Politics* (Oxford, 1969). Also useful are E. E. Ramsaur, jnr., *The Young Turks—Prelude to the Revolution of 1908* (Princeton, 1957); *Lewis*, Chap. VII and *Zeine*, especially Chap. V. Lowther has been characterised as a 'calm, fair-minded, outspoken, north country squire'. P. Graves, *Briton and Turk* (London, 1941), p. 181. Quoted in *Busch*, p. 314, n. 30.
14. Lowther to Grey (For. Secy.) June 28, 1910 (L), No. 9852/23953; FO 371/1007. [Foreign Office files, series 371 (Turkey) Vol. 1007, Public Record Office (PRO)].
15. G. de Gaury, *Rulers of Mecca* (London, 1951), p. 262. Hereafter *de Gaury*.

THE PRE-WAR ERA: 1910–1914

16. *Ibid.*, p. 264.
17. *Ibid.*, pp. 257–262. See also C. Snouck Hurgronje, *Mekka in the Latter Part of the Nineteenth Century* (Luzac, 1931). There was a Turkish Vali in the Hedjaz and, in addition to Turkish barracks in the main cities, there was a considerable garrison in Medina.
18. Monaghan (British Consul at Jedda) to Lowther, June 11, 1910, (L.), No. 23946; F.O. 424/224. [*FO* Confidential Print 424 (Turkey), Vol. 224 (P.R.O.).]
19. For the positions of Arabian tribes, see Map II.
20. See p. 18. For further details on *the Araif*, see Philby, *Sa'udi Arabia*, pp. 256, 257.
21. Shakespear to Cox, Nov. 6, 1910 (L), No. 1906; LFI, Vol. 245. The sum was in Maria Theresa Thalers (1 pound equals 13.33 Maria Theresa Thalers).
22. *Ibid.*
23. For a report on Shakespear's visit, see Shakespear to Cox, April 8, 1911 (L.), No. 899; L.F.I., Vol. 248. Philby in his *Arabian Jubilee*, p. 33 is wrong in asserting that this meeting was the first between Shakespear and ibn Sa'ud.
24. The Hedjaz Railway linking Constantinople with Medina was completed in 1908.
25. Minute by Sir W. L. W.[arner], June 20, 1911, No. 889; *L.F.I.*, Vol. 248.
26. Minute by A. H.[irtzel]; *ibid.*
27. *Ibid.*
28. IO to FO, June 8, 1911 (L), No. 22208; *FO* 424/227.
29. Cox to McMahon (Secy. to the Govt. of India in the Foreign Dept.), July 23, 1911 (L), No. 1419; *LFI*, Vol. 251.
30. *Ibid.*
31. *Ibid.* By the terms of such an agreement ibn Sa'ud would undertake to observe the maritime truce, prohibit gun-runing and piracy and maintain friendly relations with the other Trucial Chiefs.
32. *Ibid.*
33. *Earle*, p. 241. The Russians approved the Baghdad Railway provided that the line would link up with any Persian line that might be constructed and in exchange for German recognition of their position in northern Persia. On Potsdam see *Taylor*, pp. 463–465; *Earle*, pp. 239–244; and *Busch*, p. 322.
34. Britain had been negotiating with Turkey on this issue on and off for some eight years.
35. *Busch*, p. 328.
36. *S. Mem.*, p. 386.
37. *Taylor*, p. 471.
38. For a comprehensive treatment of these negotiations, see *Busch*, pp. 322–347 and *Earle*, pp. 252–255. For a copy of the Convention, see *BD*, Vol. X, Pt. II, pp. 190–193.
39. ' Abd al-Rahman (Acting Consul at Jedda) to Lowther, Oct. 11, 1911 (L), No. 4710, encl. in Lowther to Grey, Nov. 2, *HC*, Vol. 284.
40. *Ibid.*

41. Philby, Sa'udi Arabia, p. 259.
42. Ibid.
43. 'Political Diary for the Persian Gulf Residency for May, 1913', No. 3126/1913; *L/P & S/10*, 2297/1919. [Political and Secret Dept., Subject Files, No. 2297/1919 (IO)]. The spelling of Abdul Jabir is that given in the Political Diary.
44. Crow to Lowther, May 18, 1913 (L), 22076/28326, encl. in Lowther to Grey, June 17, 1913; *FO* 371/1820. Sayyid Talib was an important notable from a prominent Basra family. He is vividly described by one authority as follows: 'An able, charming, unscrupulous, and ambitious statesman, gang-leader, and patriot, he had been Mutasarrif of al-Ahsa (Hasa) had close contact in Najd, Kuwayt and Muhammera, and dominated Basra. He was at the opening of the century already well known in Istanbul as a man of the highest promise or danger, prepared to adopt whatever allegiances would favour his rise to an independent Amirate of southern Iraq'. See S. H. Lonrigg, *Iraq 1900–1950* (London, 1953), p. 45. Hereafter *Longrigg*.
45. Ibid.
46. Minute by A. P.[arker], May 20, 1913, No. 22076/23972; *FO* 371/1820.
47. The 'treaty' here referred to between Britain and ibn Sa'ud's forbears is the Pelly agreement of 1866. See pp. 17, 18.
48. Shakespear to Cox, May 15, 1913 (L), No. 22076/29150, encl. 2 in IO to FO, June 25, 1913; *FO* 371/1820.
49. Comments by A. P.[arker] on the above; *ibid*. Undoubtedly Shakespear's last sentence was dramatic, but given ibn Sa'ud's later demands to the Shaikh of Qatar to expel the Turkish garrison, there was substance in Shakespear's warnings.
50. See p. 52.
51. GI [Govt. of India] to Marquess of Crewe (Secy. of State for India 1910–1915), May 31, 1913 (T), 22076/253777; *FO* 371/1820.
52. *Ibid*. My emphasis. Hardinge was Viceroy from 1910 to 1916. In view of his former position in the Foreign Office (he was Assistant Under-Secretary, 1903–1904; Permanent Under-Secretary, in effect head of the Office, 1906–1910), he was well aware of the overriding issue of the Baghdad Railway.
53. Crewe to GI, June 10, 1913 (T), No. 22076/27217, encl. in IO to FO, June 13, 1913; *FO* 371/1820.
54. FO to IO, June 7, 1913 (L), No. 25653; *ibid*. From the tone of many despatches of this time plus the number of times his minutes were translated into despatches, Alwyn Parker played an integral part in shaping British policy towards ibn Sa'ud. Parker was also in charge of the Baghdad Railway negotiations. See Sir A. T. Wilson, *S.W. Persia, A Political Officer's Diary, 1907–1914* (London, 1941), p. 236.
55. FO to IO, June 18, 1913 (L), No. 27206; *ibid*.
56. Cox to GI, June 27, 1913 (T), No. 22076/29667, encl. in IO to FO, June 28, 1913; *FO* 371/1820.
57. Viceroy to IO, July 1, 1913 (T), No. 22076/30369; *FO* 371/1820.
58. FO to IO, July 2, 1913 (L), No. 22076/29150; *ibid*.

59. Minute by L. M[allet] on draft of the above despatch, July 2, 1913, No. 22076/29150; *FO* 371/1820.
60. Minute by A. N[icolson] on above, date: same; *ibid*. Nicolson had succeeded Hardinge in 1910 as Permanent Under-Secretary. He held the post until 1916.
61. Crewe to GI, July 3, 1913 (T), No. 22076/31140, encl. in IO to FO, July 5, 1913; *FO* 371/1820.
62. Minute by Crewe, July 3, 1913, No. 2630 on a note from A. H[irtzel] to SSI of the same date; *L/P & S/10*, 2182/1913, Pt. 1.
63. A. P[arker] to Hirtzel, July 3, 1913 (L), No. 2640; *ibid*.
64. Minute by A. H[irtzel] on the above; *ibid*. Shakespear's visit did in fact contravene the orders in Brodrick's (then the Secy. of State for India) telegram. See Memorandum by E. Parkes... July 3, 1913, No. 22076/30802; *FO* 371/1820.
65. IO to FO, July 9, 1913 (L), No. 22076/31610; *FO* 371/1820.
66. Draft despatch to GI, n.d., encl. with the above; *ibid*.
67. *Beloff*, p. 113. Although the criticism is perhaps overdone it is interesting to note that Cambridge's great Orientalist, Professor E. G. (" Persian ") Browne, described Grey as so ignorant of Asian affairs ' that he hardly knew the Red Sea from the Persian Gulf '. *Thornton*, p. 114. Thornton's source is W. S. Blunt, *My Diaries* (London, 1919), II, p. 98.
68. *Kumar*, pp. 210–212.
69. Philby implies this when he writes that Sa'udi overtures to Britain were rejected because, owing to the policy of appeasing Turkey, she 'had no stomach for involvement in desert adventures'. See his *Sa'udi Arabia*, p. 260. Graves (p. 105) thinks that Britain should have supported ibn Sa'ud as early as 1906. Although appreciating the importance of the higher diplomatic considerations of the time he wrote: ' Nevertheless the history of the subsequent relations of the British government with the Arab world leaves an impression that they may have missed a great chance in 1906 '.
70. Cox to GI, July 11, 1913 (T), No. 22076/31971, encl. in IO to FO, July 12, 1913; *FO* 371/1820.
71. Viceroy to SSI (Secy. of State of India), Aug. 1, 1913 (H), No. 22076/35805; *FO* 371/1820.
72. Same to same, Aug. 2, 1913, No. same; *ibid*.
73. See *S. Mem.* for details of the Muscat Rebellion, pp. 318, 319 and Kelly, *Eastern Arabian Frontiers*, p. 109.
74. GI to Crewe, Aug. 10, 1913 (T), No. 22076/37510, encl. in IO to FO, Aug. 13, 1913; *FO* 371/1820.
75. *Ibid*.
76. Minute by Sir L. M[allet], Aug. 14, 1913, No. 22076/37510; *FO* 371/1820.
77. Crewe to GI, Aug. 21, 1913, No. 22076/39535, encl. in IO to FO, Aug. 26, 1913; *ibid*.
78. Viceroy to Crewe, Sept. 5, 1913 (T), No. 22076/41141; *ibid*.
79. ' A necessary condition to ratification was British agreement with Germany on the railway. The ensuing negotiations were lengthy, for

before Britain and Germany could agree, Germany and the Ottoman Empire had to come to terms. By June of 1914, however, a draft agreement was reached. The terminus was to be Basra, with guaranteed equality of rates to all. Britain was to control 40 per cent of a new company to run the ports of Baghdad and Basra, and no line was to be run from Basra to the Gulf without British approval. No formal share of the line itself was to be under British control, for the problems of international financing proved impossible of settlement. Both the Anglo-Turkish [Draft Convention of 1913] and the Anglo-German agreements remained unratified, for the outbreak of World War I put a rapid end to the negotiations'. See *Busch*, p. 345.

80. Section on El Katr [Art. II] in Anglo-Turkish Agreement, reproduced in BD, Vol. X, Pt. II, p. 193. The arguments for and against the Anglo-Turkish Convention's "blue line" are many and varied. For the present suffice it to say that the Foreign Office thought that ibn Sa'ud was peripheral to the larger considerations in the Gulf and that the arbitrary designation of Najd and Hasa—then held by ibn Sa'ud—as Ottoman was an anomaly to be expected as local realities took second place to questions of greater importance. For further discussion of this point, see Kelly, *Eastern Arabian Frontiers*, pp. 107–114 and my n. 111.
81. Hakki to Parker, Sept. 24, 1913 (L), No. 22076/43979; *FO* 371/1820.
82. Ibn Sa'ud also wanted guarantees that his enemies would not be permitted to take refuge in Qatar. Both the *Araif* and the 'Ajman are said to have been granted sanctuary in Qatar and Trucial Oman. See Officiating Res. to GI, Jan. 4, 1914 (L), No. 251, encl. 1 in IO to FO, Feb. 9, 1914; *FO* 424/251.
83. Pol. Agent, Bahrain to Pol. Res., Dec. 20, 1913 (L), No. 6117, encl. 4 in IO to FO, Feb. 9, 1914; *ibid*.
84. Pol. Agent, Bahrain to Pol. Res., Dec. 20, 1913 (L), No. 6117, encl. 2 in above; *ibid*.
85. Officiating Resident to GI, Jan. 4, 1914, (L), No. 251, encl. 1 in IO to FO, Feb. 9, 1914; *ibid*.
86. FO to IO, March 7, 1914 (L), No. 10244; *ibid*.
87. Minute by A. P[arker], March 7, 1914, No. 10244, encl. in *ibid*.
88. Minute by A. H[irtzel], March 16, 1914, No. 1030/1914; *L/P & S/10*, 2182/1913, Pt. II.
89. In view of the inherent difficulties in attacking ibn Sa'ud by sea except via Bahrain, it is curious that Britain apparently did not use her declaration of 1893 to answer Sa'udi requests for a British guarantee.
90. 'Memorandum communicated to Hakki Pasha', March 9, 1914, No. 10569, *FO* 424/251.
91. Mallet to Grey, March 18, 1914 (L), No. 13871; *FO* 424/251. Sir Louis Mallet 'had had practically no diplomatic experience whatever in twenty-five years of service mainly spent in secretarial posts at the Foreign Office'. See P. Graves, *Briton and Turk* (London, 1941), p. 180.
92. Ibn Sa'ud to Pol. Agent, Bahrain, Feb. 26, 1914 (L, Trans.), No. 17636, encl. 3 in IO to FO, April 21, 1914; *FO* 424/252.

THE PRE-WAR ERA: 1910–1914   71

93. Mallet to Grey, April 2, 1914 (T), No. 1990/14632; FO 371/2123.
94. FO to IO, April 1, 1914 (L), No. 12320; *FO* 424/252.
95. *Ibid*. My emphasis. Crowe became Assistant Under Secretary in 1912 and was Permanent Under Secretary from 1920 to 1925.
96. Grey to Mallet, April 1, 1914 (T), No. 13871; *ibid*.
97. Minute by A. H[irtzel], April 2, 1914, No. 1278; *L/P & S/10*, 2182/1913, Pt. 2.
98. *Ibid*.
99. IO to FO, April 4, 1914 (L), No. 15023; *FO* 424/252.
100. FO to IO, April 6, 1914 (L), No. 15023; *ibid*.
101. Trevor to Knox (Officiating Pol. Res.), April 10, 1914 (L), No. 1990/22424, encl. in 'Bushire Correspondence of the 19th of April'; *FO* 371/2124. The Turks also approached the Shaikh of Moheammera requesting him to help facilitate negotiations. The Shaikh declined, holding that he was in Persian territory and had nothing to do with ibn Sa'ud.
102. GI to Crewe, April 14, 1914 (T), No. 16801, encl. 4 in IO to FO, April 16, 1914; *FO* 424/252.
103. Memo by Holderness, April 16, 1914, No. 1396/1914; *L/P & S/10*, 2182/1913, Pt. II.
104. Comment on the above by Crewe, d., same; *ibid*.
105. Grey (Pol. Agent at Kuwait) to Pol. Res., April 29, 1914 (L), No. 1990/24823; *FO* 371/2124.
106. Ibn Sa'ud to Mubarak, April 16, 1914 (L, Trans.), sub. encl. 3 in the above; *ibid*.
107. These desiderata were the usual: no interference in the territory or politics of the Trucial States or Qatar, suppression of piracy and maintenance of maritime truce, suppression of arms traffic, and British traders to be admitted to Qatif and protected.
108. The Turkish deputation consisted of Sayyid Talib, president of the delegation; Maj. Beda al-Din, chief of the Baghdad staff; Maj. Omar Fauzi, Chief of the Basra staff; Samir Efendi, Mutasarrif of Hasa; Sayyid Omar Bey, a Basra lawyer; Muhammed al-Nama, an Arab notable and 'Abd al-Wahhab Mandil, the Sa'udi representative in Basra.
109. Col. Grey to Pol. Res., May 6, 1914 (L), No. 1990/26063; *FO* 371/2124.
110. Pol. Res. to GI, June 30, 1914 (T), No. 1990; *ibid*.
111. Grey to Mallet, July 11, 1914 (T), No. 1990/31123; *FO* 371/2124. The somewhat confusing character of the 'Blue Line' was further complicated by the above agreement and another convention of the same time. Although the Anglo-Turkish Draft Convention of 1913 was never ratified, the Turks accepted the Blue Line as the demarcation of their territories in Eastern Arabia. On March 9, 1914, the Porte 'concluded a second frontier convention, defining the limits of Ottoman jurisdiction in north-western Arabia, which contained an express reference to the Blue Line. This convention was ratified by the Ottoman Government on 5 June, 1914'.
It has been argued that as this second treaty was ratified a few

weeks after the Turko-Sa'udi agreement, ibn Sa'ud was legally bound ' to abide by it and to observe the Blue Line, which was given legal effect by the 1914 Convention, as the eastern frontier of the *sanjaq* of Najd, over which he ruled as the Ottoman Vali '.

One expert stated that this Blue Line constituted no hardship because the Wahhabis had not ruled east of Jafura for fifty years. However, the anomaly of the ' Ottoman sanjaq of Najd ' lying east of the Blue Line was to persist and later complicate matters after the War. See Kelly, *Eastern Arabian Frontiers*, pp. 111, 112. For the complete text of the aforesaid ' second convention ', see *BD*, Vol. X, Part 11, p. 341.

112. Knox (Officiating Political Resident) to GI, July 11, 1914, (T), No. 1990/33437; *FO* 371/2124.
113. See App. II for a copy of the treaty.
114. Shakespear to Pol. Res., Jan. 4, 1915 (L), No. 975; *L/P & S/10*, 2182/1913, Pts. 4, 5. This report tends to cast doubt on Philby's assertion that ibn Sa'ud ' had regarded him [Mubarak] as a second father and had always sought his advice on important political matters, maintaining the most cordial relations with him until his death in 1916 '. See his *Arabian Days* (London, 1949), p. 152. Seven years later in his more serious work, *Sa'udi Arabia* (p. 273), he stated more correctly that Mubarak ' had become jealous and critical in his old age of one who might fairly be regarded as his pupil in politics '.
115. Mallet to Grey, May 12, 1914 (T), No. 22042; *FO* 424/252.
116. *Ibid*.
117. Minute by E. G[rey], May 18, 1914, No. 1990/22042; *FO* 371/2124.
118. There is virtually nothing in the files which could explain what prompted Mallet to change his position.
119. Mallet to Grey, May 15, 1914 (L), No. 1990/22677; *FO* 371/2124.
120. Minute by E. G[rey] on the above, May 25, 1914; *ibid*.
121. FO to IO, June 4, 1914 (L), No. 23753, *FO* 424/252.
122. Crewe to Viceroy, June 5, 1914 (T), No. 1990/25405; *FO* 371/2124.
123. ' Notes communicated by IO to FO, June 27, 1914, No. 28966; *FO* 424/252.
124. The expression is Busch's.
125. Quoted in Lady Gwendolen Cecil, *The Life of Robert, Marquess of Salisbury* (London, 1921), Vol. II, p. 288. Cited by M. S. Anderson, *The Eastern Question, 1774–1923, A Study in International Relations* (London, 1966), pp. 210, 211. Hereafter *Anderson*.

CHAPTER III

Anglo–Saʿudi Relations during the First World War

For obvious reasons few periods in this century have received as much scholarly study as the First World War and the Middle East naturally forms a great part of that study. The general history of the partition of the Ottoman Empire and British policy in the Middle East from 1914 to 1918 is well known and needs no labouring here.[1] However, as the description of British policy towards ibn Saʿud during this crucial period unfolds, it must not be forgotten that Anglo–Saʿudi relations constituted only a small facet of the larger mosaic of British policy in the Middle East. From late 1914 to the beginning of 1916, while Britain negotiated a treaty with ibn Saʿud, the more important and fateful Husain–McMahon and Sykes–Picot negotiations proceeded simultaneously. The first two years of the War also witnessed the allied setback at Gallipoli and the disastrous British–Indian campaign in Mesopotamia. It must also be borne in mind that as Turkey entered the War late, and in view of the primary importance accorded to the Western Front, the Middle Eastern theatre and its needs were always subordinated to the European arena of conflict.

The last two years of the War saw the turning of the tide in favour of the Allies and the gradual disintegration of the Turkish Army and Ottoman Empire. The latter stages of the hostilities also witnessed the addition of the Balfour Declaration to the already existing profusion of contradictory promises and agreements between the British and the French and the British and the Arabs. In the heat of war, expediency had assumed its normal role. The consequence was the absence of a coherent and unified policy and a plethora of irreconcilable undertakings. And if Anglo–French, Anglo–Arab and Anglo–Zionist relations contributed to the absence of a unified policy in the Middle East, so, too, did inter-office rivalry. Indeed, as will become clear, the edge of rivalry between the Government of India and the India

Office on the one hand and the Foreign Office on the other was sharpened during the War. The conflict was especially keen between the Foreign Office's deputies in Cairo and the Indian government's subordinates in Mesopotamia.[2]

In brief, London and Cairo viewed the Arabs differently from Delhi and her officials, first at Basra and later at Baghdad. Among other reasons, the fact that British authorities in Cairo had had experience of sophisticated intellectuals and nationalists made them more inclined to support Anglo–Arab co-operation against the Turks. The Government of India, however, had a far more paternalistic attitude towards the Arabs. The British 'Raj' had long dealt with the less sophisticated inhabitants of the Persian Gulf and South Arabia. Delhi's experience of 'Arabs', therefore, was markedly different from Cairo's Moreover, British–Indian encounters with the Arabs during the early stages of the Mesopotamian campaign was not such as to endear the 'noble Arab' to British forces in that theatre.[3] Two other factors are important in understanding Delhi's attitude. Firstly, the Indian government's experience of nationalism was not likely to make her favourable to Arab nationalism.[4] Secondly, when British authorities in India thought of 'Moslem', they thought of a large sector of their own population. They viewed Moslem–Arab developments from this standpoint. It must not be forgotten that many Indian Moslems—and not a few non-Moslem Indians who admired the Young Turks—felt great sympathy for Turkey. This sympathy had been inspired initially through Abdul Hamid's use of Pan-Islamism to dramatise his position as Caliph of all Moslems and by Moslem sensitivity to Christian dismemberment of the Ottoman Empire, the last great Islamic state.[5]

In view of the Indian government's attitude and experience it is not surprising that they looked with dismay on the encouragement by their Cairo colleagues of Arab nationalism. The fact that Turkey was at war with Britain was difficult enough, but by encouraging an Arab revolt Delhi feared that Britain might be accused of dividing Islam, further attacking the Caliphate and perhaps involving the Holy Cities of the Hedjaz in the War. Moreover, the Government of India had to deal with ibn Sa'ud, whose feelings towards Husain were hostile.

It will be shown in the following pages that British wartime relations with ibn Sa'ud are distinguished by three major developments. Firstly, there was the British decision to support Husain as the leader of the Arab revolt. Secondly, the negotiation of the Anglo–Sa'udi Treaty of 1915 was to mark a turning point in British relations with ibn Sa'ud. Thirdly, ibn Sa'ud's role in the British offensive in the Middle East will be seen to be one of secondary importance while most of the gold and glory was to be channelled to Sharif Husain.

With the decision to back Husain as the major figure in Arabian politics, Anglo–Sa'udi relations were compromised and inevitably strained. However, unlike Husain, who was later to suffer because he had failed to negotiate a treaty with Britain, ibn Sa'ud insisted on having a formal agreement before allying himself with the British. It is of great significance that by the terms of this treaty, Britain departed from her traditional policy of non-involvement in central Arabian affairs. After the proclamation of the Arab Revolt in 1916, ibn Sa'ud's activities were greatly subodinated to Husain's British-backed campaign in the western desert. Throughout the war ibn Sa'ud's role was but a sideshow in comparison with that of his rival in the Hedjaz.

Ibn Sa'ud and Husain: A comparison in Importance

Throughout much of the nineteenth century, British policy towards the Ottoman Empire was determined mainly by two considerations. Although questions of preserving the balance of power in Europe and safeguarding the British position in the eastern Mediterranean were also involved, Britain sought to preserve Turkey primarily to keep open the British routes to India and secondly to promote reforms in the Ottoman administration. Although the second consideration was no doubt rooted in the English liberal tradition, it could be said that the policy of championing reforms was primarily motivated by the desire to achieve the first objective: the imperial necessity of preserving Turkey. Britain feared that internal Turkish decay complemented by external Russian pressure would hasten the demise of the 'Sick Man', thereby endangering British communications with India. It was this great importance of India which was to determine British wartime policy in the Middle East.

On the commencement of military operations with Turkey in November 1914, Britain's immediate military objectives were to secure Egypt, the Suez Canal and Red Sea and to occupy the head of the Persian Gulf. The achievement of the first objective was facilitated by the presence of British troops in Egypt and the second by despatching the Mesopotamian Expeditionary Force. Both objectives were governed by the traditional policy of maintaining British communications with the East. England feared the establishment by the Central Powers of naval bases flanking the British lines of communications. Moreover, in the Persian Gulf she had to protect her Arab allies and guard her new oilfields.[6]

On the western side of the Arabian peninsula from the religious, political,[7] strategic and—to a lesser extent—military points of view, Husain, though devious and ambitious, was the logical choice for British support. From the religious standpoint, Husain ibn 'Ali, was in many respects one of the most important men in Islam. As a member of the Hashim family of the Quraish tribe, he was generally held to be a descendant of the Prophet and was custodian of the Holy Places. He was also appointed by imperial *firman*. It must be remembered that after Turkey entered the war, the fear that the Turkish sultan would declare a *jihad*, or holy war, greatly worried the British government. The British were apprehensive that a Turkish proclamation of *jihad* would have a grave effect on Indian Moslems. ' British India, where the Middle East is concerned, is Moslem India, and Indian Moslems as a result of political agitation which started during the Balkan Wars, attached great importance to the Caliphate of the Sultan of Turkey '.[8] Had the Grand Sharif echoed the Sultan's proclamation of *jihad* of November 14, 1914, his support, whole-hearted or otherwise, would have greatly reinforced the Sultan's appeal. It was conceivable that not only India's loyalty, but the British position in Egypt would have been threatened. ' Even a partially successful *jihad* might have proved a serious threat to the allies, which neither England with some twenty million Moslems in India and sixteen million in Egypt and the Sudan, nor France with her twenty million in Africa, nor Russia with a like number within her borders could afford to disregard '.[9] There was also the importance of the pilgrimages to the Hedjaz and Husain's influential position in this regard.

It should be stressed that it was primarily the British officials in Egypt and the Sudan who pressed for support of Husain. Faced with Moslem hostility in those areas, they argued that ' A

British understanding with the Sharif, advertising a split in Muslim ranks, would bring them welcome relief and enable them to rebut Ottoman charges that Britain was waging an anti-Muslim war '.[10]

Many members of the British government, especially those in the Government of India and the India Office, were to contest the value of a Sharifian-led movement. Indeed, there is the impression that these two authorities were not merely at variance but, as it were, at war with the policy of fostering an Arab Revolt. However, the fact remains that at the outset of hostilities, those authorities in Egypt and the Sudan who thought that only Husain could help to counteract the call to holy war were to prevail.[11]

Politically, Husain again emerged as an individual who held a unique position. At this juncture, nascent Arab nationalism was stirring in several areas of the Arab Near East. This incipient nationalism took two distinct and separate forms. First, there were the small groups of intellectuals and army officers mainly in Beirut and Damascus who thought in terms of nationalist politics. These groups were influenced basically by traditional nineteenth-century European nationalist ideals and movements. Impetus was probably given to these individuals by recent national uprisings in European Turkey. Secondly, in the more remote and less sophisticated areas of the Middle East, discontent prevailed among the proudly independent Arab chiefs over whom in the past the Turks had exercised only a shadowy form of suzerainty, if any. Their rebellion was motivated chiefly not by nationalism, but by Young Turk attempts to consolidate their crumbling Empire. This centralisation impinged on the Arab tribes' freedom and their traditional disdain of any central authority.[12]

In 1914, Husain and his second eldest son, 'Abdullah, apparently constituted the prinicpal link between these two sectors of Arab discontent. Both Husain and 'Abdullah had lived in Constantinople for more than a decade; 'Abdullah had actually sat in the Turkish Parliament as a representative of the Hedjaz. He was also in touch with the secret societies in Syria. Moreover, on a visit to Cairo in August of 1914, he had even approached Kitchener on the British position towards a possible Arab rising. On the other hand, in addition to his cosmopolitan background, Husain had long been involved with the

Bedouin of the Hedjaz. He held, as Amir of Mecca, the position of a local Arab prince and possessed a force of armed tribesmen. Husain was ideally situated to exploit and co-ordinate the two distinct movements. Militarily this was of some significance. 'The intellectuals of Damascus possessed no force, the tribesmen of Arabia no political objective.' Husain had both.[13]

While still dealing with political considerations, it must be mentioned that by mid-1915 several officials in Cairo and Khartoum were thinking in terms of a future Arab union stretching from Egypt to the Persian Gulf. Chief among these proponents of a future Arab union were the Governor-General of the Sudan, Sir Reginald Wingate, and the head of Intelligence in Egypt, Colonel (later Sir) G. F. Clayton. There was also talk of the possibility of Husain becoming an Arab Caliph. Although admitting the difficulties of such a policy, Wingate wrote: 'I conceive it to be not impossible that in the dim future a federation of semi-independent Arab states might exist under European guidance and supervision linked together by racial and linguistic bonds, owing spiritual allegiance to a single Arab primate and looking to Great Britain as its patron and protector'.[14] However, this dream of a pan-Arab union under British tutelage was rudely disturbed by London's hostility and the Sykes–Picot agreement.

From a strategic standpoint, the territory in which Husain exercised influence stretched for almost a thousand miles along the flank of one of Britain's vital lines of communications, the Red Sea. Moreover, the Sharif's territory was rendered directly accessible from Constantinople by the Hedjaz Railway which terminated in Medina. He was able to deny these strategic advantages to the Central Powers.[15] From the imperial viewpoint, the Hedjaz flanked the corridor through which Indian troops would be brought to the Western Front. 'In the first decade of this century, approximately half the British army was stationed in India, and in addition the Indian army, in which all but the most junior officers were British, numbered nearly a quarter of a million, with an almost inexhaustible reserve of manpower at its back.'[16]

Military considerations become intertwined with strategic considerations when it is noted that some military authorities thought that were the Turks denied Arab support they could not invade Egypt.[17] At the outbreak of war with Turkey, the

British faced forces in Palestine which were in a position to threaten the Suez Canal and Egypt.[18] Moreover, the Imam of Yemen declared for the Turks, and two Turkish divisions threatened Aden. Finally, to add further to British difficulties, in the desert to the west of Egypt, the Chief of the Senussi sided with the Turks.

In 1915, the costly failure of the Gallipoli Campaign appears to have convinced the British to take a Sharifian-led rebellion seriously. Kedourie cites the following statement by the High Commissioner in Egypt, Sir Henry McMahon, as evidence of this contention.

> It was the most unfortunate date in my life when I was left in charge of this Arab movement (he said) and I think a few words are necessary to explain that it is nothing to do with me : it is purely military business. It began at the urgent request of Sir Ian Hamilton at Gallipoli. I was begged by the Foreign Office to take immediate action and draw the Arabs out of the war. At that moment a large portion of the Turkish force at Gallipoli and nearly the whole of the force in Mesopotamia were Arabs, and the Germans were then spending a large amount of money in detaching the rest of the Arabs, so that the Arabs were between the two. Could we give them some guarantee of assistance in the future to justify their splitting with the Turks? I was told to do that at once and in that way I started the Arab movement.[19]

It should also be added that the worsening British situation at Kut al Amara in Mesopotamia from December 1915 until April 29 1916, when the Turks captured the city and 10,000 British Indian troops along with it must also have hastened the decision to raise an Arab revolt.

Turning now to the other side of the Arabian peninsula, on the outbreak of war with Turkey, Britain's immediate military objectives were to protect her Arab allies, the Shaikhs of Kuwait and Mohammera, and to safeguard her oil interests. The Government of India stressed the former objective, the Admiralty the latter. The British in India feared the establishment of a hostile power in Mesopotamia for several reasons. Given their alliance with Britain, India thought that the Shaikhs of Mohammera and Kuwait were directly threatened by the enemy. The British also feared that Turko–German pressure 'might bring Persia into the enemy camp, and that would expose India and Afghanistan to the penetration of enemy agents'.[20] One officer who actually served in Mesopotamia during the war maintained afterwards that German submarines 'carried overland in sections might operate from the head of the Persian Gulf'.[21] This same authority argued that oil played a secondary role in the hierarchy of British interests and that the older interests of safeguarding British protégés and forestalling enemy domination of lower Mesopotamia led to the despatch of the Indian Expeditionary Force.[22]

Before the actual outbreak of hostilities between Britain and Turkey, a division of the Indian Army was concentrated at Bahrain. In less than a week after the shelling of the Russian ports by the *Goeben*, this force landed at the entrance of the Shatt-al-Arab. It occupied Fao on November 6th and Basra on the 22nd. The commander of this division proclaimed to local Arabs that this force was friendly to them. The British government took special care to declare their friendship for Arabs on both sides of the peninsula. Britain promised to respect the Moslem Holy Cities and to treat Arabs as friends as long as they did not align themselves with the Turks. She also undertook not to disturb Jedda so long as Indian pilgrims were not interfered with. But there were differences between the Indian and—after the proclamation of the Arab Revolt in June 1916— the Egyptian methods of handling the Arabs.

Rather than encouraging an Arab revolt in Mosopotamia, the Government of India chose to follow the more traditional policy as employed in India of supporting local leaders, in this case Arab shaikhs, directly with subsidies. The invading British–Indian army found considerable confusion in lower Mesopotamia where Turkish attempts at centralised administration had weakened the already tenuous authority of the tribal shaikhs without effectively replacing it. The British authorities decided to reverse this policy and subsidise various tribal chieftains in an attempt to secure their lines of communications. Unlike the policy which was to be followed in the Hedjaz, of supplying large quantities of British gold to Husain to help fire and sustain his Bedouin levies, the Indian government administered subsidies directly to local shaikhs. When necessary, the British encouraged Arabs to refer disputes to local shaikhs for judgement.

Also, when indicated, they used troops to enforce a shaikh's authority over his rebellious tribe.²³ At this juncture one of the most important local shaikhs to receive British backing was the Amir of Riyadh, ibn Sa'ud.

It has often been asserted that Great Britain 'backed the wrong horse' in supporting Husain. This view is held especially by those who contrast the unfortunate career of Husain with the achievements of ibn Sa'ud. Philby even attributed ibn Sa'ud's inferior role in the British war effort in the Middle East to an accident of history. As we shall see in the pages to follow, in January 1915, Captain Shakespear, while on a mission to Najd to secure ibn Sa'ud's support for the Mesopotamian Expeditionary Force, was killed in a clash between ibn Sa'ud and ibn Rashid. Shakespear had insisted on accompanying ibn Sa'ud and his forces on an expedition against ibn Rashid. He was killed at the battle of Jarrab when ibn Rashid's forces overran the hill from which he was viewing the tribal clash. Philby wrote:

> His death ... was a great loss to his country, but it was a disaster to the Arab cause. It must certainly be reckoned in the small category of individual events which have changed the course of history. Had he survived to continue a work for which he was so eminently fitted, it is extremely doubtful whether subsequent campaigns of Lawrence would ever have taken place in the west.... It is probable that a less tragic outcome of Shakespear's mission would have resulted in his [ibn Sa'ud] being actively supported by Great Britain with money and arms.²⁴

It will be seen in the following pages that Philby's opinion is patently untenable. Shakespear's untimely death would not have altered the factors which led Britain to concentrate her support on Husain. Although ibn Sa'ud was recognised by some British officials at this point as possessing potential both militarily and politically, this potential was greatly over-shadowed by the actual power of Husain. Using the same scale of religious, political, strategic and military importance, it is readily apparent that ibn Sa'ud ran Sharif Husain a very bad second at the outset of the war—and for some time to come.²⁵

From the religious viewpoint, ibn Sa'ud stood at the head of a movement which was looked upon with a mixture of fear and disdain by many Moslems. His importance in this field was, in comparison with Husain, manifestly negligible. Politically, the Wahhabi leader had no influence outside the confines of central and eastern Arabia. He could not put himself at the head of an Arab movement which could to some extent co-ordinate comparatively sophisticated nationalist movements with tribal discontent.

Although it has been argued that strategically ibn Saʻud's eastern domain of Hasa acted as a buffer between the Turks in lower Mesopotamia and the Trucial Shaikhs of the Arabian littoral,[26] his position vis-à-vis the Turks was not as significant as Husain's. Militarily, ibn Saʻud 'was not in touch with Turkish forces'.[27] He could, it is true, directly engage ibn Rashid, his traditional enemy who sided with the Turks, thereby forestalling the latter's whole-hearted co-operation with the enemy. However, since the two chieftains were at this time fairly evenly matched, while ibn Saʻud partly neutralised ibn Rashid, he himself was effectively neutralised by his rival. Moreover, it should be emphasised that although ibn Saʻud combined religion and tribal leadership and his courage and prowess as a desert fighter were legendary even in the early years of his life, he was plagued throughout the War by rebellious tribes. It will be obvious that his military and strategic importance could not compare with that of Husain, who could disrupt the operations of the four Turkish divisions 'spaced out between the Hedjaz, Asir and the Yaman'.[28]

Those who argue that ibn Saʻud should have led the Arab Revolt also overlook another important factor. Had Shakespear lived, there is little reason to believe that the Government of India, under whose jurisdiction ibn Saʻud came, would have embarked on a policy on anything like the scale of Cairo's support of Husain. Delhi's attitude towards nationalism and Arabs combined with her concern for Moslem opinion, her traditional methods of handling 'natives' and her parsimony would all have militated against such a policy. And as one writer has recently noted, had the British backed ibn Saʻud, such a policy would have resulted in the 'likelihood of an active Husain–Ibn Rashid–ʻAjman alliance'—with Turkish support—against ibn Saʻud.[29]

In conclusion, to assert that Britain backed the wrong horse is to view the situation prevailing at the time in the light of ibn Saʻud's subsequent career. One of the greatest experts of the time, D. G. Hogarth, Lawrence's mentor, who served with the Arab Bureau in Cairo, summed up the reasons behind British support for ibn Sa'ud's rival, the Sharif of Mecca. In addition to being the 'only possible spokesman for the Arabs from the British point of view',[30] Husain

> could exert throughout the Moslem world a moral influence which would, and did, make a very great difference indeed. His action, involving secession of the Holy Land from the Caliph's War would, we know, be received variously—with at least as much reprobation as approbation; but everywhere it would create division and prompt action. In adopting this policy we were not looking beyond the War.[31]

Although ibn Sa'ud was to be greatly disappointed in the British support for his rival, a combination of his own political sagacity and the exigencies of war culminated in the fulfilment of the Sa'udi leader's long-desired ambition of an Anglo–Sa'udi treaty. And it is on this subject that attention will now be focused.

The Anglo-Sa'udi Treaty

It will be recalled that owing to Britain's consistent refusal to treat with ibn Sa'ud, he was forced on May 15, 1914 to sign a treaty with the Ottoman government.[32] One of the main reasons why ibn Sa'ud signed this treaty with the hated Turks was because he greatly feared a Turkish invasion by sea owing to his expulsion of their garrisons from Hasa. On October 31 1914, the Ottoman government, having learned that ibn Sa'ud was embarking on a campaign against ibn Rashid, wired Sayyid Talib in Basra to stop him.[33] It was later learned that the Turks had requested the Sa'udi Amir to assist them by defending Basra and feinting towards the Sinai peninsula and Egypt.[34] In the meantime, prevalent rumours that ibn Sa'ud would join the Turks prompted the India Office to send Captain Shakespear on a special mission to the Amir.

Before the actual outbreak of hostilities between Britain and Turkey, ibn Sa'ud had been informed by letters from the Shaikh of Kuwait and the Political Resident that in the event of war, Great Britain would like him to help keep peace in Arabia. Moreover, as early as September 14th, the Officiating Resident in the Gulf had drafted letters to be despatched in the event of war to the various Gulf chiefs. In brief the letter to ibn Sa'ud requested him to join the Shaikhs of Kuwait and Mohammera in assisting the British to take Basra. He was also requested to prevent the plundering of British merchants, to safeguard Europeans in Basra and to help protect property in the town. In return, the British promised to recognise him as the independent Ruler of Najd and Hasa, to guarantee him against attack by sea, to secure him against Turkish reprisals and to enter into treaty relations with him. This draft was approved by the Indian authorities and apparently despatched to the Amir on November 3rd. 'The ... assurances contained in it became the basis of subsequent negotiations'.[35]

On November 28th, ibn Sa'ud replied to the above letter. He affirmed that co-operation with the Shaikhs of Kuwait and Mohammera

> is incumbent upon us (and so is it for us to) use our good offices with our friends, the illustrious Government, in all useful actions which may be required by her. And I am using my endeavours and efforts in furthering the common interests of all friends. You should rest fully assured and be confident in this question.[36]

However, the Sa'udi leader preferred to discuss personally the promises made to him by the British government. He therefore set out for Kuwait in order to carry on the negotiations verbally with Shakespear.[37]

The Political Agent finally arrived at ibn Sa'ud's camp on December 31st and began discussions with the Amir. Ibn Sa'ud dwelt at some length on the letter of November 3, 1914. He stressed that the assurances were vague and that it was not specified whether they were 'limited merely to the present war or also included the future, gave no hint whether other conditions would be required of himself later, and that the document could not be regarded as a binding instrument between the two parties for the future'.[38]

From these conversations Shakespear concluded that ibn Sa'ud

> had no intention of abandoning his neutral position, with freedom to make his own arrangements with the Turks (and he was confident that he could secure from them a very good 'second best') until he held a signed and sealed treaty with the British Government; nor would he move a step

further towards making matters either easier for us or more difficult for the Turks as far as the present war was concerned, until he obtained in that treaty some very solid guarantee of his position with Great Britain practically as his suzerain.[39]

Shakespear advised the Sa'udi Amir to draw up a preliminary treaty setting forth his desires and what he was prepared to accept so that the Political Agent could forward it to the Indian government. Ibn Sa'ud complied with this suggestion and in early January Shakespear forwarded a rough translation of the Amir's desiderata.[40]

Captain Shakespear, when submitting this report, added some observations which were to transcend immediate wartime considerations. He maintained that ibn Sa'ud only asked for that which was basically conveyed in the Officiating Resident's letter if those assurances were to apply also for the post-war period. In return, the Sa'udi Amir offered, in Shakespear's view, to attach himself completely to Great Britain. Shakespear went on to argue that the accretion to British responsibilities was not onerous. Although Great Britain would have to protect ibn Sa'ud against the Turks, recent history had shown that they constituted no great threat. Moreover, as ibn Sa'ud would be guaranteed against sea invasion if trouble did arise, the Amir could cope with it himself. It was also pointed out that while Great Britain would act as arbiter in case of conflict between the shaikhs of the Arab littoral and the Amir, this was to Britain's advantage.[41]

On the positive side, Shakespear stressed that by meeting ibn Sa'ud's demands, Britain would gain complete control of the western littoral of the Gulf, control of the arms traffic, and virtual exclusion of all foreign powers from central Arabia. In addition, Great Britain would enjoy the security effected by the Amir's strong control over the Bedouin and it was also possible that much of the trade, then diverted through the Red Sea, would pass through the Gulf ports. Furthermore, ibn Sa'ud exercised great influence over Moslem opinion in Arabia which would be of no mean importance were the Turkish Empire to break up and the Caliphate to be questioned. Finally, the Sa'udi Amir's influence with many Arab tribes and especially those who inhabited lower Mesopotamia would be important to the British.⁴²

In forwarding Shakespear's report Cox pointed out *inter alia* that as ' Central Arabia is practically inaccessible by land to any Power but ours ... I venture to think that we should incur little risk by giving the desired undertaking, subject to [the] reservation that aggression be unprovoked '.⁴³ He also added that as no territory would be annexed Britain's allies would not be antagonised and that ibn Sa'ud's help ' would be no mean asset to the joint cause of us all '.⁴⁴ Cox urged that he should be authorised to draft a treaty on the lines of ibn Sa'ud's draft. However, the Government of India saw great difficulties arising from the definition of boundaries, harbouring refugees, law and jurisdiction, arms traffic and arms facilities which were embodied in the Amir's draft. They thought—and rightly so—that such considerations would require long and drawn-out negotiations; as time was a major factor, the Indian government advocated a preliminary treaty on broad lines. They suggested the following:

1. British Government recognises Bin Saud as independent ruler of Najd, Hasa, and Katif and guarantees hereditary successions to his dynasty, subject to the acceptance of successors by tribesmen and approval of His Majesty's Government;
2. In the event of unprovoked aggression on his territories by any foreign Power, British Government are prepared to aid Bin Saud to such extent and in such manner as the situation may require;
3. In return, Bin Saud agrees to have no dealings with any other foreign Power, except on the advice of the British Government, which advice he will unreservedly follow;
4. British Government and Bin Saud agree to conclude, as soon as this can be arranged, a detailed treaty in regard to other matters jointly concerning them.⁴⁵

While the British authorities were deciding on the terms of the treaty, on January 24, 1915 Captain Shakespear was killed in a Sa'udi–Rashidi battle at Jarrab. Shakespear, who was—according to the majority of accounts a—spectator in this affair, lost his life when the Rashidi forces turned ibn Sa'ud's flank and swept over the small hill where the Political Agent was observing the Bedouin battle. Complete details of his death are not known.⁴⁶ It was genuinely felt at the time that Shakespear's death was a tragic loss to the British government. Cox telegraphed succinctly but eloquently : " In the deceased officer the Service loses an able and gallant officer whose loss I deeply deplore '.⁴⁷ Ibn Sa'ud to whom the deceased officer showed more than a purely official devotion expressed ' his great sorrow at the loss of his intimate and trusted friend and begs expression [that] his sorrow and condolence may be submitted to His Majesty's Government '.⁴⁸

At this juncture it was particularly important that ibn Sa'ud arrive at some agreement with the British. He had violated his obligation—as stated in Article 12 of his treaty with the Turks—to aid the Sultan and had instead marched on the Turk's ally, ibn Rashid. On the other hand, he had disappointed some quarters in the British government by not helping their advance on Basra. However, as Cox argued, ibn Sa'ud could not have advanced on Basra because he did not have time to muster troops. Given ibn Sa'ud's many disappointments in trying to arrive at an agreement with the British, he now would make no further overt moves on their behalf until he possessed a definite guarantee. Ibn Sa'ud informed Cox that if he did not receive this guarantee, he might be forced to make some demonstration of intent to side with the Turks.⁴⁹

On January 30, 1915 the India Office forwarded the Government of India's telegram which set forth the four points around which the Anglo–Sa'udi treaty was to be constructed. They mentioned some of Shakespear's reasons for coming to an agreement with ibn Sa'ud and added that the Amir's friendship would be necessary given the disappearance of Turkish control in Basra after the war. Their observations with Grey's approval were embodied in a despatch to the Viceroy on February 1, 1915.

Your proposals are approved subject to the following :

1. In dynastic guarantee condition of acceptance of tribesmen should be secured if possible, but you will remember difficulty which this caused in case of Mohammerah, and negotiations should not be allowed to break down over this point.
2. You are presumably prepared for Shiekh [sic] of Koweit to ask for similar guarantee when both Bin Saud and Sheikh of Mohammerah have it.

3. Pledge against unprovoked aggression should be so worded as to make His Majesty's Government sole judges of nature and extent of assistance.
4. Please consider whether this treaty should not contain clause binding Bin Saud, subject to eventual definition of boundaries, not to interfere with Koweit, Bahrain, al-Katar, and Trucial Chiefs. But I leave this to your discretion.[50]

These instructions were communicated to Cox who immediately set about drawing up a treaty for despatch to ibn Sa'ud. It should be mentioned that this treaty was subject to confirmation by India. Ibn Sa'ud wrote in February asking that a new Political Officer be deputed to him or that negotiations be carried on via Basra. Cox urged that he be authorised to send the Sa'udi Amir the draft treaty and to have him sign it, after which 'an officer can then be deputed to discuss details of [a] second treaty'. Cox received permission to carry out this plan and on April 24th he received a reply from ibn Sa'ud. The Wahhabi wrote that 'modifications (which are not important) were found necessary for cogent reasons, necessitated by local conditions, the need to reassure the inhabitants and the governing family of Bin Saud, and also in view of the knowledge we possess as to the circumstances of the Arabs'. Cox replied that as the original wording had been altered he had to refer the treaty to the Government of India. On June 26th he forwarded translations of the two drafts—his and ibn Sa'ud's—set out in parallel columns.[51]

Ibn Sa'ud's modifications had been as follows. In Article I he had omitted the words 'subject to approval of British Government after consultation' as regards the selection of a successor. In Article II he had changed the wording to read: 'In the event of aggression by any foreign Power on the territories of countries belonging to the said Bin Saud and his descendants, the British Government will aid Bin Saud in all circumstances and in any place'. Here he had deleted the word 'unprovoked' and had altered the words 'to such extent and in such manner as the situation may seem to require'. In Article IV, he had added that he would only follow the advice of the British government 'where his interests require it'.[52]

After making the usual rounds to the governmental authorities concerned, the India Office despatched the following telegram to the Viceroy, August 16, 1915.

> Article I of treaty. Cox, after suitable explanation, should press for restoration of original words to which His Majesty's Government attach great importance. There seems no objection to election in default of designation, provided method of election is practicable and recognised as valid according to Arab custom by all tribes concerned. Otherwise we may become involved in intertribal disputes.
> Article II. 'Unprovoked' should be restored. His Majesty's Government do not like leaving ambiguity as to their aid, and if Bin Saud will not agree to original words they would prefer ' to such extent and in such manner as British Government after consultation with Bin Saud may consider most effective for protection of his interests '.
> Article IV. Cox should secure omission of Bin Saud's addition if possible; if not, substitution of his own proposal.
> As regards other alterations he should exercise his discretion.[53]

Sir Percy Cox carried out the above instructions and was able largely to implement at least variations of the above suggestions in the Anglo–Sa'udi treaty. This Agreement was signed on December 26, 1915 and ratified by India on July 18th of the following year. For all practical purposes, the British viewed the treaty as a success in achieving its immediate objectives. However, trouble was shortly to arise between ibn Sa'ud and the British as regards the interpretation of Article II. The Amir of Riyadh interpreted it to apply, among others, to the Sharif of Mecca. The British were quick to point out that 'foreign Power' did not apply to other Arabs. This issue will be treated in detail in another section.

Summary

As the Anglo–Sa'udi Treaty marked not only a turning point in relations between the British and ibn Sa'ud but a distinct departure from Britain's traditional policy of avoiding entanglement in central Arabia, it might be well to draw together in the form of a brief summary the various strands which were finally woven into the fabric of the agreement. Although the most recent writer touching upon this subject has rightly noted that this agreement 'was the most flexible of the Gulf network',[54] strangely enough, neither Philby nor any other writer on Anglo–Sa'udi relations has remarked the fact that this instrument constitutes a turning point in Anglo–Sa'udi relations. It will be seen that the decision to conclude a treaty with ibn Sa'ud was governed by two considerations. Firstly, it was necessary to arrive at an agreement with the Amir in order to secure his allegiance for participation in the war. It was necessary to pay an 'immediate price for his friendship' and it was also seen that after the war, his friendship would be vital. Secondly, a definite treaty was necessary as ibn Sa'ud was unprepared to give effective aid to the Indian Expeditionary Force until he had secured his long-desired agreement with the British.

It soon became clear that while ibn Sa'ud was interested in a detailed treaty, the British were interested primarily in concluding a broad temporary document which would be expanded later. The treaty as signed reflected the British viewpoint. It was general and confined to immediate essentials. The important questions of keeping peace at sea, arms-regulation and the status of British nationals were 'postponed for later consideration'. However, even this relatively limited agreement contained the attributes of a trucial treaty. Articles III and IV covered the alienation of territory and renunciation of relations with foreign powers while Article II and the last clause in Article IV implied the British right to arbitrate in disputes between ibn Sa'ud and his neighbours.[55]

As indicated previously, in practice on one point this treaty differed greatly from Britain's traditional trucial treaties. In the past, British agreements with the shaikhs of the Gulf littoral involved her at most in maritime disputes, with a narrow strip of land constituting a natural barrier between the coast and the inner fastness of Arabia. Her new engagements with ibn Sa'ud and Husain—and later with the Idrisi of 'Asir—drew Britain into central Arabia and marked a significant departure from the traditional British policy of avoiding entanglement in central Arabian affairs. In essence her new treaty with ibn Sa'ud in its promises of protection against foreign powers and references to the demarcation of boundaries involved Britain in controlling Arab relations on land where her maritime supremacy counted for very little. The principal example of the awkwardness of the new British obligation was reflected in the rising antipathy between ibn Saʿud and Husain and the former's attempt to apply Article II of his treaty to the latter. Reluctantly but inexorably Britain was drawn into the vortex of inner Arabian politics.

The Saʿudi Wartime Role: 1916 to 1918

The year 1916 was to prove a particularly eventful one for Great Britain. It began with the final withdrawals from Gallipoli and ended with the fall of the Asquith government. The intervening period was marked by a series of fateful events: the battles of Ypres, Jutland, the Somme and the surrender of Kut. It also witnessed the Easter Rising in Dublin and the Indian National Congress's demand for full self-government for India. This period also saw the conclusion of the Sykes–Picot Agreement and the raising of the Arab Revolt. And the latter was to have a significant impact on Anglo–Saʿudi relations.

At the beginning of 1916 the two principal powers of the Arabian peninsula, ibn Saʿud and Husain, had yet to make a definite move to assist the British forces in the Middle East. On the western side of the peninsula Husain was still negotiating with the British in Cairo,[56] and was not to proclaim the Arab Revolt for another six months. On the eastern side of the peninsula, ibn Saʿud, having just signed his treaty with the British, was not to march on ibn Rashid for some time. As regards purely wartime considerations, the British desired ibn Saʿud to neutralise ibn Rashid and later—after Husain raised the standard of revolt in the Hedjaz—to unite with the Sharif and support the Arab confederation against the Turks. It was also hoped that the Saʿudi Amir would enforce the British blockade on goods either going up from Kuwait or coming down from the north to the enemy. In the last analysis, ibn Saʿud played largely a negative—some would say a negligible—role during the Great War. The reasons for his nominal contribution to the Allied offensive are many, complicated and greatly intertwined.

Suffice it to say that in general ibn Saʿud was too weak to assist effectively the British offensive. He was plagued by tribal revolts which threatened his flank and by the growing enmity of Shaikh Mubarak's successors. He had also lost heavily to ibn Rashid at the battle of Jarrab and this defeat had the result of knocking him out of action for a year. Moreover, the Wahhabi Amir lacked the funds to subsidise his vassals or to buy weapons. To add to his difficulties, ibn Saʿud had to pacify his people who were daily becoming more disenchanted with interrupted trade owing to the war in general and the British blockade in particular. Finally, he greatly feared Sharif Husain's designs and the favour and pre-eminence accorded by the British to his adversary. These limitations of ibn Sa'ud's wartime co-operation were further confused by the division of opinion in the various sectors of the British chain of command as to what ibn Sa'ud should do and how he should do it. India and London both had their views on what was important and of course the issue was further complicated by rivalry between Cairo and Baghdad. As indicated earlier, the inability of the British government to co-ordinate departmental efforts and pursue a common policy towards its allies in Arabia was greatly detrimental to the British cause.

In the sense that many of the issues which arose during the war carried on after 1918, in many respects Anglo–Sa'udi wartime relations can be seen as prefiguration on a small scale of the postwar difficulties which were to occupy British attention for much of the period under consideration. In the long run, ibn Sa'ud was to consolidate his power over the greater part of the entire peninsula but during the immediate period—1914 to 1918—he was still troubled by tribal revolts.

During most of 1915, ibn Sa'ud was occupied with the revolt of the 'Ajman tribe of Hasa. His trouble with this tribe stemmed from his occupation of Hasa in 1913. It was reported that up to that time the Sa'udi Amir's relations with the tribe had been cordial and that the 'Ajman acknowledged his suzerainty.[57] However, ibn Sa'ud's extension of direct authority over the tribe strained their allegiance. Relations reached the breaking point when ibn Sa'ud attempted to tax the tribe and sought to prevent them from collecting a toll from the caravans which passed through their territories. The situation was further exacerbated by the fact that the *Araif* pretenders who claimed the Sa'udi throne were aligned with the 'Ajman.[58] Ibn Sa'ud maintained that it was due to the desertion of an 'Ajman contingent at the Battle of Jarrab that he lost to ibn Rashid.

In 1916, in an attempt to avenge himself for the 'Ajman desertion at Jarrab, ibn Sa'ud, after agreeing to an armistice with the 'Ajman leaders, was talked into attacking them by his brother, Sa'd. Not only was ibn Sa'ud worsted but his brother Sa'd was killed during the fight and ibn Sa'ud himself was wounded.[59] In September 1916 the ʿAjman were engaged once again, this time suffering defeat. They proceeded to seek sanctuary inside the borders of Kuwait. In what could be interpreted on one hand as Bedouin practice and on the other as an affront by Mubarak to ibn Saʿud, the ʿAjman were granted asylum. This refuge granted by the Shaikh of Kuwait to the ʿAjman helped to worsen the already deteriorating relations between the once friendly houses of Al Saʿud and Al Subah. After Mubarak's death in December 1915, the harbouring of the ʿAjman proved too troublesome to his son and successor, Jabir. The new shaikh feared that if he expelled the tribe they would join ibn Rashid and foment trouble in Kuwait territory. ' He wrote clearly and reasonably to ibn Saʿud on the matter. But in February 1916 ibn Saʿud insisted that they should be ejected, which was accordingly done. As was expected they joined ... ibn Rashid.'[60]

Although ibn Rashid had concluded an agreement with ibn Saʿud in June 1915 in which he implicitly agreed to support Great Britain, he later resumed hostilities against the Al Saʿud by marching on Qasim.[61] Ibn Saʿud, now further weakened by the revolt of the Al Murra, another tribe in the south, was greatly in need of material assistance from Great Britain. In the latter part of July 1915 ibn Saʿud wrote to Sir Percy Cox at Basra [62] and requested arms. He also explained ' that owing to [the] war his people were unable last year to dispose of [their] date crop to [the] Hedjaz or livestock to other parts of Arabia as usual so that he has been getting no revenue and at the same time has been put to very heavy expenditure owing to [the] necessity for keeping large forces under arms for a long time past '.[63] Cox sent the Amir 300 captured Turkish rifles and 10,000 rupees as temporary assistance. Ibn Saʿud had asked for 3,000 rifles but owing to the policy of sending all captured Turkish rifles to the Western Front, the Government of India decided that they could only spare him 1,000 Mausers. He was also given 200,000 rounds of ammunition and a £20,000 loan. This decision was taken in October 1915.[64] However, owing to the shortage of rifles, ibn Saʿud did not receive his first instalment until sometime after March of the following year.

While ibn Saʿud was preoccupied on three sides by hostile elements, the British authorities in Cairo were still negotiating with Husain.[65] In January of 1915 the Sharif had written to ibn Saʿud through his second son, ʿAbdullah, to ascertain the

Wahhabi's attitude towards the Turks and the British. In reply, ibn Sa'ud had advised the Sharif to 'temporise'. The Sharif was obviously undecided as to which side to turn to and ibn Sa'ud informed him that he saw no advantage in siding with the Porte.[66] While both ibn Sa'ud and Husain were negotiating with the British in 1915, the former's fear of the latter's designs was confirmed by an incident which occurred towards the end of that year. In November 'Abdullah marched into western Najd. There were differing reports on the objectives of this incursion but it appeared that it was something of a repetition of the 1910 Hashimite intrusion into the same area: to assert Sharifian authority over the eastern section of the 'Ataiba tribe of southern Qasim. Ibn Sa'ud was enraged ' and he protested to His Majesty's Government that if they could not restrain the Sharif's activities he would do so himself '.[67]

On June 5 1916, Sharif Husain proclaimed the Arab Revolt. Henceforth it was a cardinal fact of British policy in the Arabian peninsula to induce ibn Sa'ud to support the Sharifian rebellion and the projected Arab confederation. But ibn Sa'ud still feared that Husain would try to bring him under his rule. In July, ibn Sa'ud wrote to Cox stating his fear that the Sharif's successes might encourage him to claim some of his territories. The Amir was also worried because the British official communiqué sent to him ' referred to the Arabs " as a compendious whole ". He added that an old feud existed between the Shareef and himself, and that he and his tribesmen would never tolerate control or interference by the Shereef.'[68]

With the proclamation of the Arab Revolt the hostility between the Arab Bureau and the Indian authorities in Mesopotamia increased. The British political authorities in Mesopotamia were upset at the ' free rein being given to nationalism by the Arabophiles in Cairo . . .' At the same time the Cairo authorities were incensed at lack of co-operation afforded them by the Indian officials.[69] The following despatch underlines this rivalry between the two centres.

> The reports from Maskat, Bahrein and Koweyt are somewhat chilly: it is not very flattering to British *amour-propre* to learn that at Maskat the story of the Sherif's rising is not credited, and does not speak very well for our methods of propaganda.

Of course allowance must be made for the fact that the CPO, Basra, had assumed that the idea of a confederation of Arab States was defunct; it naturally follows that there could not be much enthusiasm in pushing what was supposed to be an abandoned idea.

The coldness shown by the Government of India towards the Arab movement since its inception will always prove a deadening influence in the Persian Gulf, and must naturally act as a damper on the keenness of our political officers there.[70]

The fact was that Delhi and the India Office always viewed the Middle East from their own vantage point and not as an imperial problem of which their interests formed only a part. From the 'Indian' standpoint, British authorities in India, Mesopotamia and the India Office saw little reason to support Cairo's activities. Many of these officials were incensed by the promises made to Husain and by the terms of the Sykes–Picot Agreement, as they hoped to annex at least part of Mesopotamia. Moreover, it was feared that Britain would appear meddlesome in Moslem religious matters as regards the idea of an Arab Caliphate. Furthermore, most of the officials in the India Office and the Government of India undoubtedly would have agreed with Lord Crewe's opinion: 'What we want is not a United Arabia: but a weak and disunited Arabia, split up into little principalities so far as possible under our suzerainty—but incapable of co-ordinated action against us, forming a buffer against the Powers in the West'.[71] Owing to bad communications among the various policy-making centres, which was complemented by misunderstandings, officials in the India Office and the Government of India were apparently unaware of Cairo's realistic interpretation of an 'independent Arab state'. As General (later Sir) G. F. Clayton, one of the most influential British officials in Cairo and at this point Director of Military Intelligence in Egypt, commented

> It is curious how they cling to their fear of a strong united Arab state on the flank of the road to India. I should not have thought that anyone who knew anything about the Arabs or Arabia (as they wish to have it) would have ever dreamed of such a possibility. I have never personally felt

> that there would be a danger to our position in Mesopotamia for the very reasons which Lord H[ardinge] gives, viz.: that the majority of the people there have no connection with the Sherif . . .'[72]

Although McMahon expressed similar sentiments,[73] it did little to assuage the anger and frustration felt by Delhi and her subordinates and the India Office at the politices pursued by London and Cairo.

By the beginning of September 1916 ibn Sa'ud had received letters from the Sharif asking for his alliance and assistance. The Sa'udi Amir replied that as regards 'assistance' he would respond to the best of his power. But as regards 'alliance', ibn Sa'ud pointed out to the Sharif that he had several times interfered with the tribes under Sa'udi jurisdiction and sponsored expeditions into Sa'udi territories. He maintained that if the Sharif was genuinely desirous of an alliance 'he should give a solemn undertaking to abstain from all interference in . . . his limits or amongst his subjects'. Ibn Sa'ud wrote to Cox mentioning that he had no wish to align himself with Husain and only considered doing so because of British desires and his own wish to expel the Turks.[74]

Cox in forwarding ibn Sa'ud's letter recommended that the Amir 'should be informed definitely that no present or future understandings between us and the Sharif would prejudice our adherence to the terms of Articles I and II of our treaty with him ...'[75] Cox was informed shortly by the Government of India that 'as the policy of encouraging an Arab State or Confederation of States was not dead, anything repudiating it should be avoided'. Cox was also instructed that any 'reference to the treaty should be confined to Article I, as we could not admit that Article 2 was binding on us as against other Arabs'. Austen Chamberlain, the Secretary of State for India, also urged that ibn Sa'ud should be pressed to unite with Husain.[76]

In what could be viewed as a shift in policy the Government of India answered Chamberlain and proposed what amounted to a negative or passive policy in contradistinction to the previously sought active role.

> We deprecate any attempt to press Bin Saud to take any specific action either to assist us or Sherif. If he does so spontaneously, well and good; but otherwise we should be

content with immense asset we have secured in the passive friendship of Nejd. We certainly cannot spare guns, while despatch of 1,000 Nejd tribesmen to support Arab revolt would be of little material value to Sherif would weaken Bin Saud vis-à-vis Bin Rashid, and might lead to subsequent embarrassing claims by Bin Saud against Sherif.[77]

This new attitude adopted by the Government of India evoked controversy on several British fronts. The Sharif was to attribute ibn Sa'ud's inactivity to 'collusion with the Turks' while his British patrons in Cairo were given more fuel to feed the fires of their hostility towards India's protégé. In the India Office, opinions on ibn Sa'ud's actions ranged from the point of view that he was doing 'practically nothing'[78] to assist the war effort to Hirtzel's caustic minute:

> The questions raised by the recent telegrams and letters is whether Sa'ud should be urged to take active steps, and if so, what.
>
> Sir P. Cox merely asks questions, without giving any advice. The G[overnment] of I[ndia] are, as usual, in favour of nobody doing anything. We did not, however, make a treaty with Bin Saud in order that he might do nothing; and the least that he can do is to pin down Bin Rashid. This he has failed to do. Only in July last Bin Rashid was on our flank in Mesopotamia and had to be driven off. Sooner or later he will, if left alone, most probably attack the Shereef. It is not clear whether in order to hold him fast it is necessary to capture Hail—a task for which Bin Saud says he requires guns.[79]

At the end of October, after a flurry of correspondence on the Government of India's views, Chamberlain bowed to India's proposals but stressed that although ibn Sa'ud's military value was small he could 'indirectly assist by holding Bin Rashid in check and preventing him from attacking the Sharif or Basra'. It was pointed out that this type of 'limited offensive' was consistent with the Government of India's view and that it 'need not involve the capture of Hail'.[80]

It will be remembered that the decision to supply ibn Sa'ud with 1,000 rifles and a 20,000 pounds loan was taken at the end of October 1915. When ibn Sa'ud had originally requested arms he had asked for several cannons with men to man them.

This had been impossible for the Government of India to supply. It is probable that one of their main reasons for recommending that ibn Sa'ud assume a passive role was due to India's inability to supply proper weapons for any Sa'udi offensive against the walled city of Hail. Moreover the growing antipathy between ibn Sa'ud and Husain was not lost on the Indian government and must have affected their decision to urge a passive role for the Sa'udi Amir.

Cox wrote to ibn Sa'ud on October 18, 1916 and communicated the Government of India's point of view to him. The essence of the message was that ibn Sa'ud should openly support Husain in some way as this would help win over other shaikhs to the Sharifian standard.

> As to how you can best do that, whether by helping him with money and men, or by attacking Ibn Rashid, or by winning the latter over to your side, this is a question which you can best decide for yourself. His Majesty's Government do not wish to press you to do this or to do that; all they wish you to understand is that your open support, whether it be moral or active, will be of great advantage to the Sherif's cause and to the common object. You know best how you can most profitably assist the Sherif without serious prejudice to important interests of your own.[81]

The effectiveness of Cox's letter—which essentially left it to ibn Sa'ud's discretion to determine how best to assist the British—was no doubt greatly undermined by recent correspondence between Husain and ibn Sa'ud.

On September 5 1916, Sharif Husain had answered ibn Sa'ud's letter in which the latter had asked the former for guarantees of his sovereignty before agreeing to align himself with the Sharif. Husain was highly insulting in his reply stating that such a letter only could have been written by a man 'bereft of his reason'. He even went so far as to return ibn Sa'ud's letter and its enclosures 'so that you may reflect in what you wrote to us in them'.[82] As ibn Sa'ud made his support of Husain contingent upon receiving a satisfactory reply from the Sharif, this move on Husain's part had grave effects on Sa'udi–Sharifian relations. To add further insult to injury, on November 5th Husain caused himself to be proclaimed by the notables of Mecca 'King of the Arabs'. The British government, who only recognised him as 'King of the Hedjaz', were not consulted. In view of the Oriental concern for 'face', this affront to ibn Sa'ud, not to mention other Arab chiefs, coupled with recent reports of substantial material assistance to the Sharif, prompted the 'Uqair Meeting of November 11th between the Sa'udi Amir and Sir Percy Cox.

At this meeting ibn Sa'ud reported that his people were greatly disturbed by the embargo which he had enforced—at British request—on traffic between Syria and northern Najd. This embargo had sorely hit Qasim—the centre of the overland trade to the north. Moreover his subjects were questioning the Sa'udi policy of supporting Great Britain who in turn supported their enemy, Husain. Cox assured ibn Sa'ud on the vital issue of Husain's new title that the British government 'had insisted on the Shereef making formal admission that he claimed no jurisdiction over other independent Arab rulers'.[83] Ibn Sa'ud ruled out as impractical any effective co-operation in the Hedjaz but offered to send one of his sons with a small force of retainers as a token of his support for the Arab Revolt. However, ibn Sa'ud would not do this unless the Sharif sent a friendly request as he was only sinking his personal differences with Husain 'in view of the common cause'.[84] During these conversations ibn Sa'ud let it be known that he was planning to visit the Shaikh of Kuwait. As a *Durbar* of Arab chiefs had been planned for November 20th, Cox invited the Sa'udi Amir to attend and urged the Government of India that while there ibn Sa'ud should be awarded the KCIE.[85] The celebrations of Kuwait afforded the British government an opportunity to take stock of the existing relations between themselves and ibn Sa'ud and to attempt to iron out the difficulties prevailing among their allies, to assure ibn Sa'ud of British support, and to clarify his wartime role.

The Great Durbar at Kuwait

On November 20 1916, ibn Sa'ud, Shaikh Jabir of Kuwait, Shaikh Khaz'al of Mohammera and Sir Percy Cox, 'with many important Beduin chiefs from El Hasa and Southern Irag', met in state.[86] Ibn Sa'ud was awarded the KCIE and Jabir the CIE.[87] After the awards the three potentates vied with one another in their protestations of loyalty to Great Britain. During the ceremonies ibn Sa'ud 'struck the keynote of the meeting in a speech " that was as spontaneous as it was unexpected " '.[88] After condemning the Turks and lauding the British he ' praised the action of the Sharif and urged the obligation of all true Arabs to co-operate with him in forwarding the Arab cause '.[89] Through this protestation of unity with the Sharif, ibn Sa'ud fulfilled the British desire of at least obtaining Sa'udi moral support for the Sharifian-led Arab Revolt. However, the Amir refused to recognise Husain's new title and it was also decided during his sojourn at Kuwait that he would send no large contingent to support Husain. At the request of the Secretary of State of India, Cox expressed to ibn Sa'ud on behalf of His Majesty's Government their approval of his action and their assurance that his rights would be protected.[90]

After the Kuwait ceremonies, ibn Sa'ud was taken to Basra as a guest of the British to be shown their military hardware. To say that ibn Sa'ud was impressed by this recognition bestowed upon him by the British government would be an understatement. He was presented with a sword of honour by the representatives of General Sir Stanley Maude, the Commander of the Mesopotamian Forces, and saw his first airplanes. In turn ibn Sa'ud impressed the British authorities with his statesmanship. Captain (later Sir) A. T. Wilson, Cox's deputy, of whom we shall hear more later, described him as ' tall, dignified, and observant ' and added that he ' looked as big a man as he was and played his part to perfection '.[91]

While still in Kuwait Cox had taken the opportunity to discuss the outstanding problems between ibn Sa'ud and his ' allies '. The Chief Political Officer effected an agreement between Jabir and ibn Sa'ud concerning the 'Ajman. This agreement stipulated that for the duration of the war ibn Sa'ud would not molest the 'Ajman as long as the tribe—under Anglo–Kuwaiti protection—did not interfere with Najdi tribes or consort with those 'Ajman sections which had joined hostile tribes. The Sa'udi Amir took the occasion of these talks to repeat his need for arms, stressing that his supplies had been virtually exhausted. He also emphasised that his main source of income, the camel trade with Syria, was interrupted by the war and his men were beginning to wish that they were not in the opposite camp to the Turks. Ibn Sa'ud also requested a subsidy as it was costing him ' one rupee per day per man in the field '.[92]

Cox urged that ibn Sa'ud's wishes be granted and that he

receive 3,000 rifles with ample ammunition and four machine
guns and that he be granted a monthly subsidy of £5,000. Cox
argued that compared to the support given by the Turks to ibn
Rashid [93] and the British aid given to Husain [94] this was minimal.
The British government agreed to these recommendations but
Delhi was doubtful whether she could supply the full 3,000 rifles
immediately. The Indian government offered to supply 1,000
straight away and to try to supply the 2,000 later on. On
January 2nd 1917, the Treasury agreed to pay ibn Sa'ud £5,000
per month for a period of six months.[95] In London Sir Mark
Sykes, the imaginative, influential and persuasive prime mover
behind many of London's decisions on Arab affairs, was favourable to Cox's suggestions.[96] ' Ibn Sa'ud's requirements seem to
be exceedingly modest and well worth complying with. He has
perhaps not considered what would be the value of a flight of
aeroplanes based upon Hufhuf; if machines are available they
should give him overwhelming advantage '.[97]

In return for this assistance, ibn Sa'ud undertook to keep
4,000 men in the field in Qasim under his personal command.

> If Ibn Rashid moves towards Irak in force he will move
> up parallel with him towards Zobeyr, and join up with our
> friendly tribes, and with a force from Koweyt. During visit
> here he will warn Shaykhs of our combine who are here to
> meet him, that if Ibn Rashid threatens them in strength
> he will move up in their support .
>
> If Ibn Rashid remains in Hail, Ibn Saud will remain at
> Qasim, and harass or attack as opportunity offers.[98]

While the various Shaikhs were still assembled in Kuwait, the
Foreign Office put pressure on King Husain to adopt a more
conciliatory attitude towards the British allies on the eastern side
of the peninsula. Husain complied and despatched a friendly
telegram congratulating the three Shaikhs on their support of
the Arab cause. The Sharif also apologised for any past slights,
blaming his shortcomings on the presures of war. This was a
timely move on the part of the Arab Bureau, as ibn Sa'ud had
stated his fear more than once that the British might recognise
Husain's lordship over the Arabs. He had written to Cox in
July, commenting on the lack of co-ordinated Middle Eastern
policy and the faulty communications between the various
branches of the Middle Eastern administration. 'Although you

yourself probably appreciate my fears, it is possible that the representative of the British Government who is actually conducting negotiations with the Sharif is not acquainted with the position'.[99] No matter how exceptional his qualities, it could not have been easy for a Bedouin chief, whose only experience of the world outside central and eastern Arabia had been his trip to Basra, to appreciate the hydra-headed political organism which made policy in the Middle East. One can imagine the difficulties he encountered explaining his adherence to the British to his less gifted followers.

Although the Kuwait *Durbar* sought to settle the outstanding questions of the 'Ajman, Sa'udi–Kuwaiti relations, Sa'udi support of Husain's Arab Revolt and ibn Sa'ud's role against the Al Rashid, these same problems persisted long after the celebration at Kuwait had ended. One of the main problems confronting Sir Percy Cox from 1917 onwards—a problem which was interwoven with the aforementioned questions—was the question of the blockade. The object of the blockade was to prevent goods from entering enemy hands in Iraq. To achieve this end it was necessary to blockade [100] the northern sector of the Arabian peninsula. As blockading the Persian Gulf ports would have been as detrimental to Britain's friends as to her enemies, she sought the aid of her Arab allies, 'namely Ibn Sa'ud and the Shaikh of Kuwait, the one to prevent leakage of supplies across his frontier to the enemy and the other to refuse access to the Kuwait market to enemy purchasing agents'. The arrangements to achieve these objects 'were left entirely to the discretion of the two rulers themselves in accordance with our consistent policy of refraining from interference in the internal arrangements of native states except when circumstances make it absolutely necessary to do so'.[101] As the scarcity of supplies during wartime drove prices up, smuggling became even more lucrative than usual. There is little doubt that contraband goods were 'traffiked' through Kuwait and Najd and that these supplies not only reached the Turks in the north but also found their way to the west.

One of the points of friction between Husain and ibn Sa'ud was this passage of Turkish supplies from Najd to the Hedjaz. By the beginning of 1917 King Husain with British assistance had driven out most of the Turks in the Hedjaz with the exception of one Turkish division under Fakhri Pasha which remained firmly entrenched at Medina. It soon became clear that Husain's 'mercenaries' could not hope to take the town by assault; Medina could only be reduced by starvation. Through the inefficient enforcement of the blockade by Kuwait and Najd, it was clear that provisions were reaching Medina from the eastern side of the peninsula. This led Husain to charge time and again that ibn Sa'ud was in league with the Turks.

Qasim was the centre of this overland trade as indeed it had been for ages. Ibn Sa'ud held that he was powerless to stop this trade as he was too weak to exert his authority over the Qasim merchants. Ibn Sa'ud also blamed the new Shaikh of Kuwait, [102] Salim, for the illicit trade. Both Salim and ibn Sa'ud exchanged countless allegations, and relations between Kuwait and Najd deteriorated still further. Salim, who was anti-Wahhabite, allegedly made an ' unnecessarily ostentatious parade of his protection of the 'Ajman tribe ' [103] while ibn Sa'ud retaliated by taxing the 'Awazim tribe, a tribe which was under the jurisdiction of Kuwait.[104]

The most flagrant contravention of the blockade took place in the latter part of September 1917. As a result of the strengthening of the Iraq blockade, Kuwait began to profit as a centre of enemy supply while Qasim enjoyed the benefits of a distributing centre.

> The climax was reached towards the end of September, when a caravan of 3,000 enemy camels came down to Kuwait through the Qasim with a passport signed by ibn Sa'ud's eldest son, Turki, who was at the time in command of the forces nominally engaged in preventing the leakage of supplies to the enemy. The debacle was completed by the clearance of the same caravan, loaded with supplies from Kuwait with the sanction or connivance of the Shaikh himself in spite of specific orders telegraphed from Baghdad that it should be detained pending further consideration.[105]

While ibn Sa'ud parried with Salim, his subjects' discontent was further excited by the British decision to win over certain sections of the Shammar confederation. Shaikh Dhari ibn Tawala, head of the Aslam section of the Shammar, had declared for the British by the time of the *Durbar*. Sometime in December of 1915 Sa'ud ibn Salah Al Subhan, ibn Rashid's brother-in-law and vizier, fell out with the Al Rashid and joined ibn Tawala, placing himself at British disposal. Cox viewed Sa'ud ibn Salah Al Subhan [hereafter ibn Subhan] as potentially powerful and thought that if treated well by the British, many other tribes would desert ibn Rashid. The prospect of detaching tribal support from the Amir of Hail was received with favour by the various offices of the British government. The thought of eliminating the last remaining stronghold of Turkish power by this method must have presented an attractive picture to a war-weary government which needed their guns for more important fronts.

The India Office held that ibn Sa'ud's claims to Jabal Shammar were not strong enough to prevent the British from giving ibn Subhan at least moral support. They were attracted by the possibility that Shammar defections might induce other Shammar tribes ' to draw in Euphrates tribes below Najaf and defeat Bin Rashid thus releasing Bin Saud to move against Medina '.[106] The Arab Bureau doubted ibn Subhan's ability to bring in the whole Shammar confederation and maintained that open support—even if limited to moral support—would commit the British to maintaining Hail against Riyadh. Fortunately ibn Subhan's presence was less embarrassing than it could have been owing to his modest aspirations. He desired only to serve Great Britain and did not wish to assume the Amirate of Hail or to seize the walled city. He had already written to ibn Sa'ud, Salim and Khaz'al ' asking them to regard him as a friend and ally '.[107] Cox was of the opinion that they need not fear ibn Sa'ud's reaction to ibn Subhan and that if assisted the Shammari could ' push forward through the desert parallel to [the] Euphrates with a view to establishing touch with Ibn Shaalan on one side and [the] Nejef tribes on [the] other. He would at the same time cut all Turkish communications between Iraq and Hail or Medina '.[108]

During the first half of 1917, ibn Rashid was relatively quiet. Owing most probably to his defecting tribes and the reverses suffered by his allies, the Turks—Baghdad was captured in March—ibn Rashid entered into a peace correspondence with ibn Sa'ud. The Amir of Riyadh replied to his perennial adversary that any friendship between them was contingent upon a a Rashidi manifestation of friendship towards Great Britain. In relaying this news to Cox ibn Sa'ud added :

I did not intend peace with him for any personal motive but only for the interests of the Arabs, otherwise my relations with Bin Rashid are not hidden from your Excellency. ... it will be proved to my friend the British Government that I have carried out the duties incumbent upon me in regard to the rights of the Arabs, and that we do not intend our own interests but we safeguard the interests of our friend and the pleasure of their friends like the Sharif.[109]

Ibn Rashid replied to ibn Sa'ud that the ' terms which you have mentioned are not agreeable to the interests of our religion as well as our world : the matter therefore stays where it was '.[110]

The British government's policy of supporting disaffected enemy elements [111] was a natural practice given the exigencies of war. However, this policy was not calculated to impress ibn Sa'ud's ignorant followers. Given the British engineered ' truce ' between the 'Ajman and the ibn Sa'ud (which did not prevent them from raiding ibn Sa'ud's tribes), the blockade, Husain's machinations and now the British support for the Shammar elements, there was great disapproval in Najd of ibn Sa'ud's support of the British.

It was freely said that we were afraid of taking strong action against potential enemies and ready to placate them at all costs. The moral was obvious; Ibn Sa'ud's policy of patient endurance of affronts and even assaults was freely criticised and disapproved.

Our dealings with the Shammar have certainly not raised us in the estimation of the people of Najd. They may have been necessitated by military considerations but that in itself was a confession of weakness dangerous to make before an ignorant and generally hostile people.

' The British Government ', said the Imam Abdul Rahman himself, ibn Sa'ud's father—and his words were endorsed by the Wahhabi High Priest—' either can and won't help us or else they would but cannot—in either case we should be prepared to help ourselves.[112]

It was true that up to this point ibn Sa'ud had exhibited no great enthusiasm for attacking ibn Rashid. His hesitance in all probability stemmed from his weakness and lack of military equipment, coupled with his fear of what Husain would do if ibn Sa'ud were to attack Hail, thus drawing his troops away from central Arabia. Ibn Saʿud himself reflected the contempt he and his followers held for ibn Subhan when he wrote: 'I neither need his aid nor do I trust him. He has about 10 followers and his attitude is no less equivocal than that of the Aslam who are with him'.[113]

Since early 1917 ibn Saʿud or one of his sons had been continuously in Qasim fulfilling his promise made at the *Durbar* to occupy ibn Rashid, thereby forestalling any Rashidi move towards the west. However as spring drew near, London and Cairo began to press the Mesopotamian Administration to have ibn Saʿud assume a more active role. On March 20th, nine days after the British had finally captured Baghdad, Wingate telegraphed to the Commanding General in Basra: 'At present juncture [the] Turks would be greatly assisted by a diversion by Ibn Rashid against Medina, and any action that can be taken by Ibn Saud and other friendly chiefs to prevent this is desirable. Nuri Shaalan is being asked to act against Rashid from the north by Faisal'. On March 24th Austen Chamberlain telegraphed: 'What is Ibn Saud doing? I hope action may be possible as suggested in Cairo telegram of 20th March ... And on May 10th Sykes sent Cox a long telegram in which he stated that 'he and Colonel Wilson and Leachman all agreed that it was most desirable for Ibn Saud to take Hail and suggesting that Leachman should proceed to Saud and see what he could do to put him in a position to do so'.[114]

The Chief Political Officer relayed these instructions to ibn Saʿud but they were crossed by the letter from the Amir mentioning the Rashidi peace overtures. This turn of events necessitated further consideration. Cox believed that the British object was 'to eliminate ibn Rashid either by winning him over or by crushing him' and that it was not of much consequence which alternative was adopted. In an aide-memoir Cox touched upon the difficulty of disposing of Hail if ibn Rashid were crushed, and the possibility of getting rid of the Rashidi Amir pacifically. Owing to the rising pressure from Cairo which was complicated by the Rashidi peace correspondence, on May 17th Cox decided to send a British officer to ibn Saʿud. He wrote to ibn Saʿud as follows: 'In order that our allied operations against the enemy may proceed on a common plan, it is very necessary that there should be close touch between our army at Gazza and the forces of the Sherif and Your Excellency and the Army on this side'.

To accomplish this object, Ronald (later Sir Ronald) Storrs, previously Sir Henry McMahon's Oriental Secretary in Cairo and presently in Baghdad as Political Officer representing the Egyptian Expeditionary Force in Mesopotamia, was to be despatched to ibn Sa'ud. Colonel Leachman was to be sent to the Sharif.[115]

The Mission to ibn Sa'ud

Cox instructed Storrs to allay ibn Sa'ud's fears concerning Salim and Husain, to discuss the Najdi–Kuwaiti rivalry and effective measures as regards the blockade, and to ascertain the Sa'udi possibilities of attacking Hail. As regards the last question, the gist of Cox's instruction to Storrs was to find out just where ibn Sa'ud stood vis-à-vis Hail and to report back how advisable it was for the Sa'udi Amir to mount an offensive. Unfortunately Storrs suffered a sunstroke on his first day out from Kuwait,[116] and the project had to be abandoned. Cox wrote that he had hoped that his mission along with the despatch to Leachman to the Sharif would have helped to dispel the 'atmosphere of distrust prevailing in the Sherif's circle' and enable the British authorities 'to decide if there were any means by which ... [they] could make Bin Saud more actively useful'. However, owing to the onset of the hot weather, the possibility of sending another officer was ruled out.[117]

Cox at this point was working under considerable strain. He was at odds with General Maude, to whom he was subordinate. Put briefly, the friction stemmed from the fact that Maude viewed things from a purely military standpoint. Furthermore, having had little experience of eastern affairs, he tended to be unsympathetic to, and ride roughshod over local problems. After threatening to resign if his position were not improved, Cox was made Civil Commissioner in July 1917. He was granted the right to send his reports on economic and political matters directly to London and not—as before—only through the Army Commander. Although weary of the daily pressures of policy discussions and the frustrations involved in building a new administration, Cox carried on in his duties. The summer was to prove an especially trying one for the new Civil Commissioner. Not only was it the hottest one on record, with temperatures over 120° in Baghdad, but in August Cox received the news that his only son had been killed in France.[118]

Although 1917 saw considerable British success in the Middle East—viz, the fall of Baghdad in March, the fall of 'Aqaba in July and the capture of Jerusalem in December—the year was generally the 'blackest'[119] yet for Britain. With the failure of the Nivelle offensive which sparked off mutinies in the French army, the onus of the fighting fell upon the British in the mud and tragedy of Passchendaele. And in November the Bolshevik Revolution took place.

1917 was also a trying time for the Government of India and the India Office. In June the Mesopotamia Commission published its findings on the Kut Disaster.[120] The report confirmed what many had thought for some time: that the Government of India was too incompetent to undertake major military operations. Among the casualties which the Commission's revelations left in its wake was Austen Chamberlain, who resigned as Secretary for India. As Lord Birkenhead said of him: 'Austen always played the game and he always lost it'.[121] Chamberlain was succeeded by Edwin Montagu, a Liberal and critic of Indian governmental methods. In addition to criticising Indian military competence, the report also raised the question of India's government generally. Although this question cannot be considered here, it is interesting to note that shortly before Montagu succeeded Chamberlain he had criticised the Indian government as '... too wooden, too iron, too inelastic, too antediluvian to be of any use for the modern purposes we have in view'.[122]

While the higher authorities in London debated the Mesopotamia Commission's report, correspondence between Cairo and Baghdad on the subject of sending a mission to ibn Sa'ud continued throughout the summer, while the questions which had prompted Cox to decide originally to despatch Storrs to ibn Sa'ud remained unsolved and grew more pressing as time wore on. By autumn it was decided that both Cairo and Baghdad should send missions to Riyadh and that Husain and ibn Sa'ud were to exchange envoys so that each of them would be aware of the other's point of view.

In answer to his request, ibn Sa'ud was to have an officer attached to him. H. St J. B. Philby of the Finance Section of the Iraq Political Department was sent to the Amir accompanied by Lt-Colonel H. Cunliffe-Owen. The latter was to assess ibn Sa'ud's military stores and determine his needs if it were definitely decided to attack Hail. Colonel Hamilton, the Political Agent at Kuwait, was to precede the Philby mission to Riyadh and represent the Shaikh of Kuwait. From Egypt, Storrs was to be despatched once again to represent the Sharifian point of view. He was also to be accompanied by a military officer.

The mission was to be beset with difficulties from the beginning, one of them being Philby's personality, which had a tendency to clash with others. Brilliant, highly individualistic, ambitious and vain, Philby was to become a great explorer, a prolific writer on Arabia and a devoted champion of ibn Sa'ud. A. T. Wilson, with whom he did not get on, described him as 'one of those men who are apt to assume that everything that they come across from a government to a fountain-pen is constructed on wrong principles and capable of amendment'.[123] Another authority wrote that 'fame was his spur'.[124] He had little of Lawrence's charm and artistry and much of his disdain for the British government. Given his character, it is not surprising that Philby threw off the shackles of officialdom, leaving the British service to become a Moslem and an advisor to ibn Sa'ud. Lawrence became a hero. Philby attached himself to one.

Soon after reaching Riyadh in late November 1917, Philby clashed with Hamilton and the latter left 'in a rage, leaving all duties to Philby and Cunliffe-Owen'.[125] In the meantime, Wingate was suggesting to King Husain that Storrs should travel to Riyadh via the Hedjaz in the 'company of an influential agent of [the] Sheriff'.[126] The High Commissioner thought that the 'military' as opposed to the political character of the mission should be emphasised. He deprecated the mention of the possibility of settling the wider issues between Husain and ibn Sa'ud as the Sharif at the time was 'in a somewhat uncompromising state of mind'.[127] The Foreign Office hoped that, once the Storrs mission reached ibn Sa'ud and held talks with him, he could be persuaded to send a personal representative to King Husain.[128] However these plans to send a mission from Egypt had to be abandoned later owing to the hostility and intransigence of Husain.

At first Husain was suspicious of the political motives of the Storrs mission and refused to take responsibility for Storrs' safety when travelling overland through the Hedjaz to Najd. Wingate prevailed upon the Sharif who then relented and guaranteed the Egyptian mission offering to provide a convoy for Storrs. However, on November 21st Wingate reported that Husain had revoked his approval. In London and Cairo frenzied attempts were made to induce Husain to lift his ban on the mission. Even in Cairo it was thought that Husain's statement that the Hedjaz was unsafe was a pretext to prevent the mission from reaching ibn Sa'ud. Philby reported ibn Sa'ud's attitude towards the Storrs' mission as follows:

> Ibn Saud heartily welcomes proposed deputation of Storrs as likely to give Egyptian authorities glimpse of other side of shield, but he expresses the opinion that Sherif's desire to disclaim responsibility after Storrs leaves Hedjaz frontier is merely a ruse to deter Egypt from pressing proposal. He agrees to send adequate escort with letters from himself and me, and there need be no anxiety about this side of frontier as Ibn Saud is delighted at projected visit.[129]

While the British authorities in Cairo and London were still trying to induce Husain to revoke his ban on the mission, Philby and Cunliffe-Owen carried on talks with ibn Sa'ud. The mission to ibn Sa'ud had two main objectives: first it sought to promote better relations between the Sharif and ibn Sa'ud and second to induce the Amir to assume a more active role in assisting his fellow Arabs. The mission also was to attempt to settle the other somewhat less important issues preventing effective Sa'udi participation in the war. It may be more convenient to leave the more important questions for the moment in order to deal first with the subsidiary issues which were capable of being settled more quickly rather than the vexed issues of Sa'udi–Sharifian relations and the role of ibn Sa'ud towards ibn Rashid.

Although ibn Sa'ud had faithfully observed his agreement with the British as regards the 'Ajman, by December 1917 the tribe had twice breached this agreement. After several programmes for settling the 'Ajman problem had proved abortive [130] owing to the bad faith of the tribe, the British government adopted the following proposal by Philby.

> Firstly, that the Ajman should be informed that, in the event of the continuance of raids, their subsidies would be stopped and their access to the local markets barred; and Secondly, that Ibn Saud should be given a free hand to deal with the tribe provided that the safety of the railway was not thereby endangered.[131]

The minor problem of the 'Awazim solved itself when ibn Sa'ud, after stipulating that he would cease taxing the tribe if Salim wrote to him and requested him 'in suitable terms' to do so, stopped taxing them anyway even though Salim never complied with his request.[132] As regards the issue of the blockade—which also involved Sa'udi–Kuwaiti antipathy—Philby seized upon the instance of the passage of the 3,000 camels through Najd to force ibn Sa'ud to apply tighter controls on his people. Pressure was also brought to bear on Salim to prevent illicit trade. Henceforth until the effective cessation of the blockade the issue was quiescent.[133]

After Philby sent off his first reports in early December regarding the estimates of what equipment and arms ibn Sa'ud would need to mount an offensive against Hail, he heard from Cox that Husain had revoked his permission for the Hedjaz mission to travel across Arabia to Riyadh. Philby took it upon himself—without reference to Baghdad—to embark upon a personal journey across Arabia in order to prove that Husain was wrong to say that the countryside was unsafe, to link up with Storrs in the Hedjaz and escort him back to Riyadh.[134] One of his motives was an ambition to follow in the steps of the great Arabian explorers. It is arguable that ' he twisted his war-time duty to suit this personal ambition '.[135] Philby, with an escort of Wahhabi retainers, reached Taif on Christmas Day 'without adventure'.[136] Husain could do little else but arrange for Philby to come to Jedda for talks. At this juncture it was thought that Storrs would join Philby, but Jerusalem had recently fallen to Allenby and Storrs had been appointed its first Governor. Instead of Storrs, Commander D. G. Hogarth of the Arab Bureau joined Philby for talks with Husain.

The talks proved completely abortive. Philby not only embarrassed and affronted Husain by crossing Arabia, but his manner antagonised the Sharif, already sensitive to the circumscription of his ambitions by the British. Relations between ibn Sa'ud and Husain, if anything, were exacerbated by Philby's actions. The Sharif was highly suspicious of the British attitude to ibn Sa'ud and also greatly feared the Wahhabi revival—the *Ikhwan* movement—and its potential strength. He was also antagonised by the actions of the Wahhabis in the little town of Khurma which he claimed. The talks dragged on until January, when Philby finally returned to Riyadh by sea, having been refused permission by Husain to return by land.[137]

Before Philby left for the Hedjaz, he had sent off his report on the arms ibn Sa'ud would need to attack Hail. It will be remembered that the main objectives of the mission to Riyadh were to promote better relations between the Sharif and ibn Sa'ud, and in Cox's words, ' to see the country and make proposals in accordance with military possibilities '.[138] The first objective—the improvement of Sa'udi–Sharifian relations—was stultified by Husain's and Philby's actions and the ensuing non-arrival of Storrs, but Philby reported on the second objective that ibn Sa'ud was

> prepared, given adequate assistance in money and arms, to mobilise 15,000 men for an attack upon Hail....
>
> Bin Saud's actual requirements for this purpose were estimated as follows : 2 siege guns, 2 field guns with necessary ammunition, 10,000 rifles and 50,000 pounds a month for period of the operations (i.e. Jan.–June 1918). Bin Saud at the same time threw out hints regarding his future political status... Mr Philby expresses himself as ' very confident that something big can be achieved... on the basis of the proposals made '; but he suggested as an alternative—in case His Majesty's Government inclined to a less ambitious programme—that he should be given discretion to make doles to Bin Saud up to a maximum of 50,000 pounds ' for minor objects actually achieved to my satisfaction '.[139]

Cairo was against such an arming of ibn Sa'ud as they feared a Wahhabi revival and the possibility that ibn Sa'ud, once so armed, might turn his efforts westwards and overrun the Hedjaz. Given the Sharifian refusal to send an envoy to Riyadh, taken together with his policy of buying Sa'udi tribes with British gold, relations between Riyadh and Mecca were reaching flashpoint. Although Wingate naturally championed Husain, he was forced to admit in late December that the latest conversations of November 24th and 25th between Colonel Wilson, the Political Agent at Jedda, and King Husain

> afford confirmation of the latter's design to become the paramount power in Arabia. The King refrained from

giving a direct indication of his future course of action but it can be inferred that he will adopt the traditional means of *divide et impera* and *vi et armis* to achieve his ends.[140]

In the India Office it was argued that ibn Sa'ud had been supplied with weapons and funds since 1915 but that the British government thus far had ' had very little value for our money '.[141] In a minute which (a) expressed the importance of the course of the war in determining what assistance was to be given to Britain's protégés and (b) the lack of appreciation of the full measure of ibn Sa'ud's problems, an Indian official expressed the following:

> ... if General Allenby succeeds in cutting the Hedjaz railway from the Jordan valley, the Turkish game will be up in Arabia, and the ' Arab Question ' will to a great extent ... disappear. In the circumstances I would hesitate to pay further blackmail to Bin Saud or anyone else until we are sure that we cannot get on without their assistance.[142]

In the margin to the above minute the Under Secretary of State for India remarked : ' I am disposed to agree '.[143]

In Cairo, Wingate held that ibn Rashid was not as strong as he was thought to be and that ' the capture of Hail . . . [was not] an object of sufficient importance to warrant paying Bin Saud a " blank cheque " for its accomplishment '.[144] Cox countered the above arguments by pointing out that large sections of the 'Anaza tribes were coming over to the standard of Fahad Bey ibn Hadhdhal, the paramount chief of the 'Amarat section of the great 'Anaza tribe of Arabia and a British protégé.[145] Cox envisaged a combination of these tribes joining with ibn Sa'ud's followers, thereby constituting a formidable force before whose tide Hail would surely be swept away. He thought that ibn Sa'ud would appoint to the Rashidi Amirate one of the members of the ibn Rashid family who had been refugees with him for many years. This amir would then rule as his deputy.[146]

In reference to King Husain, Cox probably gave the opinion of most Baghdad authorities when he added

> realising that he will never again after war be in such a strong position as he is now, either tribally or financially, Sherif is bent on doing his utmost to weaken his rival both by discrediting Ibn Sa'ud in our eyes and achieving during

the war such a prominent position for himself as Ibn Sa'ud will never be able to challenge. As regards Ibn Saud on the other hand, it is clear from Philby's reports not only that he will never accept a position of vassalage to the Sherif but that he aspires to a status in Najd not inferior to that of King Husain in Hedjaz.[147]

Cox stressed further that it would be impossible to effect an understanding between the two and mentioned the advisability of having a man in Najd who would ' form an adequate counterpoise to the Sharif in the Hedjaz'. In what for Cox was an unusual manifestation of the Mesopotamian Administration's hostility towards Cairo's protégé he added that ' such an arrangement will certainly tend greatly to simplify our work in Iraq, and will automatically correct any *inconvenient pre-eminence which our war has obliged us to accord to the Sheriff* '.[148]

At this juncture the necessity for a co-ordinated Middle Eastern policy was beginning to make itself more keenly felt while Husain's intransigence and expansionist tendencies did not go unnoticed. The deteriorating political situation in the peninsula prompted Wingate to telegraph as follows:

> Internal situation in Arabia presents certain disquieting features and careful co-ordination of policy seems to be necessary if future collision between our Arab protégés is to be prevented. ... Shareef's policy appears to be to defer cultivating relations with his neighbours until Turkish menace to Hedjaz is removed and Faisal makes good in north. Ibn Saud dreads development of this policy which if successful may place him at a disadvantage and a Wahhabi revival—recently reported from independent sources—is probably encouraged by him as counterpoise to Sherif's expansion.[149]

Although cognisant of Husain's ambitions, Wingate quite naturally emphasised the pre-eminence of the Sharif. The High Commissioner feared a repetition of the Wahhabi terror of the early nineteenth century when they overran the Hedjaz. He suggested that after the war ' our policy will be to preserve [the] balance of power between [the] Great Chiefs with the King, official custodian of the Sacred Cities, *Primus Inter Pares* '.[150] The sharpening divergence of views between Cairo and Baghdad was pointed out in a minute by an India Office official when he commented that as regards the Saʻudi Sharifian question there was a marked tendency for 'Baghdad to back the former, and Cairo the latter, which will not make it easier for H.M.'s Govt. to hold the balance fairly between the two potentates'.[151]

At this point the Government of India gave its opinion on the policy to be pursued towards ibn Saʻud and their views were to be accepted and to stand as British policy towards ibn Saʻud and their views were to be accepted and to stand as British policy towards ibn Saʻud until the end of the war. Obviously aware of the implications of claims and counterclaims on Hail by ibn Saʻud and Husain were the city to fall, taken together with the threat to the Holy Places that the *Ikhwan*, if armed, would constitute, India decided on a policy which gave the impression of giving ibn Saʻud just enough assistance to divert his attention from the Allied offensive in the Hedjaz.[152] In other words Delhi was to follow the traditional Indian policy, not unlike that of the Turks, of playing off one tribe against another.

> Ibn Rashid is at present in no position to do us much harm, and affords an occupation to Ibn Saud, while his total elimination from Arab politics might be an embarrassment to us. His retention will assist us in the maintenance of balance of power between Ibn Saud and Sherif. We therefore recommend that Cox should keep Ibn Saud in play by presents of money, but that assistance in arms and instructors should not be given except very sparingly. Otherwise we seem to risk establishment of two powers in Arabia mutually hostile, but to both of whom we have given pledges of support. We realise fully our obligations to Ibn Saud and have no wish to play unfairly by him. But we wish to avoid possibility of our generosity putting him in a position to upset equilibrium of Arabia.[153]

In the India Office Sir Arthur Hirtzel held that a policy of maintaining the 'balance of power' in Arabia between ibn Rashid, ibn Saʻud and King Husain would 'entangle' Britain in central Arabian affairs. Whereas if ibn Rashid were eliminated that would only leave two important personages in Arabia and they both had seaports on which Great Britain could exert pressure.[154] There was an element of truth in Hirtzel's opinion but he appeared to overlook the fact that Britain had already been forced to abdicate her traditional position of avoiding entanglement in central Arabia when she undertook in her treaty with ibn Sa'ud 'to discuss and determine' his borders after the war.[155]

Although Cairo had continually urged Baghdad to have ibn Sa'ud assume a more active role in the war, Wingate agreed with the Government of India's policy. Pointing out the success of the British offensive in Palestine coupled with the power of British gold, the High Commissioner remarked: 'Military success in [the] North, British gold via Shereef and Ibn Saud, combined with such pressure as latter can exert, should secure his adherence to [the] Arab cause or his replacement by a pro-Arab successor'.[156] In Baghdad, Cox maintained that ibn Sa'ud should be pressed to capture Hail and Husain to take Medina. Then after the Turks were eliminated from Arabia a British official could settle the boundary between the two.[157]

Philby, already captivated by ibn Sa'ud's personality, was bitterly disappointed with India's decision. In a plethora of voluminous telegrams he stressed—'while fully realising that Najd operations must be subordinated to [the] general scheme, both military and political'—that it would be disastrous to Anglo–Sa'udi relations to abandon the projected offensive on Hail. He also held that the Turks were far from beaten and that their loss of Hail might hasten victory in the Hedjaz. Philby argued, moreover, that if the offensive were scrapped, ibn Sa'ud's war-strained friendship would definitely cool. Finally, he emphasised above all that the abandonment of the Hail offensive would appear to ibn Sa'ud as a clear manifestation of British deference to Sharifian importance.[158]

Philby's arguments were to no avail. The increasing success of Allenby's offensive in the northwestern desert coupled with the *Ikhwan* threat, India's inability to provide ibn Sa'ud with extensive arms, Sa'udi–Sharifian antipathy and the 'subordination of Najd operations to the general scheme' at this point determined British policy towards ibn Sa'ud. As regards Philby's emphasis on the 'abandonment of the Hail offensive' Shuckburgh wrote:

> The special Mission had for its military object merely 'to see the country and make proposals, in accordance with military possibilities'. . . . An attack by Bin Saud upon Hail

was by no means regarded as a necessary corollary of the negotiations.[159]

At this juncture Cox left Baghdad to become the British Minister at Tehran and Captain A. T. Wilson—brilliant, forceful, indefatiguable and a supreme exemplar of the Indian paternalist school of administration—took his place as Acting Civil Commissioner. He was only thirty-four. Wilson had come first of the candidates entering the Infantry Branch of Sandhurst and passed out of the Royal Military College at the top of his class, winning the Sword of Honour. An ardent exponent and practitioner of the Imperial creed, he followed in the footsteps of Curzon. 'To me the message is carved in granite, it is hewn out of the rock of doom—that our work is righteous and that it shall endure'. In Wilson's own words:

> Before the Great War my generation served men who believed in the righteousness of the vocation to which they had been called, and we shared their belief. They were the priests, and we were the acolytes, of a cult—pax Britannica —for which we worked happily and, if need be, died gladly. Curzon, at his best, was our spokesman, and Kipling, at his noblest, our inspiration . . .[161]

Although ibn Sa'ud's attention was to be diverted from the Hedjaz towards a piecemeal offensive—supported by small doles—against ibn Rashid, his attention was shortly to be drawn back to the Hedjaz owing to the Khurma dispute. On this particular issue ibn Sa'ud and King Husain were to clash dramatically and it was to be two years before the hostilities centering on this small town and later on Turaba to the north were to subside.

Notes

1. On British policy in the Middle East generally during the period the most recent work is B. C. Busch, *Britain, India and the Arabs,* 1914–1921 (Berkeley, 1971), chaps. I–IV, hereafter Busch, *Britain.* Also important are Kedourie, *England,* chaps. 2–6, and his essay 'Cairo and Khartoum on the Arab Quesiton' in his *The Chatham House Version and other Middle Eastern Studies* (London, 1970), chap. 2, hereafter Kedourie, *Cairo*; H. N. Howard, *The Partition of Turkey, A Diplomatic History, 1913–1923* (New York, 1966), chaps. III–VII; and E. Monroe, *Britain's Moment in the Middle East, 1914–1956*

(London, 1963), chap. I, hereafter *Monroe*. On Anglo-French diplomacy in the Middle East, a recent monograph is J. Nevakivi, *Britain, France and the Arab Middle East, 1914–1920* (London, 1969, chaps. I–IV, hereafter Nevakivi. On Anglo-Arab relations, in addition to the above works, see *Antonius*; Zeine, *Arab-Turkish Relations* and especially his *The Struggle for Arab Independence: Western Diplomacy and the Rise and Fall of Faisal's Kingdom of Syria* (Beirut, 1960), chaps. I–IV, hereafter Zeine, *Struggle*. The Husain–McMahon correspondence is found in Cmd. 5957 (1938–1939). On the Anglo-Zionist issue the standard work is L. Stein, *The Balfour Declaration* (London, 1961). Of the many memoirs of British officials in the Middle East, easily the best written and one of the most illuminating is Sir R. Storrs, *Orientations* (London, 1937), hereafter *Orientations*. For the purposes of this work the most important sources for the Mesopotamian campaign and especially for the British administration of Mesopotamia are Wilson's *Loyalties I* and his *Mesopotamia, 1917–1920 A Clash of Loyalties* (Oxford, 1931), hereafter Wilson, *Loyalties* II.

2. On the importance of this rivalry and its adverse affect on British policy, see the work by Busch just cited. As will be seen, the situation was not helped by the bad communications existing among the multitude of British authorities advising on policy. In 1916, including those at home and abroad, civil and military, there were eighteen separate authorities who had to be consulted and who offered advice on policy in the Middle East. See *Monroe*, p. 36 and for a list of the authorities, Busch, *Britain*, p. 205.
3. It must be remembered that British forces in Mesopotamia not only fought Arabs, but that many of the best Arab officers in the Ottoman army were Iraqis. With the exception of the political officers who met the more responsible shaikhs and notables, Busch notes that 'most British authorities in Iraq . . . could view the Arabs they encountered only as assassins, thieves, and mutilators of the dead'. See Busch, *Britain* pp. 52, 53. Similar sentiments are expressed in Wilson, *Loyalties* I, p. 54, and *Longrigg*, p. 81.
4. For example, in 1912 Hardinge had almost been killed by a bomb thrown by an agitator.
5. The cumulative effect on Indian Moslems of European (Christian) incursions upon the Ottoman Empire may be imagined. To mention only a few: in 1882 Britain had occupied Egypt. In 1911 Italy invaded Tripoli (and Britain did not condemn this action). In 1912 the first Balkan War broke out. And in 1914, Britain, Russia and France declared war on Turkey. In India the British government had greatly antagonised many Indian Moslems through its annulment of the Partition of Bengal in 1911. In view of these circumstances it is obvious why British authorities were concerned about Indian Moslem opinion.
6. The British oilfield in southwest Persia, 130 miles north-east of Moheammera, was of special interest to the Admiralty. By the outbreak of war with Turkey ' 25,000 tons of oil per month were . . .

being exported from the new oil fields in south Persia'. See *Monroe*, p. 25.
7. As will be obvious to students of the Middle East, it is difficult when dealing with the Moslem East fifty years ago to separate religious from political considerations. Because of the fundamentally theocratic nature of Islam, religion and politics are, in many cases, inextricably intertwined.
8. H. Young, *The Independent Arab* (London, 1933), p. 271. Hereafter *Young*.
9. *Antonius*, p. 135.
10. Kedourie, *Cairo*, p. 16.
11. *Ibid*. For this controversy and an analysis of British relations with Husain from 1914 to 1918, Kedourie's article offers some penetrating insights.
12. J. B. Glubb, *Britain and the Arabs* (London, 1959), p. 58. Hereafter *Glubb*. For a full treatment of Arab nationalism, see the works already cited.
13. *Ibid*.
14. Wingate to Lord Hardinge, Aug. 26, 1915, in the *Wingate* Papers (hereafter *WP*), School of Oriental Studies, Durham University, File 139/6, quoted in Kedourie, *Cairo*, p. 17.
15. Committee of Imperial Defence (CID), 'Historical Summary of Events in Territories of the Ottoman Empire, Persia and Arabia affecting the British Position in the Persian Gulf, 1907–1928'; *L/P & S/18*, p. 274 A. [Political and Secret Department Memoranda (IO)]. Hereafter *Sum*.
16. *Monroe*, pp. 11, 12.
17. Sir Edmund Barrow, military secretary of the India Office, put forth this view in a minute written on September 26, 1914. See Zeine, *Arab-Turkish Relations*, p. 98.
18. In late January 1915, a Turkish force numbering 25,000 marched on the canal zone. By February 5, this expedition had been defeated.
19. *WP* 141/3, quoted in Kedourie, *Cairo*, p. 16.
20. Sir R. Bullard, *Britain and the Middle East* (London, 1951), p. 76. Hereafter *Bullard*.
21. *Ibid*., p. 77.
22. *Ibid*., p. 78.
23. *Glubb*, p. 125.
24. H. St J. B. Philby, *Arabia* (London, 1930), pp. 233, 234. Philby expressed similar sentiments in his *The Heart of Arabia*, Vol. 1 (London, 1923), p. 386, and *Arabian Days* (London, 1948), p. 157. Echoing the same theme, A. T. Wilson wrote: " The World would have been deprived of an epic, and the British Treasury would have been saved many millions of pounds sterling; the Sharifian family might never have emerged from the obscurity of the Hedjaz and the arms of the Turks, with whom until April 1916, they were in active negotiation; Palestine might have remained Turkish and Zionism a dream. In the event, however, it was left to the military authorities in Egypt, to accomplish what, with better luck and more imagination,

especially on the part of the Government of India, might have been accomplished with our assistance by Ibn Sa'ud'. Wilson, *Loyalties* I, p. 161. For other passages in this vein, see *Marlowe*, p. 39, *Howarth*, p. 87 and R. O. Collins (ed.), *An Arabian Diary, Sir Gilbert Falkingham Clayton* (Berkeley, 1969), p. 23, hereafter *Collins*. J. B. Glubb seems to appreciate the realities of the Husain-ibn Sa'ud issue when he writes: ' In the light of subsequent events, it has sometimes been argued that Britain should have adopted Ibn Saud rather than the sherif, as her Arab champion. But whatever might be the fighting qualities of the tribes which acknowledge Ibn Saud as their leader, his assistance would have been of little value to counteract the call to holy war, which exercised the minds of the Allied leaders in 1914 and 1915 '. See his p. 59. Curiously, on the following page he appears to revert to a view consonant with those given above when he notes: ' If Shakespear had survied and remained with Ibn Saud, the course of history might well have been different...' (p. 60).

25. This theme and indeed much of the material in this section has been published as an article entitled ' Ibn Sa'ud and Sharif Husain: A Comparison in Importance in the Early Years of the First World War ', *Historical Journal,* Vol. 14, No. 3 (1971).
26. *Marlowe*, p. 43.
27. *Antonius*, p. 140.
28. *Antonius*, p. 138.
29. Busch, *Britain*, p. 264.
30. *Young*, p. 273.
31. D. G. Hogarth, ' Wahhabism and British Interests ', *Journal of the British Institute of International Affairs,* IV (1925), p. 72.
32. See pp. 60, 61. For detailed treatment of Anglo-Sa'udi negotiations see ' Memorandum on British Commitments to Bin Saud ', Nov. 16, 1918, No. 5120; *L/P & S/10,* 2182/1913, Pts. 7, 8. Hereafter *Memo.* As this memorandum comprehensively and meticulously draws together the correspondence concerning the negotiation of the Anglo-Sa'udi Treaty I have usually referred to it in this section. The negotiations may also be followed in *FO* 371/2479, file 1385.
33. Viceroy to IO., Oct. 31, 1914 (T), No. 46261/66303; *FO* 371/2140. After contacting ibn Sa'ud, Sayyid Talib defected from the Turks, seeking asylum at Riyadh.
34. CGS (Commander of the General Staff), India to War Office [WO], Jan. 19, 1915 (T), No. 1385/11837; *FO* 371/2479.
35. *Memo.*
36. *Ibid.*
37. *Ibid.*
38. *Ibid.*
39. *Ibid.*
40. *Ibid.*
41. *Ibid.*
42. *Ibid.*
43. *Ibid.*

44. *Ibid.*
45. Viceroy to IO, Jan. 29, 1915 (T), No. 1385/11224; *FO* 371/2470.
46. Philby wrote that Shakespear was directing the fire of Wahhabi guns when his hill was taken. See Philby, *Sa'udi Arabia*, p. 272.
47. Cox to GI, Feb. 16, 1915 (T), No. 1385/19085; *ibid.*
48. Viceroy to IO, Feb. 26, 1915 (T), enclosing a letter from ibn Sa'ud, No. 1385/26311; *ibid.*
49. Viceroy to IO, Jan. 25, 1915 (T), No. 1385/11837; *ibid.*
50. IO to GI, Feb. 1, 1915, No. 1385/11837; *ibid.*
51. See App. III.
52. See *ibid.*
53. *Memo.*
54. Busch, *Britain*, p. 235.
55. *Ibid.* For text of final treaty, see J. C. Hurewitz, *Diplomacy in the Near and Middle East: A Documentary Record.* Vol. II: 1914–1956 (Princeton, 1956), pp. 17, 18. It is also reproduced in *Aitchison*, pp. 206–208.
56. See 'Report of the Interdepartmental Conference on the Establishment of the Arab Bureau', by CID, Jan. 10, 1916, No. ARB/16/4; *FO* 882/2 [FO, Arab Bureau file (882) (PRO)]. For a discussion of the formation, composition and operation of the Bureau see Busch, *Britain*, pp. 99–109.
57. 'Memorandum on Relations with Ibn Sa'ud', Jan. 1917, No. 1458/35392; *FO* 371/3044. Hereafter *Memo* on ibn Sa'ud. For location of 'Ajman', see Tribal Map.
58. Philby writes that the *Araif* pretenders were related to the 'Ajman through Sa'ud ibn Faisal's mother who came from the tribe. The pretenders claimed unbroken 'Ajman descent on their mother's side and were senior in their claim to the Sa'udi throne. See Philby's 'Najd Report', No. 122; *L/P & S/10*, 2182/1913, Pts. 9 and 10. Hereafter *Najd Report.*
59. *Ibid.* Sa'd was the same brother who had been captured by Husain in 1910. See pp. 38, 39.
60. 'Memorandum on Relations Between the Ajman and the Recent History of the Latter'. July 25, 1916, No. 3508; *L/P & S/10*, 2182/1913, Pts. 4, 5. Hereafter *'Ajman Memo.*
61. Cox to GI, Jan. 13, 1916, No. 4650/41345, enclosing a 'Trans of Agreement Between Ibn Sa'ud and Ibn Rashid'. *FO* 371/2769.
62. Cox at this time was stationed at Basra as Chief Political Officer with the Indian Expeditionary Force.
63. Cox to GI, Sept. 5, 1915 (T), No. 1385/150190; *FO* 371/2479.
64. Viceroy to IO, Oct 7, 1915 (T), No. 1385/150190; *FO* 371/2479.
65. For a record of the Husain-McMahon Correspondence, see *Cmd. 5957.*
66. *Sum.*
67. *Ibid.*
68. *Ibid.*
69. *Monroe*, p. 36. Monroe also adds that bad communications complicated the situation. '... the McMahon letter of October 24, 1915 did not dovetail with a treaty of independence signed six weeks later

with Ibn Sa'ud by Sir Percy Cox, ... and the Sykes-Picot agreement was communicated to Cairo but not to Basra ...; *ibid.*

70. 'Appreciation of Arabian Report' (by Sir Mark Sykes), Sept. 27, 1916, No. 201201; *FO* 371/2781.
71. Crewe to Hardinge (Private tel.), Nov 12, 1914, National Archives of India, For. Dept. Proceedings, Secret, War. Quoted in Busch, *Britain*, p. 62. Hardinge had described the Husain-McMahon negotiations as 'fatuous proceedings'. Hardinge to Nicolson, Nov. 15, 1915 (private letter) Nicolson Papers; *FO* 800/378. Hardinge also wrote: "I devoutly hope that this proposed independent Arab State will fall to pieces; if it is ever created. Nobody could possibly have devised any scheme more detrimental to British interests in the Middle East than this. It simply means misgovernment, chaos and corruption, since there never can be and never has been any consistency or cohesion amongst the Arab tribes. Had it not been for opposition from India Cairo would months ago have appointed a new Khalif! I cannot tell you how detrimental I think the interference and influence of Cairo have been'. Quoted in Busch, *Britain*, p. 80.
72. Clayton even went so far as to say that 'an Englishman would naturally avoid producing such a Frankenstein' as a politically strong Arab Caliphate. Clayton to Wingate, Jan. 6, 1916 (private letter) *Wingate Papers*, box 136. Quoted by Busch, *Britain*, p. 91. It is interesting to note that although the 'majority of people' in Iraq had 'no connection with the Sherif' this did not deter Britain after the war from setting up Husain's son Faisal as King of Iraq.
73. See Busch, *Britain*, p. 78.
74. Cox to Arab Bureau, Sept. 8, 1916 (T), No. 4650/180581; *FO* 371/2769.
75. Cox to Arab Bureau, Cairo, Sept. 8, 1916 (T), No. 4650/183725; *FO* 371/2769.
76. SSI to Viceroy, Sept. 19, 1916 (T), No. 4650/191509; *FO* 371/2769.
77. Viceroy to IO, Sept. 30, 1916 (T), No. 4650/196560; *ibid.*
78. Minute by J. E. S[huckburgh], Oct. 3, 1916, No. 4050; *L/P & S/10*, 2182/1913; Pts. 4, 5. Shuckburgh was Assistant Secretary of the Political Department. He was, in Philby's words, Curzon's 'beau ideal of the perfect Secretary'. See Philby, *Arabian Days*, p. 184.
79. Minute by A. H[irtzel], Oct. 17, 1916, No. 4174; *ibid.*
80. SSI to Viceroy, Oct. 27, 1916 (T), No. 4650/ 219650; *FO* 371/2769.
81. CPO to ibn Sa'ud, Oct. 18, 1916 (L. Trans.), No. 201201/244263; *FO* 371/2781.
82. Husain to ibn Sa'ud, Sept. 5, 1916 (L, Trans), No. 201201/24463; *ibid.*
83. *Sum.*
84. 'Arabian Report', Nov. 29, 1916, Nov. 201201/24463; *FO* 371/2781.
85. Knight Commander of the Most Eminent Order of the Indian Empire.
86. *Graves*, p. 214.
87. Companion of the Indian Empire.
88. *Graves*, p. 214.
89. *Memo on ibn Sa'ud.*

90. 'Arabian Report', Nov. 20, 1916, No. 201201/236383; *FO* 371/2481.
91. Wilson, *Loyalties* I, p. 160. For further positive impressions of ibn Sa'ud see E. Burgoyne, *Gertrude Bell, from Her Personal Papers* (London, 1961), p. 48.
92. 'Arabian Report', Nov. 20, 1916, No. 201201/23683; *FO* 371/2781.
93. On October 29, 1916, Cox had received via Bahrain an open letter from ibn Sa'ud in which the latter stated that the Ottoman government had sent ibn Rashid ' 25 German and Turkish Officers, and 300 soldiers, guns and supplies...' See Viceroy to IO, Oct. 31, 1916 (T), No. 4650/219650; *FO* 371/2769. Even taking the traditional Bedouin propensity for hyperbole into account, it was apparent that the Turks were supplying their protege with ample material.
94. Husain received 200,000 pounds per month.
95. Treasury to FO. Jan. 2, 1917 (L), No. 1458/13928; *FO* 371/3044.
96. Sykes was attached to the CID, and therefore included in the Cabinet secretariat. He was well-placed to make his opinions known and rarely refrained from doing so. Unfortunately, the standard biography is S. Leslie, *Mark Sykes: His Life and Letters* (London, 1923). A better if briefer characterization is found in C. Sykes, *Two Studies in Virtue* (N.Y., 1953), pp. 173–176. See also *Orientations*, p. 196 and Busch *Britain*, p. 67.
97. 'Appreciation of Arabian Report', Nov. 29, 1916, No. 201201–24463; *FO* 371/2781.
98. *Ibid.*
99. Ibn Sa'ud to Pol. Res., July 20, 1915 (L, Trans), No. 4166; *L/P & S/10*, 2182/1913, Pts. 4, 5.
100. Although various writers on this period use the terms blockade and embargo interchangeably, blockade is the correct usage.
101. *Najd Report*.
102. Jabir died in early 1917 and was succeeded by his brother Salim.
103. *Najd Report*. It should be pointed out that while Philby attributed the main blame for smuggling to Salim, Colonel R. E. A. Hamilton, the Political Agent at Kuwait, ascribed Salim's actions to Sa'udi offenses giving the impression that generally Salim played defensively in the perennial chess game of central Arabian politics.
104. In the old days when friendly relations prevailed between Riyadh and Kuwait, this tribe was free to seek pasture in both territories while only paying taxes to Kuwait.
105. *Najd Report*.
106. IO to Viceroy, Jan. 9, 1917 (T), No. 4541/8400; *FO* 371/3076.
107. Cox to GI, Jan. 24, 1917 (T), No. 4541/19620; *FO* 371/3046.
108. *Ibid.* Nuri al Sha'lan, who was allied with the British was head of the Ruwalla section of the great 'Anaza tribe. He exercised influence in an area stretching from the Jabal Druze in Syria to Jauf in northern central Arabia. See Tribal Map.

109. Ibn Saʿud to Cox, June 3, 1917 (L, Trans), No. 3699; *L/P & S/10*, 2182/1913, Pt. 6.
110. Ibn Rashid to Ibn Saʿud, May 20, 1917 (L, Trans), No. 3699; *ibid.*
111. For example Dhari ibn Tawala, head of the Aslam section of the Shammar, was paid a monthly subsidy of 3,000 rupees. See *ibid.*
112. *Najd Report.*
113. ' Aide Memoir for Mr Storrs Regarding Affairs of Bin Saud ', n.d., No. 3661; *L/P & S/10*, 2182/1913, Pt. 6. Hereafter *Memoir.*
114. Cox to GI, Dec. 28, 1917 (T), No. 675; *FO* 371/3383. The two other officers Sykes mentioned were Col. C. E. Wilson, British Agent at Jedda, and Brevet Lt. Col. G. E. Leachman, Political Agent of the Desert.
115. *Ibid.* Storrs wrote in his *Orientations* that ' Preoccupied by the constant strife between Ibn Saʿud ... and King Husain ... I had offered to return to Egypt across Arabia, to visit them both, and to attempt to reconcile them '. See *Orientations*, p. 261.
116. The mission is also described in Busch, *Britain*, pp. 248–262.
117. Cox to GI, Sept. 28, 1917 (T), No. 191347; *FO* 371/3061.
118. Maude had been appointed Commander of the Mesopotamian Forces in August 1916 after the War Office had relieved Delhi of military responsibilities for Mesopotamia in the wake of the Kut fiasco. The clash with Maude is described in more detail in Busch, *Britain*, pp. 147–151. See also Wilson, *Loyalties* I, pp. 260–264; Graves, pp. 223–225 and *Orientations*, p. 218.
119. *Beloff*, p. 246.
120. See Cmd. 8610.
121. Birkenhead is quoted in Lord Beaverbrook, *Men and Power 1917–18* (London, 1956), p. XII. The same quote also appears in A. J. P. Taylor, *English History*, 1914–1945 (Pelican edn., 1970), p. 103, n. 1, hereafter Taylor, *English History*; and Busch, *Britain*, p. 133.
122. S. D. Waley, *Edwin Montagu: A Memoir and an Account of His Visits to India* (London, 1964), p. 127. Hereafter *Waley*. Quoted in Busch, *Britain*, p. 134.
123. Wilson, *Loyalties* I, p. 281. Also quoted in Busch, *Britain*, p. 249.
124. D. Van Der Meulen, *The Wells of Ibn Saud* (London, 1957), p. 83. Hereafter *Van Der Meulen*. Van Der Meulen was Consul in Jedda and later Dutch Minister to Saʿudi Arabia. Before coming to Arabia, he had studied under the great Orientalist Snouck Hurgronje at Leiden. He knew Philby and describes his impressions of him on pp. 22–28. See also Busch, *Britain*, p. 249. On Philby generally see E. Monroe, *Philby of Arabia* (London, 1973).
125. Busch, *Britain*, p. 250. For Hamilton's side of the story see Lord Belhaven, *The Uneven Road* (London, 1955), pp. 22–26. Hamilton later became the eleventh Lord Belhaven and Stenton. The book is by his son. For Philby's account of the Mission see his *Najd Report* and his *The Heart of Arabia: A Record of Travel*, 2 vols. (N.Y., 1923). His activities after June 1918 are described in *Arabia of the Wahhabis* (London, 1928).
126. Wingate to Cox, Nov. 2, 1917 (T), No. 191347/210178; *FO* 371/3061.

127. *Ibid.*
128. FO to Wingate, Nov. 5, 1917 (T), No. 191347/210178; FO 371/3061.
129. Cox to Wingate, Dec. 15, 1917 (T), No. 191347/238873; *ibid.*
130. See *Najd Report* for alternative plans for settling the 'Ajman question.
131. *Ibid.*
132. *Ibid.*
133. *Ibid.*
134. Philby wrote that Husain 'had presented me with an opportunity to hoist him with his own petard'. As concerned the reception of his actions in Baghdad, he expressed the following: 'A day before my departure I sent off a dispatch to Sir Percy Cox, explaining the action I had decided to take and apologising for my inability to await his consent owing to the urgency of the matter. He must have chuckled when he read that'. Philby, *Arabian Days*, p. 155.
135. *Howarth*, p. 103. As Philby said himself: 'I should confess, perhaps, that my motives in making that proposal were of a mixed character, and not wholly based on the actual requirements of the situation, but that is a trifle, and I have never regretted my action'. Quoted in *Howarth*, p. 103.
136. Philby, *Sa'udi Arabia*, p. 276.
137. The talks and Philby's impact are described in Busch, *Britain*, pp. 254, 255. Philby described them in *Sa'udi Arabia*, pp. 158–163. The *Ikhwan* and Khurma issues will form the basis for the next chapter.
138. 'Notes for Middle East Committee Meeting' by J. E. S[huckburgh], Jan. 18, 1918, No. 7664; *FO* 371/3394. Hereafter *Notes*.
139. '*Notes* for Middle East Commiteetee Meeting' by Same, Jan. 10, 1918, No. 337; *L/P & S/10*, 2182/1913, Pts. 7, 8. Hereafter *Further Notes*.
140. Wingate to Balfour, Dec. 25, 1917 (L), No. 146/12076; *FO* 371/3380.
141. Minute by J. E. S[huckburgh], Dec. 24, 1917, No. 5153; *L/P & S/10*, 2182/1913, Pt. 6.
142. *Ibid.*
143. T. W. H[olderness], *ibid.*
144. *Further Notes.*
145. Fahad Bey headed a powerful confederation which exercised great influence in western Mesopotamia. Col. Leachman was later attached to him. [See Tribal Map.]
146. Cox to GI, Dec. 23, 1917 (T), No. 5140; *L/P & S/10*, 2182/ 1913; Pt. 6.
147. *Ibid.*
148. *Ibid.* My emphasis.
149. Wingate to FO, Dec. 23, 1917 (T), No. 99430/242590; *FO* 371/3056.
150. Wingate to FO, Dec. 28, 1917 (T), No. 99430/24470; *ibid.*
151. Minute by J. E. S[huckburgh], Dec. 28, 1917, No. 5142; *L/P & S/10*, 2182/1913, Pt. 6.
152. Or as Philby put it: 'From the beginning of 1917 onwards... [one of Cox's main preoccupations was] diverting Ibn Sa'ud's attention from

Allied activities in the Hijaz by encouraging him to take action against Ibn Rachid'. See Philby, *Sa'udi Arabia*, p. 274.
153. Viceroy to IO, Jan. 5, 1918 (T), No. 2240/4279; *FO* 371/3389.
154. Minute by A. H[irtzel], Jan. 8, 1918, No. 66; *L/P & S/10*, 2182/1913; Pts. 7, 8.
155. See App. III, Article I.
156. Wingate to FO, Jan. 10, 1918 (T), No. 875/6696; FO 371/ 3383.
157. Cox to IO, Jan. 19, 1918 (T), No. 675/10166; *ibid*.
158. *Notes*.
159. *Ibid*.
160. Cox to GI, Mar. 9, 1918 (T), No. 4402/46301; *FO* 371/3389.
161. See Introduction to his *South West Persia*. Wilson's desire to turn Iraq into an Indian province or a British colony and his methods of administration are well-known to students of modern Middle Eastern history. For his own account of events in Mesopotamia see *Loyalties* I and especially *Loyalties* II. See also the competent biography—already cited—by J. Marlowe, *Late Victorian*, especially Chap. XIII. In addition to being a Lt. Col. and an M.P. Wilson accumulated a KCIE, CSI, CMG and DSO.

CHAPTER IV

The Khurma and Turaba Dispute

The dispute between ibn Sa'ud and King Husain over the possession of the villages of Khurma and Turaba is important for two reasons. Firstly, it marks the first major clash between the two Arabian rulers; secondly, the British were faced for the first time with the threat of a Wahhabi invasion of the Hedjaz and the effect that this would have primarily on their Moslem subjects. Essentially, as will be seen, the Khurma–Turaba dispute was both a religious and a political issue. Fearing that the Wahhabi revival which was beginning to assume significant proportions in Najd might successfully attract many of his followers to the Sa'udi standard, Husain endeavoured to prevent the penetration into the Hedjaz of militant Wahhabi tenets and to assert his ownership of Khurma and Turaba to which ibn Sa'ud now laid claim.

Britain, above all, was determined to prevent a Wahhabi invasion of the Hedjaz. Conditioned by historical experience, the British feared that a Wahhabi seizure of the Holy Cities would result once again, as it had in the early nineteenth century, in depredations and interrupted pilgrimages. There was a genuine fear that history would repeat itself. The repercussions of such an event would be far-reaching. In India, Britain was confronted by many of her own Moslem subjects who were angered by the harsh terms imposed on Turkey by the Treaty of Sèvres. Many Indian Moslems were genuinely concerned about the future of Turkey and Islam. Other Indian Moslem nationalities —joined and reinforced for a time by Ghandi's Hindu nationalists—used religious issues to discredit their British rulers. At Versailles, Britain asserted her special position in Arabia: a sort of 'Arabian Monroe Doctrine'. Naturally the spectre of a war between her protégés centering on the Holiest Cities in Islam and the effect that this would have on Allied as well as hypersensitive Indian Moslem opinion exercised the British.

In trying to prevent a holocaust in the Hedjaz, however, Britain found herself placed precariously on the horns of a dilemma. Although the terms of the Anglo–Sa'udi agreement specified that Britain would demarcate ibn Sa'ud's boundaries after the war, the British government was hesitant to lay down any specific boundary. Obviously whatever decision she made, one or the other of her Allies would be estranged. However, it will be seen that although ibn Sa'ud's increasing power and ambition no longer permitted the British the luxury of ignoring him, Britain's policy during this period remained a 'Husain policy'.

Before turning to a detailed treatment of this period it is well to emphasise that the Khurma and Turaba troubles occurred during one of the most difficult times in British history, namely the immediate post-war era.

Recovering from the dislocation of war, Britain had trouble on the home front with the trauma of demobilisation and Ireland while the aforementioned problem of Indian nationlism—further excited by the Amritsar Massacre—occupied government attention in Britain's principal colonial possession. Many authorities also feared that the Bolshevik tide might spread to India, Persia, Turkey and the Arab countries as it had in central Europe. At the Peace Conference the question of Germany dominated the attention of the Allies, while in the Middle East rising national consciousness frustrated by broken promises, 'eastern and western' Arabian rivalry and unco-ordinated policy further complicated the diplomatic scene. The particular difficulties of British policy towards Husain and ibn Sa'ud were complemented by the general difficulties plaguing Britain in the Middle East. In March 1919, a rebellion broke out in Egypt and in June 1920 the Syrian nationalists resisted the San Remo decisions while in Iraq another rebellion erupted. As elsewhere in Asia, the winds of nationalism were beginning to blow with increasing ferocity throughout much of the Middle East. As Hugo said: 'There is one thing that is stronger than armies, and that is an idea whose time is come'.[1]

The Ikhwan

With the first Najdi–Hedjazi clashes over Khurma the Ikhwan movement came to be viewed with alarm by the British government. During the period from late 1917 to 1930 this militant movement helped ibn Sa'ud to unify the Arabian peninsula but by the end of the 1920s he was forced to crush Ikhwanism in order to preserve his gains and develop peaceful relations with his neighbours. Before examining the Khurma and Turaba dispute, a brief account of the origin and character of Ikhwanism will be given.[2]

One of the serious problems which ibn Saʻud encountered in his rise to power was the lack of an organised military force. Various desert tribes each paid allegiance to their respective chiefs and the Bedouin's fickleness was notorious while his incentive to fight generally depended on the amount and accessibility of the booty involved. Only on rare occasions, under the influence of a great personality or cause, would several tribes band together. In essence, the parochial took precedence over any wider sense of loyalty. The result was fragmentation with little inherent substance in the tribal culture to weld the many tribes together in a common purpose. This began to change with the advent of the Ikhwan movement.

Ikhwan meant Brethren and was an institution based on a return to the strict fundamentalist ideas of Wahhabism. The movement, however, was distinguished mainly from original Wahhabism by its religio-military settlement. Initially Ikhwanism probably originated from a Wahhabi revival. In 1912 ibn Saʻud established an Ikhwan agricultural community at Artawiya near Riyadh. The mosque was the centre of the community and the settlement doubled as a military cantonment being armed by ibn Saʻud provided that its men were always at his call.[3] Soon other groups of religious zealots settled and formed their own religio-military agricultural communities. Ibn Saʻud provided these settlements with agricultural necessities, money, teachers, mosques, not to mention arms and ammunition. As Philby wrote: ' Villages sprang up in every suitable centre with surprising rapidity : each having a present stake in the land as well as a contingent one in eternity '.[4]

Ikhwanism provoked great criticism in many quarters. In peacetime, forcible conversion to the Brethren excited anger, while in war, the Ikhwan were reputed to take no prisoners, cutting the throats of all male adversaries regardless of age. While ibn Saʻud undoubtedly put himself at the head of this movement, it was said time and again throughout the period under consideration that he was not always responsible for, nor strong enough to control some sections of the Ikhwan. This was especially true in the late 1920s as regards the great Ikhwan leader

Faisal al Dawish, Shaikh of the Mutair. Perhaps it would be well to emphasise here that although many of ibn Sa'ud's followers were zealous to a degree—especially the Ikhwan—he was much too shrewd to be described as 'fanatical'. In addition to Philby, several other officials who knew ibn Sa'ud stress this point. Characteristic of this opinion is the following observation by H. R. P. Dickson, Political Agent in Bahrain in 1920 and later to serve in Kuwait for some years in the same capacity: 'No one who knew him intimately could accuse Ibn Saud of being a Wahabi fanatic himself, or ever having possessed any of the religious frenzy that he managed to instil into his Ikhwan followers'. Despite the severe Wahhabi strictures against alcohol and tobacco, for example, Dickson records that during one of their meetings in 1919 or 1920 ibn Sa'ud provided him with 'a couple of tins of superb Egyptian cigarettes, with the request that I should only smoke them in the privacy of my room'. Amin Rihani, the Lebanese writer and friend of ibn Sa'ud, who was present at the 'Uqair Conference of 1921—which will be discussed later—notes that Sir Percy Cox's tents were well supplied with bottles of Johnny Walker and Havana cigars.[5]

Whether ibn Sa'ud founded this movement or harnessed a religious revival for his own ends is undecided.[6] However, regardless of its origins, the movement provided communities of Bedouin turned yeoman who could be counted on as a territorial army. Tribal affiliations took second place to the wider subjugation of earthly considerations to the next life. In this way the religious fervour and warlike tendencies of the Arabs were harnessed and channelled into a more constructive direction. With the development of Ikhwanism, a step was taken to preclude the age-old dissipation of power resulting from tribal raids.

Khurma

Before embarking on analysis of Britain's position on the Khurma dispute, it is necessary for reasons of perspective to turn to the immediate genesis of the problem.[7] In view of the obviously partisan approaches of Cairo and Baghdad to questions affecting Husain and ibn Sa'ud, an account of the origins of the dispute will be discussed first from the Egyptian and then from the Mesopotamian standpoint.

In 1914, the Amir of Khurma, a Sharif named Khalid, appointed by King Husain before the outbreak of the war, was said to have embraced Wahhabism.⁸ Towards the end of 1916, Husain, fearing Khalid's enthusiastic support of the Ikhwan movement, summoned the Amir to Mecca and held him under ' " open arrest " as he refused to return to the orthodox fold '.⁹ At 'Abdullah's request Khalid was permitted to go to the former's camp. In late 1917, after 'Abdullah was convinced of Khalid's protestations of loyalty, the latter was allowed to return to Khurma.¹⁰

It will be recalled that in the early nineteenth century the Wahhabis overran the Hedjaz.¹¹ After the Wahhabi tide had receded to the confines of Najd, parts of the population of several villages distant from Riyadh remained Wahhabi and Khurma was one of these villages. As Wahhabism followed the conservative Hanbalite school of Islam, the Sharifs of Mecca are said to have usually appointed Hanbalites as official *qadis* of Khurma. In 1917 the Qadi of Khurma whom Cairo maintained was appointed by Husain was twice sent for by the Sharif and admonished strongly against preaching Wahhabi ¹² tenets. After returning to Khurma the second time, the Qadi openly joined the Ikhwan movement attracting many followers. He ignored a further summons to Mecca by Husain. When the Sharif responded by appointing another Qadi, however, Khalid refused to let the new official take up his post.¹³

Philby, representing the Mesopotamian viewpoint, put forth the following thesis. He argued that the great majority of the inhabitants of Khurma were Wahhabi (or Hanbali) since the early nineteenth century and had turned Ikhwan owing to the Sharif's aggression. Philby claimed that the Khurma area was peopled ' wholly by the Subai tribe, which is essentially a tribe of Najd...'; he went on to state that Khalid succeeded his couson Ghalib as Amir of Khurma and had ' regularly received a subsidy and presents ever since as his predecessor did before him'. Moreover, it was held that Khalid's connection with Mecca was limited to his being recorded in the Turkish registers on Ghalib's death as the recipient of a stipend (*Hajj Surra*)— as was any other chief who might disturb the pilgrimage—to prevent him from annoying the annual pilgrim caravans. Philby also pointed out that the ' present Wahhabi priest of Khurma and his father before him have occupied the post without break for 60 years, the father having been appointed by Faisal '.¹⁴

It was emphasised by the Egyptian authorities that Khurma

was only eighty miles in a direct line from Taif. Moreover in a rebuttal of Philby's arguments, Col. C. E. Wilson quoted Philby's article in the Arab Bulletin (No. 81) of March 9 1919, recounting the latter's visit to Khurma in December 1917. Philby had written:

> The cause of the exodus of the tribesmen with the local Emir—a shereef—appeared to be that the latter had incurred the displeasure of the Shereef of Mecca by embracing the Wahhabi faith, or perhaps had embraced the Wahhabi faith because he had incurred the Shereef's displeasure, and that the Shereef of Mecca has commissioned the Emr iof Turaba and the Buqum tribe to attack *the rebels of Khurma* as occasion offered.[15]

Wilson seized upon the words 'rebels of Khurma' to emphasise that by virtue of this terminology it followed that the 'rebels' were rebels against Husain; hence, the village was under his jurisdiction. Wilson also pointed out that Khalid had been an official under ibn Sa'ud, it was strange that the Amir of Riyadh had not protested against Khalid's arrest. Moreover, the Political Agent stressed that had the Qadi been appointed by ibn Sa'ud the latter would hardly have remained quiet knowing that his official had been summoned and lectured by Husain.[16]

Philby with his unique experience in travelling through much of Sa'udi Arabia put forth the following as his most interesting argument for the Wahhabi claim to Khurma.

> I venture to think that His Majesty's Government will revise opinion based on distance of Khurma from Taif. As already pointed out Khurma is only 10 miles east of unquestionable boundary of Buqum and Subai tribes, namely, Shaib Shaba. Question at issue, therefore, is jurisdiction over western section of Subai tribe, whose capital is Khurma, and whose boundary is Wadi Naim, 120 miles east of Khurma. Adjudication of Khurma to Sherif, therefore, necessarily implies extending boundary of Hejez to a line about 200 miles or more east of Taif. This brings up question of Ataiba highlands extending another 100 miles east of Wadi Naim; and as Sherif claims jurisdiction over Ataiba, the boundary of Nejd falls back very nearly to the line Tuwaiq.[17]

On balance it would appear that neither side had an irrefutable claim to Khurma, the ownership of which seemed to depend largely upon whether Najdi or Hedjazi power was pre-eminent. Although both the British authorities in Egypt and Mesopotamia were manifestly partisan in their views, it would appear that Husain had a slightly better claim. Philby himself admitted the validity of the oft-repeated accusation of Ikhwan proselytising activities but argued further that in the case of Khurma all the inhabitants had ' always been Wahhabi and are now all Akhwan and as such require no proselytising '. He claimed that the Sharif was interfering with the religious freedom of the inhabitants.[18] On the other hand, the Sharif could argue that given the ' fanaticism ' of the Ikhwan, peaceful Hanbalites were being intimidated into becoming members of a revivified and militant Wahhabism and could use Khurma as a staging area from which they could interfere with the religious freedom of his Sunnite followers in the Hedjaz.[19] In sum Philby was probably right when in an apparently more reflective mood he wrote *inter alia* in his detailed *Najd Report* that ' Khurma was always in the past too insignificant, either to form a bone of contention between the authorities concerned or to be mentioned specifically in any public agreement '.[20]

The first clash over Khurma took place in May 1918 when Husain despatched a force of eight hundred Bedouin to restore order in the village. Although it was claimed that this force had accomplished its objective, the Sharif ' sent reinforcements in June, consisting of 82 men, 2 old guns, and 2 machine guns. This force was surprised by a party of Ikhwan, losing fourteen killed and all of its guns '.[21] Husain defended his action by maintaining that it was necessary ' to check transgression by Ibn Saud against 'Ataiba and other tribesmen properly subject to Shereefial Government '.[22] Wingate instructed Col. Wilson to urge Husain ' to avoid cause of friction with Ibn Saud '.[23] On the other side of the peninsula Philby was told on June 6th ' to request Bin Saud to refrain from forward policy in Khurmah and recall any agents he may have sent there '.[24] However, fighting in the area soon broke out again.

Around the middle of July, Husain sent a force under the Amir Shakir to attack Khurma. The latter's force again consisted of approximately eight hundred men with four guns and six machine guns. Husain directed Shakir ' to occupy Khurmah as Emir of the Ataibah tribe '.[25] Part of Shakir's force attacked the Ikhwan in Khurma but were routed. 'Abdullah now threatened to attack Khurma but was warned against doing so by the British government. With the war still going on against the Turks the British did not want its allies' attention diverted from the main offensive. Moreover, the Turkish garrison at Medina was still stubbornly holding out under Kahri Pasha. A dual communication was sent to ibn Sa'ud and Husain appealing to them to avoid further conflict.[26]

In Cairo, Sir Reginald Wingate urged that the British government adopt a stronger attitude towards ibn Sa'ud. He argued that ibn Sa'ud should adopt a ' hands off ' policy as regards Khurma and refuse all support to Khalid.[27] Philby refused to convey the High Commissioner's message to ibn Sa'ud holding that thus far ibn Sa'ud had taken no action in respect to Khurma except to prevent the Ikhwan of Ghatghat from attacking the Sharif's forces and to forbid the inhabitants of Khurma from avenging themselves.[28] Ibn Sa'ud was content to leave the settlement of the dispute in the hands of the British government but warned Philby that

> if the Sheriff's forces march upon Khurma a third time he will assume that we are unable or unwilling to protect his interests from aggression and being pledged to the people of Khurma and his Akhwan everywhere he will consider himself bound to take the field.[29]

India favoured a conciliatory message being despatched to ibn Sa'ud expressing appreciation of his restraint.[30] In London the India Office agreed to this suggestion but went on in their despatch to put forward the prevailing Foreign Office view at that time.

> No objection to Philby conveying conciliatory message to Bin Saud if you think it necessary, but if ... Khurmah is only 80 miles from Taif it seems clearly to fall within King Husain's sphere ... Philby should impress this view of case on Bin Saud while assuring him that his future interests are receiving active attention from His Majesty's Government at present time. We have no intention of disregarding Bin Saud's equitable claims but it must be realised that neither his services or commitments in the past, nor his potential

utility in future, will bear any comparison with those of King Husain, and that we cannot allow latter's interests to be prejudiced or his attention to be distracted from primary task of defeating enemy by ill-timed activities on part of Bin Saud.[31]

With the hardening attitude towards ibn Sa'ud, the Wahhabi Amir was nearing the end of his patience with the British government. He was having trouble explaining to his followers his restraint over Khurma; moreover, his ' on again off again ' offensive against Hail was alienating those Shammar sections which had defected to him from ibn Rashid.[32] Ibn Sa'ud was also plagued by flanking attacks by the 'Ajman and Kuwait's anti-Sa'udi machinations. In desperation ibn Sa'ud forwarded four demands of which—for the present—the following two were most important. He sought a British guarantee of absolute immunity of his people and territory from Husain: this comprised Khurma and the 'Ataiba borderland pending settlement. Ibn Sa'ud also wanted a guarantee from Britain that once he began a concerted offensive against Hail Britain would not leave him in the lurch by withholding war matériel and money.[33]

Philby wrote in favour of these demands as did A. T. Wilson, the Officiating Civil Commissioner in Baghdad. The latter urged *inter alia* that Article II of the Anglo-Sa'udi Treaty be applied to aggression by King Husain and that ibn Sa'ud should restrain his Ikhwan while the British would determine his boundaries after the War.[34]

While attempts were being made to avoid further hostilities centering on Khurma and ibn Sa'ud's demands were being considered, in August Shakir clashed with the Ikhwan at Hannu Wells, sixteen miles east of Khurma ' where his force was annihilated '. During the battle it was reported that a section of Shakir's 'Ataiba defected to the Ikhwan. The blame for the outbreak of this battle was put on Shakir. After this clash ibn Sa'ud declined further responsibility for the people of Khurma. In Cairo, the British claimed that Khalid was definitely acting as ibn Sa'ud's agent. Captain Garland of the Arab Bureau pointed out that ' a letter written to Ibn Saud by Khalid, after the Hannu Wells fight . . . which was seen by Philby, contained a full report of the action, and stated that the captured guns were being kept pending the order of Ibn Saud as to disposal '.[35]

With the third clash between Najd and the Hedjaz, arguments for diverting ibn Sa'ud's attention to the much talked about offensive against Hail met with the reluctance of the 'western Arabians' to agree to providing ibn Sa'ud with the proper arms for an advance on the city. Cairo feared that he would turn these arms on the Hedjaz; moreover, from the strict military viewpoint, British successes in Palestine and Mesopotamia coupled with peace overtures by Shammar elements—and an alleged overture from ibn Rashid himself to Husain—eliminated the necessity of a Sa'udi offensive.[36]

Having failed thrice to deter Husain from attacking Khurma, the British government gave up trying to prevent Sharifian punitive expeditions against the village but 'received firm assurances that [the] Shereefial expedition will not penetrate eastwards'.[37] The British agreed generally to ibn Sa'ud's other demands and recognised that if the matter were not settled in Khalid's favour, he would never agree to the decision and even if he did his followers would never accept this. As so often in the past, the Wahhabi leader implied his intention to overrun the Hedjaz when he wrote in the same letter

> All that what [sic] belonged to my father and forefathers in the past has been inherited to me. I do not want anything more than that and by the Will of God and that of yourself the British Government I am quite ready for discussion if you want.[38]

At this juncture Anglo–Sa'udi relations were further exacerbated by the issue of 1,000 inferior rifles to ibn Sa'ud. In March 1918 Cox had suggested—and received approval—for the issue of 1,000 rifles and 100,000 rounds of ammunition to ibn Sa'ud. A. T. Wilson in Baghdad recommended that ibn Sa'ud be sent another 1,000, not as a replacement but in addition to the inferior weapons. However, owing to a copyists error at the India Office, the Eastern Committee, meeting on August 22 1918, sanctioned the despatch of 100 and not 1,000 rifles. The mistake was discovered but as 100 and not 1,000 rifles had been approved it was held by some members of the Foreign Office that ibn Sa'ud should consider himself lucky to receive 100.[40]

Around this time it was decided by the British government that ibn Sa'ud should be kept quiet and not attack Hail and that British policy should 'mark time'.⁴¹ Feeling against Philby was growing stronger as the War drew to a close.⁴² Even A. T. Wilson, who although he did not get along with him formerly backed many of Philby's proposals, felt that as British policy had been modified as regards Cox's telegram of March 9th, Philby's 'views and sympathy have a contrary trend' and that the officer had 'reached the end of his tether'. Wilson suggested that Wingate nominate a successor as this would improve relations with Husain 'and put an end to the belief that our Arabian policies are not co-ordinated'.⁴³ Needless to say, most of the Foreign Office staff concerned with the Middle East agreed with him.

Although the British government had decided against the Sa'udi offensive, events in central Arabia outran British decisions and ibn Sa'ud mounted an attack on Hail. Philby reported that he was paying ibn Sa'ud 10,000 pounds a month 'so long as he continued his activities to my satisfaction'.⁴⁴ And while the British were discussing who would replace Philby, ibn Sa'ud attacked Hail but did not have the strength to take the city. To complicate matters still more, Philby reported that Husain had returned unopened the friendly letter which Philby had induced ibn Sa'ud to send to the Sharif, and had ordered the Sa'udi messenger to leave on pain of death. Moreover, in late September or early October reports came in of a fourth attack— this time by a section of the Sharif's 'Ataiba—on Khurma. Ibn Sa'ud promised not to intervene personally but would not agree to restrain the people of Najd.⁴⁵

Philby telegraphed that the orders not to attack Hail crossed with his telegram reporting the outbreak of hostilities.⁴⁶ He attempted to keep the news from ibn Sa'ud because he feared that such orders coming so closely on Cox's transfer would make ibn Sa'ud think that the British had changed their policy towards him. However, as the Sa'udi agent at Kuwait had already reported the stoppage of the rifles, Philby was forced to inform ibn Sa'ud of the Government's decision. Ibn Sa'ud angrily maintained that he could not withdraw from the campaign now unless the British guaranteed him immunity from Rashidi counter-attack. Philby reported that ibn Sa'ud was full of bitterness and stated that the Amir had posed the question: 'Who... will trust you after this?'⁴⁷ Ibn Sa'ud sent the following ultimatum:

1. That the present active alliance against enemy should be reaffirmed and vigorously prosecuted by us by provision of arms, etc, or
2. If British Government desire him to remain inactive he is perfectly willing to fall in with their wishes provided that they guarantee him absolutely from all aggression by Ajman, Shammar friendlies and Sharif.[48]

Philby added that ibn Sa'ud was going to give his followers one month's leave and that the Amir was sending him to Kuwait to present his case. Philby concluded by stating 'that failing substantial acceptance of one of alternatives given above he [ibn Sa'ud] would consider himself free to act for the protection of his own interests and would not expect me to return'.[49]

Ibn Sa'ud was informed by Wilson of the fall of Damascus and the 1,000 rifles were despatched to placate him. As Hail had already been attacked, Wilson urged—and his suggestion was adopted—that he congratulate ibn Sa'ud on this *fait accompli* and inform him that he need not 'put himself to trouble and expense of further military operations in any directions'.[50] Philby now left Riyadh and Wilson pressed for his replacement by Col. Leachman 'whose virile handling of Arab tribes has been of such value to this Force...'[51]

With Philby gone and the diversion of Hail eliminated, the prospect of a Sa'udi offensive westwards loomed threateningly. Wingate favoured direct negotiations between ibn Sa'ud and Husain, assisted by the British government as a third party.[52] In Baghdad, A. T. Wilson pressed for British arbitration, maintaining—as Philby had—that the issue was not one that would lend itself to peaceful settlement.[53] Wingate objected as direct arbitration would render Britain responsible for internal peace in Arabia.[54] Moreover, as Col. C. E. Wilson later pointed out, if the British were to arbitrate in the dispute, Husain would probably abdicate and there would be anarchy in the Hedjaz.[55]

While the Cairo and Baghdad views were being considered, on November 15th the Civil Commissioner in Baghdad informed ibn Sa'ud of the Turkish defeat and sent him a copy of the Anglo-French Declaration. Wilson held that ibn Sa'ud could not 'fail to interpret latter as reaffirmation of resolution of Allies to allow Arab communities, including Nejd element, to determine their own destinies'.[56] However, a few weeks later it was reported that a force of Ikhwan had attacked a Hedjazi supply base at Dighaibiya, approximately forty-five miles north of Taif.[57]

In Egypt the High Commissioner wanted an ultimatum addressed to ibn Sa'ud ordering him to disperse his Ikhwan concentrations within thirty-five days as he feared Husain's abdication; he also urged that ibn Sa'ud be informed of Husain's suzerainty.[58] On December 10th Husain reported that a force of Ikhwan under ibn Bijad, Amir of Ghatghat was advancing towards Mecca.[59] On December 13th the British government decided

> to warn Bin Saud plainly that if he does not at once abandon and cause his followers to abandon all aggressive action against Hedjaz, and withdraw all militant Ikhwan west of Khurma, his subsidy will be stopped and we shall consider ourselves free to take such further measures as we may deem desirable for maintenance of peace in Central Arabia.[60]

The Egyptian authorities did not think that the ultimatum went far enough as it only specified the withdrawal of the Ikhwan 'west of Khurma' and not from Khurma itself. On the other hand, Wilson in Baghdad wanted more material for the ultimatum other than 'ex parte allegations by King Husain, the veracity of whose previous reports as to Bin Saud is not such as to inspire confidence'.[61] In the meantime the War Office called for the despatch of war matériel and Moslem troops to the Hedjaz to prevent Mecca from being captured.[62]

With the Khurma crisis threatening to culminate in a Wahhabi attack on the Holy Cities, the British government found itself in an apparently insoluble dilemma. They were faced with the following alternatives: (1) either assign Khurma to Husain or ibn Sa'ud or (2) let the adversaries 'fight it out' in the hope that the struggle would be localised. The case against an immediate settlement was obvious. The advice of the local officers involved was conflicting to a degree which would make an equitable decision impossible. On the one hand Husain would probably abdicate if the decision went against him; on the other hand, if Philby's reports were accurate the residents of Khurma had 'freely' accepted 'Wahhabi' (now largely Ikhwan) tenets and their expulsion or forcible reconversion 'would be unpleasantly suggestive of religious persecution'. The argument against letting matters take their course, namely open hostilities, was obvious. It was the avowed policy of Britain to promote peace and goodwill among the Arabs, not open hostilities. Moreover, there was the question of the Indian reaction to conflict in the Hedjaz and the embarrassment of civil war between Britain's protégés. And with the Peace Conference in the foreground of Allied affairs, the British government was aware of the effect of war between their Arab allies on the British claims to a powerful position in the Arab world.[63]

In the light of the fall of Medina, the ultimatum to ibn Sa'ud was cancelled.[64] On February 26th 1919—after much debate on the wording—the following communication was addressed to the two Arab leaders. It was stated that if hostilities persist the following would be Britain's position.

> So long as fighting is confined to area immediately in dispute we should not think it necessary to interfere, but we desire to state in plainest possible terms that Bin Saud can in no circumstances be permitted to advance westwards of disputed area into what is unquestionably Hedjaz territory. We should be prepared to render King Husain all assistance in our power short of provision of troops in resisting any attempt of this kind.[65]

However, before the above message could be forwarded to Husain and ibn Sa'ud, A. T. Wilson, now in Cairo en route to Paris for the Peace Conference, despatched a telegram advising a stronger pro-Husain policy. He suggested that as he had been notified by the Treasury that all abnormal expenditure would lapse in March 1919 he 'did not feel justified in asking His Majesty's Government to sanction continuance to ibn Sa'ud of his present subsidy' and that he did 'not propose to make any further payments to him'. Wilson, whose attitude to ibn Sa'ud had been hardening for some time now, urged at the end of his telegram that 'If King Husain wishes to occupy Khurma he should be allowed to do so'.[66]

The Acting Civil Commissioner suggested that his views given above should be communicated to ibn Sa'ud instead of the February 26th telegram which, he claimed, would not have the desired effect. Philby, now in London, as could be expected, violently opposed this course, averring that ibn Sa'ud would

THE KHURMA AND TURABA DISPUTE

take the Hedjaz anyway. Holderness and Shuckburgh backed Philby while Wingate and Clayton supported A. T. Wilson. A compromise was effected, though it comprised a stronger attitude of British support for Husain. Ibn Sa'ud's subsidy was to be cut by one-half and he was to be told that

> The spread of militant Wahabism in this region [Khurma] would in their opinion constitute direct menace to Hedjaz, security of which they are bound to safeguard against external aggression from any quarter. In these circumstances they advise him as a friend to modify his attitude and to dissuade his followers from further opposition to administrative measures taken by King Husain at Khurma.[67]

Although at this juncture ibn Sa'ud wrote to Baghdad professing loyalty to the British government and asking for the appointment of a boundary commission, the message went forward anyway.[68]

This message, however, was never delivered to ibn Sa'ud. In November 1919 when controversy over the continuation of ibn Sa'ud's subsidy was in full swing Wilson was contacted by the India Office and asked to explain the continuation at full rate of the Sa'udi subsidy. The Civil Commissioner telegraphed that the message contained in the March 12th telegram never reached Bahrain. Wilson, of course, was away from Baghdad at the time and on his return he claimed to have overlooked the despatch. Moreover the Political Agent in Bahrain, Captain Bray, was seriously ill during this period and left Bahrain on April 26th before his successor could be appointed. A closer reading of the records, however, gives a slightly different picture of the non-delivery of this important message.[69]

The March 12th message did reach Bahrain but owing to the arrival of ibn Sa'ud's message its despatch was delayed pending reference to Wilson.[70] In early April Wilson telegraphed Baghdad direct from Paris instructing the immediate despatch of the message to ibn Sa'ud.[71] And it was apparently this message which was lost.[72] The most significant aspect of this confusion was the fact ' that the attitude of Ibn Saud was judged, and important decisions were taken on the assumption that he had received a message of very definite and unambiguous nature which we know he actually never did receive '.[73]

Turaba

On May 21st 1919, 'Abdullah, recently freed from his preoccupation with the Turks at Medina, attacked and occupied Turaba which lay approximately thirty miles southwest of Khurma. He declared his intention—after consolidating his position there—to advance on Khurma. During the night of the 25th–26th May, Khalid, at the head of a party of Ikhwan, attacked and virtually destroyed 'Abdullah's regular forces, capturing all his guns and machine guns. Around this time ibn Sa'ud was reported to have arrived at Sakha, eighty miles northeast of Khurma. He was said to be at the head of a force of 12,000 men.[74]

'Abdullah's defeat, taken together with ibn Sa'ud's arrival at Sakha, confonted the British with yet another threat of a direct—and this time a more immediate—clash between their Arab protégés. Strategically, Taif, the summer retreat of Meccan nobles, was separated from Turaba by forty miles of open country and Mecca lay only some twenty-five miles northeast of Taif. Militarily, it was clear from 'Abdullah's total defeat that his comparatively professional soldiers were no match for the Ikhwan. Politically, the usual fears of the effect in India of a Wahhabi invasion of the Holy Cities haunted British government officials. There was also the threat that Faisal, then in Damascus having been proclaimed King of Syria by the Arab nationalist congress there, would come to his father's assistance. The future King of Iraq voiced fears of losing Syria if he were forced to return to the Hedjaz.[75]

Owing to the imminent threat of invasion the following ultimatum was sent to ibn Sa'ud:

> ... His Majesty's Government have been astonished to receive reports apparently indicating that Akhwan have even advanced to Tarabah in the Hejaz. They desire to warn him solemnly that if he does not immediately withdraw his forces from Hedjaz and Khurmah area they must regard him as having adopted attitude of definite hostility towards themselves. In that event rest of his subsidy will at once be discontinued and he will forfeit irrevocably all advantages secured under Treaty of December 1915.[76]

While a bearer for the above message was being sought, the military command in Egypt proposed that a flight of airplanes be despatched to Husain and that they be accompanied by an escort of Indian Moslems.[77] The first suggestion was adopted but the second, meeting with strong objection from the Secretary of State for India, Edwin Montagu, and the Viceroy, was rejected. The Indian officials naturally feared the effect on troublesome Indian nationalists of using Moslem Indian soldiers in the Holy Cities. Aside from the Indian implications, the crisis was further complicated by the diminution of Husain's supporters owing to the defection of many of his followers to the Wahhabi standard.

Although the ultimatum of May 30th was finally despatched, it was feared by several members of the Interdepartmental Conference of June 13th, including Lord Curzon himself, the Chairman, that ibn Sa'ud had not the strength to restrain his fanatical Ikhwan. The British were also coming to the conclusion that apart from the threat to his subsidy—and even the effect of that measure on restraining ibn Sa'ud was doubtful—they were actually powerless to check a concerted Wahhabi advance. As regards attacking ibn Sa'ud from the Persian Gulf, Montagu argued that it was not feasible to invade Najd nor was there anything to bombard in Hasa. Moreover, the effect of an embargo on Sa'udi ports was dubious. Fortunately the British government were spared the embarrassment of war in the Hedjaz by ibn Sa'ud's conciliatory reply to their ultimatum.[78]

Ibn Sa'ud replied that he would return to Najd if he received a satisfactory guarantee that Husain would refrain from aggression. He voiced his readiness once again to submit to arbitration.[79] Husain's repeated attacks and subsequent defeats coupled with his obstinacy and continual threats to abdicate, when viewed against ibn Sa'ud's apparent consummate restraint and deference to British wishes, were beginning to have their effect on London's attitude towards King Husain. In another Interdepartmental Conference on June 17th, Curzon, in reply to a suggestion by Gertrude Bell that Husain might abdicate, ' confessed that he contemplated his complete disappearance, not only without apprehension, but even with satisfaction '. At this same meeting arbitration was decided upon and the conference elected to send Philby on a mission to ibn Sa'ud. This mission had two objectives: (1) to stop the advance of the Ikhwan pending arbitration and (2) to secure the withdrawal of Sa'udi forces to Khurma as a preliminary to negotiations. Curzon admitted that the second objective of Philby's mission ' amounted to a reversal of ... [the policy] hitherto adopted but in view of Ibn Saud's strong position he did not see how it was possible to adhere to the latter '.[80]

Philby, under Allenby's orders during his mission, departed immediately for Cairo. However, events once again outran British decisions and ibn Sa'ud, after consulting with his Moslem leaders, elected to return to Najd to prepare for the annual pilgrimage. He gave his word that as long as Husain refrained from aggression there would be no trouble from Najd.[81] On reaching Cairo, Philby was ordered to proceed to Riyadh immediately via Jedda and Taif. He was instructed *inter alia* to dissuade ibn Sa'ud from performing the pilgrimage. The British thought that the possibility of violence in the Hedjaz was too great to risk thousands of Najdis converging on the Holy Cities. Philby's progress was slowed down owing to Husain's refusal to grant him permission to travel via the Hedjaz. Probably remembering Philby's past affronts to his dignity, Husain alleged that the journey would be 'prejudicial to British prestige'.[82] He also refused arbitration, maintaining that ibn Sa'ud had appointed governors in Turaba and Khurma.[83] In London the Foreign Office, whose patience with Husain was daily wearing thinner, despatched the following brusque message to be conveyed to Husain: ' as he has refused arbitration no further action to be taken '.[84] Accordingly Philby's mission was cancelled and ibn Sa'ud was notified by letter of the British disapproval of the projected Najdi pilgrimage. Ibn Sa'ud agreed to postpone the pilgrimage until the following year.

With ibn Sa'ud's withdrawal and promise not to perform the pilgrimage, the immediate threat of a clash between Husain and the Wahhabi leader abated but concerted efforts were still being made by the British to settle the vexed question. In the spring of 1919 the Foreign Office had extended an invitation to ibn Sa'ud's son to visit England. The invitation was accepted and the visit took place the following autumn.[85] Before a joint conference of the India and Foreign Offices, ibn Sa'ud's spokesman, Ahmad ibn Thunaiyan, presented ibn Sa'ud's requests, the essence of which was as follows:

1. Protection of Sa'udi independence and avoidance of interference in ibn Sa'ud's internal affairs. Realisation of

the provisions in the Treaty of 1915 and its ratification anew in order to give effect to it.
2. Boundaries of Najd to be recognised as including Khurmah and Tarabah. If a commission cannot be sent, ibn Saʻud undertakes to defend these territories against aggression.
3. Removal of the embargo on the pilgrimage and guarantee that the Najdi pilgrims will not be obstructed in the Hedjaz.
4. Enhancement of and grant in perpetuity of ibn Saʻud's subsidy for the rehabilitation of his territories ruined by internal wars and their occupation by ibn Rashid and the Turks.
5. Despatch of Philby as Political Agent to ibn Saʻud.[86]

These requests were considered at an Interdepartmental Conference on November 24th. In a recapitulation of the previous meeting of June 17th, it was mentioned that at the time the danger of a Wahhabi invasion of the Holy Cities had been so great ' that the Conference had more or less gone back on their original policy of supporting King Husain. They had, as it were, been stampeded by the military danger to the Holy Places '. It was further said that Husain regarded Khurma as an integral part of the Hedjaz and that he would lose prestige if he submitted to arbitration. However, although ' the policy of His Majesty's Government was essentially a Husain policy ' and ibn Saʻud was ' not so important to them as the Sherif of Mecca ', it was held that ' His Majesty's Government were being made to look rather ridiculous by the stubbornness of this sensitive old man ...'[87]

Curzon, chairing the meeting, suggested that ibn Saʻud and Husain or at least their respective plenipotentiaries should meet and hopefully settle their problems without British interference. It was decided that Col. C. E. Wilson should return to Jedda and inform Husain that the Foreign Secretary was in favour of a meeting between the two adversaries and that Husain had an ' excellent case '. Husain was to be told that the British government thought that his claim was so good that they did not understand why he was hesitant about presenting his proofs of his ownership of Khurma.[88] As regards the Najdi delegation's requests, Curzon met the Saʻudi delegates in person. Curzon stressed the projected meeting as a solution for the Najdi–Hedjazi feud but did not inform them that the British government 'were inclined to accept King Husain's contention that he was the rightful owner not only of Turaba... but also of Khurma'. However, as the Najd delegation would not reach Riyadh for some time, Hirtzel urged that ibn Sa'ud need not be informed of Curzon's statement right away.[89]

Montagu was greatly perturbed by Curzon's actions regarding the Najd delegation. In a minute which illuminated divided opinion, inter-office rivalry, the need for a single office responsible for Arabian affairs and the less than friendly relations between Montagu and Curzon, the Secretary of State for India wrote

> I still think all this seems most irregular. I think that either I should have conveyed the message to the Nejd Mission or been consulted by Lord Curzon or been with him. I am responsible for Nejd. The FO should take these matters over or leave them to me. I object to being a telephone for the FO. I am not sure I agree as to Khurma.[90]

While efforts were being made to implement the British plan for a meeting between ibn Sa'ud and Husain, two new factors gave added impetus to the drive for reconciliation. In Syria, frustrated Arab nationalist ambitions were rapidly hardening into a solid anti-French feeling and Faisal was still the paramount Arab figure there. Also ibn Sa'ud's followers—whose failure to appreciate the vicissitudes of British policy towards Najd had long made them resentful of Great Britain—were incensed at not being permitted to make the pilgrimage in 1919. As this was the second year in succession that the pilgrimage had been postponed, it was thought that the pilgrimage could not be put off again. 'Otherwise the pot of trouble now simmering will certainly boil over'.[91]

Before continuing with the account of the much sought after meeting it is interesting at this juncture to note the impressions of ibn Sa'ud and Husain as held by different British officials. Although even Philby had admitted that ibn Sa'ud was growing more ambitious,[92] the Wahhabi leader still impressed almost all of those with whom he came into contact. H. R. P. Dickson, newly appointed Political Agent at Bahrain, described him as 'head and shoulders finer than any Shaikh I have ever met...'[93]

THE KHURMA AND TURABA DISPUTE 147

Contrariwise Husain who pressed for 'recognition of position as leader of all Arabs'[94] was described at best as 'difficult and unreasonable' and at worst as the 'parmpered and querulous nuisance'[95] and as a 'puppet dependent on British gold'.[96] Even Col. C. E. Wilson's successor attached to Husain, Col. Vickery, commenting on Husain's and 'Abdullah's actions over Turaba, wrote that 'the whole affair has been most woefully mismanaged politically and strategically... neither of them showed the rudest grasp of... statesmanship, strategy or tactics'.[97] However, even though Husain was held in varying degrees of disrepute, British policy for many reasons already mentioned remained essentially a 'Husain policy'.

The British government first asked ibn Sa'ud to meet King Husain at Jedda. Ibn Sa'ud declined as a meeting in the Hedjaz would offend his dignity. In a confidential interview with Dickson on February 5th 1920, ibn Sa'ud told the Political Agent that Britain was making his position difficult by lack of support and that his people were angered by the British position in Syria.[98] Ibn Sa'ud referred to the Hashimite position in Syria as 'the northern landing stage of Najd' and stressed that his people believed that Britain had deprived them of the fruits of their victories over Husain while simultaneously denying them their rightful position in Oman, Qatar and Bahrain.[99] Dickson reported that he had been struck by 'the affection of Bin Saud for everything British, and his almost pathetic trust in H.M.'s Government'.[100] The Political Agent also informed the Government that ibn Sa'ud had been sounded out by Syrian nationalists as regards his possible participation in a *jihad* against the French and British.[101]

Ibn Sa'ud suggested that he meet Husain in Baghdad or, if that were inconvenient, in Bombay. A. T. Wilson vetoed these alternatives while in London Lord Curzon, no doubt sensing the reluctance of either party to compromise his dignity, suggested that Husain and ibn Sa'ud meet aboard a British ship.[102] By April 1920 the need for a reconciliation between the British protégés increased greatly with the assignment of mandates at the San Remo Conference. Moreover, ibn Sa'ud was further antagonised by the British advocacy of 'Abdullah's and Faisal's kingship in Mesopotamia and Syria. It appeared to the Najdi ruler that he was being outflanked by his Hashimite adversaries. Ibn Sa'ud warned that 'the British Government has no sincere friend among the Arabs, except myself whose personal interests are strong. *Consider the matter before anything happens and bridge the gulf before it widens*'.[103] While efforts were being made to arrange the meeting and to dissuade the Treasury in its economising measures from choosing this juncture to stop ibn Saʿud's subsidy, A. T. Wilson telegraphed:

> Probability of Bin Saud seizing Mecca is being discussed with frankness in Bahrain and elsewhere in Persian Gulf and in Mesopotamia. General opinion appears to be not unfavourable to such a consummation as it is believed that this would be in interests of religion and would make pilgrimage safe.[104]

On hearing Wilson's views, Curzon's opinion of the Civil Commissioner's suggestions were embodied in a sharply worded letter from the Foreign Office to the India Office written on May 1st. As this correspondence summed up the position to date and gave an official expression of the many factors influencing the British position it deserves to be quoted at some length:

> Lord Curzon concurs in Mr Secretary Montagu's opinion that immediate steps should be taken with a view to the reopening of the Nejd pilgrimage, but he is strongly of the opinion that the scheme for a meeting between the two rulers should not be abandoned. His Lordship contemplates the possibility of a Wahhabi invasion of Mecca with the greatest misgiving and trusts that Lord Allenby is mistaken in the inference which he draws from Colonel Wilson's telegram of the 15th April. A Wahhabi occupation of the Holy Places of Mecca and Medina, and the consequent growth of Wahhabi power and influence might, in His Lordship's opinion, lead in future, as it did in the past, to massacres such as those of 1801 at Kerbela and of 1802 at Taif; to repeated raids on Iraq; to the turning back from the Holy Places of all Pilgrims who were unwilling to profess Wahabi tenets; and possibly to costly and difficult military operations, or failing these, to a loss of prestige for His Majesty's Government which His Lordship would regard as a capital disaster.
>
> His Majesty's Government have supported and financed

an Arab revolt against the Turks, headed by King Hussein, who has consequently been recognised by the Allied Powers as an independent sovereign. They are also claiming from the peace conference a special position in Arabia exclusive of the Hejaz. His Lordship considers that these two considerations inevitably commit His Majesty's Government to doing everything in their power to prevent the overrunning of the independent Hejaz by one of the rulers for whom they will in the future be solely responsible.[105]

Curzon thought the alternative meeting places had not been conveyed to ibn Sa'ud and directed that Wilson execute London's decisions.[106]

The Civil Commissioner had been guilty of delaying the despatch which suggested a meeting aboard ship. He had done so pending the receipt of further reports and the assurance that a ship would be available. The second reason was justified to some extent owing to the recent embarrasment to Anglo–Persian relations caused by the inability of the British government to provide a ship for the Shah of Persia. However it was argued that the British in Egypt were not altogether free from criticism. The High Commissioner, it was held, had been instructed to prevail upon King Husain to meet ibn Sa'ud in Jedda or 'elsewhere' and that from the reports it appeared that only Jedda—which would have been inconsistent with Sa'udi dignity—had been suggested.[107] On May 5th, the India Office directed that both rulers be invited to meet aboard ship in Aden Harbour.[108]

While the British endeavoured to arrange the Aden meeting the incongruity of war between Britain's subsidised protégés was not lost on the British public and Parliament. In the May 27th edition of the *Daily Express* the Arabian war was highlighted in an article. The following day the same paper published a letter signed by many influential MPs urging Lloyd George to establish a single ministry responsible for Middle Eastern affairs. In this same issue, Lawrence wrote an anti-Wahhabi article.[109] Contemporaneously with the MPs pressure for reform the Army Council wrote to the Foreign Office stating that

> if it is proposed to arm either of these Chiefs against the other, the Council should be given a definite expression of the policy His Majesty's Government....[110]

With the time of the pilgrimage growing nearer, Allenby telegraphed on May 29th that he had received a report from Col. Vickery in Jedda which stated that Husain had ' angrily agreed to meet Saud and that he will put no obstacles in the way of Pilgrimage if Nejdis come unarmed and in charge of some responsible person '.[111] Ibn Sa'ud agreed to meet Husain but requested the presence of Cox or Wilson attended by Dickson. He argued that the conference take place after the Hajj and requested that an Indian officer accompany the Najd pilgrims. Alternatively, ibn Sa'ud volunteered to accompany the pilgrimage to Mecca and meet Husain somewhere in the Hedjaz.[112]

A short time later Husain went back on his promise to meet ibn Sa'ud and on hearing of ibn Sa'ud's offer to head the Wahhabi pilgrimage and meet him in the Hedjaz, Husain objected, holding that such a manoeuvre would provoke violence. He suggested that ibn Sa'ud come with a small following and that the other pilgrims come by sea. Owing to the impossibility of Husain's suggestions, his action amounted to a rejection of reconciliation. Once again the Sharif threatened to abdicate if his demands were not met.[113]

In London, the Foreign Office still tried manfully to salvage the proposed meeting by requesting ibn Sa'ud to meet Husain's conditions.[114] While ibn Sa'ud was being informed of Husain's stipulations, the King of the Hedjaz further complicated matters by stating that he had only agreed to ibn Sa'ud's coming with several hundred men as an escort.[115] From the despatches it is impossible to ascertain whether the condition of limiting ibn Sa'ud's contingent to a specific number was an additional obstacle or an original stipulation which had not been reported. Whatever the case may be, it is well to bear in mind that the many disappointments which the British dealt to Husain—i.e. mandates, Balfour Declaration and his frustrated ambition to become the head of all the Arabs—were not calculated to make the Sharif a paragon of amenability. Moreover, owing to the Treasury's failure to sanction the continuation of Husain's subsidy, he had not received for over four months the financial assistance which was originally given to him by the Turks.[116]

On hearing of Husain's restrictions, ibn Sa'ud—who had set July 18th as the latest he could hold up the pilgrimage—was understandably angered. He accused the British of ' tying his hands by compelling him to refer important matters at 11th hour'. The Wahhabi leader asked that either he be allowed to make the pilgrimage in full or he would abstain from sending his pilgrims and instead would send a small following under a chief who would act as his representative. This mission would have as its objective the preparation of the way for further negotiations. Moreover, he would inform his people that 'a small party will proceed to Mecca through good offices of His Majesty's Government'.[117]

In order to pave the road to negotiation the Treasury sanctioned the grant of £30,000 to Husain and £5,000 to ibn Sa'ud.[118] However, in the light of Husain's recalcitrance, certain conditions were attached to his grant. Cairo was authorised to pay him £10,000 ' provided that it is only spent in the Hedjaz'. This was done because there were reports that Husain was helping to finance the anti-French movement in Syria. Secondly, Husain was to receive £10,000 when he agreed to sign the treaty and finally the remaining £10,000 when he actually signed it.[119] Husain refused to accept the grant, holding that it was beneath his dignity to accept £30,000 in lieu of his subsidy. He also declined to give any guarantees concerning his meeting with ibn Sa'ud, the purchase of supplies by Najdis or the maintenance of peace during the pilgrimage. However, British persistence prevailed and the meeting between representatives from Najd and the Hedjaz finally took place. Again the perennial importance of India played a great part in the immediate need for negotiations and a pacific pilgrimage.

> In view of large Indian attendance including 1,000 Indian soldiers it is important to His Majesty's Government that Hajj should pass peacefully ...[120]

A delegation from Najd headed by ibn Thunaiyan accompanied, among others, by an Indian officer and 32 Najd pilgrims travelled to the Hedjaz. The objective of the Najdi party was to discuss with the Hedjaz authorities the preliminaries of peace.[121] There was no delimitation of boundaries; an armistice was signed which suspended hostilities pending British arbitration. After much objection Husain was induced to sign the agreement. However he averred that he would never accept arbitration which did not include Khurma and Turaba in the Hedjaz.[122]

Through the signing of the armistice, war in the Hedjaz was

postponed for four years. Although the British were beginning to appreciate more ibn Sa'ud's rising stature and comparatively steadfast pro-British policy, they were to continue, though with some reluctance, to follow a 'Husain policy' for several years to come. In the 1920s this policy owed more to Faisal's and 'Abdullah's positions than to Husain's. Many London officials, and a growing number of Cairo people, probably agreed with Curzon when referring to Husain in a minute, he wrote: ' I don't think we shall ever have peace until he has gone. But I do not want to administer the final kick '.[123] In the India Office, Sir Arthur Hirtzel reflecting a more manifest frustration with the Arabs in general and 'western Arabians' in particular put it more acidly: ' Major Noel [Political Officer in Kurdistan] in a recent report quoted a Kurdish proverb which the events of the last four years seemed to have amply justified, and which our Arabofiles would do well to remember: " Do not encourage an Arab, or he will come and commit a nastiness on the skirt of your coat " '.[124]

Although the Najd–Hedjaz feud was put on ice for the moment, there was no lull in Anglo–Sa'udi relations. British attention was drawn to eastern Arabia where border problems first between Najd and Kuwait and later between Najd and Iraq threatened to erupt into new hostilities.

Notes

1. On Britain's immediate post-war problems see *Beloff*, chaps. VI, VII; Taylor, *English History*, chap. IV; W. N. Medlicott, *Contemporary England 1914–1964* (London, 1967), chaps. III–IV; C. L. Mowat, *Britain Between the Wars* (London, 1956), chaps. I, II; and for a survey of the literature on the effect of the war on British society, see A. Marwick, ' The Impact of the First World War on British society ', *Journal of Contemporary History*, Vol. 3 (1968). For events in the Middle East see Kedourie, *England*, chaps. 6, 7; Busch, *Britain*, Pt. 2; Monroe, chap. 2; *Howard*, chaps. VII–XI; *Nevakivi*, chaps. VI–XII; Zeine, *Struggle*, chaps. III–XII; and *Antonius*, chaps. XIV–XVI.
2. Much of the material and construction in this section is taken from Philby, *Sa'udi Arabia*, pp. 260–262.
3. Philby, ' The Triumph of the Wahhabis ', *Journal of the Central Asian Society*, Oct. 1926, Vol. XIII, Pt. IV, pp. 299–301. Hereafter Philby, *JCAS*.
4. Philby, *Sa'udi Arabia*, p. 262.
5. See his *Ibn Sa'ud, His People and His Land* (London, 1928), p. 55. Hereafter *Rihani*.

6. Of those officials who had direct contact with ibn Saʻud during the Ikhwan period, Philby inclined to the former and Dickson (p. 149) inclined to the latter view.
7. Busch competently surveys the British reactions to the Khurma Turaba dispute, but as this issue only constitutes a small part of his general scope and treatment he never quite brings out the complicated claims to the villages, or goes into great detail. For his treatment see his pp. 257–266 and 321–334 in *Britain*.
8. 'Note by Capt. Garland of the Arab Bureau on the Khurma Dispute...', June 4, 1919, encl. 1 in Allenby to Curzon, June 11, 1919 (L), No. 6995; *L/P & S/10*, 2182/1919, Pts. 9, 10. Hereafter *Garland's Note*. Garland states in the beginning of his 'Note' that he uses Ikhwan and Wahhabi interchangeably. See further notes for a distinction between Wahhabism and Ikhwanism. For the location of Khurma and Turaba, see Map of Arabia.
9. 'Some Notes on the Ownership of Khurma' by Col. C. E. Wilson, (Pol. Agent, Jedda), Aug. 8, 1919, No. 6995; *ibid*. Hereafter *Wilson's Notes*.
10. *Ibid*.
11. See pp. 13, 14.
12. 'Wahhabi' in this instance is apparently used interchangeably with 'Ikhwan'. As a further indication of the Wahhabi claim to Khurma, Col C. E. Wilson, obviously less inclined to being pro-Wahhabi than Philby, pointed out in his *Notes* that 'owing to the number of Wahhabis in Khurma the Emirs of Mecca usually appointed a Hanbali as the official cadi'. Given this practice it is arguable that Husain would not object to Wahhabism in Khurma—probably moribund there, its initial (19th century) fervour having long been spent. It was the ominous threat of revived Wahhabism in the form of militant Ikhwanism on his doorstep that Husain dreaded.
13. *Wilson's Notes*.
14. Memo from Philby to CC, Aug. 13, 1918, No. 5335; *L/P & S/10*, 2182/13, Pts. 7, 8. Hereafter *Philby's Memo*. As regards the alleged payment of Khalid by ibn Saʻud, it is quite probable that Khalid received some form of payment from both Najd and the Hedjaz, thus playing both ends from the middle.
15. *Wilson's Notes*. My emphasis. 'By embracing the Wahhabi faith' Philby most probably meant here 'Ikhwanism'. Philby usually made the distinction between the two terms whereas his contemporaries used them frequently—and confusingly—as interchangeable labels.
16. *Ibid*.
17. *Philby's Memo*.
18. *Ibid*.
19. As regards the conversion of an Arab to the Ikhwan movement Wilson emphasised that 'an Arab strongly objects to leaving his own country, and as remaining entails sudden death or an outward profession of the Akhwan faith, it is not surprising that the latter is the course usually taken'. See *Wilson's Notes*.
20. *Najd Report*.

21. *Garland's Notes.*
22. Wingate to FO, May 25, 1918 (T), No. 2240/93419; *FO* 371/3389.
23. *Ibid.*
24. Pol./Bagh [Political Department in Baghdad], to GI, June 28, 1918 (T), No. 2240/116176; *ibid.*
25. *Garland's Notes.*
26. FO to Wingate, Aug. 26, 1918 (T), No. 2240/147381; *FO* 371/3390.
27. Wingate to FO, July 30, 1918 (T), No. 2240/133039; *ibid.*
28. *Philby Memo.*
29. *Ibid.*
30. Viceroy to IO, July 30, 1918 (T), No. 2240/133928; *FO* 371/3390.
31. SSI to Viceroy, Aug. 2, 1918 (T), No. 2240/135458; *FO* 371/3390.
32. Ibn Sa'ud complained bitterly that British policy regarding the Shammar was detrimental to the Allied effort. He argued that the British policy of forcing him to banish the Shammar from his territory and then supplying them with food resulted in the hostility of disaffected Shammari tribes towards Riyadh and their gradual return—well supplied by the British—to ibn Rashid's standard. See *Philby Memo.*
33. Philby to CC, July 24, 1918, encl. in Pol./Bagh. to GI; Aug. 8, 1918 (T), No. 2240/ 139460; *FO* 371/3390. The other two demands dealt with the British practice of supplying food to the 'Ajman and Shammar and the Kuwaiti duplicity in blockade operations. See pp. 102–104.
34. Pol/Bagh to GI, Aug. 8, 1918 (T), No. 2240/140184; *ibid.*
35. *Garland's Notes.*
36. C-in-C [Commander-in-Chief] (Egypt) to WO, Aug. 17, 1918 (T), No. 3660; *L/P & S/10*, 2182/1913, Pts. 7, 8.
37. Wingate to FO, Aug. 26, 1918 (T), No. 2240/147594; *FO* 371/3390.
38. Ibn Sa'ud to Philby, Aug. 30, 1918, (L, Trans), No. 5870; *L/P & S/10*, 2182/13, Pts. 7, 8.
39. 'Relations with Bin Saud' by J. E. S[huckburgh], Sept. 22, 1918 (Note) No. 4138; *ibid.*
40. Note by IO Pol. Dept. on 'Supply of Rifles...',Sept. 10, 1918, No. 3931; *L/P & S/10*, 3182/13, Pts. 7, 8.
41. SSI to Viceroy, Sejt. 13, 1918 (T), No. 2240/162677; *FO* 371/3390.
42. In a memo for Mark Sykes, William Ormsby-Gore of the Cabinet Office argued that Philby was 'trying to build up ibn Sa'ud's power by asking for the 1,000 rifles'. He also suggested that ibn Sa'ud was using Philby as a tool to build up Wahhabi power. Sykes agreed. See 'Memo for Sykes' by W. O[rmsby]-G[ore], Sept. 10, 1918 and accompanying Minute by Sykes, Sept. 11,, 1918, No. 2240/154498; *ibid.*
43. Minute by J. E. S[huckburgh], Oct. 21, 1918, No. 4618; *L/P & S/10*, 2182/1913; Pts. 7, 8. Hereafter *Shuckburgh's Minute.*
44. Philby to CC [Civil Commissioner], Bagh., Sept. 26, 1918, encl. in Pol./Bagh. to SSI, Oct. 11, 1918 (T), No. 2240/172858; *FO* 371/3390. This was one of the alternative suggestions put forward by Cox in his March 9th telegram. It is not clear whether this was ibn Sa'ud's subsidy or an addition thereto.

THE KHURMA AND TURABA DISPUTE 155

45. Philby to CC, Bagh., Oct. 5, 1918, encl. in Pol./Bagh. to SSI, Oct. 9, 1918 (T), No. 2240/171797; *ibid.*
46. Communication with Philby at times took up to one month.
47. Philby to CC, Bagh, Oct. 12, 1918, encl. in Pol./Bagh. to SSI Oct. 16, 1918 (T), No. 2240/174691; *FO* 371/3390.
48. *Ibid.*
49. *Ibid.*
50. SSI to Viceroy, Oct. 17, 1917 (T), No. 2240/176864; *FO* 371/3390.
51. Pol./Bagh. to SSI, Oct. 16, 1918 (T), No. 2240/17469; *ibid.*
52. Wingate to FO, Oct. 21, 1918 (T), No. 2240/175525; *ibid.*
53. Pol./Bagh. to GI, Oct. 22, 1918 (T), No. 2240/178003; *ibid.*
54. Wingate to FO, Oct. 24, 1918 (T), No. 2240/178255; *ibid.*
55. *Wilson's Notes.*
56. Pol./Bagh. to GI, Nov. 18, 1918 (T), No. 2240/191471; *FO* 371/3390. On November 9, 1918 the British and French governments declared 'that they would "encourage and assist the establishment of native governments in Syria and Mesopotamia...as also in those territories for whose liberation they are striving"'. See *Anderson*, pp. 351, 352, and Kedourie, *England*, chaps. 6, 7.
57. Note by J. E. S[huckburgh] on 'Nejd-Hejaz Feud', Jan. 7, 1919, No. 873; *L/P & S/10*, 2182/1919, Pts. 9, 10. Hereafter *Shuckburgh's Note.*
58. Wingate to FO, Dec. 6, 1918 (T), No. 2240/202098; *FO* 371/3390.
59. Wingate to FO, Dec. 16, 1918 (T), No. 2240/203387; *ibid.*
60. *Shuckburgh's Note.*
61. *Ibid.*
62. WO to FO, Dec. 23, 1918 (L), No. 2240/210939; *FO* 371/3390.
63. *Shuckburgh's Note.*
64. SSI to CC, Jan. 16, 1919 (T), No. 84; *L/P & S/10*, 2182/1913, Pts. 9, 10.
65. FO to Cheetham (Acting High Com.), Feb. 26, 1919 (T), No. 1079; *ibid.*
66. Wilson to FO, March 2, 1919, encl. in Cheetham to FO, Same d., No. 1254; *ibid.* Although from the tone of his despatches it was obvious that Wilson was losing patience with ibn Sa'ud, the Civil Commissioner's concluding suggestion is difficult to understand.
67. FO to Cheetham, March 12, 1919 (T), No. 1314; *ibid.*
68. Allenby to FO, March 31, 1919 (T), No. 1763; *FO* 371/3390.
69. CC to SSI, Dec. 12, 1919 (T), No. 8059; *L/P & S/10*, 4931/1916. For details on the Sa'udi subsidy, see pp. 162–164.
70. Allenby to FO, March 31, 1919 (T), No. 1763; *L/P & S/10*, 2182/1913, Pts. 9, 10.
71. FO to Allenby, April 11, 1919 (T), No. 1896; *ibid.*
72. Minute by J. A. Simpson, Feb. 20, 1920, No. 486; *L/P & S/10*, 4931/1916.
73. *Ibid.*
74. *Garland's Report.* See 'Extract from Intelligence and Pol. Report' by Vickery, Oct. 26 to Nov. 21st, 1919, encl. in CC to SSI, Jan. 3, 1920 (T), No. 1099; *L/P & S/10*, 2182/1920.

75. Allenby (now High Commissioner) to FO, June 9, 1919 (T), No. 3252; *L/P & S/10*, 2182/1913, Pts. 9, 10.
76. SSI to CC, May 30, 1919 (T), No. 2903; *L/P & S/10*, 2182/1913, Pts. 9, 10. The ultimatum was actually despatched to ibn Sa'ud on June 9th through the Hedjaz. See Allenby to FO, June 10, 1919 (T), No. 3252; *ibid*.
77. GHQ (Cairo) to WO, June 2, 1919 (T), No. 3030; *ibid*.
78. Inter-Departmental Committee (IDC), June 13, 1919, No. 3280; *ibid*. In 1919 the IDC replaced the Eastern Committee. ' It worked in spurts rather than regularly because all its important members had other and more pressing duties'. See *Monroe*, p. 52.
79. Allenby to FO, June 14, 1919 (T), No. 3298; *L/P & S/10*, 2182/1919.
80. IDC, June 17, 1919, No. 3340; *ibid*.
81. Allenby to FO, June 25, 1919 (T), No. 3566; *ibid*.
82. Col. French [for the HC] to FO, June 29, 1919 (T), No. 3874; *L/P & S/10*, 2182/1913, Pts. 9, 10.
83. Allenby to FO, June 25, 1919 (T), No. 3736; *ibid*. The governor at Khurma was Khalid.
84. FO to Allenby, July 25, 1919 (T), No. 4340; *ibid*. Owing to the sensitivity of Husain, Allenby was able to dissuade the Foreign Office from issuing this message to the King. Presumably a less harsh version was conveyed.
85. For an account of the bungled reception and treatment of ibn Sa'ud's son, Faisal, see ' Report of the Sec., Govt. Hospitality Fund, on the Arab Missions ', Oct., 1919, No. 6775; *L/P & S/10*, 4006/1919, Pt. 1.
86. ' Note read by ibn Thunaiyan to FO and IO Conference ', Nov. 1, 1919 (Trans), No. 142/152298; *FO* 371/4147.
87. IDC of Nov. 24, 1919, No. 7943; *L/P & S/10*, 2182/1913, Pts. 9, 10.
88. *Ibid*.
89. SSI to CC, Jan. 24, 1920 (T), No. 446; *L/P & S/10*, 2182/1913, Pts. 11, 12. Curzon also was in favour of not informing ibn Sa'ud immediately of the decision.
90. Minute by E. S. M[ontagu], n.d., No. 446; *ibid*. For Montagu's differences with Curzon see *Waley*, especially chap. XII.
91. Minute by C. C. Garbett, of the IO, Jan. 4, 1920, No. 8349; *L/P & S/10*, 2182/1913, Pts. 9, 10.
92. Note by Philby, March 23, 1920, No. 2312; *L/P & S/10*, 2182/1913, Pts. 11, 12.
93. Dickson to Cox, Feb. 10, 1920 (L), No. 2635; *ibid*.
94. Allenby to FO, Jan. 11, 1920 (T), No. 393; *ibid*.
95. Minutes by A. H[irtzel], July 9, 1919, No. 3896; *L/P & S/10*, 2182/1913, Pts. 9, 10.
96. Pol./B. to SSI, June 14, 1919 (T), No. 3298; *ibid*.
97. ' Extract from Intelligence and Political Report ' by Vickery (Pol. Agent, Jedda), Oct. 26 to Nov. 21, 1919, encl. in CC to SSI, Jan. 3, 1920 (T), No. 1099; *L/P & S/10*, 2182/1913, Pts. 11, 12.
98. CC to SSI, Feb. 12, 1920 (T), No. 1202; *ibid*.
99. Ibn Sa'ud to Dickson, Feb. 6, 1920, (L, Trans), No. 2780; *ibid*.

100. Dickson to CC, Feb. 10, 1920 (L), No. 2780; *ibid.*
101. CC to SSI, Feb. 15, 1920 (T), No. 1264; *ibid.*
102. FO to IO, March 16, 1920 (L), No. 2123; *ibid.*
103. Ibn Saʻud to Pol. Agent, Bahrain, April 2, 1920 (L, Trans), No. 4132; *ibid.* Emphasis in original.
104. CC to SSI, April 15, 1920 (T), No. 3060; *ibid.*
105. FO to IO, May 1, 1920 (L), No. 3496; *L/P & S/10*, 2182/1913, Pts. 11, 12. Wilson, characteristically relentless in his advocacy of paternalist administration, had cabled earlier: ' The Arab Movement is becoming steadily more anti-foreign and anti-British. It shows however no sign of being constructive nor does it promise to develop on peaceful lines. Arabia never has and never can be united and the present movement is a natural reaction against Arab idea. The abdication of King Husain should go far to hasten collapse of Arab Movement in its present form and will thus facilitate a settlement of the questions in Mesopotamia, Syria, and Palestine on lines acceptable alike to the allies and to the mass of the local population '. See Pol./B. to SSI, June 14, 1920 (T), No. 3298; *L/P & S/10*, 2182/1913, Pts. 9, 10.
106. *Ibid.*
107. ' Note by the India Office on British Commitments '..., No. 3496, n.d., *L/P & S/10*, 2182/1913, Pts. 11, 12.
108. IO to CC, May 5, 1920 (T), No. 3496; *ibid.*
109. *Daily Express*, May 27, 28, 1920.
110. Army Council to FO, June 9, 1920 (L), No. 4561; *L/P & S/10*, 2182/1913, Pts. 11, 12.
111. Allenby to FO, May 29, 1920 (T), No. 4278; *ibid.*
112. CC to SSI, June 8, 1920 (T), No. 3496; *ibid.*
113. Allenby to FO, June 30, 1920 (T), No. 5173; *ibid.*
114. F.O. to Allenby, July 2, 1920 (T), No. 5282; *ibid.*
115. Allenby to FO, July 8, 1920 (T), No. 5492; *ibid.*
116. FO to Treasury, July 16, 1920 (T), No. 5602; *ibid.* From his intervention in the War until February 1, 1919, Husain received 200,000 pounds per month. During the following year these payments were diminished until their complete cessation. See A. Toynbee ' Arabia, The Rise of the Wahhabi Power ', *Survey of International Affairs, The Islamic World Since the Peace Settlement*, Vol. 1, 1925 (London, 1927), p. 273. Hereafter *Survey*. The subsidy question will be treated further in Section I of Chapter V.
117. CC to SSI, July 27, 1920 (T), No. 5754; *L/P & S/10*, 2182/1920.
118. It should be stressed that although the Treasury had to cut expenditure, the discontinuation of Arab subsidies put Arab leaders in a difficult position. These rulers had become dependent on these subsidies to buy the allegiance of their followers. Husain, lacking ibn Saʻud's assets of charismatic leadership and the Wahhabi's position as the head of a religious revival, suffered especially as his followers were leaving his standard in great numbers. In ibn Saʻud's case, his total revenue was about 20 lakhs of rupees [1 lakh equals 100,000 rupees or £6,666.13.4], hardly sufficient to run an efficient

government. As Bedouin tribes had for centuries supported themselves by terrorising the countryside ibn Sa'ud stressed that it was necessary to subsidise them now that he had forced them into a law-abiding life. See CC to SSI, Sept. 5, 1920 (T), No. 6689; *L/P & S/10*, 488/1920.
119. FO to Cairo, Sept. 28, 1920 (T), No. 7250; *ibid.*
120. Scott to FO, Aug. 9, 1920 (T), No. 6077; *ibid.*
121. 'Report on Najd Mission' by Sadiq Hasan (Indian Political Officer) to British Agent (Jedda), Aug. 20, 1920, No. 7439; *ibid.*
122. Scott to FO, Sept. 23, 1920 (T), No. 6305; *ibid.*
123. Minute by C[urzon], Oct. 6, 1920, No. 9/E 12144; *FO* 371/5064.
124. Minute by A. H[irtzel]. Sept. 7, 1919, No. 3896; *L/P & S/10*, 2182/1919.

CHAPTER V

British Policy 1920 to 1922: Subsidies and Frontiers

The period from the end of World War I to the signature of the 'Uqair Protocols in December 1922 which defined the Kuwait–Najd and Iraq–Najd frontiers is distinguished mainly by three factors. Firstly, ibn Sa'ud, his power ever on the increase, endeavoured relentlessly to extend his frontiers to the limits of the early nineteenth century Wahhabi Empire. In 1920 he conquered the mountain districts of 'Asir.[1] In 1921 ibn Sa'ud captured Hail and in 1922 he annexed Jauf in northernmost Arabia. Given this Sa'udi expansion and the British policy of king-making in Iraq and Transjordan, ibn Sa'ud proceeded to clash not only with Kuwait but with Iraq and before long, with Transjordan.

Secondly, the following pages will show that just as Britain had bought allies in Arabia during the War she now found that she was forced to continue the same policy of ' financial assistance ' as the only means by which to exert any control over the contentious leaders of the peninsula. It will be noted in the pages to follow that this policy of subsidies was the subject of heated controversy in British governmental circles.

The third major factor in Anglo–Sa'udi relations of this time was the drawing by Great Britain of European-style bounaries between Najd and her neighbours, Kuwait and Iraq. It will be shown that these boundaries, ignoring as they did such desert realities as annual tribal migrations, did not alleviate the tension existing between Najd and Iraq.

A Question of Subsidies

The issue of the continuation of ibn Sa'ud's subsidy was of such importance in the formulation of British post-war policy in Arabia that it merits special—if brief—attention in a section of its own. Ever since the end of the War ibn Sa'ud had been pressing for an increase in his subsidy. As his appeals coincided with past-war attempts at home to reduce foreign expenditure and the growing pressure for a co-ordinated Middle Eastern policy, the question of the Sa'udi subsidy became involved with the larger question of British subsidies to all Arab chiefs. Hence treatment of the issue of ibn Sa'ud's subsidy must be viewed not only against the background of British post-war policy in Arabia but also as inextricably intertwined with the question of subsidising all the Arabian chiefs.[2]

After the end of World War I, Britain sought to secure her position in the Arabian peninsula. Her reasons were the traditional considerations involving the area's proximity to imperial routes to a communications with India, and the British relationship with the Arab Shaikhs on the coast of the peninsula stretching from Kuwait to Aden. Britain's problems regarding subsidies arose in part from the difficulties of trying to reconcile her political aspirations with her economic stringency.

> His Majesty's Government are now faced with the double task of substantially reducing their financial commitments in Arabia and at the same time of securing the special position for which the good-will of the chiefs is as necessary as is the consent of the Principal Allied Powers.[3]

The financial difficulties of Great Britain after the end of the War are too obvious to stress. As there was great pressure at home to reduce foreign spending, the question of subsidising distant desert chieftains who spent much of their allowance intriguing against one another was especially open to criticism and hotly debated. Moreover, the necessity of a clear and general policy in the Middle East became interwoven with the subsidy debate. In June 1920 in reply to a Foreign Office request to resume Husain's subsidy until the independence of the Hedjaz had been ratified by the Peace Treaty, the Treasury 'intimated that they were unable to sanction these payments until some general policy with regard to Arab rulers could be laid down'.[4] The situation was further complicated by the expected transfer to the Colonial Office of responsibility for the Middle East. The Treasury's obstinacy, however, was continually assailed by the arguments in favour of adopting a policy of subsidies. One of the biggest obstacles to the continuation of ibn Sa'ud's subsidy was the section of official opinion which held that owing to the moral prestige attached to subsidies and the jealousy of one shaikh towards another, to subsidise one meant to subsidise all. It is submitted that the only practical method of securing the influence which His Majesty's Government hope to deny to other Powers is by extending the principle of financial support to all the independent rulers of Arabia.⁵

There were many general reasons for a policy of subsidies which were prefaced by Allenby's dictum that ' to gain a predominant influence in Arabia without being prepared to pay for it . . . will result in failure '. Through a policy of buying friends, Britain might recover her prestige in the Middle East. Additionally, the problems confronting Britain in Syria and Palestine could be offset by consolidating her position in Arabia. The peninsula was comparatively free from foreign rivalries and conditions were favourable for the recognition of Britain's predominant position there. Moreover, there was the fear, which was very real at the time, that Turkish and Arab nationalists would successfully unite Islam against the Allies. A friendly Arabia would act as a counterpoise to this contingency. The geographical and religious importance of the peninsula was always in the foreground while the possibilities of opening up the interior to trade were mentioned. And finally there was the British desire to deny to any other Power(s) the opportunity of gaining a predominant position in the peninsula.⁶

Another important factor in subsidising various shaikhs was the fact that they in turn bought their influence with this money. This was especially true in Husain's case. The King of the Hedjaz maintained power and the allegiance of his followers only as long as he could afford to pay for it. Allenby touched upon this fact and the post-war implications of the Arab Revolt when he warned Curzon against the discontinuation of subsidies.

> As your Lordship is aware, the Arab Revolt was not regarded with sympathy either in India or in our other Mohammedan countries. This feeling still exists today. The revolt can only be justified by its success, and we shall undoubtedly lay ourselves open to severe criticism if the Peninsula passes into a state of anarchy.⁷

As to the reasons for the continuation of the Sa'udi subsidy, in particular, the question will first be considered from ibn Sa'ud's point of view. The Wahhabi leader was reported to be heavily in debt and repeatedly besought the British government for an increase in his subsidy.⁸ While Wilson was still in Baghdad he had recommended that ibn Sa'ud be granted a loan of £50,000 to be secured on the customs revenues of his ports and that direct trade with his Hasa port be developed. The Civil Commissioner suggested that British India steamers, if necessary, be subsidised to call there.⁹ Later, when Cox replaced Wilson as High Commissioner in Baghdad, he pressed for the development of Sa'udi ports and also urged that ibn Sa'ud's subsidy be increased to £100,000 annually.¹⁰

The arguments for continuing ibn Sa'ud's subsidy were met with the following rebuttals. It was held that as the Sa'udi subsidy grew out of wartime conditions, now that the War had ended so should his subsidy. There was also the argument that Britain could not afford to subsidise him while others maintained that his threat to the Holy Places was negligible because if ibn Sa'ud attacked the Hedjaz he would be counter-attacked by a combination of forces from the north. Moreover, as it was held that a subsidy to one would necessitate subsidies to all shaikhs ' considering the extent to which the chiefs are influenced by personal jealousy of one another, it ought not to be impossible to settle with them on a basis of no subsidies to any of them '. It was also put forward that subsidies upset the natural equilibrium of desert politics and that in Wahhabism, Britain was supporting a heresy.¹¹

The Treasury was also incensed because ibn Sa'ud's subsidy had not been discontinued in June 1917 according to their original stipulation. The subsidy was originally sanctioned for only six months: from January to June, 1917.¹² This six-month sanction, however, was overlooked and the subsidy was continued throughout the War and indeed until November 1919 when at an Inter-Departmental Conference this discrepancy was brought to light. London was also antagonised on discovering that during the growing hostilities between Husain and ibn Sa'ud, a London decision to reduce ibn Sa'ud's subsidy by half was not executed. As regards the original Treasury sanction, Montagu explained that through an oversight the India Office telegram to the Viceroy sent on January 4th 1917, authorising the payment of the subsidy, neglected to mention the time limitation. Moreover, the Treasury letter of January 1st 1917 which had sanctioned the subsidy for six months was not communicated officially to Montagu's predecessor by the Foreign Office until after the despatch of the telegram to the Viceroy. 'A copy of the Treasury letter was forwarded to the Government of India in the ordinary course, without comment; and it appears to have escaped notice both in India and in Mesopotamia'.[13] The Treasury now hotly contested the India Office's claim from them of a refund for much of India's expenditure on ibn Sa'ud in excess of the six-month limitation. The Treasury proposed that the Sa'udi subsidy be debited against the accrued surpluses of the Mesopotamian revenues.[14]

Exception was also taken to the failure of the Civil Commissioner in Baghdad to reduce ibn Sa'ud's subsidy in March 1919. Wilson explained that the telegram of March 12th 1919 directing the reduction to £2,500 per month never reached Bahrain.[15] At this time Wilson was en route for Paris and he maintained that on his return to Baghdad he had overlooked this despatch. On July 16th 1920, another telegram from the Secretary of State for India to Wilson mentioned the continuation of the reduced subsidy but Wilson took this to mean £5,000 per month or 'half the 10,000 he had been receiving till December 1919'.[16] Hence, with little interruption, ibn Sa'ud had been receiving his subsidy continuously from January 1917.

In spite of much opposition, the arguments in favour of continuing subsidies were to prevail. From the strictly central Arabian standpoint, the following facts were inescapable. With the disapearance of the Turks from the fringes of Arabia and Mesopotamia, Britain now had become definitely involved in the interior. Given the British subsidy to Fahad Bey of the Amarat and her traditional and treaty relationship with ibn Sa'ud, she faced inevitable entanglement in central Arabian affairs. Strategically, ibn Rashid's and Fahad Bey's territories bordered the British Mandates of Palestine and Mesopotamia. Ibn Sa'ud shared a common border with British-protected Kuwait, the Trucial Shaikhdoms and Oman. These chiefs controlled the territory through which caravan, pilgrim, and projected air and railway routes extended. As military operations were impossible against these shaikhs, and the blockades ineffectual, subsidies were 'the normal, and infinitely the cheapest way' of controlling the tribes. Not only did these chiefs actually require financial assistance in order, in turn, to subsidise their own minor shaikhs but each subsidy to an important shaikh had 'a moral significance out of all proportion to its cash value, and it is that which counts most.'[17]

Again from the strategic viewpoint, the major central Arabian shaikhs were important owing to the proximity of the French in Syria. France, jealous and suspicious of England, could extend her influence as far south as Jauf which lay in the far north of desert Arabia. '... there is in the desert a great field for French intrigue: the tribes want money, and will turn where they can get it. It is worth our while to pay them a retaining fee.' [18]

There was also the belief that Britain had a moral responsibility, now that they had ousted the Turks from Arabia, to replace them. Moreover, the British had championed Arab civilisation ['whatever that may be' as Hirtzel put it] and were honour-bound to employ a policy superior to the former Turkish policy which played off one tribe against another. It was also argued that if the Arabs were left to their own devices, anarchy and rapine would ensue.[19]

In many ways ibn Sa'ud was the lynchpin of Arabia. Although his zealous Wahhabis menaced not only the Holy Lands but their other neighbours, a few prescient observers saw in ibn Sa'ud's Ikhwan settlements the genesis of a future settled Arabian state.

> The real problem is Central Arabia, which is on a much lower cultural level. So long as it remains a cockpit in which Beduin fight over wells and grazing ground, all Arabia is liable to be kept in a turmoil. The key to the situation here, I think, is Bin Saud. Unlike most of the blood-stained scoundrels generically termed 'the noble Arabs', he is a man with some real ideas as to the advancement of his people.[20]

While the London authorities continued to debate the issue of subsidies there was still at this time (autumn 1920) the possibility of effecting a meeting between ibn Sa'ud and King Husain. In view of this and the Sa'udi–Kuwaiti friction, the moment for any cessation of financial assistance was patently unpropitious.

On December 7th 1920, the whole question of subsidies was discussed at an Inter-Deparmental Conference. Austen Chamberlain, the Chancellor of the Exchequer, voiced the opinion that as subsidies in ibn Sa'ud's and Husain's cases had grown out of the War, they should now be reduced to a minium.

He also suggested that 'subsidies should only be paid where they could be supported as an insurance against military commitments'. However, this suggestion came under fire as it would have entailed subsidising British adversaries such as the Imam of Yaman who constantly threatened Aden. Chamberlain reiterated his objection to supporting mutually hostile shaikhs and the fact that Husain (and Faisal) were allegedly using their subsidies to finance anti-French nationalists.[21]

Curzon recounted the successful policy of subsidising recalcitrant tribes on India's northwest frontier and held by way of analogy that the threat of withdrawing their subsidies was the only way to control them. After much arguing back and forth the Conference decided to adopt Hubert Young's plan of providing for Arabian subsidies the provisional annual sum of £100,000 to be distributed among the various shaikhs in proportion to their importance. The cost of this subsidy was to be shared equally between the Imperial Exchequer and the Government of India. The conference also agreed to adhere to treaty obligations and ask other Powers interested in the pilgrimage to contribute to the Hedjaz.[22]

Colonel Kinahan Cornwallis, formerly of the Arab Bureau and now in London, drew up a memorandum outlining the distribution of subsidies. Ibn Sa'ud and Husain were to receive equal amounts while ibn Rashid was to be considered for a subsidy in the year 1921 to 1922 as at present he was too harmless to worry the British. The leaders were to be paid in rupees and not in sovereigns. However, as none of these suggestions, if approved, could come into effect until the following financial year, it was suggested that the Sa'udi susbsidy be reduced progressively until ibn Sa'ud would be receiving by March 1921 only £2,500 a month. Of the total £100,000, ibn Sa'ud could not hope to receive more than £25,000 per annum, or less than half his original subsidy.[23]

Fortunately for British policy in the Arabian peninsula, Churchill, then the Secretary of State for Colonies, opposed the Inter-Departmental Conference's views. He explained that with the shift to the Colonial Office of responsibility for policy and expenditure in the Middle East the position was altered.

> In the circumstances Mr Churchill would strongly deprecate any final decision on the question of subsidies at the present

juncture. He is convinced that expenditure so incurred may prove to be the truest economy in the long run. The subsidy paid to Bin Saud for example, even if it were raised to the figure recommended by Sir P Cox 100,000 pounds per annum, is a negligible quantity as compared with the vast expence of maintaining regular troops in Mesopotamia and elsewhere.[24]

The whole question of subsidies was to be taken up when Churchill framed his budget proposals for 1921–1922. By the spring of 1921 it was decided that ibn Sa'ud was to continue receiving his £5,000 but in rupees as opposed to sovereigns. Husain, contingent upon his agreeing to certain stipulations, was to receive £5,000 per month as well. Both leaders were to receive a grant of £20,000 in addition to their subsidies.[25] Husain, however, refused to come to an agreement with the British; hence, he never received these amounts. Thus after several years of debate it was decided to continue ibn Sa'ud's subsidy at its normal rate. The British also recognised ibn Sa'ud as ' Sultan of Najd and its Dependencies '.

With the shift of responsibility for the Middle East to the Colonial Office, the British sought to end their previous arrangement of divided control in Middle Eastern policy-making. A Middle East Department under the Colonial Office was formed which was responsible for controlling British policy in all Arab countries except the Hedjaz which remained under the Foreign Office. The Colonial Secretary was to be ' held responsible to Parliament not only for civil but also for military expenditure in connection with the Middle East '. It was hoped to reduce spending in the Middle East from an estimated £33½ million in 1921–1922 to around £6 million by 1923–1924.[26]

In February 1921, recovering from the impact of the recent rebellion in Mesopotamia [27] and facing inexorable pressure at home for a definite statement of policy and reduced commitments in the Middle East, Churchill took charge of Middle Eastern affairs. As Colonial Secretary he was to have unified control of and responsibility for British interests in the Middle East. This would eliminate the tortuous arrangement whereby responsibility was shared—and fought over—by the Foreign, India and War Offices on one side and the Government of India on the other. Churchill was directed to establish stable governments and reduce spending and garrisons in the Middle East. A Conference was convened in Cairo under Churchill's chairmanship. The Cairo Conference assembled most of the leading British experts on the Middle East and the details of British policy were formulated.

The following projects discussed at the Conference were to affect ibn Sa'ud.[28] Churchill emphasised the importance of a policy of Imperial aerial development. In view of Sa'udi expansionist tendencies one of the most significant developments of the Conference was the decision to adopt ' Sir High Trenchard's idea of keeping order in Iraq by means of the Air Force '.[29] British plans were to constitute a strong deterrent to Ikhwan raids. The possibilities of air, rail and motor routes spanning the desert from Palestine to Mesopotamia were discussed while Sir Arnold Wilson, now Managing Director of the firm which operated the British-controlled Anglo–Persian Oil Company, was consulted about the possible construction of a trans-desert pipeline.[30]

One of Churchill's first decisions after assuming responsibility for the Middle East was to prove detrimental to Anglo–Sa'udi relations. Working with Lawrence in an attempt to redress the grievances suffered by Husain at the hands of the British, Churchill placed Faisal on the Iraqi throne while ' entrusting his brother 'Abdullah with the government of the vacant lot which the British christened the Amirate of Transjordan '.[31] Ibn Sa'ud's capture of Hail in 1921 brought him into direct contact with both of these British-protected Hashimite rulers.

The End of Rashidi Rule

By the spring of 1918 even a figure so friendly to ibn Sa'ud as Sir Percy Cox had begun to think about the post-war situation in central Arabia and the possible position there which ibn Rashid might occupy. On March 23rd 1918 at a meeting at the Residency in Cairo concerned with the political future of Arabia, Cox had suggested a post-war policy of maintaining a balance of power in Arabia. As it was put at the time:

> ... it would seem that the continued independent rule of ibn Rashid there would better preserve the balance of power in Arabia.[32]

After the War had ended, Cox's suggestion, supported by Cairo, was rejected. Had Britain adopted this policy they would, in effect, have been perpetuating the traditional Turkish policy of pitting one chief against another. However, in spite of Britain's avowed policy to reduce her Arabian commitments to a minimum and her wish—albeit unattainable—to avoid entanglement in central Arabian affairs, Saʿud ibn Rashid's importance could not be overlooked.[33]

As has been mentioned elsewhere, the Rashidi Amir's influence extended to the western borders of Iraq while his domains lay across pilgrim and caravan routes.[34] In view of his strategic importance, the Foreign Office favoured subsidising him to insure themselves against the possibility that ibn Rashid might use his position to the detriment of British interests. While still Civil Commissioner in Baghdad, A. T. Wilson had suggested that ibn Rashid be granted a subsidy of £37,500 per annum.[35] Although the possible effect of this subsidy on Anglo–Saʿudi relations was not overlooked, the arguments for a Rashidi subsidy gained impetus when the Amir of Hail's followers captured Jauf and Sakaka in the northernmost reaches of desert Arabia, thus consolidating the Rashidi position against the Ruwalla.[36]

While the London authorities debated which office was to foot the bill for this subsidy, the entire situation was altered by the assassination of Saʿud ibn Rashid by one of his relatives. After the assassin himself was put to death, the Amirate was assumed by a thirteen-year-old boy, ʿAbd al-ʿAziz ibn Mitʿab. One of his uncles was appointed regent.[37] By this example of Rashidi self-destruction, ibn Saʿud's position in central Arabia was greatly strengthened. Soon after the assassination, ibn Saʿud sought to consolidate his power by concluding an agreement between himself and the leaders of Hail. This Saʿudi–Rashidi agreement declared that: (1) Hail's foreign relations were to be conducted only through Riyadh, (2) the Shammar were to be entirely under Saʿudi control and all disputes were to be submitted directly to ibn Saʿud and, (3) the Amirate was to remain independent in internal affairs but with ultimate control resting in Saʿudi hands.[38] The ramifications of the new accretion to ibn Saʿud's power were aptly summed up in a minute by an India Office official.

> Bin Saud by re-establishing the influence of Nejd over the Shammar has thus doubled his territory: and he will now

have influence presumably over the whole of the western half of the Syrian desert. He is in close touch with the Anaizah, and if they too accept his supremacy, the whole desert between Syria and Mesopotamia will be his and he will be the one person with whom Mesopotamia must not quarrel. The omen of 1790 will not be lost on Bin Saud. The last time the Shammar accepted his house, he was about to take Mecca. They have again accepted it.[39]

Although, by ibn Sa'ud's reckoning, two-thirds of Hail's inhabitants accepted the Sa'udi–Rashidi agreement, fighting soon broke out betwen the Ikhwan and certain sections of the Shammar who objected to his rule.[40] These hostilities culminated in the capitulation of Hail the following year. On November 4th 1921 ibn Sa'ud occupied Hail 'by negotiation and without bloodshed'.[41] The members of the Rashidi family were arrested and taken to Najd to live in honourable capitvity.[42] Unlike many of the other Bedouin leaders, ibn Sa'ud usually treated the adversaries he vanquished with benevolence. As a result they became devoted to him and other tribes were impressed by both his strength and magnanimity. In commenting on the capture of Hail, Cox's gifted Oriental Secretary, Gertrude Bell—described by Hardinge as a 'remarkably clever woman with the brain of a man'[43]—underlined the importance of the Sa'udi conquest and offered a contemporary insight into the influence exercised by Cox, not only on ibn Sa'ud, but on many of the shaikhs of Arabia.

> The conquest of Hayil will have far-reaching consequences. It will bring Ibn Saud into the theatre of Trans-Jordanian politics and probably into the Franco–Syrian vista also—it's difficult as yet to see with what result. I should, however, feel much greater anxiety if I weren't so certain of Sir Percy's power to guide him. It's really amazing that anyone should exercise influence such as his. ... I don't think that any European in history has made a deeper impression on the Oriental mind...[44]

The legendary influence of Sir Percy Cox was soon to find expression in the definition of the Iraq–Najd and Kuwait–Najd borders which took place at Mohammmera in 1922. The following two sections give ample indication of Sa'udi expansionism and

The Najdi-Kuwaiti Border Dispute

The long-standing feud betwen ibn Sa'ud and Shaikh Salim [45] continued to worsen after the War had ended and by 1920 hostilities broke out between the two leaders. These clashes were occasioned by Salim's assertion of his jurisdiction over the area assigned to Kuwait by the Anglo–Turkish Agreement of 1913 [46] and ibn Sa'ud's refusal to accept this assertion.

The Anglo–Turkish Agreement had assigned to Kuwait direct control over a small expanse of land immediately around the town of Kuwait, and 'indirect control, with the power of levying taxes on the tribes, over a much larger area to the south...'.[47] The frontier ran 'from Jabal Manifah on the sea to Hafar al Batin in the west, and up the Batin valley to opposite Jabal Sanam, etc. in the north'.[48] This gave Kuwait indirect control over an area stretching from about 135 to 160 miles from Kuwait town. Early in 1920, Salim, determined to press his claims, announced that he intended to build a fort at Dauht Balbul which lay on the coast to the north of Jabal Manifa, 'to signify that this was his southernmost boundary'.[49] Events once again developed into an exercise of move and countermove; the perennial chess game of desert politics. Ibn Sa'ud answered Salim's challenge by instructing the Mutair Shaikh, ibn Shuqair, to seize Jariya which was claimed by Salim. The Shaikh of Kuwait retaliated by sending the commander of the Kuwaiti forces 'with his warflag' to Hamdh which lay only fifteen miles east of Jariya.[50] Thus the stage was set for conflict.

Ibn Shuqair, fearing imminent attack, apparently invoked the assistance of Shaikh Faisal al Duwish, chief of the Mutair tribe. On the morning of April 18th 1920, Faisal, at the head of a force of Ikhwan, attacked and routed the Kuwaiti forces.[51] As Dickson, the Political Agent at Bahrain, put it: '... Kuwait trod on a lion's tail and caught a tartar'.[52] As the remaining members of the Kuwaiti force marched back to Kuwait town, Salim, fearing an imminent Ikhwan attack on the town itself hastened to build his famous wall around Kuwait proper. 'It was completed in two months, the whole population taking a hand in the form of a *levée en masse*'.[53]

Shortly after this incident, ibn Sa'ud wrote to Dickson asking the British to settle the matter or to let the two chiefs 'fight it out'.⁵⁴ While the British government was considering the issue, a letter from Salim to ibn Sa'ud reached the Political Agent in Bahrain. This letter remonstrated with ibn Sa'ud and ended with a threat of war if Faisal al Duwish were not induced to compensate for Kuwaiti losses.⁵⁵ On June 1st Salim followed up his letter by sending a deputation to ibn Sa'ud demanding the aforementioned compensation. This deputation returned to Kuwait accompanied by a Sa'udi emissary who presented a letter from ibn Sa'ud to Salim. In this correspondence ibn Sa'ud not only claimed Jariya but issued an ultimatum for Salim's signature. Had Salim signed, his signature would have been 'tantamount to giving away all the country he claimed east and west of Jariya'.⁵⁶ Ibn Sa'ud ended his letter with an unambiguous threat.

> I advise you to accept my ultimatum and sign attached paper otherwise I shall attack you when you next annoy me.⁵⁷

At this point it is desirable to consider the respective bases of ibn Sa'ud's and Salim's claims and the legal and political considerations surrounding this dispute. Ibn Sa'ud based his claim on the extent of his forefathers' territories. This would have brought the Najd frontier 'to within 20 miles of the town, as in Col. Lewis Pelly's report on his journey from Kuwait to Riyadh in 1865 ...'. Moreover, by the conversion to Ikhwanism of the Mutair who resided in the disputed area, ibn Sa'ud had a strong practical case. The boundaries as fixed by the Anglo–Turkish Agreement were based on Shakespear's information which in turn was based on Mubarak's power to impose order and levy taxes on his surrounding tribes. Shakespear had summed up the 'unwritten desert law' when he defined a Shaikh's power in the following terms.

> All Arab shaikhs base the territorial extent of their power upon their ability to enforce some order over the adjacent tribes, their power to enforce the payment of 'zikat' by Beduin, and their capacity to prevent and to avenge outrages and raids within the territorial limits claimed.⁵⁸

By the above standards Mubarak had been sovereign within the area assigned to him by the Agreement of 1913. However, by the same standard, the ebb and flow of desert politics had now seen the ascendancy of ibn Saʻud accompanied by the corresponding decline of Mubarak's successors. In essence, ibn Saʻud based his claim on desert law while Salim based his ʻon a document as would a civilised state'. There were further issues to be taken into consideration. Legally, the Anglo–Turkish Agreement had never been ratified; moreover, the Ottoman Empire had ceased to exist. In addition, Clause 6 of the Anglo–Saʻudi Treaty was thought to have superceded the 1913 Agreement. The issue was further complicated by the fact that ibn Saʻud could argue logically from the tribal point of view that while Mubarak had been strong Salim was weak and hence could not claim the same boundaries. However, ibn Saʻud himself had refuted this line of argument when in signing his 1915 Treaty, he agreed in Clause 1 that his descendants would rule after him. These descendants, like Salim, might conceivably someday be weaker than ibn Saʻud. The British also faced the problem that while only ibn Saʻud could control the tribes in the disputed area, some sections of local opinion attached importance to the Anglo–Turkish Agreement and any decision against Salim would be viewed as a breach of faith by the British and alienate Kuwaiti feeling.[59]

After weighing these considerations, the British decided on arbitration. Salim was told that the Anglo–Turkish Agreement was drawn up under conditions which no longer obtained, that he was not a party to this agreement and that in any case the 1913 Agreement had been superceded by Clause 6 of the Anglo–Saʻudi Treaty of 1915. He was advised not to sign ibn Saʻud's ultimatum and to invoke the arbitration of the British government. The Kuwaiti leader was also advised to take no further action in or around Jariya. In Baghdad, A. T. Wilson evinced predilection for ibn Saʻud's case when he stated that ʻthe result ... [of arbitration] is in my opinion likely to restrict his [Salim's] territory to an area less than that given in the Anglo–Turkish Convention but this need not be told him'. Ibn Saʻud was accordingly warned against hostilities pending arbitration.[60]

While the plans for arbitration were being made, Sir Percy Cox returned to Baghdad as High Commissioner, replacing Wilson. On his way to Baghdad Cox met ibn Saʻud at ʻUqair. The Wahhabi leader asserted his demands, maintaining that he was unaware of any boundaries as laid down by an Anglo–

Turkish Agreement. On the one hand Cox pointed out to ibn Sa'ud that Kuwait had to have a hinterland otherwise it would never be free from the fear of raids, on the other hand, he informed Salim that Britain could not support frontiers that she had been willing to obtain against the Ottoman Empire. Both parties agreed to accept arbitration. Cox also expressed his view to the Government that this border dispute resulted from the bad relations prevailing between the two shaikhs and that if they would 'bury the hatchet', the dispute would disappear. The High Commissioner urged further that as the boundary would be difficult to settle owing to fickle tribal allegiances, ibn Sa'ud and Salim should meet during the winter and the British should only arbitrate if the two were unable to come to an agreement themselves.[61] This was accepted.

On Cox's arrival in Kuwait he learned that Salim had raised a large force at Jahra at the head of Kuwait bay. The High Commissioner advised him to demobilise. Salim refused and on 10th October, the day of Cox's arrival in Baghdad, Faisal al Dawish and his Ikhwan attacked and defeated Salim's forces.[62] Salim himself was trapped with other leaders in a fort to the southwest of the city. Faisal later withdrew and Salim returned to Kuwait; both claimed victory. Major J. C. More, the Political Agent at Kuwait, reported that the Kuwaitis had lost 200 men, whereas the Ikhwan, with characteristic disregard for life, were estimated to have lost 1,200 dead.[63]

Faisal later demanded that all Kuwaities become Ikhwan. The Shaikh of Kuwait called on the British for assistance. Major More informed a Mutair delegation that any attack on Kuwait town would be opposed by the British 'by every convenient means'. Immediate hostilities were prevented by Britain's unequivocal intention to protect Kuwait town. Warnings were dropped by airplanes on the Mutair tribes. No attack occurred.[64]

In January 1921 the Shaikh of Mohammera offered to arrange a truce between the Kuwaitis and Sa'udis. A mission consisting of the Shaikh's eldest son, Chasib, and Salim's nephew, Shaikh Ahmad, the next ruler of Kuwait and a friend of ibn Sa'ud's, was sent to Najd. After the mission's arrival at Riyadh, it was announced that Salim had died. Ibn Sa'ud declared immediately that the dispute was ended and that there was 'no need for a boundary between his territory and Wuwait'.[65] However, with the temporary cessation of Najdi–Kuwaiti friction, British

The Najdi-Iraqi Dispute

In 1921 trouble flared up on the frontier between Najd and Iraq owing to the influx into Iraq of certain Shammari and other tribal elements who rejected Sa'udi overlordship. Ibn Sa'ud's capture of Hail had brought the Ikhwan to the ill-defined borders of southern Iraq. Raids and counter-raids—the traditional Bedouin pastime—were exchanged as the Ikhwan confronted the Iraqi Amarat, Dhafir and Muntafiq. The situation was further exacerbated by the appointment of a Sa'dun of the Muntafiq to command the Iraqi Desert Police on the Najd frontier. This Iraqi shaikh was personally hostile to one of the Dhafir shaikhs who followed ibn Sa'ud. Friction on the frontier was, of course, worsened by the traditional enmity prevailing between the Sa'udi and the Hashimite families. While on the one hand the capture of Hail had no doubt increased Sa'udi ambitions, on the other ' it was even whispered that the ' Iraqi monarch, in his private or dynastic capacity, was not unwilling that the anti-Hashimite Najdi prince should be thus harassed '.[66]

There was also another aspect of these problems which cut across the existing political pattern. From the economic standpoint, the tribes of northern and northeastern Najd, especially the Shammar, Harb, Mutair, 'Awazim, Ajman and Dhafir, had from time immemorial migrated in autumn towards Kuwait and the Euphrates ' to obtain the necessities of life '.[67] The political enmity existing between Riyadh and Baghdad, coupled with local tribal troubles, interrupted these natural migratory habits. As the Iraqi state began to take shape and Sa'udi power increased, the political issue was complicated by the economic one.

On March 11th 1922, matters came to a head with the unprovoked attack by Faisal al Dawish at the head of a force of Ikhwan—whose numbers were given at somewhere between 500 and 2,000—on Iraqi tribesmen at Abu Ghar. After slaughtering many of the tribesmen and capturing their camels and livestock, they advanced on a nearby contingent of the Iraqi Desert Police. Cox sent airplanes to keep the Ikhwan under surveillance and although instructed not to fire upon them unless their planes were attacked, the small group of British pilots were forced to attack the Ikhwan when they met heavy fire from the retreating raiders.[68] This encounter not only tried the patience of the British officials in Baghdad who were endeavouring to build a new administration in Iraq, but also had implications which transcended tribal politics.

Faisal prevailed upon Cox to bomb the Ikhwan but this course threatened to rupture not only English but also Iraqi relations with Najd. There was, moreover, the fear that if Anglo–Sa'udi relations were disrupted, ibn Sa'ud might turn his energies towards the Hedjaz. Faisal argued that as the mandatory power Britain was obliged to protect Iraq. In what, for the comparatively upright Faisal, was the first of several dramatic instances of *Realpolitik* taking precedence over filial allegiance, he stated 'that the interests of the Hedjaz must be disregarded'. The Iraqi monarch urged 'very strongly that unless we [the British mandatory] retaliate by bombing at once he cannot carry on his government'. Faisal concluded his importunities by threatening that if Britain could not protect him then they should 'stand aside and let him rally his tribes to attack Bin Saud's Akhwan'.[69] In view of the above dangers, a conference was convened at Mohammera in May 1922. Its purpose was to settle the differences between Najd and Iraq.

On May 5th 1922 in the presence of Sir Percy Cox, the Treaty of Mohammera was signed by delegates from Najd and Iraq. Article I of this agreement stipulated that the Shammar of Najd appertained to Najd while the Amarat, Dhafir and Muntafiq belonged to Iraq. The boundary between the two countries was to be based on the location of pastures and wells used by the said tribes. It was further decided that a party of delegates from both sides should meet in Baghdad under the presidency of a British official to work out the details of this boundary. Article II ensured the safety of pilgrims and Article III provided for normal commercial intercourse between the two countries. Articles IV and V dealt with freedom of travel and grazing fees while Article VI declared that if there should occur a breach of relations between Najd, Iraq and Great Britain, the treaty would become null and void. Pending the decision of the projected meeting in Baghdad, the Ikhwan were pledged not to attack Iraqi tribes. The Treaty was subject to ratification by Faisal and ibn Sa'ud.[70]

No definite frontier was fixed owing to the nature of the Bedouin's annual migrations.

> The Nejed delegates were far more vividly aware than were the Iraqis or the British that the very existence of nomadic tribes depended on their power to migrate and graze freely. So fickle was the desert rainfall that in some years, the greater part of Nejed might be afflicted with drought. In such cases, it was essential for the very survival of the Nejed tribes that they be able to move northwards towards Iraq or Syria in search of some desert area where rain had fallen. Conversely the northern tribes might at times be obliged to migrate for a whole season to Nejed. To draw a hard and fast frontier across the desert wastes seemed to the Nejdis to threaten the very existence of those tribes... constituted a great part of Ibn Sa'ud's armed forces.[71]

With the singing of the Mohammera Treaty the imminent danger of a large scale conflagration on the Iraqi–Najd frontier abated. Attention, however, soon shifted from one Hashimite problem to another. The annual pilgrimage to Mecca was approaching and ibn Sa'ud's followers were making ready to visit the Holy City. Although minor skirmishes between the Ikhwan and Husain's followers occurred intermittently throughout the early 1920s, tension was mounting as the Hajj approached in 1922.

Ibn Sa'ud wrote to Cox stating that it would be impossible to prevent his subjects from making the pilgrimage for the fourth consecutive year. He guaranteed that there would be no aggression on the part of the Najdis.[72] The British contacted Husain and demanded reciprocal guarantees from him for the Najdi pilgrims. The situation, however, was complicated by reports coming into the Foreign Office from Jedda which stated that Ikhwan tenets were spreading rapidly in the Hedjaz. Faisal was contacted by his brother Zaid and informed that the Hedjaz was in great danger. Faisal expressed his fears to Cox and attributed the situation to the 'mad obstinacy of his father which has alienated his subjects as well as hostilized [sic] his neighbours'. Demonstrating the ever-growing British dissatisfaction with Husain, the High Commissioner asked Faisal about the possibility that he and his brothers might depose their father. Faisal 'replied that in principle that would be a salutary measure which he would welcome at heart but it would be impossible to bring it off just at the time of the pilgrimage '. Faisal urged that ibn Sa'ud be requested to postpone the pilgrimage yet again.[73]

The Foreign Office suggested that the Najdis surrender their weapons at Taif to a British Agent. Churchill rejected this proposal because if any disaster were to befall the Najdis, Great Britain would be held directly accountable. The Colonial Secretary felt that any further interference with the pilgrimage would be useless.[74] Cox had already been instructed to impress upon ibn Sa'ud the seriousness of good conduct and had requested that the Sa'udi pilgrimage be limited in numbers. The High Commissioner, confronted by Faisal's threat to leave his throne to help his family in the Hedjaz,[75] displayed rare emotion in a telegram to the Colonial Office in which he accused Churchill of ' disinterestedness '. Cox continued in his depatch to remonstrate with London and vividly portray the implications of a possible conflagration in the Hedjaz.[76]

> Is it that danger of conflagration is not considered serious in view of Bin Saud's guarantee or is it that His Majesty's Government are tired of Hussein and all his works and consider any change that may come in Hedjaz would be welcomed as being an improvement on existing state of affairs?
>
> If former is the principal ground, I would respectfully observe that no guarantees have been given by Husain, that he is practically demented and that there is no suicidal act of provocation of which he might not be capable. Faisal admits as much.
>
> It latter is the principal ground, I can only repeat the conviction that any untoward incident in the Hedjaz during the pilgrimage is bound to re-act injuriously upon our interests throughout Islam. In India for instance, it would bring grist to the mill of Khilafat propaganda and support their contention that the Arabs are not suitable rulers for the Hedjaz; it would encourage Kemalists in their claim as an Islamic military power to regain control over the holy places; and generally the blame for any bloodshed either at Mecca or Medina would undoubtedly be laid at our door; we should be charged with inability to secure the safety of pilgrims and neglect to bring the existing danger to the notice of other Islamic states concerned.[77]

Churchill, however, refused to be alarmed by Cox's fears. The Colonial Secretary telegraphed to the High Commissioner that the Government was 'by no means indifferent' but as they possessed no means of threatening Husain and military intervention was 'out of the question' the British government were 'unwilling to menace . . . ibn Sa'ud with stoppage of his subsidy to cover the hypothetical contingency of his breaking his promise'.[78] In spite of much fear and trepidation in Baghdad and an apparently equal amount of *sang froid* in London, the pilgrimage passed without event. One thousand, eight hundred Najdis performed the pilgrimage, causing no trouble.[79]

In spite of the Ikhwan raids into Iraq, ibn Sa'ud repeatedly demonstrated characteristic statesmanship which was not duplicated by Husain. Although the Najdis had caused no trouble in the Hedjaz, Husain confiscated £5,000 in gold from the returning pilgrims declaring that the 'export of gold was illegal'.[80] The King of the Hedjaz also wrote ibn Sa'ud a letter in which he demanded the restoration of Rashidi rule in Hail and the surrender of certain tribes and some villages in Qasim.[81] Husain also manifested his anti-British attiudes which led London officials such as Sir Arthur Hirtzel to write: 'The feeling is growing that it would be a good thing if Ibn Saud did establish himself at Mecca, though no doubt we would have one or two bad quarters of an hour before things settled down'.[82] Ibn Sa'ud reported that Husain had declared that

> he was ready to *abdicate in my favour* if I would join him in helping to expel European powers from Arabia, and cease to be a partisan of British and a tool in their hands for intimidation of Iraq and weakening of Arabs by setting one against another. . . . He talked lot about Palestine and made it to be Jewish state from which Moslems were expelled to make room for Jews which was also due to British.[83]

With the peaceful passing of the pilgrimage, British attention was re-directed to northeastern Arabia. Whereas Faisal had ratified the Treaty of Mohammera, ibn Sa'ud repudiated the agreement. The reason given by the Wahhabi leader for this repudiation was that his representative had disobeyed his instructions in assigning the Dhafir, Amarat and western Muntafiq to Iraq. It was speculated that one of the possible reasons for the repudiation might have been Sa'udi fears of Transjordan's hostile activities in the direction of Jauf.[84] Ibn Sa'ud claimed this area which Philby described as ' the northernmost principality of desert Arabia '.[85] Perhaps Sa'udi fears of being outflanked by hostile Hashimite monarchs led the Wahhabi leader to reject the treaty and reclaim as many tribes as he could.

In the autumn of 1922 as the Chanak Crisis in Turkey which was to bring down Lloyd George's government reached its apex, Cox endeavoured to prevent another Middle Eastern crisis in northern Arabia by arranging a further meeting between Iraq and Najd. Ibn Sa'ud had already written to the High Commissioner complaining of attacks on him in the Iraq press and requesting a meeting with Cox to settle his Hashimite problems.[86]

At the end of November 1922, Sir Percy Cox met ibn Sa'ud at the port of 'Uqair. The purpose of the meeting was to solve the frontier problem between Najd and Iraq and to fix a boundary between Najd and Kuwait. Cox was accompanied, among others, by Faisal's delegate, the Iraqi Minister of Communications and Works, Sabih Bey and Fahad Bey, chief of the Amarat, the Iraqi division of the 'Anaza. Major J. C. More, the Political Agent at Kuwait, represented the interests of the Shaikh of Kuwait. Major Dickson, the Political Agent in Bahrain was present, as was Amin Rihani. Ibn Sa'ud arrived with a bodyguard of about 300 men. Some idea of the contrast between Cox, the sophisticated representative of the greatest imperial power of the time and ibn Sa'ud, the Bedouin leader from a country little changed for millennia is preserved in a picture taken of the two at the conference. Ibn Sa'ud in his tribal attire is seated next to Cox who is dressed in a lounge suit, high-laced boots and a trilby.[87]

Ibn Sa'ud based his claim on the Dhafir and Amarat, both now considered Iraq tribes, on the fact that they had belonged to his ancestors, thereby indicating once again that he intended to expand his power to the confines enjoyed by the early nineteenth-century Wahhabi empire. He maintained that both tribes had formerly resided in Najd but had since migrated to Iraq.[88] Cox was in a somewhat difficult position. He had been friendly with ibn Sa'ud for over a decade and was in turn greatly trusted by him; Cox was also the High Commissioner of Iraq and morally bound to protect Faisal's interests. In the end there was little alternative for Cox, he was forced to prevail upon ibn

Sa'ud to relinquish his claim to the two—presently—Iraq tribes. Ibn Sa'ud, however, fought against a clearly demarcated boundary between the two states.[89]

Ibn Sa'ud pressed for a tribal boundary marked by a system of wells and grazing grounds as opposed to the European expedient of an arbitrary line drawn in the desert. Any wells which were the common property ' such as existed between the 'Anizah 'Amarat division and the Dhafir and between the Dhafir and the Mutair—should be declared neutral '. The Iraqi delegate rejoined by claiming that Baghdad would accept ' nothing less than a frontier at least two hundred miles south of the Euphrates '. As the conference neared the end of its first week, Cox neared the end of his patience. The negotiations had got nowhere. Sir Percy then stepped in and took matters into his own hands.[90]

Cox informed both sides that they were achieving nothing. At a private meeting with ibn Sa'ud, Cox reprimanded him ' like a naughty schoolboy ' for his ' childish attitude ' regarding his desire for a tribal boundary. After this meeting, according to Dickson, ibn Sa'ud left the decision on his boundaries to the High Commissioner. Cox proceeded then to draw unilaterally the borders between Iraq and Najd and Najd and Kuwait. The following passage by Dickson describes Cox's action, the reasoning behind the borders and offers one of the first expressions of the future importance of oil.[91]

> At a general meeting of the conference, Sir Percy took up a red pencil and very carefully drew in on the map of Arabia a boundary line from the Persian Gulf to Jabal 'Anaizan, close to the Transjordan frontier. This gave Iraq a large area of territory claimed by Najd. Obviously to placate Ibn Sa'ud, he ruthlessly deprived Kuwait of nearly two-thirds of her territory and gave it to Najd, his argument being that the power of Ibn Sabah was much less in the desert than it had been when the Anglo–Turkish Agreement had been drawn up. South and west of Kuwait proper, he drew out two zones, which he declared should be neutral and known as the Kuwait Neutral Zone and the Iraq Neutral Zone. Replying to the mild expostulations of ... [ibn Sa'ud's advisor] against the need for a Kuwait Neutral Zone, Sir Percy said that the Kuwait tribes proper

must have more grazing room. Pressed by ... [the Sa'udi advisor], he snapped out: 'Why, pray, are you so anxious that this area go to Najd?'

'Quite candidly,' the Pasha replied, 'because we think oil exists there.' 'That,' retorted Sir Percy, 'is exactly why I have made it a neutral zone. Each side shall have a half share.' [92]

The Political Agent in Bahrain also reported the following remarkable scene. After Cox drew the boundaries ibn Sa'ud asked Cox to come and see him. Ibn Sa'ud proceeded to break into tears bewailing the loss of land to Iraq. Cox too became upset and began to weep. In answer to ibn Sa'ud's lamentations Cox replied: 'My friend, I know exactly how you feel and for this reason I gave you two-thirds of Kuwait's territory. I don't know how Ibn Sabah will take the blow.' [93]

Cox's boundary between Iraq and Najd has remained until this day. The drawbacks of a western-type boundary in a nomadic society were partly offset by the neutral zone. Moreover, the neutral zone between Kuwait and Najd was the only practical solution to the possibility of oil being discovered there and the inevitable dispute arising over drilling rights. However, Cox's action did not escape criticism.

Dickson took rather a dim view of the rejection of the Sa'udi tribal boundary and the adoption of the European demarcation. There was substance in the Political Agent's opinion that the Najd–Kuwait settlement was based purely on expediency. Dickson believed that Cox's action had the aura of a cavalier assignment for the purposes of appeasement of a small and weak state's territory to its stronger and more troublesome neighbour. It is also true that Cox was bound to damage his reputation by his actions. The effect on Kuwait of losing nearly two-thirds of her territory was less than salutary.[94]

As a result of these Protocols, and, probably of the Sa'udi desire to avoid possible conflict with hostile neighbours, ibn Sa'ud

> apparently decided on a policy of slowly but surely diverting his people from their old and time-honoured communication with Iraq and Kuwait, trying instead to force them to get the necessities of life and daily requirements from 'Uqair, Qatif, and Jubail, his ports on the Persian Gulf.

> ... But natural lines of trade cannot thus be lightly interfered with or laid aside, and, as a result of this policy, we have seen nothing but trouble. Had Ibn Sa'ud left well alone, it is not improbable that we should not have had the Ikhwan rebellion of 1929–30, or the friction between Iraq and Najd that preceded it, or the long-drawn-out fourteen years' agony of the Kuwait blockade.[95]

With reference to the Iraq–Najd border, Amin Rihani, who assisted Cox with translations several times during the conference, offers an interesting contemporary insight into British methods and the reasoning behind these actions. With regard to a cable sent by Cox to Churchill—which he translated to ibn Sa'ud—suggesting that Qoraiyat ul-Milh (Rihani's spelling) in the neighbourhood of Jauf be assigned to ibn Sa'ud, Rihani concluded an entry to his diary with the following words:

> This is a part of the compensation made to him [ibn Sa'ud] for conceding to Iraq his right of sovereignty over the 'Amarat and Dhafir. We take from Ibn Sa'oud to satisfy Iraq, and we take from Trans-Jordania to placate Ibn Sa'oud.[96]

While it can be argued that a clearly defined boundary in such a nomadic area is anomalous, it can equally be argued that in view of the hostility prevailing between Iraq, Najd and Kuwait, some line had to be fixed to avoid constant claims and counterclaims. Also, with the westernisation of Iraq and the Middle East in general—not excluding the potential settlement of Arabia owing to the Ikhwan movement—it could be said that a western-style boundary was inevitable.

Notes

1. During the First World War Muhammad ibn 'Ali Al Idrisi of the 'Asir had declared for Great Britain and fought against the Turks. ' Following the war the Wahhabi forces of Ibn Sa'ud conquered ' Asir in 1920 as part of the Hijaz campaign, but the Idrisi still controlled the northern Tihameh and the port of Al-Hudaydah which the British had handed over to him after his withdrawal in 1921. The following year Sayyid Huhammad Al Idrisi died, and a civil war ensued between his son, 'Ali Al Idrisi, and his brother, Husayn for control'. See *Collins*, pp. 208, 209, n: 13. For further reference to ibn Sa'ud's incursions into 'Asir, see p. 235, n. 71.

2. In view of the limitations imposed by the need for selectivity, attention will be directed mainly to ibn Sa'ud and secondly to the paramount north central Arabian shaikhs. By 1921, Britain assisted financially by way of direct subsidies ibn Sa'ud (£60,000 annually), the Sultan of Muscat (186,400 rupees annually), the Sultan of Shehr and Mokalla (Hadhramaut) (720 rupees annually), Fahad Bey-Shaikh of the Amarat—(204,000 rupees annually), and the Aden protectorate chiefs (70,000 rupees annually). Also, until the end of the War, Husain had received £200,000 per month and more than a few high-ranking officials urged the resumption—on a lesser scale—of his subsidy. See 'Memorandum by Col. Cornwallis...', Dec. 16, 1920, No. 9035; *L/P & S/10*, 488/1920, Pts. 1, 2. Hereafter *Cornwallis' Memo*.
3. *Ibid.*
4. 'FO Memorandum on the Subsidies to King Husain and ibn Sa'ud', July 7, 1920, in Appendix D. of 'Foreign Office Memorandum on Arabian Policy', n.d. (Hereafter *FO Memo*), No. 497; *L/P & S/10*, 7251/1920, Pts. 2, 3.
5. *FO Memo.*
6. Allenbq to Curzon, May 28, 1920 (L), in App. D., *FO Memo*, No. 497; *L/P & S/10*, 7251/1920, Pts. 2, 3. In his urgings for an increased subsidy for ibn Sa'ud, Cox cited the growing anti-European and nationalist sentiment in the Middle East. Morevore, there was trouble on the Mosul frontier an Husain was reported to be in correspondence with Mustafa Kemal. As a Bolshevist-inspired nationalist-cum-Pan-Islamic movement in the Middle East was thought possible, Cox continually stressed ibn Sa'ud's importance. See HCB [High Commissioner, Bagdad to SSI, Oct. 21, 1920 (T), No. 8376; *L/P & S/10*, 7251] 1920, Pt. 1.
7. *Ibid.*
8. Dickson reported from Bahrain that ibn Sa'ud owed Qasim merchants six lacs of rupees. He also owed one lac to his agent in Bahrain. See memo on the 'Political Situation in Nejd' by Dickson, Aug. 12, 1920, No. 7564; *L/P & S/10*, 7251/ 1920, Pt. 1.
9. CC [Civil Com. Bagh] to SSI, Aug. 19, 1920 (T), No. 6281; *L/P & S/10*, 488/1920, Pts. 1, 2. Ibn Sa'ud received his goods through Kuwait and Bahrain, thereby losing the customs duties to these two shaikhdoms; moreover, the resentment of ibn Sa'ud prevailing in these two countries made this arrangement impractical. Dickson believed that were the ports of 'Uqair and Jubail developed, ibn Sa'ud could probably earn 40 lacs of rupees annually. See an 'Extract on the Ikhwan Movement' byk Dickson, June 5, 1920, no No. *L/P & S/10*, 756/1917.
10. 'The policy of subsidies' by A. H[irtzel], n.d., No. 2274; *L/P & S/10*, 488/1920, Pts. 1, 2. Hereafter *Hirtzel's Note*.
11. 'Question of Future Policy, Subsidies to Chiefs...', by J. E. S[huckburgh], Oct. 29, 1920, No. 7950, *L/P & S/10*, 7251/1920, Pt. 1.
12. See p. 101.
13. IO to FO, April 8, 1920 (L), No. 1885; *L/P & S/10*, 493/1916.

Hirtzel claimed to have been at fault in overlooking the six-month stipulation. See minute to the foregoing by A. H[irtzel], June 5, 1920. Given the many IDC gatherings at which their respective representatives discussed, among other issues, the Sa'udi subsidy, it is curious that none of the various governmental departments—including the Treasury—ever commented on the fact that subsidy had exceeded its sanction.

14. Treasury to FO, April 20, 1920 (L), No. 3122; *ibid*. This suggestion was vehemently opposed by Wilson and later by Cox. It also raised a legal question. An Army of Occupation could apply to any liberated (hence friendly) as opposed to a conquered (or enemy) territory; therefore, a case could be made against the Treasury's suggestion. See Minute by C. C. Garbett, June 8, 120, No. 3334; *L/P & S/10*, 4931/1916.
15. See p. 141.
16. CC to SSI, Dec. 12, 1919 (T), No. 8059; *ibid*. Wilson here and in other despatches confused the dates of the period during which ibn Sa'ud received an enhanced subsidy of £10,000 as opposed to his usual £5,000 per month. From the records and Philby's *Najd Report*, ibn Sa'ud received £10,000 per month in September and October 1919 as a reward for his attack on Hail and to placate him as British advances in the north all but eliminated his military usefulness. For a breakdown of the total expenditure made to ibn Sa'ud until March 1920 (which totalled £265,000) see J. A. Simpson's Minutes of Feb. 20th and March 30th, 1920, Nos. 486 and 1885; *L/P & S/10*, 4931/1916. For wartime expenditures, see Philby's *Najd Report*.
17. *Hirtzel's Note*.
18. *Ibid*.
19. *Ibid*.
20. *Ibid*. In view of this quotation and his many other less than charitable comments, it need not be emphasised that the Under Secretary of State for India, Sir Arthur Hirtzel, was not exactly sympathetic to Arabs. Even such a hard-line imperialist as Arnold Wilson wrote of Hirtzel, in relation to the post-war settlement in Mesopotamia, that he was 'too anti-Turk and anti-Mohammedan to be quite a safe guide for HMG in these matters...' See Wilson to Cox, May 9, 1919 (Private L); Wilson MSS [British Museum], Add. 52455–747 E.
21. Minute of IDC, Dec. 7, 1920, No. 3082; *L/P & S/10*, 488/1920, Pts. 1, 2.
22. *Ibid*. Hubert Young was Secretary to the IDC and later Secretary to the Middle East Department of the Colonial Office. By virtue of treaty relationships as opposed to custom or policy, the British subsidised the Sultans of Shehr and Mokalla and Muscat and the Aden protectorate chiefs. The suggestion of sharing the cost subsidies was strongly opposed by the Viceroy. He argued that Indian public opinion was hostile to the spending of Indian revenues outside India. He was especially opposed, in view of Indian feeling, to India's helping to subsidise King Husain who was regarded by many

SUBSIDIES AND FRONTIERS 185

Indian Moslems as a rebel against the Turkish Sultan and ibn Sa'ud who threatened to wreak havoc in the Hedjaz. See Viceroy to SSI, Feb. 20, 1921 (T), No. 1055; *L/P & S/10*, 488/1920.

23. *Cornwallis' Memo.* For details of the allotments to other Arabian shaikhs, see the aforementioned Memo. For the position of the Rashidi dynasty at this time see the following section.
24. Shuckburgh to Treasury, Feb. 11, 1921 (L), No. 695; *L/P & S/10*, 488/1920, Pts. 1, 2.
25. CO [Colonial Office] to Treasury, May 13, 1921 (L), No. 2279; *L/P & S/10*, 4931/1916.
26. See 'Memorandum by Hubert Young' n.d. (but probably written sometime between Oct. 1922 and Jan. 1923); Young MSS at St Antony's College, Oxford. For members of the new Middle East Department, see Young, *The Independent Arab*, pp. 324, 325.
27. Mesopotamia's role in precipitating the transfer of control to the Colonial Office is reflected in the following extract from a letter by Churchill to Sir George Ritchie, President of Dundee Liberal Association. '... by means of Arab Government, supported by a moderate military force, we may be able to discharge our duties without imposing unjustifiable expense on the British Exchequer. The fact that we should be calling into being an Arab administration in Baghdad made it indispensible that we should treat the Arabian question as a whole so far as it concerned the British interests'. *The Times*, March 4, 1921, quoted in M. A. Fitzsimmons, *Empire by Treaty* (London, 1965), pp. 25, 26, n. 13. Hereafter *Fitzsimmons*.
28. It should be noted that although the Conference was in favour of granting ibn Sa'ud an increased subsidy of £100,000 a year his subsidy continued at the previous rate until it was stopped altogether in 1923.
29. *Monroe*, p. 68.
30. 'Report on the Middle East Conference', No. 533/E8001, *FO* 371/6343.
31. *Monroe*, p. 68.
32. 'Eastern Report LXVI', May 2, 1918, No. 1927; *L/P & S/10*, 705/1916, Pts. 3, 4.
33. FO to Allenby, June 24, 1919 (T), No. 4298; *L/P & S/10*, 4929/1918.
34. See p. 163.
35. CC to IO, March 12, 1920 (T), No. 2000; *ibid*.
36. *Ibid*.
37. Pol.:/B. to IO, April 4, 1920 (T), No. 2854; *L/P & S/10*, 4929/1918. For an account of this murder and a brief history of other Rashidi inter-family assassinations, see *Rihani*, chap. XIV. As D. G. Hogarth noted: '... no other dynasty of Arabs is so blood-guilty as this'. See his *Arabia* (Oxford, 1922), p. 100.
38. CC to IO, May 7, 1920 (T), No. 3690; *ibid*.
39. Minute by C. C. Garbett, May 10, 1920, No. 3690; *ibid*.
40. CC to IO, May 31, 1920 (T), No. 4313; *ibid*.
41. HCB to SSC, Dec. 6, 1921 (T), No. 5407; *L/P & S/10*, 7251/1920.

42. *Ibid.*
43. Quoted in Busch, *Britain*, p. 123.
44. G. Bell to Sir Hugh Bell [father] Dec. 18, 1922 in *The Letters of Gertrude Bell*, ed. by Lady Bell, Vol. II (London, 1927), pp. 659, 660.
45. See pp. 102, 103.
46. For Kuwait's frontiers see Arts. V and VII of the Anglo-Turkish Agreement in *BD*, Vol. X, Pt. II, pp. 190–194.
47. *Dickson*, p. 251. Much of the material for this and the following two sections is taken from *Dickson*, pp. 250–257. The writer has also generally used his spelling of Kuwaiti place names.
48. *Ibid.*
49. *Ibid.*
50. *Ibid.*
51. Given the conflicting reports on who actually started the battle and the perennial hyperbole, duplicity and special pleading of various informants, it is difficult to determine precisely who touched off the clash. The most plausible account was given by ibn Sa'ud's agent in Bahrain who reported that a skirmish between two scouting parties flared into a full scale conflict. See 'Abd al-'Aziz al Qusaibi to Dickson, June 3, 1920 (L, Trans), No. 6317; *L/P & S/10*, 6499/1920, Ptes. 1, 2.
52. P. [Pol.] A. [Agent], Bahrain to CC, May 26, 1920 (T), No. 6317; *ibid.*
53. *Dickson*, p. 251.
54. PA Bahrain to CC, June 3, 1920 (T), No. 6417; *ibid.*
55. Salim to ibn Sa'ud, May 29, 1920 (L, Trans), No. 6317; *ibid.*
56. Dickson, p. 252.
57. PA Kuwait to CC, July 5, 1920 (T), No. 6317; *L/P & S/10*, 6499/1920, Pts. 1, 2.
58. Memo from PA Kuwait to CC, June 13, 1920, No. 6317; *ibid.*
59. *Ibid.*
60. CC to PA Kuwait, July 9, 1920 (T), No. 6317; *ibid.* Oddly enough, the fact that the 1913 Agreement was unratified is not stressed in many of the deliberations on the pros and cons of the dispute.
61. Cox to SSI, Oct. 11, 1920, No. 7555 (T), *L/P & S/10*, 6499/1920.
62. Cox to SSI, Oct. 13, 1920, No. 7620 (T), *ibid.* Jahra was important to Kuwait as it was the main and virtually the only seat of agriculture in the Shaikhdom. See *Dickson*, p. 61.
63. *Ibid.* pp. 255–257.
64. *Ibid.* p. 256.
65. *Ibid.* p. 257. It should be added in passing that the spelling of Chasib is Dickson's. Although the name appears odd the writer has not been able to find an alternative spelling.
66. *Longrigg*, p. 137.
67. *Dickson*, p. 266. For tribal migratory routes, see *Dickson*, pp. 266, 267.
68. HCI (High Com., Iraq) to SSC, March 16, 1922 (T), No. 1214; *L/P & S/10*, 7251/1920, Pts. 2, 3. Such was the ferocity of the *Ikhwan* and ibn Sa'ud's difficulty in restraining his stronger chieftains,

especially Faisal al Dawish, that many times it was far from certain that ibn Saʻud was behind various raids.
69. HCI to SSC, March 13, 1922 (T), No. 1124; *ibid.*
70. For a copy of the Treaty of Mohammera see *Report on Iraq Administration*, April 1922–March 1923.
71. J. B. Glubb, *War in the Desert* (London, 1960), pp. 62, 63. Hereafter Glubb, *War in the Desert*. Sir J. B. Glubb had much experience in southern Iraq during the 1920's as British commander of the Iraqi Desert Police.
72. HCI to SSC, April 26, 1922 (T), No. 1751; *L/P & S/10*, 7251/1920, Pt. 1.
73. HCI to SSC, May 23, 1922 (T), No. 2200; *L/P & S/10*, 7251/1920, Pt. 1.
74. CO to FO, May 30, 1922 (L), No. 2315; *L/P & S/10*, 7251/1920, Pt. 1.
75. HCB to SSC, June 1, 1922 (T), No. 2328; *ibid.*
76. HCB to SSC, June 5, 1922 (T), No. 2376; *ibid.*
77. *Ibid.*
78. SSC to HCB, June 8, 1922 (T), No. 2400; *ibid.*
79. Marshall (Consul at Jedda) to FO, July 31, 1922 (T), No. 3212; *ibid.*
80. HCB to SSC, Sept. 15, 1922 (T), No. 3860; *ibid.*
81. *Ibid.*
82. Minute by A. H[irtzel] June 10, 1922, No. 2376; *ibid.*
83. HCB to SSC, Sept. 15, 1922 (T), No. 3860; *ibid.* Emphasis in original with the marginal comment 'the same old story'.
84. HCI to SSC, June 12, 1922 (T), No. 2480; *L/P & S/10*, 7251/1920, Pts. 2, 3.
85. Philby, *JCAS*, p. 307.
86. HCI to SSC, June 17, 1922 (T), No. 2564; *L/P & S/10*, 7251/1920, Pts. 2, 3. It is probable that this propaganda also had the purpose of creating alarm in Iraq 'which was exploited for internal political purposes'. See *Longrigg*, p. 160.
87. The picture may be found in *Rihani*. Both *Dickson*, pp. 270–275 and *Rihani*, chaps. VIII and IX, give detailed colourful eye witness accounts of the conference. See also Glubb, *War in the Desert*, pp. 61–64.
88. *Rihani*, p. 60. At this juncture—shortly before Cox's arrival at 'Uqair and during the conference—the Muntafiq's allegiance is not mentioned by either Dickson or Rihani. Moreover, Dickson only mentions ibn Saʻud's claim on the Dhafir. He does not mention the allegiance of the 'Amarat.
89. *Dickson*, pp. 272, 273.
90. *Ibid.*, pp. 273, 274.
91. *Ibid.* p. 274.
92. *Ibid.*, pp. 274, 275. Major Holmes, representing the Eastern and General Syndicate, was present at 'Uqair and was later granted a concession to prospect for oil and minerals in an area roughly between the Kuwait Neutral Zone and Qatar and exteending inland to a point roughly 60 miles from the sea. See *Dickson*, p. 278.

93. See *Dickson*, p. 275.
94. For Kuwaiti reactions to the boundary, see *Dickson*, pp. 278–280. '... Kuwait's new frontier started in the west at the junction of the Wadi al Aujah with the Batin valley. From this point, leaving Riq'ai under the control of Najd, it ran in a straight line to the junction of the 29th parallel of latitude with the red semi-circle referred to in the Anglo-Turkish Agreement, and then followed the red semi-circle to a point on the coast just south of Ras al Qalai'ah (or Jilai'ah). South of this line of demarcation was the Kuwait Neutral Zone, bounded on the west by the wide and shallow depression called Ash Shaqq, on the east by the sea, and on the south by a line drawn from Ash Shaqq, through 'Ain al 'Abd to a point on the coast just north of Ras al Misha'ab '. See *Dickson*, p. 275.
95. *Ibid.*, p. 277.
96. *Rihani*, p. 79.

CHAPTER VI

Conflict in the Wadi Sirhan and the Kuwait Conference 1922-1924

With the exception of the Arabian peninsula, the Treaty of Lausanne settled the problem of the disposal of the territories lost by Turkey in World War I. The mandates of Iraq and Palestine, however, were left with their inland frontiers undefined. It will be seen in the pages to follow that the period from late 1922 until early 1924 is characterised by two major problems. Firstly, there was the struggle in north central Arabia between Anglo–Hashimite aggrandisement and Sa'udi expansionism. Secondly, there was the attempt by Britain to settle through a general conference the outstanding problems between ibn Sa'ud and his Hashimite neighbours.

In north-central Arabia the area of dispute was the Wadi Sirhan. This long depression was an important avenue for caravan trade between Najd and Syria and therefore of significant economic value to ibn Sa'ud. On the British side, the High Commissioner in Jerusalem, who was responsible for Transjordean as a subdivision of Palestine, stressed the strategic importance of the Wadi Sirhan for Britain. With Colonial Office backing he argued that it was important for Britain to have a continuous belt of dependencies stretching from the Mediterranean to Persia. One of the chief reasons for this connection was the imperial necessity of keeping within the British mandatories the motor and air routes linking Britain with the east. These lines of communications crossed the northern section of the Wadi. Moreover if ibn Sa'ud, who had no desire to be completely surrounded in the north and west by Hashimite enemies, possessed the Wadi he would be in an important position to threaten Amman and the Hedjaz.

The second major event of this period will be seen to be the British conference which endeavoured to settle the Sa'udi–Shrarifian problems. However the enmity and intransigence of both sides were to thwart what came to be called the Kuwait Conference.

Jauf, Qaf and the Wadi Sirhan

By ibn Sa'ud's defeat of ibn Rashid in 1921 the Jabal Shammar ceased to be a buffer between Najd and the Hashimite domains in the north. Not only did ibn Sa'ud come into direct contact with Faisal but in early 1922 by annexing Jauf in northernmost Arabia [1] the Wahhabi leader arrived at the doorstep of 'Abdullah's undelimited southern frontier. The inevitable friction between the two rulers once again put Britain and her High Commissioner for Palestine, Sir Herbert Samuel, in an awkward position. At this point the British were interested in building a trans-desert railway from Iraq to the Mediterranean.[2] Britain had been interested in such a railway since the middle of the nineteenth century when Lt-Colonel F. R. Chesney had surveyed the Euphrates Valley route. In 1916 by the terms of the Sykes–Picot Agreement, which like the Chesney expedition was to prove abortive, ' France " accorded " to Great Britain the Palestininan ports of Haifa and 'Akka and consented that Great Britain should build, administer, and be sole owner of a railway from Haifa to Baghdad; and south of a French Syria and of an international Palestine, a tenuous but unbroken zone of British influence was drawn on the map ... from the south-eastern corner of the Mediterranean to the north-western corner of the Persian Gulf'. Although air and motor routes were to replace the rail line, this trans-desert connection proved to be one of the governing factors in the British desire that Transjordan should abut upon Iraq. These routes gained added importance owing to the post-war economic revival of Persia and Iraq.[3]

In January 1922, Cox drafted a telegram to ibn Sa'ud stating the possibility of a rail line proceeding via Jauf. An exploratory group was to examine the proposed route. After requesting Sa'udi protection of this party, Cox acknowledging Sa'udi influence in this area, added that whereas in the past Rashidi dominance in Jauf had made such exploration impossible ' now your friendly influence in Jauf has happily changed the situation ...'[4]

The High Commissioner in Palestine disputed the Sa'udi claim to Jauf, favouring its inclusion in Transjordan. In London, the Colonial Secretary, now the Duke of Devonshire, sided with Samuel, arguing that Jauf still belonged to Nuri al Sha'lan of the Ruwala.⁵ Cox, refuting Samuel's contention, reported: 'Shaalan, it is stated, definitely accepted Bin Sa'ud's lordship over Jauf according to our information and . . . [has?] agreed to hold it on his behalf'. The High Commissioner of Iraq warned against the possibility of the French 'meddling in Jauf through Nuri Shaalan and [the] consequent advantage of recognising Bin Saud's claim to its overlordship'.⁶

The problem of Nuri al Sha'lan's allegiance was a familiar one in the post-war Middle East. The Ruwala's grazing grounds extended from Jauf at the southern end of the Wadi Sirhan northwards, spanning the entire Wadi finally to end in the vicinity of Homs in Syria. As submission of this tribe could conceivably cut off Transjordan from Iraq, the British were most interested in Nuri's relation with ibn Sa'ud. Nuri's real allegiance since the end of the war had been something of an open question. Between 1919 and 1922 he is reported to have declared his allegiance to Faisal and, after his expulsion, to the French in Damascus. After antagonising the French he turned to 'Abdullah in Amman and later to ibn Sa'ud. After 1922, relations between Nuri and ibn Sa'ud were—to use Toynbee's adjective—'ambiguous'. It is true to say that tribes suffered owing to the post-war policy of dividing the former Arab provinces of the Ottoman Empire into states whose frontiers ignored the desert realities of seasonal migration and economic geography. It is equally true that the tribes themselves exploited this situation by crossing borders at will to avoid any control.⁷

While London, Jerusalem and Baghdad argued back and forth, the exploration was postponed. Philby, who was at this time chief British Representative in Transjordan, having succeeded Lawrence in this capacity,⁸ was directed by Samuel to visit Jauf and report on the conditions there. Philby's orders were 'to proceed to Jauf and to establish a basis for friendly relations after satisfying himself that no risk of extending Imperial commitment in Transjordan was involved therein'. Much to the chagrin of his superiors 'Philby duly proceeded to Jauf and concluded a full-dress offensive and defensive treaty with one of the Shalan sheikhs and a representative of the present ruler of Jauf by which Jauf is annexed (or attached) to Transjordania and the British Government undertakes to find the necessary funds for military operations " if the common interests of the parties require an attack on their neighbours or any of their neighbours attack them "'.[9] Philby's act was immediately repudiated by the Colonial Office; however, they still admonished Cox to indicate to ibn Sa'ud that he should not 'give [the] impression that we have acknowledged or propose to acknowledge Bin Sa'ud's suzerainty over Jauf'.[10]

The position at Jauf remained unsettled throughout the first half of 1922 and it was feared by the British in Palestine that, if the situation at Jauf was not regularised soon, the Transjordanian Bedouin would be forced, albeit reluctantly, to convert to Wahhabism as the only way to put an end to incessant warfare. Samuel also pointed out that the Palestine Garrison could not be reduced if Wahhabi tenets flooded Transjordan.[11]

British fears of a Wahhabi attack on Transjordan were vindicated in August of 1922 when an estimated three to four thousand Ikhwan penetrated to within twelve miles of Amman. This force, however, was virtually annihilated by British planes and armoured cars at Umm at Ahmad.[12] In order to protect 'Abdullah's little Amirate the Colonial Secretary approved Transjordan's occupation of Qaf, whose occupation by ibn Sa'ud would have rendered Transjordan especially vulnerable to attack. The Colonial Secretary pressed for the drawing up of a frontier, the chief significance of which was its inclusion within 'Abdullah's frontiers of the British trans-desert air route and its exclusion of the Hedjaz Railway and its immediate vicinity from possible Sa'udi encroachments.[13] In an attempt to consolidate their Middle Eastern position, the British sought also to draw Transjordan's boundaries in such a way as to make the Amirate contiguous with Iraq, thus forming a solid line of British protectorates from Persia to the Mediterranean.

Owing no doubt to Wahhabi power and influence in the area, the Colonial Office's desire to include Jauf in Transjordan was shown not to be feasible.

> It is clear that while certainly we should have been glad if the Transjordan sphere of influence could have embraced Jauf this must now be recognised as an impossibility. ... Provided that south of [the] desert air route and east of [the] Hedjaz Railway a wide strip of desert is rendered secure from raids we must leave the interior of Arabia alone.[14]

Although the British were forced to abandon the idea of incorporating Jauf into Transjordan,[15] their projected boundary line was still unacceptable to ibn Sa'ud as it cut across the middle of the much contested Wadi Sirhan.

Ibn Sa'ud objected to the British line on the following grounds. Firstly, the Wadi Sirhan would be bisected, the jurisdiction being divided between Najd and Transjordan. This boundary was impractical from the economic standpoint because al Geraya, on whose salt deposits the inhabitants of the whole Wadi depended, would fall within the Transjordan frontier. Secondly, the people of the Wadi viewed Jauf as their chief city and spent part of each year there.[16] Ibn Sa'ud desired that the boundaries be drawn so as to include the whole Wadi in Sa'udi territory, thus achieving what was undoubtedly one of his primary aims: cutting off Transjordan from Iraq. Glubb touches upon the area's importance both economically and strategically when he writes: ' The Wadi as Sirhan, a long depression containing great numbers of wells, opened a highway before him [ibn Sa'ud] to Syria. ... This was precisely the route always used by caravans and travellers and was commanded at its northern end by Roman forts '.[17]

While continued efforts were being made to effect a meeting between ibn Sa'ud and his Hashimite adversaries to solve their border problems, Anglo–Sa'udi relations were exacerbated by the British decision to discontinue ibn Sa'ud's subsidy. In early spring 1923, London decided to make a single payment of £50,000 to ibn Sa'ud for the year 1922–3. After March 31 1923, his subsidy was discontinued. On the other side of the peninsula, Husain was to be given £50,000 ' if and when he signs a satisfactory Treaty '. Ibn Sa'ud's subsidy was to be paid in two equal instalments of £25,000 at six-month intervals. With diplomatic endeavours giving little satisfaction, the British in London were thinking once again in terms of buying peace in Arabia. With reference to the Sa'udi payment, the Colonial Secretary wrote: ' Opportunity might be taken ... to consider [the] question of [the] Nejd–Transjordan boundary ... a satisfactory arrangement ... being the condition on which [a] second payment would be made '.[18]

Ibn Sa'ud, who had recently asked Cox for a loan, was informed by the High Commissioner that not only was a loan impossible but his subsidy was to be discontinued. However, Cox did veto the suggestion that any conditions be attached to the second payment.[19] Shortly after the message concerning the cessation of the subsidy was relayed to ibn Sa'ud, another Ikhwan attack took place in the disputed area between Transjordan and Najd.

Towards the end of June 1923, a force of Wahhabis attacked Qaf at the northern end of the Wadi Sirhan but were repulsed. Fourteen Wahhabis were killed. 'Abdullah received British permission to re-occupy the village. However, he had to depend on his own resources; the British declined to assist him either financially or militarily.[20] In view of Britain's desire to retain Qaf—which will become evident in the succeeding pages—Britain's reluctance to support her protégé does appear odd. Perhaps by withholding financial and material assistance the British sought to dissuade the rather sanguine 'Abdullah from any precipitate action such as extending his power south of Qaf. There is also the possibility that they were just reluctant to pour any more money into Arabia. Ibn Sa'ud proceeded to deny any knowledge of the raid and stated that he had instructed his chief to avoid raids against the Beni Shakhr and to respect Transjordan's frontier.[21] It is impossible to ascertain whether this raid was sanctioned by ibn Sa'ud. On many such occasions the British were ready to accept ibn Sa'ud's denials of any knowledge of the said raids. The relevant authorities believed that the Wahhabi leader could not always control his more distant zealous followers.

Before continuing the narrative of events leading to the Kuwait Conference it is advisable to pause for a moment to examine the importance of Qaf and its immediate vicinity. Strategically there was a fortress adjacent to the village of Qaf which formed a valuable observation post for the detection of raids coming up the Wadi towards Amman. Owing to its strength, the fort required only a small garrison. Economically, the northern half of the Wadi Sirhan and its smaller tributary wadis were the customary and natural grounds of the Ruwala and Beni Shakhr. By assigning this territory to ibn Sa'ud, these two tribes would be cut off from their economic necessities. Politically, both the aforementioned tribes had to this point been unaffected by Wahhabi tenets. Were ibn Sa'ud to come into closer contact with these tribes, the chances of conversion would be increased.[22]

The importance of effecting a settlement of the outstanding questions between ibn Sa'ud and 'Abdullah was growing daily.

In Iraq the British faced the prospect of Faisal coming to his brother's assistance if the Ikhwan attacked Transjordan. Faisal on more than one occasion made it ' quite clear ... that in the matter of supporting 'Abdullah his honour was involved. He said that if Kaf was attacked by Nejd forces he and his ministers are agreed that, in order to create a diversion, an attack by Iraq tribes on [the] West of [the] Euphrates must be launched against Najd, since Ibn Saud's domination over [the] Beni Sakhr and Rualla would be the preliminary to a serious attack on [the] Hedjaz, and the end of Transjordan.' [23]

Faisal had offered on several occasions to mediate between ibn Sa'ud on the one side and Husain and 'Abdullah on the other. However, ibn Sa'ud did not view this expedient favourably. While the British dealt with the last-minute details of the approaching Kuwait Conference to settle these border problems, strong warnings were despatched to ibn Sa'ud to refrain from hostilities in or near Transjordan.[24]

At the end of the summer of 1923, Faisal visited Amman. Philby gave Faisal the impression that ' his representing Transjordan in discussions with Ibn Saud would be agreed to by His Majesty's Government '. By the tone of the despatches dealing with Faisal's visit, it is clear that Philby had no authorisation to speak as he did. In London a somewhat perturbed Duke of Devonshire thought ' Iraq intervention ' to be ' undesirable '.[25] The following despatch emphasises the ramifications of Philby's action and the British desire to settle once and for all not only the Transjordan but also the Hedjaz border with Najd.

> His Grace adheres to the view that it would be undesirable that King Faisal should represent either Trans-Jordan or the Hedjaz at any meeting with Ibn Saud, but in view of the fact that he was apparently given to understand during his recent visit to Amman that this course would be viewed with favour by His Majesty's Government, His Grace sees no alternative to suggesting that the scope of the meeting should be extended to cover any outstanding questions between Nejd and Iraq. With regard to oustanding questions between Nejd and the Hedjaz, His Grace has always been of the opinion that in order to secure a satisfactory frontier between these two states it might be necessary to combine any negotiations for this frontier with

negotiations for the frontier between Najd and Trans-Jordan.[26]

On October 21st 1923, Trevor succeeded Knox as Political Resident in the Persian Gulf. Before leaving the Gulf area, Knox accepted the chairmanship of the Kuwait Conference. Husain, 'Abdullah, Faisal and ibn Sa'ud were requested to send delegates for the purpose of settling their border and other oustanding questions. Before turning, however, to an examination of this Conference, it would be well to touch briefly on an issue which coincided with these border disputes: the means by which ibn Sa'ud and the British were to communicate.

Channel of Communication

In 1921 when the Colonial Office assumed responsibility for the Middle East, an Interdepartmental Committee approved a report by J. Masterton-Smith, Under Secretary, Ministry of Labour, which recommended that political jurisdiction on the Arabian coast of the Persian Gulb be transferred from the Government of India to the Colonial Office. As regards the Arabian coast, India would only be responsible for administrative and local matters. Paragraph 12 of the Masterton-Smith Report stipulated ' that the Secretary of State for the Colonies ... should communicate with them [the Political Agents at Kuwait and Bahrain] through the Resident at Bushire, it being understood that in cases of great urgency the Colonial Office would communicate direct with the official in touch with Ibn Saud or the Shaikh of Kuwait '.[27]

Although the above report came out in 1921, owing to Sir Percy Cox's personal friendship with ibn Sa'ud and the fact that Cox had been dealing with ibn Sa'ud for over a decade,[28] he continued to deal with the Wahhabi leader. No doubt impressed by his new successes and feeling that news regarding his affairs was not always accurately represented, ibn Sau'ud designated a certain British subject, Dr Mann, to be his personal representative in London. Mann had been despatched by Cox to Riyadh to advise ibn Sa'ud on medical problems. Having come to trust Dr Mann, ibn Sa'ud prevailed upon Cox to support his choice of the Doctor as his representative. In support of ibn Sa'ud's appointment, Cox pointed out that in view of his own imminent retirement and the fact that his dealing with ibn Sa'ud was based on expediency, ibn Saʻud could not be expected in future to accept the High Commissioner of Iraq to represent and protect Saʻudi interests. On several occasions in the past, Cox had been put in an awkward position.[29] As High Commissioner in Iraq he was responsible for the protection of Faisal's interests; however, he was a personal friend of ibn Saʻud. Obviously after his retirement, ibn Saʻud would not wish to communicate with London but sending copies of despatches to Baghdad and Bushire.[30] While the prospect of appointing a British Agent to Arabia was being considered, London agreed to Mann's appointment as ibn Saʻud's personal representative while Cox was to continue dealing with ibn Saʻud until he retired.

Shortly before the ʻUqair Conference of 1922, the Colonial Office received India Office and Foreign Office approval for their proposal that after Cox's retirement the Colonial Office would correspond direct with the Political Agency at Bahrain concerning Saʻudi affairs. The Resident was to receive copies.[31] During their negotiations at ʻUqair, Cox had discussed the channel of communication with ibn Saʻud who had agreed to communicating in future through the Political Agent at Bahrain. Ibn Saʻud did stipulate, however, that the officer must be of sufficient status, seniority and experience. He also requested to be dealt with in London by the Foreign Office, probably because Husain was handled through that Office.[32]

The Political Resident in the Persian Gulf, supported by the Government of India, objected to Bahrain's dealing exclusively with ibn Saʻud. The Resident pointed out that owing to Bahrain's climate, officers seldom remained there long: senior officers certainly could not be expected to do so. Also, Bushire offered quicker mail and telegraphic communication. Further, the Ikhwan could threaten the southern part of the Trucial Coast and Oman as well as Kuwait. Owing to his experience and the fact that the records for the Shaikhdoms of the Arab littoral were kept at Bushire, the Political Resident was in a better position to know about these areas. Finally, the Indian Government emphasised the fact that Bahrain was subordinate to Bushire.[33]

The Colonial Office acceded to the importunities of India and agreed to follow the policy as suggested in paragraph 12 of the Masterton-Smith Report. Ibn Saʻud's request to be dealt with through the Foreign Office was rejected. Unfortunately, this disappointment coincided with several other disillusioning events. Owing to troubles between Bahrainis and Najdis resident in Bahrain, ibn Sa'ud's agent, with British assistance, was expelled from the island. The various slights which ibn Sa'ud suffered at the hands of his British friends at this point—coupled with Cox's retirement—must have strained the Wahhabi leader's friendship to the utmost. As an India Office official commented: 'There has been recently a most unfortunate conjuncture of circumstance in our relations with Ibn Saud—the withdrawal of his subsidy, the expulsion of his agent from Bahrain, and the change in the channel of communication must have had a deplorable cumulative effect'.[34]

Ibn Sa'ud initially refused to accept Bushire as a channel of communication owing to the 'delay involved'. He requested that he be granted the right to send telegrams direct to London. He also requested permission to send a representative to London.[35] Curzon vetoed the idea of receiving a Najdi representative because of ibn Sa'ud's relatively minor diplomatic status. Curzon favoured the possibility of sending an agent to Arabia.[36]

Ibn Sa'ud was to accept Bushire in due course, while the proposition to send a British Agent to Riyadh was to be debated off and on for the next few years. The Kuwait Conference, however, is of more immediate importance.

The Kuwait Conference

In late 1922 the British first began to talk about holding a conference which would settle the outstanding problems between Najd on the one hand and Transjordan, Iraq and the Hedjaz on the other. 'Abdullah and Faisal were informed of this possibility. It appears that Husain was not consulted about these negotiations 'until the questions had been under discussion for almost a year'. Hence he refused to send a delegate when the conference actually assembled. On September 23rd 1923, the Colonial Office suggested that this conference should be held at Kuwait. On October 21st 1923, the Political Resident telegraphed the Colonial Secretary that ibn Sa'ud had accepted the suggestion that the conference should discuss all matters relating to his Hashimite adversaries. Faisal and Abdullah agreed to send delegation.[37]

Colonel Knox, former acting Political Resident in the Persian Gulf, was appointed chairman of the conference. For the duration of the negotiations he was under the jurisdiction of the Colonial Office and reported directly to the Colonial Secretary. In addition to Sa'udi–Hashimite border problems, the conference was to settle certain provisions of the Treaty of Mohammera which ibn Sa'ud found objectionable. In Baghdad the new British High Commissioner, Sir Henry Dobbs, protested against the inclusion on the agenda of the Mohammera Convention. He argued (rightly) that Iraq had never suggested this and (wrongly) that ' so far as I am aware ' nor had ibn Sa'ud.[38] The Colonial Secretary pointed out quickly that it was the High Commissioner's telegram of September 24th, mentioning Sa'udi displeasure with the Convention, which had resulted in its inclusion on the agenda.[39]

While the British were awaiting the arrival of the various deputations, Faisal al Duwish led a raid across the Hedjaz Railway in the vicinity of al Ulla. A strong remonstrance was addressed to ibn Sa'ud and he was asked to ' deal with Faisal Dawish as *he deserves* '.[40] This ill-timed exploit of ibn Sa'ud's unruly chief must have further convinced Husain not to send a representative to Kuwait. However, the British still endeavoured to induce him to despatch a delegate, pointing out ' that a a settlement of the Nejd–Hedjaz issue is more likely to be in favour of the Hedjaz when discussed at a Conference where there can be so much more latitude for give and take elsewhere, whereas if the Trans–Jordan Nejd questions are definitely settled at Kuwait the King's frontier will have to be decided on its own merits and he may suffer as a result '.[41]

While the British attempted to elicit Husain's cooperation, they also had to deal with an anxious Faisal who feared that Ikhwan penetration to within eighty miles of Medina presaged the imminent Wahhabi seizure of the city. Dobbs favoured addressing a British threat to ibn Sa'ud stating that ibn Sa'ud's supplies which came primarily from Iraq and India would be cut off if he infringed ' the well known Hedjaz boundaries '.[42] In view of the patently undefined nature of the Najd–Hedjaz boundary and the fact that this boundary had been in dispute for so long, it is difficult to take Dobbs' wording seriously.

Although normally predisposed to accord ibn Sa'ud the benefit of the doubt, British patience with him was showing signs of wear. Ibn Sa'ud's letter to Trevor, the Political Resident, suggesting that the conference be postponed while he studied his borders and formulated his desiderata provoked a strong reproof. The Colonial Secretary telegraphed that he 'strongly deprecate[d] delay in [the] assembly of [the] proposed conference'. The telegram continued: 'There are other indications that the wishes of His Majesty's Government do not carry the weight with Ibn Saud that they have a right to expect in view of the friendly relations which have subsisted for so many years between the two Governments' The despatch ended with the following threat:

> In the event of the Nejd representative not reaching Kuwait by the end of the first week in December, His Majesty's Government will be reluctantly compelled to assume that the Sultan has decided to incur the grave displeasure of His Majesty's Government. They are confident that this is not the case, but they would point out to the Sultan that in the present condition of scarcity in Nejd it is of the greatest importance to that territory that he should remain on the friendliest possible terms with the great maritime power whose interests are so closely associated with his own.[43]

Husain, undoubtedly seizing upon the latest Wahhabi incursions near Medina, agreed to send a delegate on three conditions—which obviously could not be met. He stipulated (1) that ibn Sa'ud evacuate ibn Rashid's former territory, and 'Asir, (2) that the amirates of Jabel Shammar and 'Asir be returned to their rightful owners, and (3) that the Hedjaz be compensated for losses suffered during recent Ikhwan attacks.[44] Faisal, taking seriously the Wahhabi threat to his father's Kingdom, pressed for the Sa'udi evacuation of the Hedjaz frontier and for assurances against further Wahhabi depredations before despatching his delegation to Kuwait. Trevor and Knox objected strongly to Dobbs' espousal of Faisal's demands. Trevor pointed out *inter alia* that to press ibn Sa'ud for such assurances would wreck the conference, as ibn Sa'ud would probably refuse to give them. The Sultan would take special exception if he knew that such stipulations issued from Faisal. Such a measure would serve to confirm his impression that the Hashimites were in league against him. Moreover, how could ibn Sa'ud be ordered to withdraw from a frontier which had yet to be defined by the conference?[45] Knox too took issue with Dobbs' views and was to continue throughout the conference to challenge the High Commissioner's demands.⁴⁶

After several postponments, the first meeting of the Kuwait Conference was held on December 17. Delegations from Iraq, Najd and Transjordan were present. Husain still declined to be represented. The essence of the British policy to be adhered to during the conference was telegraphed to the Political Resident on November 8.

> H.M.G. are directly concerned with the frontier of [the] mandated area of Palestine. Provided that Trans Jordan has access to [the] Gulf of Akaba that Nejd does not encroach upon [the] Hedjaz railway and that Khurma and Taraba are included in [the] Hedjaz they are prepared to exclude [the] whole [of the] Wadi Sirhan from Kaf inclusive and to allow [the] Hedjaz to extend northwards along [the] railway as far as Mudawwara.
> ... Thus Kaf would be given up for Akaba by Abdullah, Khurma and Taraba would be given up by Ibn Saud for Kaf and any claim to territory north of Mudawwara would be given up by Hussein for Khurma and Taraba.
> ... Should [the] Hedjaz not be represented H.M.G. will not discuss Trans Jordan boundary beyond [the] Nefud salient at which point they consider [the] Nejd-Hedjaz boundary should take off. In this case [the] cession of Kaf must be made conditional upon Ibn Saud giving [a] written understanding in which he agrees to [the] subsequent inclusion in [the] Hedjaz of Khurma and Taraba should H.M.G. so desire.⁴⁷

In order to present as clearly as possible a picture of the complicated demands and counter-demands put forward by each delegation, the Iraqi claims against Najd and vice versa will be given first. Thereafter, the issues between 'Abdullah and ibn Sa'ud will be considered.

At the first meeting of the Kuwait Conference, Iraq put forward the following nine points:

1. Consideration of allegations made by Ibn Saud that Mohammera Convention has been infringed by Iraq.
2. [Consideration] that agreement should be concluded for prevention of raiding by tribes.

3. Arrangement that Bin Saud shall only communicate through his agent in Baghdad with any of his tribes that may be in Mesopotamia. Agent to be stationed in Riyadh.
4. Mesopotamian officials or Sheikhs not to be communicated with direct by Bin Saud.
5. Mutual undertaking that Nejd tribes in Iraq shall not be required to raise armed forces in Iraq and vice versa.
6. Except by mutual agreement neither Iraq nor Nejd forces to pursue offenders across the frontier.
7. Other political offenders to be subject of extradition agreement.
8. Flags or other badges of office to be discarded by Sheikhs having official positions before crossing the frontier for grazing.
9. An inspector of boundaries to be appointed by each Government to be posted at al Hafar by whom grazing permits to tribes crossing the frontier will be issued, who will supply his [Faisal's] Government with information, serve as a medium by whom loot may be returned, and work in agreement for prevention of aggression and robbery.[49]

The Najd delegates put forward seven points:

1. Return of the Nejd Shammar.
2. Immediate return of the loot taken after Ojair ['Uqair] Conference.
3. Expulsion of certain Najd tribes who in hostile spirit recently fled to Iraq for shelter.
4. An agreement for the return in future of refugee tribes whom their suzerain alleges to be a menace to the peace of the border.
5. Declaration to be made in favour of Nejd authorities, giving them right at tribute season, on giving 15 days' notice to Mesopotamian officials supplying names of collectors to collect tribute from Nejdis in Mesopotamia.
6. Apology for insult to Nejd flag and for manner in which . . . [Nejdi official who was imprisoned in Baghdad] was treated.
7. Iraq to admit Ibn Mijlad [a shaikh, allegedly from

Najd, residing in Iraq but claiming allegiance to ibn Sa'ud] is a subject of the Sultan of Nejd.

8. ... (further point) is tacked on ... [to the above and] demands that no tribe shall be allowed to cross the frontier without a permit from its suzerain's representative.[49]

Considering first the Iraqi points, some measure of agreement was reached on all points except number five. Najd and Iraq agreed that each possessed the right to 'send and call to arms'. However, Najd took great exception to the following Iraqi provision: 'In such [an] event tribe(s) men [sic] may ... obey the call.... However they must go in that case with wives, children and cattle as [the] enemies of Nejd will otherwise complain that Iraq is sheltering women, children and property of raiders in arms.'[50]

As regards the Najd points, although Iraq objected initially to most of the Najdi demands, points two, three and four caused the most trouble. The Iraqi delegation argued that the acceptance of three and four would have been contrary to tribal tradition and hospitality. It was also pointed out that the return of refugees would not only have been against international practice but would have been impractical as Iraqi coercion would just drive these refugees to settle on the Turko–Iraqi border. Najd proceeded to suggest that raiding be classified as an extraditable offence.[51] While Cox was being contacted to find out what had been agreed upon between himself and ibn Sa'ud pertaining to point two,[52] Knox endeavoured to record the progress made thus far by the negotiations.

On December 22nd, the attempt to register the agreement achieved by the conference foundered on the rocks of Hashimite intransigence. The Iraqi delegation insisted on the adoption of a clause that their agreement depended on a satisfactory agreement being achieved with Husain. Perceiving a hostile alliance in this provision, Najd refused to sign the document. Knox suggested that the conference be adojurned until January 18th, 1924. This adjournment would enable the Najd delegation to contact ibn Sa'ud on various issues and give Husain a few weeks to send a representative.[53]

When confronted by Dobbs with the Colonial Secretary's plea to negotiate on purely Iraqui–Najdi problems to the exclusion of the Hedjaz, Faisal pointed out that owing to the following considerations this was impossible. Firstly the predominantly Moslem character of his people and his familial relationship with the Hedjaz made it impossible for him to look the other way when the Holy Cities were threatened. Secondly, the argument that the Wahhabis could not logically be required to withdraw from Khaibar on the Hedjaz frontier as this frontier had yet to be defined was fallacious. Thirdly, were Faisal and 'Abdullah to sign an agreement while ibn Sa'ud was in possession of part of the Hedjaz, this would imply acquiescence.[54]

Knox took issue with Faisal's arguments and with Dobbs' support of these demands. He pointed out that without the assistance of British troops, Husain could not drive ibn Sa'ud out of the Hedjaz. Even Faisal confessed that Medina itself was ready to fall and the British Consul in Jedda had reported that the city's inhabitants were not likely to oppose a Wahhabi takeover. Knox emphasised that there were countless instances where a country was forced to negotiate with an enemy in possession of conquered territory.[55] Faisal relented somewhat and agreed to concentrate on Iraq's and Transjordan's problems, leaving the Hedjaz until last.[56]

Returning to the outstanding points at issue, the following remained to be settled: (a) the claims involving pre-'Uqair plunder, (b) compensation for raids, (c) the question of whether raiding could be classed as an extraditable offence and (d) expulsion of raiders. As regards (a), Cox was consulted on the negotiations during the 'Uqair Conference. The former High Commissioner stated that no agreement had been reached on compensation and that as far as he was concerned the policy should be: 'let bygones be bygones'.[57] With reference to (b), Faisal suggested that a special tribunal consisting of Najdis and Iraqis should deal with raids on a tribal basis, seeing that property was returned. If this was not sufficient, individual Shammar raiders would be expelled from Iraq. With specific reference to compensation, Faisal proposed that his coronation date should be taken as the point after which loot should be mutually restored. With reference to (c), the King of Iraq argued that extradition should be forgotten as Najd had no regularly constituted courts. And finally, Faisal touched upon the comparatively minor point of ibn Mijlad by suggesting that he and his tribe should return to Najd if he chose to belong to ibn Sa'ud.[58]

At the tenth meeting of the conference on January 18th and 19th, agreement was reached on all the Iraqi points except the fifth. The Najdi delegation objected mainly to the Iraqi clause that if ibn Sa'ud required his tribes living in Iraq for battle, they could leave but had to take their families. Knox thought that Iraq offered obstruction on this point and on the Sa'udi demand that refugee tribesmen from Najd be returned. In order to extricate the negotiations from this quagmire of deadlock, Knox suggested that the Colonial Secretary's recommendation be adopted. Devonshire suggested the following plan; Najdi tribes who desired to enter Iraq would give, as a guarantee against raiding, either cash or cattle. This would be confiscated if the tribe raided. As the possibility of agreement seemed near, Knox even went so far as to adopt the officially ' frowned-upon ' suggestion put forward by Najd and Iraq that Britain should arbitrate on those issues preventing agreement.[59]

Less than a week after the tenth meeting, Knox reported that the settlement on all issues, which had seemed imminent, had been lost when the Najd delegation ' went back on their undertaking regarding the Ojair plunder settlement and the undertaking that the proposed tribal tribunal should decide the matter '.[60] Knox decided to adjourn the conference until March 5th, and write to ibn Sa'ud informing him of the Najdi breach of faith and requesting that two members of the Najd delegation, whom the British found objectionable, be replaced.[61]

With deadlock reached between Najd and Iraq, attention will now be focussed upon the problems between Najd and Transpordan. On December 26th 1923, 'Abdullah's delegation put forward the following points:

1. Restoration of Jauf and Sakaka in the Wadi Sirhan to Nuri al Sha'lan.
2. Resident agents to be exchanged between Najd and Transjordan.
3. Blood money to be paid by Najd for raids in the neighbourhood of Amman.
4. Agreement for the prevention of raiding to be concluded.
5. Numbers crossing the Transjordan frontier without permission from both sides to be limited.
6. No correspondence with various tribes in Transjordan.
7. Political refugees not to be surrendered.[62]

Najd objected primarily to Transjordan's first point. The Sa'udi delegation repeated its usual argument that the Wadi had formerly belonged to ibn Rashid, to whose territory they had succeeded and latterly was under the jurisdiction of Nuri al Shalan—whose family traditionally held the area—who had recently signed the district over to ibn Sa'ud. 'Abdullah's delegates based their claim to the Wadi Sirhan on the argument that it belonged to the tribes of Syria—i.e. the Ruwalla of the Sha'lan family—and now that they were heirs to that part of Syria, the Wadi belonged to them. In a word, Najd based their claim on a traditional tribal argument, while Transjordan claimed the Wadi on a more modern, albeit artificial European expedient, namely territorial basis. Stalemate was reached when the Sa'udi demand that they must have a corridor between Najd and Syria through which their caravans could pass freely was met by the Transjordan demand—vigorously backed by England —that Iraq and Transjordan must be joined together.[63]

While the Transjordan and Najd delegations sought to have their demands met, Husain was continually requested to despatch a delegate to Kuwait. As the British endeavoured to induce the King of the Hedjaz to co-operate, ibn Sa'ud grew daily more disenchanted with his British mentors:

> ... certain of your officers wish to make difficulties and to set up numerous obstacles, whereby the spirit of sincerity of love (between our two countries) is disturbed.
>
> Yea! I have observed, since the day of ... Cox's departure from Iraq a great change in the behaviour and disposition of the officers in the Persian Gulf ...[64]

Knox wrote to ibn Sa'ud allaying the latter's fears of an attack by Husain. He stated that the King of the Hedjaz had agreed not to attack ibn Sa'ud during the conference and had finally been persuaded to send a representative. Knox also mentioned that ibn Sa'ud's 'extravagant' claims in the north could be safeguarded in ways other than by extending his borders to an extreme degree. Knox emphasised Britain's position as the mandatory of Palestine and her desire that Transjordan's boundary coincide with that of Palestine.[65]

While Knox was awaiting ibn Sa'ud's reply, Mulla Hafiz, leader of the Najd deputation, gave the reasoning behind the Sa'udi position:

1. Except [for] the salt villages, which he has only deferred capturing because of the expressed wish of the British Government, he is in practical possession of [the] Wadi Sirhan.
2. This being so, the suggested price for abandoning Turaba, Khurma and Khaibar is not sufficient. He would however be prepared to give up Turaba, or consent to Khaibar and Turaba being made [an] independent buffer state but in no case can Khurma be given up.
3. This concession would however depend on an undertaking by King Husain to abandon Qunfidah and not to interfere in affairs of Asir. He should further, as Iraq had done, acknowledge territories of Nejd according to the Mohammerah Convention [presumably this meant that Husain would recognise Najd and its Dependencies].[66]

In view of the intransigence of ibn Sa'ud and his Hashimite adversaries on various points, Knox, ill with dysentery and virtually at the end of his patience, began to talk of closing down the conference. On January 30th he suggested that his illness afforded the British an opportunity to withdraw from the conference if they saw fit. As one of several alternatives, Knox proposed that he meet ibn Sa'ud and coerce him into a more conciliatory mood. The Colonial Secretary disapproved of this second alternative ,and it was decided to adjourn the conference until March owing to Knox's illness.[67]

After the conference had adjourned, Knox again requested the Colonial Secretary's permission to meet ibn Sa'ud and threaten him with economic sanctions if he did not modify his position. The Colonial Secretary thought that Knox's suggestions were too harsh, emphasising that it was of the utmost importance to avoid a rupture of the negotiations.[68] However, it was reasserted that under no circumstances would the British government agree to the separation of Iraq and Transjordan.

Knox wrote to ibn Sa'ud informing him of the progress of the conference and reasserted British policy. He also requested ibn Sa'ud to send one of his sons with the returning Najd deputation as Husain had finally been induced to send his son Zaid to Kuwait.[69] Ibn Sa'ud answered Knox's letter, offering 'to negotiate direct with Britain as [the] Mandatory power for [the] protection of his commerce and abandons claim to [the] mandate'.[70] Knox suggested that a buffer state be created out of the Wadi Sirhan with the High Commissioner in Palestine guaranteeing the duty free safe passage of caravans making their way to and from Syria.[71]

At the end of February the Najdi delegation returned to Kuwait. They informed Knox that, as the letter requesting ibn Sa'ud to send his son gave the impression that the conference would reassemble at the end of February, ibn Sa'ud found it impossible to send Faisal with the delegation. Ibn Sa'ud also wrote to the Political Resident complaining of raids into Najd by members of the Mutair tribe, who then sought refuge in the Neutral Zone between Najd and Iraq. He ended his complaint with the following threat:

> Either tell me definitely that a stop will be put to these acts of aggression and that the plunder and refugees will be returned on the responsibility of my friends the British Government or I must ask to be excused for any turn the affair may take. I am awaiting your reply with great eagerness.[72]

In Baghdad, Dobbs professed inability to control the Mutair raiders as they had sought refuge in the neutral territory. He added by way of a warning concerning possible impending hostilities on the part of Najd:

> There have been persistent rumours for the last few days that Faisal al Dawish is moving north to attack Iraq tribes and [the] Air Officer Commanding is making every possible effort to keep in close touch with the situation.[73]

To add further to British problems Husain, on finding out that ibn Sa'ud was not sending one of his sons to the conference, refused to despatch Zaid. Knox summed up some of the frustration attaching to his efforts when he wrote:

> We are in a vicious circle, Husain promises to send an exalted representative whom Ibn Saud never asked for and then says that if Ibn Saud will not despatch [a] corresponding dignitary he will not send his man nor even appoint [a] substitute of lesser importance.... In the meantime accord-

ing to Ibn Saud all malcontents are flocking to [his] borders creating disturbances in his territories and crossing to Iraq at the first signs of retaliation.[74]

Knox continued in his despatch to mention the possibility of ibn Sa'ud 'blazing out' and attacking his Hashimite adversaries.[75] Knox stressed that were such an attack to take place, ibn Sa'ud could argue ' with some justice that [it was] unreasonable to play fast and loose with him ... [and that the] Hashimites forced these steps upon him when he was ready to treat and showed [that] he was so ready '.[76]

Knox, manifesting the contempt in which many India officials held Husain and his sons, added that the present ' is not time for such mushroom monarch(s) as the Hashimites insisting on their royal dignity ...' [77]

At this juncture the possibility of a settlement being achieved was greatly undermined by Husain's assumption of the Caliphate. On March 3rd, the Turkish Grand National Assembly abolished the Caliphate and two days later King Husain—albeit, as has been asserted, reluctantly and at the urging of 'Abdullah —assumed the office.[78] The effect this had on ibn Sa'ud will be obvious from the future sequence of events.

On March 13th, Dobbs once again reported war preparations in Najd. He telegraphed that ibn Sa'ud's father admitted militant preparations in the neighbourhoods of Karama, ninety miles north-east of Artawiya. The High Commissioner in Iraq rejected ibn Sa'ud's allegation that Iraq had encouraged the Mutair to attack Najd and then sheltered them. He urged that ibn Sa'ud ' be pressed for an immediate official denial of [a] concentration with hostile intent '.[79]

Less than a week later, Dobbs telegraphed that a raid of Ikhwan, whose numbers were estimated at 2,000, attacked some sections of the Diwaniya and Dhafir shepherds.[80] The casualties initially were put at roughly 70 men, 20 women and 40 children killed. The Iraq delegation, which at the time of the raid was en route for Kuwait to resume negotiations, was held up by Baghdad and an official apology was demanded by Iraq. In view of the magnitude and excesses of the raid, Dobbs felt that no practical purpose could be served by continuing the Kuwait Conference, and telegraphed that he considered it ' impossible in these circumstances to suggest that delegates of Iraq should proceed to Kuwait...'.[81] On April 3rd, Knox telegraphed to Devonshire that ibn Sa'ud's complicity in the raid had been confirmed. In view of this and his belief that Britain was only compromising her dignity by continuing futile negotiations, Knox recommended that the conference be dissolved.[82] After seventeen sessions, the new Colonial Secretary, J. H. Thomas, telegraphed to Knox on April 11th authorising the dissolution of the Kuwait Conference.

As regards the raid itself, three factors served to inflame both British and north Arabian opinion in general against the Ikhwan: (1) the size of the raid, (2) the fact that the Ikhwan attacked defenceless shepherds, only the few wealthy among whom possessed horses by which to escape and (3) the casualties, especially women and children. Traditional tribal raids were colourful clashes in which few, if any, bedouin were killed. Indeed, it was not uncommon for a victorious raiding party to return some of the loot if their chief considered the vanquished tribe to be especially poor. These raids were an integral part of desert life, and had certain rules governing their conduct. However, with the advent of the Ikhwan, extreme religious fervour turned comparatively unsanguine traditional encounters into massacres. In many instances, the Ikhwan killed all males, regardless of age.[83]

Although ibn Sa'ud was generally considered by the British officers in the Gulf to have known of the raid, opinion was divided as to whether he could actually have prevented it. The Sultan of Najd was known to have fallen out with his powerful follower, Faisal al Duwish. His tribes were outraged owing to the many raids from Iraq and the fact that raiders could take sanctuary in either the Neutral Zone or in Iraq itself. It would be no exaggeration to say that many of ibn Sa'ud's followers were incensed at their leader's deference to the British, which prevented them from attacking their Hashimite enemies. A report from the Political Agent in Bahrain to the Resident mentioned that ibn Sa'ud's insecurity was shown by the fact that he was appointing ' near relatives to govern his outlying districts '.[84] The assumption of the Caliphate by King Husain added to his subjects' as well as to his own frustration.

The British Consul at Jeddah, Mr. (later Sir) Reader Bullard, reported that ' Jeddah was taken completely by surprise' by Husain's assumption of the Caliphate. 'The announcement,' he added, 'was listened to without enthusiasm, and a speech from a young Syrian, ending with "Long live the Caliph Husain!" was received in dead silence. The Jeddah people are greatly depressed. The assumption of the Caliphate by King Husain they regard as a farce, but the abolition of the Turkish Caliphate has given a check to the hope that had sustained them: that sooner or later the Turks would recover the Hedjaz and the nightmare reign of King Husain come to an end.'[85]

These factors set the stage for the assault on the Hedjaz.

Notes

1. See Map of Arabia.
2. See HCI (High Commissioner, Iraq) to SSC, Jan. 10, 1922 (T), No. 450; *L/P & S/10*, 450/1922, Pt. 1; and Minutes by J. A. Simpson, March 9, and July 20, 1922, Nos. 990 and 3006 in *L/P & S/10*, 450/1922, Pt. 1. See also 'Notes on Trans-Arabian Railway' by Maj. A. C. Griffin, Jan. 6, 1922, No. 990; *L/P & S/10*, 450/1922, Pt. 1. According to Foreign, India and Colonial Office sources, British interest in a trans-desert railway continued until spring, 1922. In stressing these motor, rail, and air routes it must not be forgotten that a projected pipeline running across the north of the Wadi Sirhan was also being discussed.
3. *Survey*, pp. 328–329. For an account of Chesney's explorations see his *Reports on the Navigation of the Euphrates* (London, 1833) and his four-volume *Expedition for the Survey of the Rivers Euphrates and Tigris, 1835–1837* (London, 1840).
4. HCI to SSC, Jan. 10, 1922 (T), No. 450; *ibid.*
5. SSC to HCI, Jan. 26, 1922 (T), No. 582; *ibid.*
6. HCI to SSC, Jan. 26, 1922 (T), No. 457; *ibid.*
7. See *Survey*, pp. 326, 327 and 337, 338.
8. Philby arrived in Transjordan at the end of 1921, resigning in January, 1924. For an account of his tenure in Trans-jordan, see his 'Transjordan', *JCAS* Vol. XI, Pt. IV (1924), pp. 296–312.
9. Minute by J. A. Simpson, July 20, 1922, No. 3006; *L/P & S/10*, 450/1922, Pt. 1. In view of Philby's critical attitude toward post-war British policy in the Middle East and his devotion to ibn Sa'ud, it is more than a little ironical that he attempted to 'filch' Jauf from ibn Sa'ud. Moreover, the following extract from one of Philby's many books does not mention the author's action, nor gives any indication why he would have acted thus. 'I have already mentioned Lawrence's anxiety to include the Sha'lan fief (Jauf) in Transjordan, though I had, and kept it to myself, strong doubts whether ibn Saud would let

us have it'. See *Forty Years in the Wilderness* (London, 1957), pp. 106, 107.
10. SSC to HCI, July 13, 1922 (T), No. 2941; *ibid.* For an account of Philby's unauthorised treaty, see Philby to HC (in Jerusalem), May 27, 1922 (L), No. 2941; *P/P & S/10*, 450/ 1922, Pt. 1.
11. HCP (High Com., Palestine) to SSC, Aug. 22, 1922 (T), No. 3495; *ibid.*
12. Geographical Handbook Series (BR 527), *Western Arabia and the Red Sea* (Naval Intelligence Division, 1946), p. 297.
13. SSC to HCP, Sept. 9, 1922 (T), No. 3761; *L/P & S/10*, 450/1922, Pt. 1. See Map of Arabia.
14. SSC to HCP, Aug. 22, 1922 (T), No. 3538; *ibid.*
15. During his visit to London in 1922, 'Abdullah was apparently induced to give up the thought of securing Jauf. The following extract illuminates 'Abdullah's desiderata and once again emphasizes the strategic importance of the Hedjaz Railway. ' After some discussion, however, it appeared that the Emir would be willing to relinquish Jauf, Provided that he were assured that the districts Kaf-Azrak-Burka were retained within the limits of Transjordan and that ibn Sa'ud were given clearly to understand that he must not encroach beyond Jauf. He added that it was very necessary also to prevent ibn Sa'ud from extending his influence from Jauf towards the Hedjaz railway between Ma'an and Medina'. Note by Sir G. Clayton, Oct. 25, 1922, Clayton MSS, Oriental Library, Durham University, Box 471/3. Hereafter, *Clayton MSS*.
16. HCI to SSC, Dec. 6, 1922 (T), No. 4861; *ibid.* As the boundary between Najd and Transjordan was not to be settled until late 1925, it is not worth tracing the various frontiers put forth by Britain and ibn Sa'ud. It is rather more important to point out the strategic and economic reasons behind these negotiations.
17. J. B. Glubb, *The Story of the Arab Legion* (London, 1948), p. 25
18. SSC to HCI and HCP, April 7, 1923 (T), No. 1355; *L/P & S/10*, 488/1920.
19. HCI to SSC, May 21, 1923 (T), No. 2041; *ibid.*
20. SSC to Pol. Res., July 4, 1923 (T), No. 2634; *L/P & S/10*, 450/ 1922, Pt. 1.
21. Pol. Res. to SSC, July 7, 1923 (T), No. 2634; *ibid.*
22. ' Memorandum on the Eastern Front of Transjordan ' by G. Antonius, n.d. (but written sometime in September 1925); *Clayton MSS*, Box 471/6.
23. (Acting HCI to SSC, Aug. 28, 1923 (T), No. 3282; *L/P & S/10*, 450/1922, Pt. 1.
24. (Acting) HCI to SSC, Aug. 25, 1923 (T), No. 3223; *ibid.*
25. SSC to Officer Administering the Government of Palestine, Sept. 12, 1923 (T), No. 3480; *ibid.*
26. CO to FO, Sept. 6, 1923 (L), No. 3395; *ibid.* Marked section in the original with the marginal comment ' Philby again!'.
27. CO to IO, Feb. 10, 1923 (L), No. 540; *L/P & S/10*, 7251/1920,

Pts. 4, 5. The Political Agent at Bahrain was in close touch with ibn Sa'ud.
28. Cox had been dealing with ibn Sa'ud since 1904 when he had been appointed Political Resident in the Gulf.
29. HCI to SSC, April 4, 1922 (T), No. 1427; *L/P & S/10*, 7251/1920, Pts. 4, 5. Cox wrote later: 'My position... became a little delicate at the time of [the] acute tension between Iraq and Bin Saud a few months ago, as I had then to act as your representative with both parties'. See HCI to SSC, Oct. 12, 1922 (T), No. 4165; *ibid*.
30. HCI to SSC, Oct. 12, 1922 (T), No. 4165; *ibid*.
31. SSC to HCI, Nov. 10, 1922 (T), No. 4550; *L/P & S/10*, 7251/1920, Pts. 4, 5.
32. Cox to Duke of Devonshire (SSC), Dec. 18, 1922 (L), No. 120; *ibid*.
33. Pol. Res. to Bray (Foreign Secy. in Delhi), Jan. 6, 1923 (L), No. 688; *ibid*.
34. Minute by J. A. Simpson, June 18, 1923, No. 2283; *L/P & S/10*, 7251/1920, Pts. 4, 5.
35. (Acting) HCI to SSC, Aug. 25, 1923 (T), No. 3223; *ibid*.
36. FO to CO, Oct. 5, 1923 (L), No. 3837; *ibid*.
37. 'Note on the invitation to King Husain to participate in the Kuwait Conference' by E. T. Richmond (India Office), Jan. 25, 1924, No. 891; *L/P & S/10*, 488/1920, Pt. 3.
38. HCI to SSC, Nov. 3, 1923 (T), No. 4232; *L/P & S/10*, 405/1922, Pt. 1.
39. See HCI to SSC, Sept. 24, 1923 (T), No. 3673; *ibid*.
40. FO to IO, Nov. 5, 1923 (L), No. 4256; *ibid*. Emphasis in the original.
41. FO to Bullard (British Consul, Jedda), Nov. 6, 1923 (T), No. 4256; *ibid*.
42. HCI to SSC, Nov. 7, 1923 (T), No. 4297; *ibid*.
43. SSC to Pol. Res., Nov. 12, 1923 (T), No. 4834; *L/P & S/10*, 450/1922, Pt. 1.
44. Naji al Assil (Husain's Foreign Minister) to FO, Nov. 16, 1923 (L), No. 56574; Colonial Office (CO), 727/6. [Colonial Office series 727 (Arabia), vol. 6 (PRO)].
45. Pol. Res. to SSC, Dec. 1, 1923 (T), No. 4653; *L/P & S/10*, 450/1922, Pt. 1.
46. Dobbs' requests for British sanctions against ibn Sa'ud if he did not subscribe to Faisal's demands elicited the following response from Knox. 'I must protest against [the] attitude of Iraq,... Faisal's... continued suggestions for impossible demands and threats by HMG appear to me as reasonable as to expect that while you are continually cracking your whip at him a horse running wild will come in... Their [Iraq's] present attitude suggests the imputation that they are resolved to produce such a state of mind in Bin Saud as to make my task impossible...' See Knox to SSC, Dec. 3, 1923 (T), No. 4673; *ibid*.
47. SSC to Pol. Res., Nov. 8, 1923 (T), No. 4303; *ibid*.

48. HCI to SSC, Nov. 27, 1923 (T), No. 4584; *L/P & S/10*, 450/1922, Pt. 1.
49. Knox to SSC, Dec. 21, 1923 (T), No. 4996; *L/P & S/10*, 450/1922, Pt. 1 (No. 32). The number in parenthesis is the actual number assigned by Knox to his telegram. It is given here—and will be given elsewhere when necessary—to differentiate between various despatches accorded the same register number by the India Office.
50. Knox to SSC, Dec. 21, 1923 (T), No. 4996; *ibid.*, (No. 33).
51. Knox to SSC, Dec. 18, 1923 (T), No. 4916; *ibid.*
52. Knox to SSC, Dec. 21, 1923 (T), No. 4996; *ibid.* (No. 32).
53. Knox to SSC, Dec. 22, 1923 (T), No. 4996; *L/P & S/10*, 450/1922, Pt. 1 (No. 35).
54. HCI to SSC, Dec. 22, 1923 (T), No. 5008; *ibid.*
55. Knox to SSC, Dec. 24, 1923 (T), No. 164; *L/P & S/10*, 450/1922, Pt. 1.
56. HCI to SSC, Dec. 27, 1923 (T), No. 5008; *L/P & S/10*, 450/1922, Pt. 1.
57. SSC to HCI, Jan. 18, 1924 (T), No. 342; *L/P & S/10*, 450/ 1922, Pts. 2, 3, 4. As regards (a), Iraq as a countermove put forward this demand in answer to Najd's second point.
58. HCI to SSC, Jan. 3, 1924 (T), No. 160; *L/P & S/10*, 450/1922, Pts. 2, 3, 4.
59. Knox to SSC, Jan. 21, 1924 (T), No. 414; *ibid.*
60. Knox to SSC, Jan. 26, 1924 (T), No. 516; *L/P & S/10*, 450/1922, Pts. 2, 3, 4.
61. The Sa'udi delegation consisted of Sayyid Hamza (president), 'Abdullah Efendi, Mulla Hafiz (better known as Hafiz Wahba), 'Abd al-'Aziz Al Qusaiba and Sa'id Hashim. The British took exception to Hafiz Wahba and Sayyid Hamza. The former, an Egyptian journalist, was said to be ' a notorious anti-British agitator and propagandist '. (See Knox to SSC, Dec. 16, 1923 (T), No. 4881; *L/P & S/10*, 450/ 1922, Pt. 1). The latter was described as a ' fugitive from justice in the Hedjaz '. (See Knox to SSC, Jan. 26, 1924 (T), No. 516; *L/P & S/10*, 450/1922, Pts. 2, 3, 4). In view of both Hamza's and Wahba's distinguished careers doubt is cast on the British impression of them.
62. Knox to SSC, Dec. 28, 1923 (T), No. 74; *L/P & S/10*, 488/1920, Pts. 2, 3, 4. These points are expressed generally in the writer's words owing to the telegraphically abbreviated (not to say, ambiguous) expression they were given in the above despatch. For further elucidation of the first and most important point see ' Report for the Eighth Session of the Kuwait Conference ', Dec. 23, 1924, No. 3393; *CO* 727/8.
63. *Ibid.*
64. Ibn Sa'ud to SSC, Jan. 19, 1924 (L), No. 989; *L/P & S/10*, 7251/ 1920, Pts. 4, 5.
65. Knox to ibn Sa'ud, Jan. 24, 1924 (L), No. 3393; *CO* 727/8.
66. Knox to SSC, Jan. 28, 1924 (T), No. 547; *L/P & S/10*, 450/1922, Pts. 2, 3, 4.
67. SSC to Knox, Feb. 5, 1924 (T), No. 666; *ibid.*

68. SSC to Knox, Feb. 14, 1924 (T), No. 801; *L/P & S/10*, 450/1922, Pts. 2, 3, 4.
69. SSC to Pol. Res., Feb. 5, 1924, No. 678; *ibid*. It should be noted here that, while the Secretary of State for the Colonies was communicating direct with Knox, all correspondence with ibn Sa'ud was through the Political Resident. Trevor, now Resident at Bushire, communicated with ibn Sa'ud, as usual, through Bahrain.
70. Knox to SSC, Feb. 22, 1924 (T), No. 974; *ibid*. Ibn Sa'ud had originally wanted his northern border to extend to a point which would have brought it parallel with Amman.
71. Knox to SSC, Feb. 29, 1924 (T), No. 1112; *L/P & S/10*, 450/1922, Pts. 2, 3, 4.
72. Knox to SSC, Feb. 29, 1924 (T), No. 10670; *CO* 727/9. It should be added that both the Political Resident and the Political Agent at Bahrain later thought that ibn Sa'ud could have sent his son if he had wanted to send him. See Pol. Res. to SSC, Mar. 19, 1924 (T), No. 1371; *L/P & S/10*, 450/1922, Pts. 2, 3, 4.
73. HCI to SSC, March 4, 1924 (T), 4/E2026; *FO* 371/9997.
74. Knox to SSC, March 8, 1924 (T), No. 11691; CO 727/9.
75. It should be noted that Knox thought that ibn Sa'ud would vent his wrath on the Hedjaz as Iraq was on the alert.
76. *Ibid*.
77. *Ibid*.
78. See *Survey*, pp. 64, 65.
79. HCI to SSC, March 13, 1924 (T), No. 1277; *L/P & S/10*, 450/1922, Pts. 2, 3, 4.
80. HCI to SSC, March 20, 1924 (T), No. 1440; *ibid*.
81. HCI to SSC, April 1, 1924 (T), No. 1600; *ibid*. Although reports on the massacre varied, one of Dobbs' sub-ordinates who had been designated to investigate the raid put forward the following figures: '... [the] Akhwan killed 146 men, 127 women and children and carried off 26,500 sheep, 3,710 donkeys, 2 camels and 5 horses. Women were spared but prisoners and wounded, both men and boys were killed; female casualties [were] caused by rifle [fire] at the time of the attack'. See HCI to SSC, April 7, 1924 (T), No. 1708; *ibid*.
82. Knox to SSC, April 3, 1924 (T), No. 1687; *ibid*.
83. See 'The Iraq-Najd Frontier' in *JCAS*, Vol. XVII, Pt. 1 (1930), p. 80. This unsigned article gives a good account of the geography, inhabitants and political situation of northern Arabia in the 1920's.
84. Copy of a Report from the PA Bahrain to the Pol. Res., n.d., No. 2697; *L/P & S/10*, 7251/1920, Pt. 1.
85. Bullard to MacDonald (Prime Minister and Foreign Secretary) March 29, 1924 (L), No. 2062; *L/P & S/10*, 1707/1924.

CHAPTER VII

The Wahhabi Capture of the Hedjaz and the Conclusion of the Hadda and Bahra Agreements

Two occurrences in March 1924 were undoubtedly important in ibn Sa'ud's decision to attack the Hedjaz in force. On March 5th 1924, Husain assumed the Caliphate which had been abolished by the Turkish Grand National Assembly two days earlier.[1] Moreover, Britain's subsidy to ibn Sa'ud ceased as of March 31st. In view of Husain's latest provocation and the fact that the termination of the British subsidy meant that ibn Sa'ud had little to lose by antagonising the British, there was little to restrain the Wahhabi leader from unleashing his zealous followers on the Hedjaz.

Britain chose to remain 'neutral' in the Najd–Hedjaz War. Her reason for this neutrality was that the issue was a religious one. Britain, however, was in no position to intervene even if she had wanted to do so. In India she was confronted by anti-British agitation on the part of a militant Indian Moslem nationalist group, the Khilafat Committee. This organisation was fervently opposed to any British interference in the Holy Cities. Moreover, Britain no longer had the leverage of threatening to withdraw ibn Sa'ud's subsidy.

The following pages will show that although Britain was to remain officially neutral, this 'neutrality' did not prevent her on behalf of Transjordan from asserting her authority in certain areas which most certainly belonged to the Hedjaz. While war raged in the Hedjaz Britain endeavoured to secure a position in Iraq and Transjordan by the Hadda and Bahra Agreements.

The Invasion of the Hedjaz[2]

On June 4th 1924 ibn Sa'ud's father, 'Abd al-Rahman, convened a congress of tribal, military, religious and Ikhwan leaders at Riyadh. The object of the congress was to discuss the pilgrimage and an Ikhwan petition for a campaign against the Hedjaz. Ibn Sa'ud urged restraint upon his followers, arguing that ' however easy it might be for the Najdis to take Mecca and Medina by force from King Husayn, it would be both unwarrantable and impolitic for them to attempt this [especially in the pilgrimage season] except as mandatories of the Islamic World, since the Holy Cities were a common possession of all Muslims '.[3]

Throughout the summer, Ikhwan raids took place against Transjordan and Iraq. As usual ,when ibn Sa'ud was confronted by the British on these raids, he pleaded provocation by tribes seeking refuge in Iraq and Transjordan. Moreover, he could not punish his raiders as they immediately sought sanctuary either in another country or in a neutral area.[4]

After a summer of Ikhwan raids and speculation on when ibn Sa'ud would strike in the Hedjaz and as the hot season drew to an end, the Wahhabi leader attacked on August 29, 1924. In view of his June declaration to postpone any attack on the Hedjaz until he had received a mandate from the Islamic world, it has been pointed out that ibn Sa'ud could not have received the Indian Khilafat Committee's sanction to attack ' if Husain rejects all our proposals ' before he actually commenced hostilities.[5] As this Khilafat movement has been the subject of much literature, its nature will only be touched upon briefly and in passing. For the purposes of this paper it should be noted that the Khilafat Committee, led by the brothers Shawkat and Muhammad 'Ali, was primarily an Indian Nationalist group of Moslems propounding allegiance to the Turkish Caliphate, but in practice using religious issues as a stick with which to beat their British rulers. They viewed Husain originally as a rebel against the Turkish Caliph and his assumption of the Caliphate as an act of grave provocation. In view of the Turkish abolition of the Caliphate and Husain's assumption of the title ' they looked to the hyper-orthodox Wahhabi ruler 'Abdu'l-Aziz b Sa'ud to act as the sword of Islam in place of the sacrilegious President of the Turkish Republic '.[6]

Returning to ibn Sa'ud's atack, his battle plans appear to have been carefully worked out. While the main contingent of the Wahhabi forces was poised at Khurma and Turaba for a strike at the Hedjaz, other contingents were despatched to raid Iraq, Transjordan and to cut the Hedjaz Railway. Supporting columns were also sent to the Wadi Sirhan. It is probable that these northern contingents were to act as diversions designed to forestall Iraq and Transjordan from assisting the Hedjaz.⁷

The Wahhabis first struck at Taif, the summer retreat of the Meccan wealthy class and chief oasis of the Hedjaz. 'Ali, Husain's eldest son, arrived at Taif at the head of a force of the Hedjaz army. However, as he received no support from the local tribes, he was soon forced to retreat to Hadda, approximately twenty miles to the north-west. Before the arrival of the senior commander of the Wahhabi forces, Sultan ibn Bijad ibn Humaid, a massacre took place. Among the casualties were several British Indians.⁸

In London, an informal conference at the Colonial Office was at first unable to decide from the reports at hand whether they were confronted by an internal Hedjazi revolution against Husain or an Ikhwan attack. After receiving proof that it was the latter, they directed that a warning be sent to the Ikhwan commander demanding that precautions be taken to safeguard the lives and property of British subjects in the Hedjaz.⁹

At this juncture, Britain was confronted by several problems. Husain had appealed to the British government, invoking the memory of his war-time role. 'Abdullah and Faisal pressed Great Britain to prevent the Wahhabis from capturing the Hedjaz. Both rulers threatened to go to the assistance of their father if Britain refused to help. 'Abdullah pointed out that if the Hedjaz came under ibn Sa'ud's control, Wahhabi influence would soon assert itself in Transjordan.¹⁰ Faisal asserted his dependence on the Hedjaz for his position in Baghdad. Moreover, if ibn Sa'ud were to overrun the Hedjaz, Faisal feared that the resultant growth of ibn Sa'ud's prestige would draw to the Sa'udi standard large numbers of Faisal's southern Euphrates tribes.¹¹ Britain was understandably hesitant to interfere in what she chose to view as a religious issue. Although concerned to protect the lives and property of her subjects resident in the Hedjaz, Britain as a Christian power could not despatch troops to the Moslem Holy Land. Moreover, owing to Khilafat agitation, she could not really countenance seriously the possibility of sending Moslem troops to intervene.

Britain finally decided to recognise the *fait accompli* of the Wahhabi invasion, but to emphasise to ibn Sa'ud the importance which Britain attached to the safety of pilgrim routes and British residents in, and pilgrims to, the Holy Land.

> H.M.G. have learnt that Taif has been taken by Arabs described as Wahhabis from outside the Hedjaz and that they are said to be advancing on Mecca. H.M.G. are not aware whether Ibn Saud is in any way party to the proceedings, but they think it necessary to remind him of article 5 of his treaty with them and to request him to assure them that British pilgrims to and residents in the Hedjaz are secure from molestation by any tribes who owe him allegiance. They take this opportunity of informing him in the most solemn and formal manner that they attach the greatest importance to and freedom of access to the Holy Places being enjoyed by British pilgrims and they are confident that he will neither do nor allow to be done by his followers anything calculated to prejudice that freedom.[12]

On September 24th, the Colonial Office wrote to the Foreign Office declaring the policy that was to be followed throughout the period culminating in the Sa'udi conquest of the Hedjaz.

> It is in the opinion of the Secretary of State [for the Colonies], out of the question that H.M.G. should in any case embark upon hostile action against Ib Sa'ud, whether direct or indirect, in defence of the Holy Places.[13]

While Husain called in vain for British support, the Hashimite position continued to deteriorate. As ibn Sa'ud's followers threatened Mecca, hundreds of the city's inhabitants fled to Jedda. Husain received little support from the Hedjazi tribes while the possibility of his receiving assistance from his sons was ruled out. Britain stated that she would ' give no countenance to interference in the Hedjaz by Transjordan and Iraq '. Reasserting her neutrality, Britain declared that she would only intervene if both sides spontaneously requested her assistance.[14]

In India, the Viceroy reported that in general Moslem opinion viewed the war in the Hedjaz as furthering the destruction of Islam. The Khilafatists, however, lauded the policy of ibn Sa'ud and were ' raising [an] outcry at [the] prospect of Britain giving support to King Husain or otherwise in the civil war in the Holy Land '. He further pointed out that while Moslems generally favoured the removal of King Husain, they did not regard the Wahhabis very highly.[15]

On October 3rd, the notables of Mecca and Jedda demanded

Husain's abdication and the unfortunate King of the Hedjaz had no other alternative but to comply with the demand.[16] The Hedjazi people then demanded a provisional government and the following day Husain's son 'Ali was appointed Constitutional Sovereign of the Hedjaz.[17] To add insult to ignominy, Husain was denied refuge at Amman as Samuel thought that he would interfere in 'Abdullah's affairs and provoke a major Wahhabi attack on Transjordan.[18] Although Husain was soon to settle temporarily in 'Aqaba, the effect of his forced exile coupled with the fact that he was not welcome to the British authorities in either Iraq or Transjordan, had an understandably adverse effect on both 'Abdullah and Faisal, especially the latter.[19]

As a Wahhabi seizure of Mecca seemed imminent, on October 5th 'Ali offered to negotiate but was turned down.[20] Within a week ibn Sa'ud's forces entered Mecca, giving a declaration that no one would be prevented from performing the pilgrimage nor would any other residents or their property be touched.[21] This time there was no massacre. With the loss of Mecca plus the capitulation of the ports of Qunfidh, Rabigh and Lith to the Wahhabis, 'Ali was left in command of only Jedda, Medina and the port of Yanbu'. At this juncture, the Khilafat Committee telegraphed to ibn Sa'ud that Husain and his sons must leave the Hedjaz, that a constitution for the Holy Land 'must be drawn up by the whole Islamic community' and that the area 'must be placed under a democratic government'.[22] On October 16th, ibn Sa'ud declared himself in agreement with the Khilafat Committee's views, replying to 'Ali's overtures for peace 'that, while the Najd had no intention of annexing or dominating the Hijaz, but would leave the new regime in the Holy Land to be determined by the Islamic World there could be no peace until both Husayn and his sons had left the country'.[23]

To clear up some of the ambiguities attaching to various declarations by ibn Sa'ud as to just what his war aims were, on October 29th a third congress [24] was held in Najd consisting of numerous military commanders, provincial representatives of Najd and several Iraqis, Egyptians and Syrians. Aware of the divided opinion in the Moslem World as regards Wahhabism in general and the invasion of the Hedjaz in particular, ibn Sa'ud made the following declaration. After reasserting 'that the sole purpose of the invasion of the Hijaz was to guarantee the liberty of Pilgrimage and to settle the destiny of the Holy Land in a manner satisfactory to the Islamic World ', he invited Muslims throughout the world to a congress at Mecca to decide the destiny of the Holy City. Basing his stand on the fact that the Indian Muslims approved his policy, ibn Sa'ud reiterated his ' ban upon the entire family of Husayn '.[25]

While ibn Sa'ud endeavoured to make his position clear to the Moslem world, he also took precautions to avoid any further excesses on the part of his levies. As early as October 3rd, he had guaranteed the British that he intended to come to ' an understanding with H.M.G. as to the deaths [of the British subjects in Taif] and say that he has issued strict orders that all non-combatants and foreigners are to be protected and the [British] captives released. He will send his son to the Hedjaz with a suitable force '.[26] Ibn Sa'ud's desire to avoid harming the foreign community in Jedda is shown by his decision to lay siege to Jedda although he was in an obvious position to take the city by force. Ibn Sa'ud arrived in the Hedjaz on December 6th 1924, and on January 6th 1925, the siege of Jedda began with Wahhabi shelling.[27]

As the year 1925 wore on, two important problems confronted the British. The first was the pilgrimage and the second was the problem of asserting British control from Transjordan over Ma'an and 'Aqaba lest ibn Sa'ud be left in possession of certain areas which would allow him to threaten 'Abdullah's Amirate.

Turning first to the pilgrimage, Britain was in a difficult position not only because of the implications in India but also owing to the fact that Moslems in general might be prevented from making the pilgrimage as a result of a conflict between her former protégés. On February 25th, ibn Sa'ud ' published a proclamation to all Muslims far and near informing them that 'Ali b. Husayn was closely blockaded in Jiddah and that he [ibn Sa'ud] would not only welcome Pilgrims but would guarantee their security on the road to Mecca from either Rabibh or Lith or Qunfudah '.[28]

Ibn Sa'ud did not really have much alternative other than to guarantee the pilgrimage. Legally, Article 5 of his treaty of 1915 with Great Britain bound him ' to keep open within his territories the roads leading to the Holy Places, and to protect Pilgrims on their passage to and from the Holy Places '. He had also justified his attack on the Hedjaz ' on the ground that King Husayn had neglected the rights of the Holy Places and had debarred the people of the Najd from making the Pilgrimage, ... [moreover, ibn Sa'ud had declared that he] would make the Pilgrim routes safe...'[29] From a purely political standpoint, assuming that ibn Sa'ud could restrain his fervent followers from committing massacres, he would gain immeasurably from a successful pilgrimage. Firstly, it would add to his stature, secondly he would obtain revenue and thirdly, he would undermine 'Ali's position.[30] In the end, the pilgrimage passed without incident.

As to the situation in the north, it will be recalled[31] that even before the Kuwait Conference, Britain had expressed the desire that Transjordan should have access to 'Aqaba and that its southern boundary should extend to Mudawwara in the vicinity of the Hedjaz Railway, thereby including Ma'an. In some respects, the incorporation of Ma'an and 'Aqaba into Transjordan merits the description as 'one of the most confused chapters in that country's history'.[32] In brief the question was: to whom did Ma'an and Aqaba legitimately belong? Prior to the dissolution of the Ottoman Empire Britain argued that the areas were attached first to the Vilayaet of Damascus, and were later appended to the Vilayet of the Hedjaz.

During the Arab Revolt, Husain had captured Ma'an and 'Aqaba from the Turks. While Faisal ruled briefly in Damascus, he and his father both laid claim to the areas.[33] After Faisal's expulsion from Damascus, the question of the ownership of Ma'an and 'Aqaba became an issue between 'Abdullah and Husain. Toynbee mentions that in 1922 it was reported that Husain transferred Ma'an to 'Abdullah.[34] As stated before, the British instructions to Knox of November 8th 1923, were worded so as to imply, if not state, the British desire to incorporate Ma'an and 'Aqaba in Transjordan. In March 1924, as the Kuwait Conference was nearing its abortive close, it was reported that on a visit to Amman, Husain transferred 'Aqaba and Tabuk to 'Abdullah. However, two days after the announcement, 'Abdullah's government officially denied this transfer.[35] Arguing that British officials had been trying to persuade Husain to transfer Ma'an and 'Aqaba to 'Abdullah for some time, Shwadran asserts that 'this time it was apparently so embarrassing to the Transjordan government that the British found it necessary to deny the report officially'.[36]

From mid-October 1924, until Clayton's mission a year later,

Britain endeavoured to secure her position first in Ma'an and later in 'Aqaba.

> H.M.G. regard Transjordan as extending to a point south of Ma'an on the Hedjaz railway. ... Abdullah should be invited to consult with his brother Ali for the immediate *retrocession* to Transjordan of the Ma'an area.[37]

On October 20th 1924, the Political Resident directed the Political Agent in Bahrain to inform ibn Sa'ud specifically what Britain desired Transjordan's southern boundary to be.[38] Ibn Sa'ud answered the Political Agent's letter stating that no mention of such boundaries had been made to him before, nor had they been disclosed during the Kuwait Conference. The Political Agent as much as admitted Britain's failure to communicate their conception of 'Abdullah's boundaries when he reported: ' I had assumed this and we wrote him details from Bahrain on October 21st '.[39] It should be noted that although the British were to prevent ibn Sa'ud from taking Ma'an and 'Aqaba, which he was to claim as Husain's successor in the Hedjaz, he was assigned almost all the Wadi Sirhan, including Qaf but excluding Azrak.

In the same letter in which ibn Sa'ud had requested details of the Transjordanian boundary, he had also offered to negotiate with Britain ' at any time and place convenient '.[40] While the British sought someone to negotiate with ibn Sa'ud, they cautiously went about extending their control over Ma'an. At this juncture the status of 'Aqaba was ' to be left indeterminate '.[41] The British were reluctant to assume—or ' resume ', as they were to put it—responsibility for Ma'an as they did for other areas more readily recognisable as part of Transjordan. They pursued a policy of gradually insinuating their control over the Ma'an vilayet. At the same time they warned 'Abdullah against assisting 'Ali from Ma'an, and also warned 'Ali that if he had to flee from Jedda, he could not expect to establish himself in Transjordan.[42]

> You will understand that the main consideration is *to stake out a claim* for Transjordan in the Maan area but this does not mean that H.M.G. will be prepared forthwith to *resume* military responsibility for the defence from [a] possible Wahhabi attack on Maan itself or other places in [the] Vilayet. Restoration of railway communication

between Amman and Maan is the first step: the rest must follow as and when circumstances permit.⁴³

In reply to the proposals of the new Colonial Secretary, L. S. Amery, Samuel telegraphed that after obtaining the views of the Chief British Representative and 'Ali Pasha al Rikabi, 'Abdullah's principal adviser, he was of the opinion that Amery's proposals would be unsuccessful. Samuel argued that

> No revenue is being collected in the Maan district under the present regime: Husain is providing all funds for administration and military purposes. It is therefore hopeless to expect the civil authorities at Maan to cooperate so long as they are paid by Husain. Nor can the General Manager of the Palestine Railways administer the railways with safety or efficiency unless he is assured of complete support and cooperation at the terminus. The question therefore resolves itself into the necessity of paying for [the] administration at Maan if we desire any adequate control.⁴⁴

In considering the evidence up to this point, it appears that both Ma'an and 'Aqaba were part of the Hedjaz. In the early 1920s, as Husain's power waned while ibn Sa'ud's increased, Britain endeavoured to include these areas in Transjordan owing to their strategic importance. If the reported transference of these areas had any validity, it is curious that this was not even mentioned in any of the unpublished British records or official British publications. Although when referring to Ma'an the Colonial Office used such terms as 'retrocession' and 'resume' implying that 'Abdullah had a prior claim to, or control of, Ma'an, these terms are contradicted by the expression 'to stake out a claim'.

No sooner had ibn Sa'ud been dissuaded from attacking Ma'an than by mid-spring 1925, a crisis evolved concerning ibn Sa'ud's intention to attack 'Aqaba owing to his legitimate complaint about Husain, who had retired to the port after his abdication and was using his place of exile to assist Jedda. To forestall a Wahhabi attack on 'Aqaba, London 'invited' Husain to leave the town within three weeks.⁴⁵ 'Ali, by this time desperate owing to mutinies among his troops for pay in arrears, protested in vain against this detachment of 'Aqaba as it would isolate Medina which received supplies from 'Aqaba.

In London, a draft ultimatum by the Colonial Office to ibn Sa'ud enjoining him not to attack 'Aqaba, provoked controversy. Amery, a staunch and pugnacious imperialist, requested the concurrence of the Foreign Secretary, Austen Chamberlain, in the proposed ultimatum which stressed that Britain would repel any unprovoked attack on territory for which she was responsible. Chamberlain believed that the attack was provoked and that Husain should be removed from 'Aqaba post-haste. Amery retorted that he did not want Husain 'hustled'. In a minute reflecting both the gravity of the situation and the point to which British regard for the leader of the Arab Revolt had sunk, Chamberlain wrote:

> Mr Amery has no objection to 'hustling' Ibn Saud with warships and landing parties, but we must not 'hustle' King Husain. If we don't 'hustle' him, he will stay where he is. Mr Amery asks my concurrence in an ultimatum which may lead to war. I will not give it unless (a) he undertakes to remove the provocation without hesitation or (b) my opinion is overruled by the Cabinet.
> ... I do think it essential ex King Husain should be got out with the least possible delay by 'invitation' if possible but otherwise if necessary. Why should we be involved in a war ... for King Husain? [46]

Ibn Sa'ud was warned against attacking 'Aqaba and a letter was drafted to him by the Foreign Office emphasising Britain's desire to 'consult with you with a view to the removal of any such grievance and to the settlement of all outstanding questions between yourself and Transjordan and Iraq'.[47] Husain was taken by a British warship to Cyprus, his new place of exile.

As regards the ownership of 'Aqaba, several unpublished records—which are comparatively devoid of the special pleading, contradictions and vague expressions usually made in defence of British policy in Ma'an and 'Aqaba—give the impression that 'Aqaba was probably Hedjaz territory. For example, the Colonial Office's instructions to Knox on the eve of the Kuwait Conference[48] were interpreted in a report on the 'Aqaba situation by the Committee of Imperial Defence as follows:

> Ex-King Hussein ... has taken refuge in Akaba, *and as that place has continued to remain under the administration*

of the Hedjaz Government, Ibn Saud has considered, and rightly considered, that it is being used as a port from which munitions are being forwarded for use against his forces . . .'.[49]

The *underlined* section of the above could indicate that it had been administered by the Hedjaz before Husain settled there. It should be noted that when Husain was first looking for a place of exile, Samuel had adamantly refused to have him in Amman, arguing firstly that he would interfere with 'Abdullah's affairs and secondly that he might provoke a Wahhabi attack on Transjordan.[50] In view of the second contention, if Transjordan had good claim to 'Aqaba, Samuel perhaps overlooked the fact that Husain's presence there might also provoke an attack on Transjordan.

In June 1925, in the House of Commons, Amery defined the assertion of British power in Ma'an and 'Aqaba by arguing that ' in pursuance of its declaration of neutrality in the Husain–Ibn Saud war ' Britain had to assume responsibility ' when it appeared that it [the Ma'an–'Aqaba area] was being used by Husain for military purposes '. The Permanent Mandate Commission, however, was displeased with British action in Ma'an and 'Aqaba, and in 1925 W. Ormsby-Gore appeared before the Commission only to repeat Amery's sentiments. The Permanent Mandates Commission was still dissatisfied with Britain's explanation and requested her ' to investigate further the legal status of the area '.[51]

In June 1925, 'Abdullah issued the following proclamation:

> On the authority of His Hashimite Majesty King Ali, King of the Holy Hejaz, we declare the districts of Maan and Akaba to be part of the Amirate of Transjordan. On behalf of our people and Government we express our heartfelt thanks to His Majesty.[52]

The above proclamation would seem to indicate that both areas were in the Hedjaz. As it would be somewhat difficult to believe that 'Ali would, during a fight for survival, gratuitously cede his two chief supply centres, it is reasonable to accept the contention of one authority that 'Abdullah allowed his brother to continue to use Ma'an and 'Aqaba for ' military purposes '.[53]

By the end of June, 'Ali's position was virtually hopeless. With the loss of 'Aqaba and Ma'an, Medina was cut off at least officially from its supply bases. Husain's exile to Cyprus prevented him from assisting his ex-kingdom directly. A safe, if small, pilgrimage further undermined 'Ali's position while he, at the same time, was plagued by the refusal of his Palestinian troops to fight without pay. Moreover, Wahhabi superiority in the field linked with the above factors resulted in the defection of various Hedjazis to ibn Sa'ud's standard.[54] However, before the final stages of the Najd–Hedjaz war are considered, attention will now be focussed on Anglo–Sa'udi negotiations between Sir Gilbert Clayton and ibn Sa'ud.

Clayton's Mission[55]

As the year 1925 wore on. ibn Sa'ud's complete conquest of the Hedjaz appeared inevitable. No doubt foreseeing the possibility of ibn Sa'ud 'in the hour of victory'[56] turning his energies towards his Hashimite adversaries to the north, Britain decided to open negotiations. In order to settle the outstanding issues between her protégés and the Sultan of Najd, Sir Gilbert Clayton, who had just retired from his post as Chief Secretary of the Government of Palestine, was despatched to negotiate with ibn Sa'ud. On October 10th 1924, Clayton arrived at a special camp set up by ibn Sa'ud at Umm al Qurun, midway between Bahra and the Hadda oasis. The object of the mission was to settle the Najd–Transjordan frontier and the problems between Iraq and Najd which had not been settled at the Kuwait Conference. Twenty meetings took place between October 10th and November 3rd when the negotiations ended.

As regards the Transjordanian frontier settlement, Britain desired that the frontier follow the same line as originally telegraphed to Knox before the Kuwait Conference[57] and repeated again[58] on October 20th 1924 by the Political Resident to Bahrain for transmission to ibn Sa'ud.[59] The only difference was that this time the British desired that Qaf be included in Transjordan. It was to be ceded to ibn Sa'ud only if a deadlock over its inclusion with 'Abdullah's frontiers were reached. The reason for this change in position over Qaf was due to a reconsideration of the village's strategic position already discussed.[60] Once again the overriding reason governing Britain's desire for a boundary joining Iraq and Transjordan was the necessity to consolidate her north Arabian position and secure her communications and pipelines.

Ibn Sa'ud was made to agree essentially to the British frontier but ultimately forced Clayton to cede Qaf to him. Ibn Sa'ud based his argument for the retention of Qaf on the fact that a boundary including Qaf had already been offered to him in the preceding October. He argued that in view of the discontent among his tribes owing to his deference to the British in not redressing the grievances suffered by his people at the hands of 'Abdullah, he had been forced to publish the contents of this letter. The Sultan told Clayton that

> A few months ago, however, when one of our messengers carrying the mail was arrested and ill-treated by 'Abdullah, the Chiefs of our tribes and certain members of our Government protested loudly to us, and in order to reassure them we had no other course than to acquaint them with the terms of His Majesty's Government's letter of the 23rd October, 1924, which recognised our right to Kaf. We placed this letter before them in support of our contention that His Majesty's Government would deal fairly with us on the question of our natural frontier.
>
> In submitting this to your impartial examination, I have to ask you to consider my position towards my people. What am I to say to them in face of these events? Can I tell them that the letter which I showed them was an invention on my part? Or am I to say that the British Government, always renowned for its loyalty and honour, had reversed its previous decision and annulled the letter which I had to parade before my people? It is out of the question for me to accept such a thing, both for my sake and for that of the British Government.[61]

As ibn Sa'ud pointed out 'his authority in Nejd rested entirely on his personal ascendancy over his subjects and that the reversal of a decision which he had published as final would mean a greater risk to his prestige than he was prepared to run'.[62]

On November 2nd 1925, the Hadda Agreement was signed. Article I ceded Qaf to ibn Sa'ud but affirmed the southern position of the western frontier of Najd and the northern frontier ' as fixed by His Majesty's Government'. It should be noted that if Clayton was compelled to cede Qaf he did manage to exclude almost the whole of the four smaller wadis adjoining the Wadi Sirhan from Najd. Articles 2, 4 and 8 secured Transjordan from Wahhabi aggression and propaganda and also stipulated that Qaf could not be fortified. Articles 5 and 6 dealt with the prevention of raids, and 7 and 8 covered the regulation of tribal movements. In Article 13 Britain guaranteed freedom of passage to ibn Sa'ud for his trade between Najd and Syria and secured exemption from customs for all goods in transit. Article 12 dealt with freedom of passage to be accorded to pilgrims and travellers. To prevent friction between Najd and Transjordan, Article 3 provided for constant communication between the Najdi Governor in the Wadi Sirhan and the Chief British Representative in Amman. Articles 9, 10 and 11 covered minor issues of frontier regulation.[63] It should be noted that by awarding most of the Wadi Sirhan to ibn Sa'ud, the agreement secured his suzerainty over much of the Ruwalla tribe. Moreover although Britain could not delimit the frontier between the Hedjaz and Transjordan owing to the conflict in the Hedjaz, Clayton, following his instructions from the Colonial Office, was able to persuade ibn Sa'ud to regard the possession of Ma'an and 'Aqaba as a ' chose jugée '.[64]

Turning now to the Bahra Agreement, Clayton was able to incorporate practically all of his instructions, which were essentially a repetition of the British desiderata put forward at the Kuwait Conference, into this agreement. With one exception [65] all the points agreed upon at the Kuwait Conference (Articles 1, 5, 6 and 7) were embodied in the Bahra Agreement. The two main points which had caused deadlock at the Kuwait Conference—the extradition of refugee tribes and the circumstances under which armed contingents could be raised—were settled. As regards extradition, Clayton was able to get ibn Sa'ud to agree to Iraqi's point of view (Article 8).[66] An extradition clause was inserted (Article 10) but again it was the re-statement of an Iraqi point [67]; this article provided for the negotiation of an agreement between Iraq and Najd for the extradition of common criminals. Clayton was also able to prevail upon ibn Sa'ud to accept the Colonial Office's proposal (Article 9) put forward during the Kuwait Conference which provided for the exaction of guarantees from a tribe which had emigrated from one territory to another and then raided in its former territory. Article 8 again embodied a proposition which the Najdi delegation at

Kuwait had rejected. This article stipulated that were a tribe in one territory called on by the other territory to provide armed contingents, it could only go if it left quietly and took its families and belongings.[68]

Articles 1 to 7 of the Bahra Agreement were similar to Articles 5 to 11 of the Hadda Agreement. The 'Uqair Conference was accepted as the starting point for compensation for raids and severe punishment was stipulated for any future raiding. A Najdi–Transjordanian and a Najdi–Iraqi mixed tribunal were to be organised to deal with tribal aggression, fix the responsibility and assess the damages. Movements of tribes were to be restricted except for grazing purposes.[69]

By the signature of the Hadda and Bahra Agreements, a significant advance was made towards the development of regular relations between Najd and her Hashimite neighbours in the north. With the exception of the frontier between the Hedjaz, which ibn Sa'ud was soon to capture, and Transjordan, the northern boundary of Najd was finally delimited.[70] It is now time to devote our attention to the final stages of the Najd-Hedjaz War.

The Wahhabi Victory

In July, the Consul at Jedda reported that he had received a letter from ibn Sa'ud stating that the Wahhabi leader had been invited by the Idrisi ruler of the 'Asir, the province between the Hedjaz and Yemen ,to take over his government.[71] The following month the Wahhabis ' bombarded ' Medina. Attacks were also made against Yanbu'.[72] The British had offered to mediate between 'Ali and ibn Sa'ud but the latter had rejected this proposal.[73] Although there were few if any Europeans in Medina or Yanbu', ibn Sa'ud was still careful about unleshing his men on these two cities, probably owing to his own doubts about his ability to restrain his followers. He had already excited much Moslem opinion against himself when it was reported that Wahhabi projectiles had badly damaged the Prophet's tomb in Medina.[74]

On November 10th the Acting British Consul in Jedda, Mr Jordan, who had recently replaced Bullard, reported that the garrison at Medina had requested that ibn Sa'ud receive the surrender of the city personally in order to avoid excesses. On December 5th the city surrendered, followed on the 21st by

Yanbu'. 'Ali, realising that to hold on any longer was useless, asked Mr Jordan to act as intermediary in his surrender to ibn Sa'ud. On December 18th, 'Ali 'announced his withdrawal from the Hijaz',[75] and the following day the Wahhabis peacefully entered the city. On December 21st, the British Consul accompanied Jedda officials to ibn Sa'ud's camp where they formally surrendered.[76] The following day, 'Ali sailed for Iraq.

On December 23rd, ibn Sa'ud entered Jedda and two days later announced officially that the Najd-Hedjaz War was ended. On January 8th 1926, the notables of the Hedjaz pledged allegiance to ibn Sa'ud and proclaimed him King of the Hedjaz and Sultan of Najd and its Dependencies. Within the next three months, he was recognised by Great Britain, the USSR, France and the Netherlands, the chief non-Moslem powers who ruled Islamic peoples.[77]

Notes

1. For a further account of local reaction see Bullard to MacDonald (Prime Minister and Foreign Secretary), March 29th, 1924 (L), No. 2062; *L/P & S/10*, 1707/1924.
2. The writer acknowledges his debt to Toynbee's *Survey*, pp. 296-310, for much of the substance and sequence of events in this chapter. As Toynbee has done a thorough job in telling the story of the siege and its ramifications in the Moslem World, only a brief outline of this story will be presented. As the writer is primarily concerned with British policy towards and reactions to the Sa'udi onslaught, the reader is referred to Toynbee for a more general account of this period. It should also be noted that in view of Toynbee's extensive use of the journal *Oriente Moderno* for much of the material for his work, the writer has usually given the references to Toynbee as being easier of access.
3. *Survey*, p. 297.
4. In August 1924, a huge Ikhwan raid estimated at between 1,500 and 3,000 raiders took place in Transjordan in the neighbourhood of Amman. They were driven off by the R.A.F. and armoured cars, suffering great losses. It was reported in one paper that the 'whole country from Kaf as far as Jauf was literally strewn with Corpses'. See Major E. W. Polsen-Newman 'The Trans Jordan Fighting' in *The Near East*, September 18th, 1924.
5. *Survey*, p. 297, quoting from the Khilafat Committee's letter reproduced in *Oriente Moderno*, IV, 10, pp. 645, 6.
6. *Ibid.*, p. 63. For an account of the abolition of the Caliphate and the Khilafat movement in India, see *Survey*, pp. 25-90. K. K. Aziz, *The Making of Pakistan: A Study in Nationalism* (London, 1967), pp. 111-115 and the same author's *Britain and Muslim India* (London,

1963), chap. 7. The most recent, and arguably the best, treatment of the Khilafat movement is to be found in F. C. R. Robinson, 'The Politics of UP Muslims, 1906–1922', unpublished Ph.D. dissertation, the University of Cambridge, 1970.
7. *Ibid.*, p. 298.
8. *Ibid.* Toynbee writes that the Ikhwan advance guard was led by Khalid ibn Luwai, the Amir of Khurma, 'who had old scores to pay off'. See *Survey*, p. 298. Bullard reported that the first news of the Wahhabi attack was received in Jedda with 'hardly concealed delight'. Bullard continued: 'The inhabitants of Mecca and Jeddah now say that but for the news of the massacres they would have deposed King Husain'. It is interesting to note that Bullard described the townsman of the Hedjaz as 'a mean-spirited and cowardly creature whose doughty deed is the swindling of a live pilgrim or the robbing of a dead one. His hatred of King Husain had hitherto been concealed under an effusive servility ,but at the sight of the Wahhabis about, as he thought, to set him free from King Husain, he began to talk treason boldly'. See Bullard to MacDonald, Sept. 28, 1924 (T), No. 4232; *L/P & S/10*, 1707/1924.
9. FO to Bullard, Sept. 12, 1924 (T), No. 3746; *L/P & S/10*, 3665/1924, Pt. 1.
10. HCP to SSC, Sept. 11, 1924 (T), No. 3705; *L/P & S/10*, 3665/1924, Pt. 1.
11. HCI to SSC, Sept. 18, 1924 (T), No. 3855; *ibid.*
12. SSC to Pol. Res., Sept. 13, 1924 (T), No. 43017; *CO* 727/8.
13. CO to FO, Sept. 23, 1924 (L), No. 44525; *CO* 727/8.
14. SSC to HC ('s) for I. and P., Sept. 30, 1924 (T), No. 3979; *L/P & S/10*, 3665/1924, Pt. 1.
15. Viceroy to SSI, Sept. 25, 1924 (T), No. 3890; *ibid.*
16. Bullard to FO, Oct. 3, 1924 (T), No. 4053; *ibid.*
17. *Survey*, p. 299.
18. HCP to SSC, Oct. 11, 1924 (T), No. 4115; *L/P & S/10*, 3665/1924, Pt. 1.
19. In Iraq the High Commissioner reported that during an interview with Faisal, the Iraqi King, who had just learned that his father would be refused refuge in Transjordan 'was overcome by acute hysteria. He sobbed, cried and threw himself about...' See HCI to SSC, Oct. 13, 1924 (T), No. 4156; *L/P & S/10*, 3665/1924, Pt. 1.
20. *Survey*, p. 300.
21. Bullard to FO, Oct. 14, 1924 (T), No. 4169; *L/P & S/10*, 3665/1924, Pt. 1.
22. *Survey*, p. 300.
23. *Ibid.*
24. The second congress is reported to have been held in Najd on September 25th. For the decisions of this congress and an account of the various policy declarations see *Survey*, pp. 302–304. In reference to the above mentioned ambiguities, Toynbee points out that at this second congress it was decided *inter alia* that Husain should be deposed and that Wahhabi military occupation should be extended

over the entire Hedjaz with the exception of Mecca. However ibn Sa'ud soon extended his war aims. After Husain's abdication he demanded that the whole family leave the Hedjaz. Moreover, he proceeded to occupy Mecca. See *Survey*, pp. 303–304.

25. *Ibid.*, pp. 303–304.
26. Pol. Res. to SSC, October 19, 1924 (T), No. 4241; *L/P & S/10*, 3665/1924, Pt. 1.
27. H. St J Philby, *Arabia* (London, 1930), p. 312.
28. *Survey*, p. 305.
29. *Ibid.*, pp. 302, 303.
30. Bullard to FO, May 8, 1925 (T), No. 2889; *L/P & S/10*, 3665/1921, Pt. 5
31. See p. 192.
32. B. Shwadran, *Jordan, A State of Tension* (New York, 1959), p. 154. Hereafter *Shwadran*. As Shwadran devotes four and a half pages to a competent discussion of the Ma'an-'Aqaba issue, relying on the relevant secondary and official published sources (which the writer himself has checked), his arguments will only be summarised briefly here and emphasis will be given to the unpublished records. For a more general treatment of the Ma'an-'Aqaba question, see his pp. 154–158.
33. *Ibid.*
34. *Survey*, p. 342.
35. *Ibid.* A usually reliable Arabic source states that at this time (March, 1924) Husain gave only administrative rights over 'Aqaba and Ma'an to 'Abdullah. Legal possession remained with the Hedjaz. See M. Al Mady and S. Musa, *Tarikh Al Urdun fi Al Qaran Al 'Ushrin (A History of Jordan in the Twentieth Century)* (Amman? 1957), p. 248. Hereafter *Al Mady and Musa*. The writer wishes to thank Dr P. A. Gubser for drawing his attention to and helping with the translation of passages from this work. For further comment on the transfer of territory in 1924 see *Oriente Moderno*, Vol. IV, No. 4, pp. 262, 263.
36. *Shwadran*, p. 156.
37. SSC to HCP, Oct. 15, 1924 (T), No. 4193; *L/P & S/10*, 3665/1924, Pt. 1. My emphasis.
38. 'The intersection of meridian 39 with parallel 32 to the intersection of meridian 37 with parallel 31 1/2. Thence along meridian 37 to parallel 31. Thence to the intersection of meridian 38 with parallel 30. Thence along meridian 38 to parallel 29 degrees 35 [minutes] or [a] point due west of [the] Nefud salient. Thence crossing the Hedjaz railway in the neighbourhood of Mudawwara to [a] point on the Gulf south of Akara. Ends. In other words [the] boundary stretches from [the] Gulf of Akaba at a point due west of Mudawwara through and Jebel Tubik up to meridian 38, 32 miles below the intersection of meridian with parallel 30. Thence north-west about 95 miles of Wakf-As-Suan, thence north about 40 miles, thence 120 miles east and slightly north to [the] intersection of meridian 39 with parallel 32, thus forming a trijunction with Iraq.' See Pol. Res to PA, Bahrain, Oct. 20, 1924 (T), No. 607 14; *CO* 727/8.

39. Pol. Res. to SSC, Nov. 25, 1924 (T), No. 4637; *L/P & S/10*, 3665/1924, Pts. 2, 3, 4.
40. *Ibid.*
41. SSC to HCP, Feb. 25, 1925 (T), No. 585; *ibid.*
42. *Ibid.*
43. SSC to HCP, Feb. 25, 1925 (T), No. 585; *L/P & S/10*, 3665/1924, Pts. 2, 3, 4. My emphasis.
44. HCP to SSC, March 7, 1925 (T), No. 707; *ibid.*
45. FO to Commander of the H.M.S. Cornflower (anchored off 'Aqaba), May 27, 1925 (T), No. 1681; *L/P & S/10*, 3665/1924, Pt. 5.
46. Minute by A. C. [Chamberlain], May 25, 1925, No. 10 E/2990; *FO* 371/10808.
47. FO to Bullard, n.d., No. 1603; *L/P & S/10*, 3665/1924, Pt. 5.
48. See p. 201.
49. Report by Sub-Committee of the CID on the Akaba Situation, June 3, 1925, No. 315; CAB 24/174. [Cabinet Memoranda (24), Vol. 174 (PRO)]. My emphasis. It is interesting to note that the British commander of Transjordan's Arab Legion, Lt. Col. Peake, wrote: 'One result of ... [Husain's] abdication was that the Maan Vilayet was added to Transjordan'. See Peake Pasha (Lt. Col. F. G. Peake), *A History of Jordan and Its Tribes* (Florida, 1958), p. 108. Moreover, Bullard—certainly no ardent partisan of the Hashimites—stated that 'Akaba is admitted to be in the Hedjaz'. See Bullard to FO, May 20, 1925, No. 1680; *L/P & S/10*, 3665/1924, Pt. 5.
50. See HCP to SSC, Oct. 11, 1924 (T), No. 4115; *L/P & S/10*, 3665/1924, Pt. 1, and Official Administrating the Govt. of Pal. to SSC, Oct. 16, 1924 (T), No. 4195; *L/P & S/10*, 3665/1924, Pt. 1.
51. *Shwadran*, pp. 156, 157. In 1928, the frontier between Transjordan was finally delimited including Ma'an and 'Aqaba in Transjordan. Ibn Sa'ud objected but 'took no action to support his claim'. See *Memoirs of King Abdullah of Transjordan*, ed. by P. P. Graves (London, 1950), n. 1, p. 217. Hereafter *Abdullah*.
52. *Abdullah*, p. 217.
53. *Al Mady and Musa*, p. 250.
54. Bullard to Chamberlain, June 30, 1925 (T), No. 2565; *L/P & S/10*, 1704/1924. Bullard had reported on several occasions that 'Abdullah had supplied Palestinian (perhaps meaning primarily Transjordanian mercenaries) to fight with 'Ali's beleaguered forces.
55. The Hadda and Bahra agreements with some of the relevant correspondence have been published as a British White Paper (Cmd. 2566, 1925) and are dealt with in printed detail in an eighty-seven page report (Clayton's Report to CO, Feb. 26th, 1926, No. 747; *L/P & S/10*, 87/26, Pts. 1, 2. Hereafter *Clayton's Report*). As they also have been summarised in Toynbee's *Survey*, and have recently been the subject of a full length book (*Collins*), only a brief summary of the negotiations and the agreements will be given here. For the Hadda and Bahra agreements see the above mentioned Command Paper. For a brief biographical account of Clayton's distinguished career in the Middle East see *Collins*, Introduction.

56. *Survey*, p. 343.
57. See p. 201.
58. See p. 213, n. 38.
59. This message was actually sent to ibn Sa'ud on October 23rd, 1924.
60. See p. 194.
61. Memorandum No. 3 of October 14th, 1925, in Annexure 4 of *Clayton's Report*.
62. *Clayton's Report*.
63. *Ibid*. See also *Survey*, pp. 343, 344.
64. Appendix to *Clayton's Report*.
65. The exception was the proposal that Inspectors of Boundaries be appointed.
66. It will be remembered that Iraq had originally objected to the extradition of refugees on the basis that it was contrary to tribal hospitality and tradition. Moreover it would have been impractical. See p. 203.
67. See No. 7 of the original Iraqi points put forward at the Kuwait Conference, p. 202.
68. *Clayton's Report* and *Survey*, pp. 343, 344.
69. *Survey*, pp. 344, 345.
70. Toynbee wrote. ' It may be noted that if, from the south-western terminus of the Transjordan-Najd frontier a line were drawn due eastwards to Red Sea, that line would assign 'Aqabah and Ma'an to Transjordan and Tabuk to the Hejaz'. *Survey*, p. 346, n. 1.
71. Bullard to Chamberlain, July 20, 1925 (T), No. 2809; *L/P & S/10*, 1707/1924. It has already been mentioned (see p. 182, n. 1) that in 1920 ibn Sa'ud conquered much of the 'Asir. In 1922 on the death of Sayyid Muhammad al Idrisi his son, 'Ali, encouraged by Imam Yahya of Yemen, ascended the throne. To years later ' Ali was deposed by his uncle, Husain. ' In 1925 the Imam Yahya seized the opportunity of this rivalry to seize Tihamah and Al-Hudaydah, while Ibn Sa'ud capitalised on it to establish a virtual protectorate in 'Asir by recognising Husayn as a Wahhabi puppet'. *Collins*, pp. 208, 209, n. 13. Collins states further than ibn Sa'ud had agreed to guarantee Husain's position as ruler of the 'Asir ' if, on his death, the region would be annexed to Ibn Sa'ud's domains'. See his p. 213, n. 22.
72. *Survey*, p. 306.
73. Bullard had written to ibn Sa'ud on July 10th to ask him if he would agree to 'Ali's request for British mediation. Ibn Sa'ud declined.
74. On closer scrutiny, the tomb was seen to have been struck and slightly marred by five ordinary bullets.
75. *Survey*, p. 307.
76. Acting British Consul (Jordan) to FO, Dec. 22, 1925 (T), No. 4517; *L/P & S/10*, 3665/1924, Pts. 7, 8, 9.
77. *Survey*, p. 311.

CHAPTER VII

Postscript

By December 1926, ibn Sa'ud had reached the summit of his career. With the conquest of the Hedjaz he had unified the greater part of the Arabian Peninsula and laid the foundation for present day Sa'udi Arabia. Today the mention of Sa'udi Arabia conjures up images of endless rivers of oil and economic power. In 1926, however, ibn Sa'ud's treasury was virtually empty and the desert wastes over which he ruled had yet to yield their vast wealth. In view of Sa'udi Arabia's present position in world affairs, it might be useful to review, however briefly,* the events of the decade following his conquest of the Hedjaz, taking our story up to the first major oil concession.

Early in 1927 Sir Gilbert Clayton returned to Arabia to negotiate a new treaty with ibn Sa'ud. The events of 1926 had made the earlier Anglo–Sa'udi Treaty of 1915 completely obsolete. On May 20th 1927 the Treaty of Jedda was signed annulling the old agreement of 1915. It was to run for seven years in the first instance. By the terms of the new treaty the British recognised 'the absolute independence of the dominions' of ibn Sa'ud. In return, ibn Sa'ud undertook to respect British treaties with the Trucial Shaikhs, to suppress slavery and to facilitate the Pilgrimage of British subjects.[1]

The problem of the Pilgrimage had long been one of ibn Sa'ud's top priorities and immediately upon his conquest of the Hedjaz, he set about ridding the province of its baser evils and making it safe for the Pilgrimage. This purification process was largely carried out by zealous members of the Committee for the Commendation of Virtue and the Condemnation of Vice. Prostitution was suppressed and the consumption of alcohol and use of tobacco were at least banished from public places for a

---

* This summary of events pretends in no way to be thorough, comprehensive or original. It is, as the title indicates, a postscript. Naturally much more work must be done on this period, especially now that records are available for the 1930s.

time. The Committee also pressed individuals to be punctual in their prayers.²

In addition to improving conditions in the Hedjaz, ibn Sa'ud began to build around him the infrastructure of an administration. Most of his original advisers had been with him for at least a few years and did not originally come from the peninsula. In 1928, Fuad Hamza, a Palestininan, took charge of the Sa'udi Foreign Office. In 1929 Abdullah Sulaiman, a Najdi, became head of the Treasury. In 1930 Hafez Wahba, an Egyptian, became Sa'udi representative and later ambassador to London. Yusif Yasin, a Syrian, was appointed Political Secretary and later became Minister of State. In these early years ibn Sa'ud wisely refrained from appointing members of his own family to important administrative posts until they were more prepared to assume these responsibilities. It is interesting to note that the above-named officials originally appointed to various posts by ibn Sa'ud were largely to remain in charge of their respective departments until ibn Sa'ud died in 1953.

In addition to building an administration and assuring a less than friendly Islamic world at large that Sa'udi rule in the Hedjaz could be a welcome change from the past, ibn Sa'ud confronted the formidable task of reconciling his fundamentalist followers to the ways and inventions of the modern world. Philby —who was soon to leave the British Service and become a Moslem, an Arabian entrepreneur as well as explorer and adviser to ibn Sa'ud—notes for example that the motor car was viewed by the orthodox Wahhabi ' as an invention of the infidel, if not the devil...'. He adds that ' the first lorry to enter the fanatical town of Hauta was burned publicly in the market place, while the driver nearly shared its fate '.³ Moreover, legend has it that the radio was accepted by some of the ardent only when they heard verses of the Quran being broadcast over the machine. More difficult was the reconciliation of some of the Ikhwan chiefs to ibn Sa'ud's moderate rule in general and his relations with the infidel British and their Hashimite satellites in particular.

Soon after the ratification of the Treaty of Jedda fighting broke out on the Iraqi border and set in motion a chain of events which were to dominate ibn Sa'ud's attention for the next few years. Arguably in contravention of Article 3 of the first 'Uqair Protocol attached to the Treaty of Muhammera which forbade the construction of forts along the border,⁴ Sir Henry

Dobbs sanctioned in 1927 the building of a police post eighty miles from the Najd border. It was to be manned by ten policemen. The Ikhwan who, along with other Najdis, had been assured by ibn Sa'ud that these agreements would not interfere with their grazing rights took matters into their own hands. A force of Mutair tribesmen attacked and massacred a working party who had started construction on the post at the wells of Busaiya in the Neutral Zone between Iraq and Najd. Ibn Sa'ud's tribes could see no distinction between police and military; moreover, the Sa'udi government made little use of maps at this time and therefore was not fully aware of the distance of Busaiya from the Najdi border.[5] This initial raid soon spread and the frontier once again went up in flames.

As the Ikhwan proceeded to raid and plunder first Iraq and then Kuwait, the RAF responded by pursuing Najdi raiding parties across the border and bombing them at will. Clayton's attempts to mediate in the dispute between Iraq and Najd foundered as the Ikhwan broke various truces and the British rejected ibn Sa'ud's demand that the post be demolished. The flames of Ikhwan zealotry were further fanned by the bombings of the RAF and several paramount shaikhs rebelled against ibn Sa'ud's accommodation with the British. The principal leaders of this rebellion were Faisal al Duwish of the Mutair and Sultan ibn Bijad of the 'Ataiba, the chiefs respectively of Artawiya and Ghatghat, the two most extreme centres of the Ikhwan movement. These chiefs were supported by, among others, the Ajman tribe which had plagued ibn Sa'ud since before the War.

Ibn Sa'ud attempted to settle the matter by consultation but this traditional tribal practice failed. The fighting dragged on until early 1930. In March 1929 a major encounter between the Ikhwan and ibn Sa'ud's forces took place on the plain of Sibba, between Zilfit and Artawiya. Faisal's and ibn Bijad's forces were thoroughly beaten. Ibn Bijad was captured and imprisoned in Riyadh and his town of Ghatghat was razed to the ground. Faisal al Duwish was badly wounded and left to die in peace. However the redoubtable chief recovered and massed his followers for one final assault on ibn Sa'ud's rule.

In January 1930 ibn Sa'ud took the field in person for the last time in his life. At Sha'ib al 'Auja near Riqai where the frontiers of Iraq, Najd and Kuwait meet, ibn Sa'ud attacked and completely broke the back of the Ikhwan Rebellion. The rebel chiefs including Faisal al Duwish ended their days in a dungeon in Riyadh. The Ikhwan Movement which had done so much to facilitate ibn Sa'ud's rise to power was effectively destroyed. It had served its purpose in the early days. It was accordingly broken when it posed an obstacle to the development of ibn Sa'ud's new state.[6]

With the Ikhwan Rebellion over, the British endeavoured to bring ibn Sa'ud and King Faisal of Iraq together in order to arrive at some accommodation between the two rivals. On February 22nd 1930 the two kings met aboard HMS *Lupin* in the Persian Gulf under the auspices of Sir Francis Humphreys, the new High Commissioner in Iraq. Glubb describes part of the meeting as follows:

> A crisis arose at one stage which nearly caused a failure of the meeting. It was agreed that the two monarchs should exchange letters, but King Feisal refused to address Ibn Saud as King of the Hejaz. King Feisal's father, King Husain, had been driven from the throne of that country by Ibn Saud only four years earlier, and the latter now refused to accept any letter addressed to him which did not give him the title of king of the Hejaz and Nejed and its dependencies. It fell to Sir Francis Humphreys to pacify the ruffled feelings of the two monarchs. After no little trouble, both agreed to address one another without titles as 'my dear brother'.[7]

The two rulers finally participated in the drafting of a Bon Voisinage Agreement which was initialled in Baghdad a fortnight later. From this meeting onwards relations between the two countries were amicable.

Soon after the settlement between Iraq and Najd, fighting broke out on ibn Sa'ud's ill-defined southern border with Yemen. Desultory clashes and negotiations dragged on until 1934 when ibn Sa'ud finally invaded Yemen, occupying large tracts of the country including the important port of Hudaidah. Ibn Sa'ud's natural caution and restraint no doubt reinforced by Great Power interest in Yemen as evidenced by the arrival of British, French and Italian warships in Hudaidah resulted in a truce. By the terms of the Treaty of Taif of 1934, hostilities ceased between the only two independent countries in the peninsula and ibn Sa'ud restored most of the occupied territory to Imam Yahya.[8]

The war with Yemen had been costly, especially as it had been fought in the wake of a world-wide depression. Ibn Sa'ud's financial situation in the early 1930s therefore was more than usually desperate. There had been talk now for some time about the potential mineral wealth of Sa'udi Arabia as the country was renamed in 1934. Although ibn Sa'ud was less than optimistic about these possibilities his financial situation made him amenable to the acquisition of any ready money. Attempts had been made as early as 1918 to obtain oil concessions in Arabia but unstable political conditions, among other factors, prevented any tangible results. As mentioned earlier,[9] Major Frank Holmes, the indefatigable New Zealander representing the Eastern General Syndicate of London, had already approached ibn Sa'ud for mineral concessions. In December 1922, during the 'Uqair Conference, ibn Sa'ud granted Holmes a concession. The syndicate agreed to pay ibn Sa'ud an annual rent of £2,000 in advance and to prospect until oil was found or proved to be non-existent. The concession was finally abandoned in 1928 after a team of Belgian economists failed several times to discover any oil deposits. Ibn Sa'ud received a total of £4,000 from the venture.[10]

In 1932 the Bahrain Petroleum Company, an Anglo–American organisation, discovered oil in Bahrain in quantities considerable enough to inspire oil companies to press on in Arabia with further explorations. In 1930 Standard of California had sought and failed to obtain rights of free exploration from ibn Sa'ud. In 1931 the Arabophile American philanthropist C. R. Crane who had earlier shown interest in the Middle East with reference to the Allied scheme to impose a French mandate on Syria, visited Jedda. Crane and ibn Sa'ud discussed the economic potential of Arabia and Crane undertook to send, at his own expense, Karl S. Twitchell, an American mining engineer, to carry out explorations. In 1932 Twitchell reported that certain features of Dhahran indicated the possible presence of oil.

Twitchell returned to the United States and after failing to interest several companies persuaded the Standard Oil Company of California to request a comprehensive concession for mainland exploration. Twitchell then returned to Jedda along with Standard's representative, Lloyd Hamilton, to negotiate with the Sa'udis. During the negotiations the British Iraq Petroleum Company (IPC), represented by Stephen Longrigg, and Holmes of the Eastern General also made offers. Ibn Sa'ud demanded gold payments which put Longrigg at a great disadvantage as the directors of IPC only sanctioned him to offer rupees. Holmes quickly withdrew from the negotiations when the Sa'udis demanded a £100,000 downpayment in gold. Longrigg was only permitted to offer £10,000 down. The concession was therefore awarded to Standard. On May 29th 1933 Hamilton and Shaikh 'Abdullah Sulaiman signed an agreement for a sixty-year concession for the Hasa province. In Longrigg's words:

> The territory covered was the whole of eastern Sa'udi Arabia as far west as the Dahana, with assurance of future preferential treatment over wide further areas which included the Sa'udi's half rights in the Kuwait Neutral Zone. An initial payment of 30,000 gold sovereigns was counted out at Jidda a few weeks later; an annual minimum payment of 5,000 sovereigns, two loans of 50,000 sovereigns each when commercial oil should be discovered, and a royalty of 4s (gold) per ton, were the other financial considerations. Exemptions were granted from taxation and custom duties.[12]

Standard assigned the concession to an affiliate especially created for the purpose, the California Arabian Standard Oil Company or CASOC.

In late September 1933, Standard's geologists embarked on the explorations. In spring 1935 the first well in Dhahran was drilled but produced nothing significant. Standard built up its complex at Dhahran and pressed on with exploratory drilling. Success came early in 1938 when at a depth of 4,550 feet, well no. 7 revealed oil in considerable quantities, a harbinger of things to come. A six-inch pipline was laid to the coast at Al Khobar and Ras Tanura was selected to receive tankers for the export of oil. On May 1st 1939, marked by a visit in state by ibn Sa'ud, the first cargo of oil was shipped from Ras Tanura. In 1939 ibn Sa'ud's hitherto impoverished kingdom received an annual royalty of around £200,000 gold.

Ibn Sa'ud never let his wealth go to his head; he governed as he had before until the end of his days. When he died in 1953 he had, however, as Philby wrote, ' the satisfaction of seeing the income on which he had started life, multiplied 2,000-fold to the respectable sum of about £100 million a year '.[13] Today the wealth of the country has become legendary and—together with the economic power resulting from it—has brought Sa'udi Arabia to a prominent position on the world stage.

Notes

1. For a copy of the Treaty of Jedda see Hurewitz II.
2. For the events of this period generally see Philby, *Sa'udi Arabia*, Chap. II.
3. *Ibid.*, p. 304.
4. For a copy of the Treaty see Report on Iraq Administration, April 1922–March 1923.
5. Glubb, *War in the Desert*, p. 193, 194. Glubb notes: ' Ibn Saud's protests were plausible. The Iraqi case was based on the fact that Busaiya was eighty miles from the Nejed border and not in its vicinity. It was, moreover, not a military fort but a police post, to be manned by ten policemen.
   ... In Nejed, there was no difference between soldiers and police, so that a point which appeared of basic importance to the Iraqis and the British, meant nothing to the king [ibn Sa'ud]. After all, it is just over a hundred years since a regular police force was established in Britain. Previous to that time, the army or the militia were the only forces used to prevent civil disturbances '. *Ibid.* For a detailed account the Ikhwan Rebellion see Glubb's chaps. XI–XIX.
6. See Philby, *Sa'udi Arabia*, pp. 306–313 and Glubb, *War in the Desert*, chap. XIX.
7. Glubb, *War in the Desert*, p. 344.
8. On the Yemeni campaign see M. W. Wenner, *Modern Yemen 1918–1966* (Baltimore, 1967), pp. 143–147 and Philby, *Sa'udi Arabia*, pp. 321–324.
9. See p. 187, n. 92.
10. Philby, *Sa'udi Arabia*, p. 329.
11. The oil negotiations may be followed, among other places, in S. H. Longrigg, *Oil in the Middle East*, 3rd Edn. (London, 1968), chap. VII; Philby, *Sa'udi Arabia*, pp. 329–332, and in Twitchell's own book, *Sa'udi Arabia* (Princeton, 1958).
12. See Longrigg, *Oil in the Middle East*, p. 108.
13. Philby, *Sa'udi Arabia*, pp. 332–333.

Conclusion

The preceding pages have reviewed in detail British policy towards ibn Sa'ud in the important period when he imposed his will on and unified the greater part of the Arabian peninsula. Some general conclusions remain to be drawn. From a traditional policy of non-involvement in central Arabian affairs it took the catalyst of World War I and the Ottoman alliance with Germany to force Great Britain into formal relations with ibn Sa'ud. The conclusion of the Anglo–Sa'udi Treaty of 1915 marked the turning point in Anglo–Sa'udi relations. Although the British still tried to avoid entanglement in central Arabian affairs they were now bound to determine ibn Sa'ud's frontiers. Try as they might, the British after 1915 could only postpone entanglement; they could no longer avoid it. Ibn Sa'ud was sophisticated enough to demand a treaty. Husain was not.

In view of ibn Sa'ud's achievements it is tempting to say, as many have, that the British should have backed him as the leader of the Arab Revolt. Not only does this contention enter the dubious realm of speculation and hindsight, but it also ignores the relative attributes of the two leaders at the time. It is also more than doubtful whether Shakespear's survival would have altered the Government of India's attitudes and assumptions any more than it would, in the political climate of the day, have detracted from the pre-eminence accorded by the British government to the ' Cairo School of thought '.

Throughout the period under consideration inter-office rivalry played a major role in Anglo–Sa'udi relations. The clash of interests and viewpoints among the various authorities concerned, coupled with the exigencies of the time and the remoteness of Arabia, provided ample opportunities for powerful personalities such as Cox, or forceful, ambitious junior officers to exercise considerable influence. As regards the importance of the junior officer, the example of Lawrence on the western side of the peninsula is well known. The role of Philby, although less dramatic in its impact, has been illustrated above. Perceiving early the potential of ibn Sa'ud, Philby relentlessly championed his cause to the British government. Disappointed with British treatment of Ibn Sa'ud in particular, and British policy towards the Arabs in general, he became as vigorous a critic of British policy as he was a champion of the attributes of ibn Sa'ud. Believing as he did that ibn Sa'ud was 'perhaps the greatest Arab since Muhammad',[1] he endeavoured through his many books to present his hero—and himself—to the West. Philby remains a very valuable source on the Wahhabis and Sa'udi history in the twentieth century. He is less reliable as a guide to the realities governing British policy towards ibn Sa'ud.

In many respects one must sympathise with Philby's admiration of ibn Sa'ud. Although certainly the most ardent and prolific of ibn Sa'ud's admirers, he was by no means alone. Ibn Sa'ud repeatedly stated his intention to recapture the Sa'udi patrimony but he was realistic and shrewd enough to know that he needed the British too much to alienate them. He played it accordingly. Although unable many times to restrain his Ikhwan he proved Delhi's greatest fear to be unfounded, namely that massacres and interrupted pilgrimages would follow a Wahhabi capture of the Hedjaz as they had done in the early nineteenth century.

For some time now it has been unfashionable for historians to speak of 'great men'. Yet in the light of his achievements it would be difficult to resist the conclusion that ibn Sa'ud was a great man. Against the general background of a Middle East in transition, gripped by the forces of rapid change and technological advance, ibn Sa'ud's legacy today—as perhaps his achievement two generations ago—must appear anomalous in the twentieth century. However, operating within the framework of traditional Arabia and judged by its standards, he stood the test of greatness. Gibbon wrote that 'the times must be suited to extraordinary characters'. In Arabia, at this time, they were. The figure of Lawrence, his legend and his works have cast a long shadow. This shadow has tended to obscure the fact that there was also another drama of great importance being played on the other side of the peninsula.

Notes

1. Philby, *Sa'udi Arabia*, Introduction.

Appendices*

* Of the appendices dealing with treaties the following are the sources: App. II: *FO* 371/2769; App. III: *Memo*, No. 5120; *L/P & S/10*, 2182/1913, Pts. 7, 8.

Appendix I

Abbreviated Genealogy of the House of Sa'ud
(Numbers and capitalisation indicate the line of major rulers)

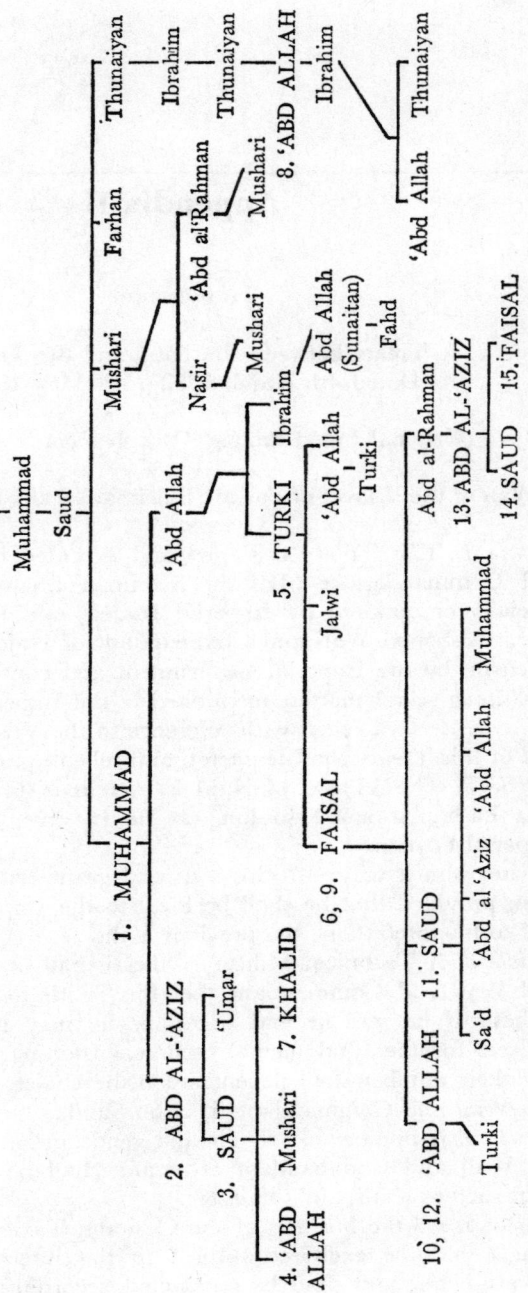

GENEALOGY TAKEN FROM *WINDER* PAGE 279

Appendix II

Translation
of
Treaty between Ibn Saud and the Turks.
Dated 4th Rajab 1332–15th May 1914.

(Original found among Turkish records at Basrah).

Wali of the Vilayet of Basrah. Suleiman Shafik bin Ali Kumali.

Article 1. This Treaty is signed and executed between the Wali and Commandant of Basrah, Suleiman Shafik Pasha, who is specially empowered by Imperial Iradeh, and H. E. Abdul Aziz Pasha Al-Saood Wali and Commandant of Najd: This Treaty is relied on by the Imperial Government and consists of 12 articles, explaining secret matters mentioned in the Imperial Firman dated .... with reference to the Vilayet of Najd. The text of this Treaty shall be secret, and relied upon.

Article 2. The Vilayet of Najd is to remain in charge of Abdul Aziz Pasha Al-Saood so long as he is alive, according to the Imperial Firman.

After him it will go to his sons and grandsons by Imperial Firman, provided that he shall be loyal to the Imperial Government and to his forefathers, the previous Valis.

Article 3. A Technical Military Official shall be appointed by the said Wali and Commandant (i.e. Bin Saud) to live wherever he wishes: if he sees fit and necessary he may introduce Turkish Officers for the fundamental technical training of Local Troops, and their number shall depend upon the choice and wishes of the said Wali and Commandant (i.e. Ibn Saud).

Article 4. A number of soldiers and gendarmerie, as deemed fit by the Wali and Commandant aforesaid, shall be stationed at seaports such as Katif, and Ojair, &c.

Article 5. All the business of the Customs, Taxes, Ports and Light houses shall be exercised subject to the international rights of Governments, and shall be conducted according to the principles of the Turkish Government under the direction of the said Wali and Commandant.

Article 6. Till the sources of the revenues reach a degree sufficient to meet the requirements of the Vilayet and the local expenditure and military dispositions according to the present circumstances and normal conditions of Najd, the deficiency in the budget shall be met from the Customs, Posts, Telegraphs and Ports revenue; and if there is a surplus, it should be sent to the Porte with a report.

If the local revenue is sufficient to meet all expenses, the income of the Posts, Telegraphs and Customs shall be remitted to their respective Departments. Also as regards local incomes other than those mentioned above, if there is any surplus, 10 per cent of it shall be sent to the Government Treasury.

Article 7. The Turkish flag shall be hoisted on all Government buildings and places of importance on the sea and on the land, and also on boats belonging to the Vilayet of Najd.

Artice 8. Correspondence shall be conducted with the Marine Department for the regular supply of arms and ammunition.

Article 9. The said Wali and Commandant is not allowed to interfere with, or correspond about foreign affairs and international treaties, or to grant concessions to foreigners.

Article 10. All the correspondence of the Wali and Commandant shall be direct with the Imperial Ministeries of Interior and Marine, without intermediary.

Article 11. Post Offices shall be established in the Vilayet of Najd, in order to facilitate communication; and arrangements shall be made to despatch posts to the necessary places in a fitting manner; Turkish stamps shall be affixed to all letters and packages.

Article 12. If, God forbid, the Government should have to fight with a foreign power or if there should be any internal disturbance in any Vilayet and the Government asks the said Wali for a force to co-operate with its own forces it is incumbent on the Wali to prepare a sufficient force with provisions and ammunition, and to respond to the demand at once, according to his power and ability.

Signed.   Abdul Aziz,
            Wali of Najd Wilayet, and Commander of its Army.
Signed.   Suleiman Shafik Bin Ali Kamali,
            Wali of Basrah Wilayet, and Commander of its Forces.

Appendix III

(Part 1)

A Comparison of the Drafts
of the
Anglo-Sa'udi Treaty of 1915

British draft	*Bin Saud's draft*
In the name of God the Merciful and Compassionate.	In the name of God the Merciful and Compassionate.
The High British Government on its own part, and Abdul Aziz-bin-Abdur Rahman-bin-Faisal al-Saud, Ruler of Najd, Al Hasa and Qatif, on behalf of himself, his heirs and successors and tribesmen, being desirous of confirming and strengthening the friendly relations which have for generations existed between the two parties, and with a view to consolidating their respective interests—the British Government have named and appointed Lieutenant-Colonel Sir Percy Cox, K.C.I.E., C.S.I., British Resident in the Persian Gulf, as their Plenipotentiary to conclude a Treaty for this purpose with Abdul Aziz-bin-Abdur Rahman-bin-Faisal al-Saud,	The High British Government on its own part, the Abdul Aziz-bin-Abdur Rahman-bin-Faisal as-Saud, Ruler of Najd, El Hasa, Qatir, *Jubail, and the towns and ports belonging to them*, on behalf of himself, his heirs and successors and tribesmen, being desirous of confirming and strengthening the friendly relations which have for a *long time* existed between the two parties, and with a view to consolidating their respective interests—the British Government have named and appointed Lieutenant-Colonel Sir Percy Cox, K.C.I.E., C.S.I., British Resident in the Persian Gulf, as their Plenipotentiary, to conclude a Treaty for this purpose with Abdul Aziz-bin-Abdur Rahman-bin-Faisal as-Saud,
The said Lieutenant-Colonel Sir Percy Cox, and Abdul Aziz-	The said Lieutenant-Colonel Sir Percy Cox, and Abdul Aziz-

bin-Abdur Rahman-bin-Faisal al Saud, hereafter known as "Bin Saud", have agreed upon and concluded the following articles :—

I.

The British Government do acknowledge and admit that Najd, Al Hasa and Qatif,

and their territories and ports on the shores of the Persian Gulf are the territory of Bin Saud and of his fathers before him, and do hereby recognise the said Bin Saud as the independent Ruler thereof,

and after him his sons and descendants by inheritance, but the selection of the individual shall be *subject to the approval of the British Government, after confidential consultation with them.*

II.

In the event of *unprovoked* aggression by any Foreign Power on the territories of the said Bin Saud and his descendants, the British Government will aid Bin Saud to such extent and in such manner as the situation may seem to them to require.

III.

Bin Saud hereby agrees and promises to refrain from

bin-Abdur Rahman-bin-Faisal as Saud, hereafter known as "Bin Saud", have agreed upon and concluded the following articles :—

I.

The British Government do acknowledge and admit that Najd, El Hasa, Qatif, *Jubail, their dependencies and territories, which will be discussed and determined hereafter,*
and their territories and ports on the shores of the Persian Gulf are the *countries* of Bin Saud and of his fathers before him and do hereby recognise the said Bind Saud as the independent Ruler thereof *and as absolute Chief of their* tribes,
and after him his sons and descendants by inheritance, but the selection of the individual shall be according to the designation of his successor (by the living Ruler) *or by the calling for the votes of the subjects inhabiting those countries.*

II.

In the event of aggression by any Foreign Power on the territories of the countries belonging to the said Bin Saud, and his descendants, the British Government will aid Bin Saud *in all circumstances and in any place.*

III.

Bin Saud hereby agrees and promises to refrain from

entering into any correspondence, agreement or Treaty with any Foreign Nation or Power and further to give immediate notice to the political authorities of the British Government of any attempt on the part of any other Power to interfere with the above territories.

IV.

Bin Saud hereby undertakes *for ever* that he will not cede, *sell,* mortgage or otherwise dispose of the above territories or any part of them, or grant concessions within those territories to a Foreign Power or to the subjects of any Foreign Power without the consent of the British Government, whose advice he will unreservedly follow.

V.

Bin Saud hereby promises to keep open the roads leading through the above territories to the Holy Places and to protect pilgrims on their way to and from the said shrines.

VI.

Bin Saud undertakes as his fathers did before him to refrain from all aggression on, or interference with, the territories of Kuwait, Bahrain, Qatar and Oman Coast, or *other tribes and Chiefs* who are under the protection of the British Government, and the limits of whose

entering into any correspondence, agreement or Treaty with any Foreign Nation or Power and further to give immediate notice to the political authorities of the British Government of any attempt on the part of any other Power to interfere with the above territories.

IV.

Bin Saud hereby undertakes that he will not cede, mortgage, or otherwise dispose of the above territories or any part of them, or (*grant*) concessions within those territories to a Foreign Power or to the subjects of any Foreign Power without the consent of the British Government, whose advice he will unreservedly follow, *where his interests require it.*

V.

Bin Saud hereby promises to keep open the roads leading *through his countries to the* Holy Shrines and to protect pilgrims on their *return* to the Holy Places.

VI.

Bin Saud undertakes as his fathers did before him to refrain from all aggression on or interference with the territories of Kuwait, Bahrain, *the Shaikhs of* Qatar and the Oman Coast, who are under the protection of the exalted Government and have Treaty relations and the territories shall be hereafter determined.

VII.
The British Government and Bin Saud agree to conclude *so soon as this can conveniently be arranged*, a further detailed Treaty in regard to *other* matters jointly concerning them.

limits of their territories shall be hereafter determined.

VII.
The British Government and Bin Saud agree to conclude a further detailed Treaty in regard to matters jointly concerning the two parties.

(Signed) ABDUL AZIZ-BIN-ABDUR RAHMAN-BIN-FAISAL-BIN-SAUD.
(Seal of Abdul Aziz-bin-Abdur Rahman-bin-Faisal-bin-Saud.)

Appendix III

(Part 2)

TEXT OF THE TREATY OF DECEMBER 26, 1915

In the Name of God the Merciful and Compassionate

Preamble

The High British Government on its own part, and Abdul Aziz-bin-Abdur Rahman-bin-Faisal Al-Saud, Ruler of Najd, El Hassa, Qatif *and Jubail, and the towns and ports belonging to them,* on behalf of himself, his heirs and successors, and tribesmen, being desirous of confirming and strengthening the friendly relations which have *for a long time* existed between the two parties, and with a view to consolidating their respective interests—the British Government have named and appointed Lieutenant-Colonel Sir Percy Cox, K.C.S.I., K.C.I.E., British Resident in the Persian Gulf, as their Plenipotentiary, to conclude a treaty for this purpose with Abdul Aziz-bin-Abdur Rahman-bin-Faisal Al-Saud.

The said Lieutenant-Colonel Sir Percy Cox and Abdul Aziz-bin-Abdur Rahman-bin-Faisal Al-Saud.

The said Lieutenant-Colonel Sir Percy Cox and Abdul Aziz-bin-Abdur Rahman-bin-Faisal Al-Saud (hereafter known as " Bin Saud "), have agreed upon and concluded the following articles :—

I.

The British Government do acknowledge and admit that Najd, El Hassa, Qatif *and Jubail,* and their *dependencies and* territories, *which will be discussed and determined hereafter,* and their ports on the shores of the Persian Gulf are the *countries* of Bin Saud and of his fathers before him, and do hereby recognise the said Bin Saud as the independent Ruler thereof *and absolute Chief of their tribes,* and after him his sons and descendants by inheritance; but the selection of the individual shall be *in accordance with the nomination* (i.e., *by the living Ruler) of his successor; but with the proviso that he shall not be a person antagonistic to the British Government in any respect; such as, for example, in regard to the terms mentioned in this treaty.*

II.

In the event of [' *unprovoked* ' *omitted*] aggression by any foreign Power on the territories of the countries of the said Bin Saud and his descendants *without reference to the British Government and without giving her an opportunity of communicationg with Bin Saud and composing the matter,* the British Government will aid Bin Saud to such extent and in such a manner as *the British Government after consulting Bin Saud may consider most effective for protecting his interests and countries.*

III.

Bin Saud hereby agrees and promises to refrain from entering into any correspondence, agreement, or treaty with any foreign nation or Power, and, further, to give immediate notice to the political authorities of the British Government of any attempt on the part of any other Power to interfere with the above territories.

IV.

Bin Saud hereby undertakes that he will *absolutely* not cede, sell, mortgage, *lease*, or otherwise dispose of the above territories or any part of them, or grant concessions within those territories to any foreign Power or to the subjects of any foreign Power,* without the consent of the British Government.

And that he will follow her advice unreservedly provided that it be not damaging to his own interests.

V.

Bin Saud hereby *undertakes* to keep open *within his territories the roads leading to the Holy Places,* and to protect pilgrims on their *passage* to and from the Holy Places.

---

* The words ' or the subjects of any foreign Power ' were accidentally omitted in the copies signed by Sir P. Cox and Bin Saud on the 26th December, 1915. Sir P. Cox drew Bin Saud's attention to this omission in a letter dated the 27th December, 1915 (38086/16), and added: ' I have duly written them in the text of the original document which I am submitting to Government, and Government will consider it in this form; so that if the same mistake occurs in the copy with you, I trust you will add the words above quoted '.

VI.

Bin Saud undertakes, as his fathers did before him, to refrain from all aggression on or interference with the territories of Kuwait, Bahrein, *and of the Sheikhs of* Qatar and the Oman Coast [" *other tribes and chiefs* " *omitted*], who are under the protection of the British Government, *and who have treaty relations with the said Government*; and the limits of their territories shall be hereafter determined.

VII.

The British Government and Bin Saud agree to conclude [*words in original draft omitted*] a further detailed treaty in regard to [*word omitted*] matters concerning the two parties.

Dated 18th Safar 1334, corresponding to 26th December, 1915.
    (Signed and sealed)   ABDUL AZIZ AL-SAUD.
                                   P. Z. COX, Lieutenant-Colonel,
                                   British Resident in the Persion Gulf.
    (Signed)   CHELMSFORD,
                                   Viceroy and Governor-General
                                   of India.

This treaty was ratified by the Viceroy and Governor-General of India at Simla, on the 18th day of July, 1916 A.D.
    (Signed)   A. H. GRANT,
                                   Secretary to the Government
                                   of India, Foreign and
                                   Political Department.

Bibliography

This bibliography lists those sources mentioned in the notes and some others which have proved useful. Although the use made of various works in the preceding pages indicates the importance of each of them, I have also called special attention in the bibliography to those sources which I found particularly useful. Sections A and B—dealing with manuscript collections and published documents—are comprehensive. Sections C and D list only the most important works consulted. I have refrained from calling the bibliography "select" only because I have cited several sources dealing generally with British (and, to a lesser extent, European) history. Although these works are not specifically relevant to Anglo-Sa'udi relations, I have listed them as they proved helpful in forming a fuller perspective of the period treated.

A. Manuscript Collections
Official Correspondence

Great Britain
    Public Record Office, London.
        Arab Bureau files, series 882.
        Cabinet files, series 24 (Cabinet Memoranda).
        Colonial Office files, series 727 (Arabia).
        Foreign Office files, series 371 (Turkey).
        Foreign Office Confidential Print, series 424 (Turkey).
    Commonwealth Relations Office: India Office Records, London.
        Political and Secret Department, Home Correspondence, 1875–1911.
        Political and Secret Department, Letters from India, 1875–1911.
        Political and Secret Department, Memoranda.
        Political and Secret Department (Regular) Files, 1912–1930.
        Political and Secret Department, Residency Files: 1 (Bushire), 2 (Bahrain), 3 (Muscat) and 4 (Kuwait).
        Political and Secret Department, Subject Files, 1902–1931.

Foreign Office Library, London.
  The Arab Bulletin : 1915–1919.

Private Correspondence

St. Antony's College, Oxford.
  The Papers of H. R. P. Dickson (partial collection).
  The Papers of Hubert Young.
  The Papers of H. St. J. B. Philby (partial collection).
School of Oriental Studies, University of Durham.
  The Papers of Sir Gilbert Clayton.
  The Papers of Sir Reginald Wingate.
British Museum.
  The Papers of Sir Arnold Wilson.

B. Published Documents

Great Britain
  Admiralty: Naval Intelligence Division, Geographical Handbook Series. *Western Arabia and the Red Sea.* Oxford, 1946.
  Foreign Office:
  British Documents on the Origins of the War 1898–1914, ed. by G. P. Gooch and H. Temperley. London, 1926–1938. 11 Vols. in 13.
  United Kingdom Memorial : *Arbitration Concerning Buraimi and the Common Frontier Between Abu Dhabi and Saʿudi Arabia.* Vol. 1, London, 1955.
    This volume is useful for an account of Wahhabi history and Anglo-Saʿudi relations. It also possesses important maps.
  Cmd. 5957 (1939) *Correspondence between Sir Henry McMahon . . . and the Sherif Hussein of Mecca.*
  Iraq—Report on Iraq Administration, April 1922–March, 1923. London, 1923.
  Palestine, Report of the High Commissioner on the Administration of Palestine, 1920–1925. London, 1926.
  Report by His Britannic Majesty's Government on the Administration of Iraq, April 1923–December 1924. London, 1925.
India
  Foreign and Political Department.
    Aitchison, C. U. *A Collection of Treaties, Engagements, and Sanads Relating to India and Neighbouring Countries.* 5th edition, Vol. XI, Delhi, 1933.

Lorimer, J. G. *Gazetteer of the Persian Gulf*, '*Oman, and Central Arabia*, 2 Vols. in 4. Calcutta, 1908–1915.
  Indispensable for the study of the history of the development of the British position in the Gulf and Anglo-Wahhabi relations.

Other Sources
Hurewitz, J. C. *Diplomacy in the Near and Middle East: A Documentary Record*. 2 Vols., Princeton, 1956.

Saʻudi Arabia: *Memorial of the Government of Saʻudi Arabia: Arbitration for the Settlement of the Territorial Dispute Between Muscat and Abu Dhabi on One Side and Saʻudi Arabia on the Other*, 3 Vols., Cairo, 1955.

C. Special Articles

Bari, M. A., 'The Early Wahhabis and the Sharifs of Makkah', *Journal of the Pakistan Historical Society*, Vol. III (1953).

Cunningham, A. 'The Wrong Horse—A Study of Anglo-Turkish Relations Before the First World War', *St. Antony's Papers*, No. 17, Middle Eastern Affairs, No. 4 (1965).

Dawn, C. E., 'From Ottomanism to Arabism', *Review of Politics* XXIII (1962).

—— 'The Amir of Mecca al-Husayn ibn Ali and the Origin of the Arab Revolt', *Proceedings of the American Philosophical Society* CIV (1960).

—— 'The Rise of Arabism in Syria', *Middle East Journal* XVI (1962).

—— 'Great Britain and the Powers, 1904–1914', *The Cambridge History of the British Empire*, Vol. III: *The Empire-Commonwealth, 1870–1919*, ed. by E. A. Benians et al. Cambridge, 1959.

Hinsley, F. H. 'British Foreign Policy and Colonial Questions, 1895–1904', *The Cambridge History of the British Empire*, Vol. III: *The Empire-Commonwealth, 1870–1919*, ed. by E. A. Benians et al. Cambridge, 1959.

Hogarth, D. G. 'Wahhabism and British Interests', *Journal of the British Institute of International Affairs*, IV (1925).

Kelly, J. B., Review of R. B. Winder's *Saʻudi Arabia in the Nineteenth Century*, *Middle Eastern Studies*, Vol. 3, No. 1 (1966), published by Frank Cass, London.

—— 'Mehmet Ali's Expedition to the Persian Gulf, 1837–

1840', *Middle Eastern Studies*, Vols. 1, 2, Nos. 4, 1 (1965), Frank Cass, London.

—— 'The Legal and Historical Basis of the British Position in the Persian Gulf', *St. Antony's Papers*, No. 4, *Middle Eastern Affairs*, No. 1 (1958).

Pelly, Lt.-Col. L. 'A Visit to the Wahabee Capital, Central Arabia', *Journal of the Royal Geographical Society*, Vol. XXXV (1865).

Philby, H. St. J. B. 'The Triumph of the Wahhabis', *Journal of the Central Asian Society*, Vol. XIII, Part IV (1926).

—— 'Transjordan', *Journal of the Central Asian Society*, Vol. II (1924).

Marwick, A. 'The Impact of the First World War on British Society', *Journal of Contemporary History*, Vol 3 (1968).

Rentz, G. S. 'Dickson's *Arab of the Desert*', *The Muslim World* XLI (1951).

—— 'The Iraq-Najd Frontier', *Journal of the Central Asian Society*, Vol. XVII, Part I (1930).

Toynbee, A. 'The Rise fo the Wahhabi Power' and 'The Delimitation of Frontiers', *Survey of International Affairs*, 1925, Vol. I (1927).

Both the above-mentioned sections are indispensable for the study of Anglo-Sa'udi relations.

Troeller, G. 'Ibn Sa'ud and Sharif Husain: A Comparison in Importance in the Early Years of the First World War', *Historical Journal*, Vol. 14, No. 3 (1971).

D. General Works, Biographies, Memoirs, and Monographs

Abdullah, King of Transjordan, *Memoirs*, ed. by P. P. Graves. London, 1950.

Ahmad, F. *The Young Turks, The Committee of Union and Progress in Turkish Politics* (Oxford, 1969).

Al Mady, M. and Musa, S. *Tarikh Al Urdun fi Al Qarun Al Ushrin* [A History of Jordan in the Twentieth Century] Amman (?), 1957.

Amery, L. S. *My Political Life*. London, 1953. 2 Vols.

Anderson, M. S. *The Eastern Question, 1774–1923, A Study in International Relations* (London, 1966).

Antonius, G. *The Arab Awakening*. London, 1955.

For years the definitive work on the rise of Arab nationalism.

Aziz, K. K. *Britain and Muslim India*. London, 1963.

Aziz, K. K. *The Making of Pakistan : A Study in Nationalism.* London, 1967.

    Both these works have useful sections on Indian Muslim nationalism and the Khilafat Movement.

Beaverbrook, Lord. *Men and Power, 1917–1918.* London, 1956.

Belgrave, Sir C. *The Pirate Coast.* London, 1966.

Belhaven, Lord. *The Uneven Road.* London, 1955.

Bell, Lady (ed.). *The Letters of Gertrude Bell.* London, 1927. 2 Vols.

    Volume II is important for contemporary insights into Anglo-Sa'udi relations, especially from the Baghdad vantage point.

Beloff, M. *Imperial Sunset, Britain's Liberal Empire, 1897–1921*, Vol. I. London, 1969.

Berque, J. *Les Arabes d'hier à demain.* Paris, 1960.

    An excellent sociological study of the modern Arab scene in North Africa and the Middle East.

Blunt, W. S. *My Diaries : Being a Personal Narrative of Events*, 1888–1914. London, 1921. 2 Vols.

Brémond E. *Le Hedjaz dans la Guerre Mondiale.* Paris, 1931.

    Brémond was the French Agent in the Hedjaz during the First World War.

Bullard, Sir R. *Britain and the Middle East : from the earliest times to 1950.* London, 1951.

—— *The Camels Must Go; An Autobiography.* London, 1961.

    Both these books are useful. The latter gives an amusing contemporary account of the siege of Jedda. The author was British Consul there at the time.

Burckhardt, J. L. *Notes on the Bedouins and the Wahábys.* London, 1830. 2 Vols.

—— *Travels in Arabia*, London, 1829. 2 Vols., reprinted 1968. Frank Cass, London.

    Both sources are still valuable as accounts of Bedouin life by the great Swiss explorer.

Burgoyne, E. *Gertrude Bell : from her personal papers*, 1889–1926. London, 1958–1961.

Burton, Sir R. *Personal Narrative of a Pilgrimage to El-Madinah and Meccah.* London, 1855–6. 3 Vols.

    One of the classics of Arabian exploration by the translator of The Arabian Nights.

Busch, B. C. *Britain and the Persian Gulf, 1894–1914.* Berkeley, 1967.

—— *Britain, India and the Arabs, 1914–1921,* Berkeley, 1971.

These two complementary works are well-written and important accounts of British policy in the Middle East, especially from the 'Indian' vantage point. They both have comprehensive bibliographies.

Chapman, M. K. *Great Britain and the Baghdad Railway, 1888–1917,* Massachusetts, 1948.

Chesney, Lt.-Col. F. R. *Expedition for the Survey of the Rivers Euphrates and Tigris, 1835–1837.* London, 1840. 4 Vols.

—— *Reports on the Navigation of the Euphrates.* London, 1933.

Collins, R. O. (ed.) *An Arabian Diary, Sir Gilbert Falkingham Clayton.* Berkeley, 1969.

Useful for a detailed account of the Hadda and Bahra Agreements. The introductory summary of the rise of ibn Sa'us is rather uncritical.

Curzon, G. N. *Persia and the Persian Question.* London, 1892. 2 Vols., reprinted 1966, Frank Cass, London.

de Gaury, G. *Rulers of Mecca.* London, 1951.

Dickson, H. R. P. *Kuwait and her Neighbours.* London, 1956.

—— *The Arab of the Desert.* London, 1949.

The former is especially good for first-hand accounts of Sa'udi-Kuwaiti problems and the negotiations leading to the signature of the Treaty of Muhammera and 'Uqair Protocols. The latter is an important work on Bedouin life, principally in eastern Arabia.

Doughty, C. M. *Travels in Arabia Deserta.* Cambridge, 1888. One of the classic accounts of Arabian life.

Earle, E. M. *Turkey, the Great Powers and the Baghdad Railway, A Study in Imperialism.* London, 1923 (for years the best work on the subject).

Fitzsimons, M. A. *Empire by Treaty: the British and the Middle East in the 20th Century.* London, 1965.

Fraser, L. *India Under Curzon and After.* London, 1911.

Garnett, D. (ed.) *The Letters of T. E. Lawrence* (Part III: 1918–1922). London, 1938.

Gibb, H. A. R. *Modern Trends in Islam.* Chicago, 1947 (one half dozen most important books on the modern Arab world).

Glubb, J. B. *Britain and the Arabs.* London, 1959.

—— *The Story of the Arab Legion.* London, 1956.

—— *War in the Desert.* London, 1960.

Glubb's books are helpful in understanding Anglo-Sa'udi relations from 1921 to 1926.

Goldziher, I. *Muslim Studies* (Muhammedanische Studien), ed. by S. M. Stern, trans. by C. R. Barber and S. M. Stern, Vol. I. London, 1967.

Originally published in 1888, this work is still an important treatise on Bedouin life and the effect of Islam on the Bedouin.

Graves, P. *Britain and Turk*. London, 1941.

—— *The Life of Sir Percy Cox*. London, 1950.

Grenville, J. A. S. *Lord Salisbury and Foreign Policy, The Close of the Nineteenth Century*. London, 1964.

Grey of Fallodon, Viscount, *Twenty-Five Years, 1892–1916*. London, 1925. 2 Vols.

Haim, S. *Arab Nationalism, An Anthology*. Berkeley, 1962.

Hay, Sir R. *The Persian Gulf States*. Washington, D.C. 1959.

Hogarth, D. G. *Arabia*. Oxford, 1922.

Hoskins, H. L. *British Routes to India*. London, 1928.

Hourani, A. H. *Arabic Thought in the Liberal Age 1798–1939*. London, 1962.

The definitive account of Arab intellectual history.

Howard, H. N. *The Partition of Turkey, A Diplomatic History*. New York, 1966.

Originally published in 1931 this work is still a useful if tedious account of the break-up of the Ottoman Empire.

Howarth, D. *The Desert King, A Life of Ibn Saud*. London, 1964.

A relatively popular but valuable account of ibn Sa'ud's life.

Hurgronje, C. S. *Mekka in the Latter Part of the Nineteenth Century*. Luzac, 1931.

An important study of Meccan life by the great Dutch Orientalist.

Ibn Khaldun, *The Muqaddimah, An Introduction to History*. Trans. by Franz Rosenthal. London, 1958. 3 Vols.

Written in the fourteenth century by one of the greatest Arab historians and sociologists, it is still a classic work on the traditional Islamic society, remnants of which are still to be found in the Arabian peninsula today.

Kedourie, E. *England and the Middle East: The Destruction of the Ottoman Empire, 1914–1921*. London, 1956.

—— *The Chatham House Version and Other Middle Eastern Studies*, London, 1970.

For the purposes of perspective, and especially for British dealings with the Hashimites, both books contain useful and stimulating sections.

Kelly, J. B. *Britain and the Persian Gulf, 1798–1880.* Oxford, 1968.

The definitive work on the British position in the Gulf throughout much of the nineteenth century with valuable sections on British relations with the Al Sa'ud.

—— *Eastern Arabian Frontiers.* London, 1964.

Helpful especially for accounts of Anglo-Turkish negotiations between 1911 and 1914 with reference to the Sa'udi position.

Kumar, R. *India and the Persian Gulf, 1858–1907, A Study of British Imperial Policy.* New York, 1965.

Valuable mainly for British relations with Kuwait and the British position towards the Al Sa'ud from 1900–1907.

Langer, W. L. *The Diplomacy of Imperialism, 1890–1902.* New York, 1951.

—— *The Franco-Russian Alliance, 1890–1894.* Harvard Historical Studies XXX. Cambridge (Mass.), 1929.

Laoust, H. *Essai sur les doctrines sociales et politiques de Taki-d-Din Ahmad b. Taimiyah.* Cairo, 1939.

One of the best treatises on the teaching of the great Moslem theologian.

Lawrence, T. E. *Seven Pillars of Wisdom: A Triumph.* New York, 1936.

Leslie, S. *Mark Sykes: His Life and Letters.* London, 1923.

Lewis, B. *The Arabs in History.* New York, 1960.

—— *The Emergence of Modern Turkey.* London, 1961.

Both books are vital sources in understanding the modern Middle East.

Longrigg, S. H. *Iraq, 1900 to 1950, A Political, Social and Economic History.* London, 1953.

—— *Oil in the Middle East,* 3rd Edn. London, 1968.

Marder, A. J. *The Anatomy of British Sea Power: A History of British Naval Policy in the Pre-Dreadnought Era, 1880–1905.* New York, 1940, reprinted 1972, Frank Cass, London.

Marlowe, J. *Late Victorian, The Life fo Sir Arnold Talbot Wilson,* K.C.I.E., C.S.I., C.M.G., D.S.O., M.P. London, 1967.

An excellent biography of Wilson.

Marlowe, J. *The Persian Gulf in the Twentieth Century.* London, 1962.

Medlicott, W. N. *Contemporary England, 1914–1964.* London, 1967.

Meulen, D. Van Der, *The Wells of Ibn Saʻud.* London, 1957.

Miles, Col. S. B. *Countries and Tribes of the Persian Gulf.* London, 1919. 2 Vols., reprinted 1966, Frank Cass, London.

Monger, G. *The End of Isolation : British Foreign Policy, 1900–1907.* London, 1963.

Monroe, E. *Britain's Moment in the Middle East, 1914–1956.* London, 1963.

    A well-written and competent survey of the British position in the Middle East from 1914 to 1956.

—— *Philby of Arabia.* London, 1973.

Mosely, L. *The Glorious Fault : The Life of Lord Curzon.* New York, 1960.

Mowat, C. L. *Britain between the Wars, 1918–1940.* London, 1956.

Moyse-Bartlett, H. *The Pirates of Trucial Oman.* London, 1966.

Musil, A. *Manners and Customs of the Rwala Bedouins.* New York, 1928.

Nevakivi, J. *Britain, France and the Arab Middle East, 1914–1920.* London, 1969.

Nicolson, H. *Curzon : The Last Phase, 1919–1925 : A Study in Post-War Diplomacy.* Boston, 1934.

Oppenheim, M. Freiherr von. *Die Beduinen.* Wiesbaden, 1939–52. 4 Vols.

    A comprehensive, not to say Germanically exhaustive, treatment of the Bedouin. Volume 3 has useful maps at the end.

Palgrave, W. G. *Narrative of a Year's Journey through Central and Eastern Arabia.* London, 1865.

Peake Pasha (Lt.-Col. F. G.), *A History of Jordan and its Tribes.* Florida, 1958.

Philby, H. St. J. B. *Arabia.* London, 1930.

—— *Arabian Days.* London, 1948.

—— *Arabia of the Wahhabis.* London, 1928.

—— *Arabian Jubilee.* New York, 1953.

—— *The Heart of Arabia: A Record of Travel.* London, 1922. 2 Vols.

—— *Forty Years in the Wilderness.* London, 1957.

—— *Saʻudi Arabia.* London, 1955.

    Virtually all of Philby's books are important for the

study of modern Arabia. The above-named sources are vital.

Rentz, G. S. 'Muhammad ibn 'Abd al-Wahhab (1703/4–1792) and the Beginnings of the Unitarian Empire in Arabia'. Unpublished Ph.D. dissertation, University of California, Berkeley, 1948.

Rihani, A. *Ibn Saʿud, His People and his Land*. London, 1928.

—— *Muluk al-Arab* (The King of the Arabs). Beirut, 1924.

—— *Tarikh Najd al-Hadith wa mulhaqatihi* (The Modern History of Najd and its Dependencies). Beirut, 1928.

Rihani was a personal friend of ibn Saʿud with considerable knowledge of Arabian affairs and personalities. His books are useful for sympathetic insights into the world of ibn Saʿud.

Robinson, F. C. R. 'The Politics of U.P. Muslims, 1906–1922'. Unpublished Ph.D. dissertation. The University of Cambridge, 1970.

Chapters 7 and 8 contain useful information on the Khilafat Movement.

Ronaldshay, The Rt. Hon., the Earl of. *The Life of Lord Curzon, Being the Authorized Biography of George Nathaniel, Marquess Curzon of Kedleston, K.G.* London, 1927–1928. 3 Vols.

Rutter, E. *The Holy Cities of Arabia*. London, 1928.

Searight, S. *The British in the Middle East*. London, 1969.

Shwadran, B. *Jordan: A State of Tension*. New York, 1959.

Steiner, Z. *The Foreign Office and Foreign Policy, 1898–1914*. Cambridge, 1969.

Storrs, R. *Orientations*. London, 1937.

A brilliantly-written book, helpful for this work for its sections dealing with British wartime and post-war policy in the Middle East.

Sykes, C. *Two Studies in Virtue*. New York, 1953.

Taylor, A. J. P. *English History, 1914–1945*. London (Pelican edn.), 1970.

—— *The Struggle for Mastery in Europe 1948–1918*. Oxford, 1954.

Both of Taylor's works are useful for purposes of perspective. They are written with his characteristic verve, perception and pungency.

—— *The Shorter Encyclopedia of Islam*, ed. by H. A. R. Gibb and J. H. Kramers. Leiden, 1953.

Thomas, B. *Alarms and Excursions in Arabia.* London, 1931.
Thomson, D. *Europe Since Napoleon.* 2nd edn. London, 1963.
Thornton, A. P. *The Imperial Idea and Its Enemies.* London. 1959.
   A stimulating and well-written book. It contains a useful section on British dealings in the Middle East.
Twitchell, K. S. *Sa'udi Arabia,* Princeton, 1958.
Vidal, F. S. *The Oasis of al-Hasa.* Dhahran, 1955.
Waley, S. D. *Edwin Montagu: A Memoir and an Account of his Visits to India.* London, 1964.
Wenner, M. W. *Modern Yemen,* 1918–1966. Baltimore, 1967.
Wilson, Lt.-Col. Sir A. T. *Loyalties, Mesopotamia: 1914–1917. A Personal and Historical Record.* Oxford, 1930.
—— *Mesopotamia 1917–1920: A Clash of Loyalties. A Personal and Historical Record.* Oxford, 1931.
   Both sources are important for first-hand accounts of British dealings with ibn Sa'ud and for insights into the personalities and politics of the British administration of Iraq.
—— *S.W. Persia, A Political Officer's Diary, 1907–1914.* London, 1941.
Wilson, Lt.-Col. Sir A. T. *The Persian Gulf: An Historical Sketch from the Earliest Times to the Beginning of the Twentieth Century.* London, 1928.
Winder, R. B. *Sa'udi Arabia in the Nineteenth Century.* New York, 1965.
   This book must be used with caution.
Woodruff, P. *The Men Who Ruled India: The Guardians.* New York, 1954.
Young, H. *The Independent Arab.* London, 1933.
   A good contemporary account of British policy in the Middle East.
Zeine, Z. N. *Arab-Turkish Relations and the Emergence of Arab Nationalism.* Beirut, 1958.
—— *The Struggle for Arab Independence: Western Diplomacy and the Rise and Fall of Faisal's Kingdom of Syria.* Beirut, 1960.

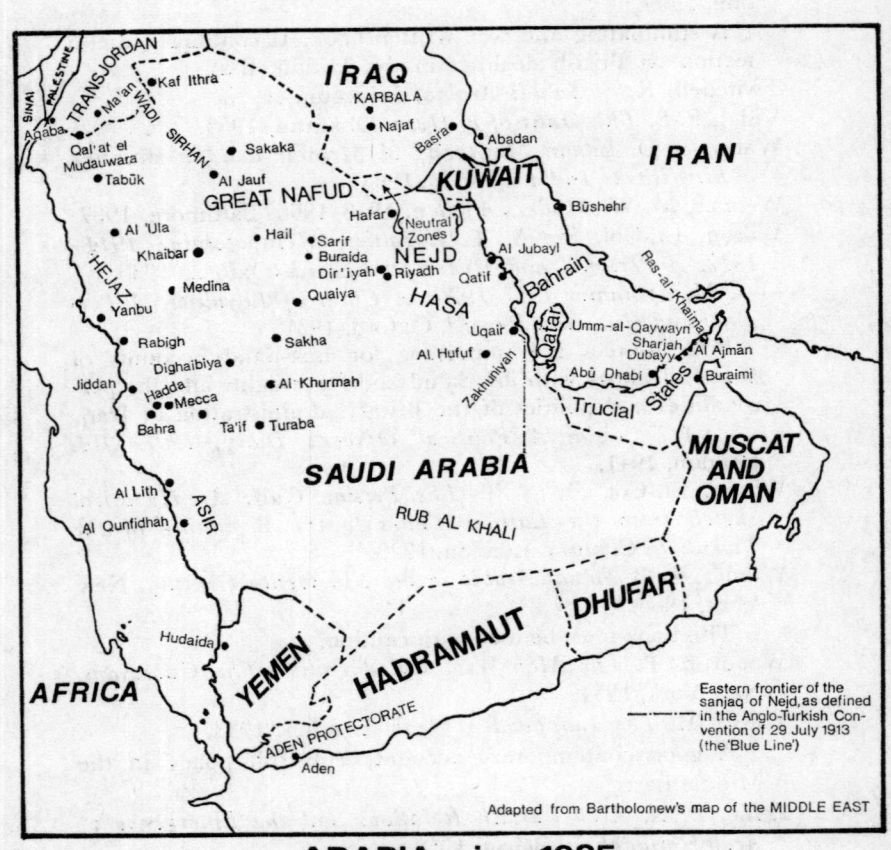

MAP OF THE GRAZING AREAS OF THE PRINCIPAL BEDOUIN TRIBES

from Glubb, *War in the Desert*,

Index

'Abd al-'Aziz ibn 'Abd al-Rahman Al Sa'ud, *see* Ibn Sa'ud
'Abd al-'Aziz ibn Mit'ab, 168
'Abd al-Aziz ibn Rashid, 19
'Abd al-Rahman, Imam (Abdullah 'Abd al-Rahman ibn Sa'ud: ibn Sa'ud's father), 17–18, 19, 20, 105, 216–17
'Abd al-Wahhab Mandil, 71n
Abdul Hamid, Sultan of Turkey, 18, 22, 34, 37, 38, 74
Abdul Jabir Bey, Colonel, 44
'Abdullah *see* 'Abd al-Rahman
'Abdullah, King of Transjordan (Husain's son), 93, 131, 134, 147, 152, 190, 191, 209; his stay in Turkey, 77; marches into western Najd (1915), 94; defeated by Khalid at Turaba, 142; proclaimed King of Transjordan, 167; dispute with Sa'udis over Jauf, Qaf and Wadi Sirhan, 192, 194–5, 212n; and Kuwait Conference, 196, 198, 204, 205–8; Najd-Hedjaz war, 218, 221; effect of Husain's abdication on, 220; 'Aqaba and Ma'an transferred to, 222–7; Clayton-ibn Sa'ud negotiations and, 227–8
'Abdullah, Shaikh of Qatar, 51, 52
Abdullah Sulaiman, head of Sa'udi Treasury, 237, 241
Abu Dhabi, 15, 23, 51
Abu Ghar: Ikhwani attack on Iraqi tribesmen at (1922), 174
Aden, 79, 149, 165
Afghanistan, 80
Agadir Crisis (1911), 42
Ahmad (Qasim ibn Thani's brother), 23

Ahmad, Shaikh (Salim's nephew), 173
Ahmad ibn Thunaiyan, 144–5, 151
Ajman tribe, 39, 70n, 92–3, 100, 102, 103, 105, 110, 121n, 135, 138, 154n, 174, 238
'Akka port, Palestine, 190
Al Khobar, 241
'Ali ibn Husain (Husain's elder son), 218; appointed Constitutional Sovereign of the Hedjaz (1924), 220; and war with Sa'udis, 220, 221, 223, 224, 226–7, 231; surrenders to ibn Sa'ud (1925), 231
Allenby, General, 111, 113, 116, 144, 148, 150, 161
Amarat tribe, 174, 175, 178, 179–80, 182
Amery, L. S., Colonial Secretary, 224, 225, 226
Amin Rihani, 179, 182
Amman, Transjordan, 189, 192, 194, 205, 224; King Faisal's visit to (1923), 195; Husain denied refuge at, 220, 226
Amritsar Massacre, 128
'Anaza tribes, 113, 179
Anglo-French Agreement (1904), 6, 12
Anglo-Persian Oil Company, 167
Anglo-Russian Agreement (1907), 6, 12
Anglo-Sa'udi Treaty (1915), 75, 83–91, 128, 142, 172, 243; Article II of, 88, 89, 96, 135; British and Sa'udi drafts compared (App. III, part 1), 250–3; and text of (App. III, part 2), 254–6
Anglo-Turkish Convention (1913),

THE BIRTH OF SA'UDI ARABIA

Anglo-Turkish Convention—*contd.*
    42–3, 45, 49, 52, 56, 70n, 71n;
    Najdi-Kuwaiti boundaries defined
    by, 170, 171–2, 173, 180, 188n
'Aqaba: fall of (1917), 108;
    Husain's exile in, 220; incorporation into Transjordan of, 221, 222–7, 229
Arab Bureau, Cairo: divergent
    views of Government of India
    officials and, 74, 94–6, 97, 101,
    104, 106, 108, 111, 112–15, 116;
    Storrs Mission to ibn Sa'ud from,
    107, 109–11; policy over Khurma
    dispute of, 130–41; *see also*
    Foreign Office
Arab nationalism, 37, 66n, 74,
    77–8, 82, 94, 146, 161, 183n
Arab Revolt (1916), 77, 82, 91, 161,
    222, 243; British support Husain
    as leader of, 75, 79, 80; Husain
    proclaims, 94; ibn Sa'ud offers
    token support for, 99, 100, 102
Arab union/confederation: British
    plans for, 78, 94
Araif pretenders to Sa'udi throne,
    38–9, 54, 70n, 92, 121n
Arms, 5, 46, 55, 85; supplied by
    British to ibn Sa'ud, 93, 97, 100–
    1, 111, 112–13, 136, 138
Artawiya, 238; Ikhwan agricultural
    community at, 129
'Asir, 90, 200, 230; ibn Sa'ud conquers (1920), 159, 182n
Asquith government, 91
Ataiba tribe, 38, 43, 94, 133, 135, 137, 238
Austria, Bosnia-Herzegovina annexed by (1908), 12, 34
Autonomy, Arab quest for, 37
'Awazim tribe, 103, 111, 174

Baghdad, 2, 18, 107; British
    Resident in, 3; fall to British of
    (1917), 104, 106, 108; policy of
    Government of India officials in,
    74, 94–6, 108, 112-15, 118n, 130–
    41

Baghdad Railway, xx, 5, 6, 8, 9–11,
    12, 21, 42, 43, 52, 67n, 69–70n
Bahra Agreement (1925), 229–30
Bahrain, 3, 16, 28n, 54–5, 147;
    Political Agent in, xxn; Britain
    obtains non-alienation bonds
    from, 2, 7, 9; Anglo-Ottoman
    relations concerning, 7; Faisal
    seeks to assert his authority in,
    16; Turkish troops retire from
    Hasa to, 44; Indian Army
    division sent to, 80; oil discovered
    in, 240
Bahrain Petroleum Company, 240
Balfour, A. J., 11
Balfour Declaration, 73, 150
Balkan Wars, 35, 42, 45, 118n
Bandar Abbas, Persia, 6
Basra, 2, 7, 10, 21, 39, 58, 83, 84,
    87; Government of India Consul
    and officials in, 3, 9, 19, 44, 56;
    Turkish troops massed against
    (1901), 19–20; as terminus for
    Baghdad Railway, 70n; occupied
    by division of Indian Army
    (1914), 80; ibn Sa'ud shown
    British military hardware in, 100
Beda al-Din, Major, 71n
Bedouins, 85, 86; character of, 13,
    129; raids (*ghazzu*) of, 14,
    174; concept of *hasab* of, 21;
    Husain's involvement with, 77–8,
    80; Great Durbar of chiefs at
    Kuwait (1916), 99–102; *see also*
    Ikhwan movement
Beirut, 77
Bell, Gertrude, 23, 143, 169
Beni Shakhr tribe, 194, 195
Birkenhead, Lord, 108
Bismarck, Count Otto von, 4
Boer War, 6
'Blue Line' (demarcation of Turkish
    territory in eastern Arabia), 52,
    70n, 71–2n
Bon Voisinage Agreement (1930),
    239
Bosnia-Herzegovina, annexed by
    Austria (1908), 12, 34

INDEX

Bray, Captain, Political Agent in Bahrain, 141

Britain, British: Sa'udi relations with, xiv–xx; overlapping administrations responsible for Arabian policy, xvii–xviii, 2–4; 19th-century policy in Persian Gulf, 1–25; Great Power rivalries and, 4–6; French relations with, 5; and Russian threat to, 5–6, 9; Anglo-French and Anglo-Russian Agreements, 6; growing hostility to Germany in, 10, 34; Baghdad Railway scheme and, 9–11, 12, 42, 52, 69–70n; Lansdowne declaration on Persian Gulf, 11, 12; and Curzon's visit to Persian Gulf, 11–12; Japanese alliance with, 12; pre-war domestic problems, 35; and Home Rule for Ireland, 35; policy towards ibn Sa'ud (1910–14), 35–65; Turkish relations with, 34, 35, 36–7, 40–1, 42, 44–65; and Anglo-Turkish Convention, 42–3, 45, 70n; interoffice rivalry in dealings with ibn Sa'ud, 49–50; against Sa'udi action in Qatar, 51–3, 55; accused by Turks of intriguing with ibn Sa'ud, 62; war declared with Turkey, 65; Sa'udi wartime relations with, 73–117; and Turkish wartime relations, 73, 75–6, 77, 78–80; Husain backed as leader of Arab Revolt by, 75, 76–7, 79, 81–2; failure of Gallipoli Campaign, 79, 91; Turkish capture of Kut al Amara, 79; Indian Expeditionary Force sent to Mesopotamia by, 80; support and subsidies for Arab Sheikhs by, 80–1; Anglo-Sa'udi Treaty, 83–91, 135, 250–6; Sa'udi role in Middle East campaign of, 91–9; and blockade of enemy supplies, 91, 102–3, 111; arms and money for ibn Sa'ud from, 93, 97, 100–1, 111, 112–13, 136, 138; negotiations with Sharif Husain, 93–4; Arab Revolt and, 94, 96, 99; Great Durbar at Kuwait, 99–102; ibn Subhan declares support for, 103–4; Baghdad captured by, 104, 106, 108; Storrs Mission and Philby Mission to ibn Sa'ud, 107–12, 116–17; 'balance of power' policy in Arabia of, 115–16; threat of Wahhabi invasion of Hedjaz and, 127–8; post-war domestic and colonial problems, 128; Khurma dispute and, 130–41; ibn Sa'ud's ultimatum to, 137–8; Anglo-French Declaration (1918), 138; Turaba dispute and, 142–4; threaten to withhold subsidy from ibn Sa'ud, 141, 143, 148; Philby Mission to ibn Sa'ud cancelled, 143–4; Faisal's visit to (1919), 144; reconciliation between ibn Sa'ud and Husain sought by, 144–52, 164; and officials' impressions of two rulers, 146–7; MPs urge establishment of single ministry to deal with Middle East affairs, 149; Arabian policy (1920–22), 159–82; subsidies to Arab chiefs from, 159–66, 183n, 184n; Colonial Office takes over responsibility for Middle East affairs, 160, 165–7; and Cairo Conference, 167; end of Rashidi rule and, 167–70; and Treaty of Mohammera, 169, 175–6, 178; Najd-Kuwaiti border dispute, 170–4; and Najd-Iraqi dispute, 174–6, 178–9; and ibn Sa'ud's 1922 *hajj*, 176–8; Chanak crisis brings down Lloyd George government, 179; Uqair Conference, 179–82; Trans-Arabian railway proposed by, 190; disputes over Jauf, Qaf and the Wadi Sirhan, 189, 190–6; ibn Sa'ud's subsidy discontinued by, 193–4, 216; Kuwait Conference convened by, 196, 198–210; channel of communication between ibn Sa'ud and, 196–8; involvement in

Britain, British—*contd.*
  Najd-Hedjaz war, 216–31; policy towards 'Aqaba and Ma'an of, 221, 222–7; Clayton's Mission to ibn Sa'ud, 227–30; and Hadda Agreement, 228–9; and Bahra Agreement, 229–30; Treaty of Jedda signed by, 236; Ikhwan Rebellion and, 237–9; ibn Sa'ud-Faisal meeting aboard HMS *Lupin*, 239
British India Steamship Company, 62
British Iraq Petroleum Company (IPC), 240–1
British Lynch Company, 2
Bukariya, Sa'udi victory at (1904), 22
Bulgaria: independence proclaimed by (1908), 12, 34
Bullard, Sir Reader, 210, 230, 232n
Buraimi, 15, 51
Bushire: British Political Resident in, 2, 3, 16, 17, 197–8; Russian consul's interview with ibn Sa'ud in, 6, 32n

Cairo *see* Arab Bureau
Cairo Conference (1921), 167
Californian Arabian Standard Oil Company (CASOC), 241
Caliphate: Husain's assumption of (1924), 209, 210–11, 216, 217
Chamberlain, Austen, 96–7, 106, 108, 164–5, 225
Chanak crisis, Turkey, 179
Chasib (son of Shaikh of Mohammera), 173
Chesney, Lt.-Col. F. R., 190
Churchill, Winston (as Secretary of State for the Colonies), 182, 185n; subsidies and, 165–6; takes charge of Middle East Affairs, 166–7; his attitude towards ibn Sa'ud's *hajj*, 177–8
Clayton, Sir Gilbert, 78, 95–6, 141, 238; Mission to ibn Sa'ud of, 222, 227–30; negotiates Treaty of Jedda, 236

Coaling station(s): French seek to establish in Gulf, 5; and Russian request at Bandar Abbas for, 6, 27n
Colonial Office, xvii, 185n, 192; takes over responsibility for Middle East affairs, 160, 165–7, 196; and Cairo Conference, 167; channels of communication between ibn Sa'ud and British, 196–8
Committee for the Commendation of Virtue and the Condemnation of Vice, 236–7
Cornwallis, Col. Kinahan, 165
Cox, Sir Percy, 112, 115, 116, 130, 136, 137, 150, 166, 174, 183n, 203, 204, 243; as Political Resident in Gulf (1904–17), 23–4, 41, 44–54 *passim*, 93, 94, 97, 98, 104; character and career of, 23, 33n; Anglo-Sa'udi Treaty and, 86, 87, 88, 89, 250, 254, 255n, 256; Uqair meeting with ibn Sa'ud, 99; attends Great Durbar at Kuwait, 99, 100–2; and blockade of enemy supplies, 102–3; sends Storrs Mission to ibn Sa'ud, 106–7, 108; appointed Civil Commissioner of Baghdad (1917), 107; death of his son, 107; on ibn Sa'ud-Husain relations, 113–14; appointed British Minister at Teheran (1918), 117; appointed High Commissioner in Baghdad (1920), 162, 172; his suggestion for post-war balance of power policy rejected, 167–8; and role in settlement of Najd border disputes, 169–70, 172–3, 175, 179–82; and ibn Sa'ud's 1922 *hajj*, 176–8; supports ibn Sa'ud in Jauf dispute, 190–1; and ibn Sa'ud's channel of communication with British, 196–7; retirement of (1923) 196–7, 198
Crane, C. R., 240
Crete, union with Greece of, 34

INDEX 275

Crewe, Marquis of, 49, 50, 51, 57, 59, 95
Crowe, Sir Eyre, 56–7, 63
Cunliffe-Owen, Lt.-Col. H., 108, 109, 110
Currie, Sir Philip, 8
Curzon, Lord, 1–2, 20, 23, 27n, 28n, 32n, 33n, 117, 161, 165, 198; tours Persian Gulf (1903), 11–12; resigns as Viceroy (1905), 12; seeks reconciliation between ibn Sa'ud and Husain, 143–4, 145–6, 147, 148–9, 152
Cyprus: Husain exiled to, 225, 227

Damascus, 77, 78, 142, 222
Damman, 17
Dane, Sir Louis, 21
Dar'iya, 14
Devonshire, Duke of, Colonial Secretary, 190–1, 195, 205
Dhafir tribe, 174, 175, 178, 179–80, 182, 209
Dhahran oilfield, 241
Dhari ibn Tawala, Shaikh (head of Aslams), 103
Dighaibiya: Ikhwan attack Hedjazi supply base at, 139
Dickson, H. R. P., Political Agent in Bahrain, 130, 146–7, 150, 170–1, 179, 180–1
Dobbs, Sir Henry, British High Commissioner in Baghdad, 199, 200–1, 203–4, 208, 209–10, 237–8

Easter Rising, Dublin (1916), 91
Eastern General Syndicate of London, 240, 241
Egypt, 7, 14, 15, 77, 79, 109, 118n; British troops in, 75–6; Storrs Mission to ibn Sa'ud from, 107, 109–10, 111; 1919 rebellion in, 128; *see also* Arab Bureau
Entente Cordiale (1904), 5

Fahad Bey ibn Hadhdhal, 113, 163, 179, 183n
Faisal al Duwish, Shaikh, 130, 170, 171, 173, 174, 187n, 199, 210

Faisal ibn Turki, King (Faisal the Great), xv; relations with Sharif of Mecca, 16, 17; and with British, 15–18; death of, 18
Faisal (son of ibn Sa'ud): his visit to England (1919), 144, 156n; as leader of Ikhwan Rebellion, 238–9
Faisal, King of Iraq (son of Husain), 152, 191, 222; proclaimed King of Syria by Arab nationalists, 142, 146; and Churchill places him on Iraqi throne, 167; Treaty of Mohammera signed by, 175; ibn Sa'ud's 1922 pilgrimage to Mecca and, 176–7; and Uqair Conference, 179; threatens to come to 'Abdullah's aid over Qaf dispute, 195; and Kuwait Conference, 195–6, 198, 200, 204–5; Hedjaz-Najd war (1924), 218; effect of Husain's abdication on, 220; his meeting with ibn Sa'ud aboard HMS *Lupin* (1930), 239
Fakhri Pasha, 102, 134
Fao, 10, 80
Fashoda, 6
Foreign Office, British, xix, 197; divided administrative responsibility and inter-office rivalry between Government of India and, xvii–xviii, 2–4, 49–50, 73–4, 76–7, 146, 148–9; Arabian policy of, 35–6, 42, 44, 51, 52–3, 56–7, 58, 60, 65; Faisal invited to England by, 144; interdepartmental conferences on ibn Sa'ud-Husain dispute, 143–5; subsidies debate and, 160, 163; Colonial Office take over responsibility for Middle Eastern affairs from, 160, 165–6; *see also* Arab Bureau
France, French, 1, 73, 155n, 190, 191; 1894 alliance with Russia, 4–5; British relations with, 5, 6; joint Russo-French visit to Kuwait, 6; Anglo-French

France, French—*contd.*
Agreement (1904), 6, 12; army mutinies, 108; Anglo-French Declaration (1918), 138; in Syria, 128, 146, 147, 151, 164
Frontiers, frontier disputes: 'Blue Line' as demarcation of Turkish territories in eastern Arabia, 52, 70n, 71–2n; Kuwait-Najd and Iraq-Najd, defined by Uqair Protocols, 159, 179–82; Treaty of Mohammera (1922), 169, 175–6, 178–9; Najd-Kuwait border dispute, 170–4; and Najd-Iraqi dispute, 174–6, 178–9; Wadi Sirhan, 189, 190–6; and Kuwait Conference to settle, 196, 198–210; 'Aqaba and Ma'an incorporated in Transjordan, 222–7; Clayton-ibn Sa'ud negotiations on, 227–30
Fuad Hamza, Sa'udi Foreign Minister, 237

Gallipoli campaign, 73, 79, 91
Garland, Captain, 135
General Treaty of Peace with Great Britain (1820), 15
al Geraya salt deposits, 193
Germany, 1, 80, 128; Kaiser William II's expansionist policy, 4; Baghdad Railway scheme of, 5, 6, 8, 9–11, 12, 42, 67n, 69–70n; British relations with, 6, 10–11, 12, 34; Turkish relations with, 7, 25; Potsdam agreement with Russia on Baghdad Railway, 142
Ghalib, Amir of Khurma, 131
Ghandi, Mahatma, 127
Ghatghat, 139, 238
Glubb, J. B., 120n, 193, 239, 242n
Greece, Crete declares union with, 34
Grey, Colonel, Political Agent at Kuwait, 59, 60, 61
Grey, Sir Edward, 44, 46, 47–8, 49, 50, 51, 54, 56–7, 62–4, 65, 69n, 87

Gulf of 'Aqaba, 201

Hadda Agreement (1925), 228–9, 230
Hafez Wahba, Sa'udi Ambassador to London, 237
Haifa, 190
Hail, 101, 178; proposed offensive against, 104, 105, 106, 107, 108, 111, 112, 113, 115, 116–17, 135, 136–7; ibn Sa'ud's attack on, 137, 138; and capture of (1921), 159, 167, 169, 174; ibn Sa'ud's agreement with leaders of, 168–9
Hakki Pasha (Turkish Ambassador in London), 51, 53, 54, 55, 60–1, 62, 63
Hamilton, Sir Ian, 79
Hamilton, Colonel R. E. A., Political Agent in Kuwait, 108–9, 123n
Hamilton, Lloyd, 240, 241
Hanbalites, Hanbali school of Islam, 13, 131, 133, 153n
Hannu Wells, battle of, 135
Harb tribe, 174
Hardinge, Lord, Viceroy of India, 46, 47, 51, 68n, 95, 122n, 169
Hasa, xix, 15, 17, 21, 32n, 39, 40, 41, 52, 53, 55, 61, 82, 86, 99, 143, 162; Turkish activities in, 7; and Turkish capture of, 18–19; ibn Sa'ud captures (1913), 43–5, 62, 83, 92; oil concession in, 241
Hashimite family/dynasty *see* 'Abdullah, King of Transjordan; Faisal, King of Iraq; Husain ibn 'Ali
Hedjaz, xiv, xx, 38, 43, 78; blockade of Turkish supplies during war from Najd to, 102–3; Husain bans passage of Storrs Mission through, 109–10, 111; Khurma dispute, 111, 117, 127, 130–41; threat of Wahhabi invasion of, 127–8; Turaba dispute, 142–4; and ibn Sa'ud's proposed *hajj*, 144, 145, 146, 148, 150–2, 176–8; Foreign Office retains responsi-

Hedjaz—*contd.*
bility for (1922), 166; Kuwait Conference and, 198, 199–201, 206, 207, 208; Husain assumes Caliphate, 209, 210–11; Sa'udi invasion of, 216–31; Husain abdicates, and 'Ali appointed Constitutional Sovereign of the, 220; fall of Mecca, 220; Husain family banned from, 220, 221; siege of Jedda, 221; 'Aqaba and Ma'an transferred to Transjordan from, 222–7; Clayton-ibn Sa'ud negotiations on frontiers with, 227–30; and Hadda Agreement, 228–9; and Bahra Agreement, 229–30; ibn Sa'ud proclaimed King of, 231; improved conditions in, 236–7; and reactions to modern technology, 237; *see also* Husain ibn 'Ali

Hedjaz Railway, 40, 78, 113, 192, 201, 217, 222, 223

Hirtzel, Sir Arthur, xix, 40, 49, 57, 115–16, 146, 152, 164, 178, 184n

Hogarth, D. G., 83, 111

Holderness, T. W., 58–9, 141

Holmes, Major Frank, 187n, 240–1

Hormuz: Russian surveyors' visit to, 5

Hudaidah, Yemen, 239

Hufhuf, 44, 45, 101

Humphreys, Sir Francis, High Commissioner in Iraq, 239

Husain ibn 'Ali, Sharif of Mecca, 56, 74, 90, 101, 107, 108, 138, 167, 195; confrontations between ibn Sa'ud and, 37–8, 39, 43; British support as leader of Arab Revolt, 75, 76–8, 79, 81, 128; ibn Sa'ud compared in importance with, 75–83; his role in British campaign in Middle East, 75, 82, 91, 102–3; religious influence among Moslems of, 82, 83; ibn Sa'ud attempts to apply Article II of Anglo-Sa'ud Treaty to, 89, 91, 96; and ibn Sa'ud's relations with, 92, 93–4, 96–9, 100, 101, 102–3, 107, 110, 111, 112–14, 115; British negotiations with, 93–4; proclaims Arab Revolt, 94; has himself proclaimed King of the Arabs (1916), 98–9; bans Storrs Mission, 109–10, 111; Philby's meeting at Jedda with, 111–12; Khurma dispute between ibn Sa'ud and, 117, 127, 128, 130–41; and Turaba dispute, 117, 127, 142–4; British efforts to reconcile ibn Sa'ud with, 144–52, 164; British officials' impressions of, 146–7, 152, 157n; armistice signed between ibn Sa'ud and, 151–2; British subsidies and grants to, 150, 151, 157n, 160, 161, 164–5, 166n, 183n, 193; ibn Sa'ud's 1922 *hajj* and, 176–8; and anti-British attitudes of, 178; Indian Moslems view of, 184–5n; Kuwait Conference and, 199, 200, 201, 203, 206, 207, 208; assumes Caliphate (1924), 209, 210–11, 216, 217; and Najd-Hedjaz war, 216–19, 221–2; abdication of, 220; denied refuge by British in Amman, 220; settles in 'Aqaba, 220, 225–6; and dispute over ownership of 'Aqaba and Ma'an, 222, 224, 225; exiled to Cyprus, 225, 227

Husain-McMahon negotiations, 73

Ibn Abd al-Wahhab, 13

Ibn Bijad ibn Humaid, Sultan (Amir of Ghatghat), 139, 218, 238

Ibn Mijlad, Shaikh, 202–3, 204

Ibn Rashid *see* Muhammad ibn Sa'ud ibn Rashid

Ibn Sa'ud (Abd al-'Aziz ibn 'Abd al-Rahman Al Sa'ud), British relations with, xiv–xx; character and appearance, xvi, 21, 59; Russian consul's interview with, 6, 32n; exiled in Kuwait, 18, 19;

Ibn Sa'ud—*contd.*
'Abd al-Rahman hands over temporal leadership to, 20; Riyadh captured by, 20–1; fails to gain British support, 21–2, 24–5; victory at Bukariya of, 22; appointed Qaimaqam of Najd by Turks, 22; ibn Rashid killed and vanquished by, 24; British policy towards (1910–14), 35–65; growing power of, 35, 36; Shakespear's meetings and relations with, 36, 39, 44–5, 47–8, 49, 53, 61–2, 83, 84–7; confrontations with Husain ibn 'Ali, 37–8, 39, 43; al Araif revolt against, 38–9, 92–3; Turks seek agreement with, 43; seizes Hasa and Qatif, 43–5; seeks to expel Turks from Qatar, 51–2; Turks propose talks with, 58; meets Col. Grey at Malah, 59; his letter to Mubarak, 59–60; Turkish Treaty with (1914), 60–2, 83, 248–9; disintegrating relations with Mubarak, 61–2, 72n; British relations during First World War with, 73–117 *passim*; role in British offensive in Middle East, 75, 81, 82, 91–9, 106; Arab Revolt and, 75, 82, 94, 96; compared in importance with Husain, 81–3; Anglo-Sa'udi Treaty, 83–91, 135, 250–6; defeated at battle of Jarrab, 81, 86, 91, 92; enforcement of British blockade by, 91, 102–3, 111; tribal revolts against, 92–3; British arms and money supplied to, 93, 97, 100–1, 111, 112–13, 136, 138; Husain's relations with, 93–4, 96–9, 100, 101, 102–3, 107, 110, 111, 112–14, 115; Uqair meeting with Cox, 99; offers token support for Arab Revolt, 99, 100, 102; attends Great Durbar at Kuwait, 99–107; awarded KCIE by British, 99; his contempt for ibn Subhan, 106; Rashidi peace overtures to, 104–5, 106; Storrs Mission to, 106–7, 108, 109–10; and Philby Mission, 108–12, 116; Ikhwan movement and, 111, 112, 115, 116, 128–30; British 'balance of power' policy towards, 114–16; Khurma dispute, 117, 127, 128, 130–41; and Turaba dispute, 117, 127, 142–4; Hail attacked by, 137, 138; his ultimatum to Britain, 137–8; threat to withhold British subsidy from, 141, 143, 148; Philby Mission (1919) cancelled to, 143–4; Britain seeks reconciliation between Husain and, 144–52, 164; and British officials' impressions of, 146–7; dispute over annual pilgrimages to Holy cities by, 144, 145, 146, 148, 150–1, 176–8, 216–17, 218, 220, 221–2; armistice signed between Husain and, 151–2; British subsidies to, 157–8n, 159–66, 183n, 184n; territorial expansionism of, 159, 169–70; Hail captured by, 159, 167, 169, 174; concludes agreement with Rashidi leaders of Hail, 168–9; Najdi-Kuwaiti border dispute, 170–4; and Najdi-Iraqi dispute, 174–6, 178–82; Treaty of Mohammera signed by, 175–6; 1922 *hajj*, 176–8; repudiates Treaty of Mohammera, 178–9; Uqair Conference, 179–82; disputes over Jaif, Qaf and Wadi Sirhan, 189, 190–6; British discontinue subsidy to, 193–4, 216; Kuwait Conference, 196, 198–210; channel of communication between British and, 196–8; invasion of Hedjaz by, 216–31; fall of Mecca to, 220; declaration of aims by, 220–1; siege of Jedda, 221; 'Aqaba and Ma'an dispute, 222–7; Clayton's mission to, 227–30; Hadda Agreement and Bahra Agreement signed by, 228–30;

Ibn Sa'ud—*contd.*
'Ali surrenders to, 231; proclaimed King of the Hedjaz, 231; Treaty of Jedda signed by, 236; improves conditions in Hedjaz, 236–7; and builds administration, 237; Ikhwan Rebellion, 237–9; meets Faisal aboard HMS *Lupin*, 239; Yemen War, 239–40; oil concessions granted by, 240–2
Ibn Shukair, Shaikh (of Mutair tribe), 170
Ibn Subhan *see* Sa'ud ibn Salah Subhan
Ibn Thunaiyan *see* Ahmad ibn Thunaiyan
Ibrahim Pasha, 14
Ikhwan tribes/movement, 111, 112, 115, 116, 128–30, 131, 133, 134, 135, 139, 142, 143, 153n, 167, 169, 170, 171, 173, 176, 185–6n, 199, 200, 210; raids in Iraq of, 174–5, 178, 209, 217; defeated by British at Umm, 192; attacks on Transjordan by, 192, 194, 195, 217, 231n; Hedjaz invaded by, 216–31; fall of Mecca to, 220; and siege of Jedda, 221; and fall of Medina, 230; Rebellion (1927–30), 237–9
India, 12; strategic importance of Persian Gulf to, 1–2, 4, 15; Russian threat to British in, 5; National Congress demand full self-government, 91; Moslem opinions on Middle East affairs, 74, 76, 118n, 127, 143, 219, 220, 221; nationalism in, 74, 127, 128, 143; Amritsar Massacre, 128; Khilafat Committee, 217, 218, 219, 220, 221
India, British Government of: divided administrative responsibility and rivalry between Foreign Office and, xvii–xviii, 2–4, 49–50, 73–4, 77, 146, 148–9; Political Resident and Agents appointed by, xix, 3; wartime Arabian policy of, 77, 79–80, 82, 89–91, 94–8, 100–1, 113; divergent views of Arab Bureau and officials in Baghdad of, 74, 94–6, 108, 112–15, 118n, 130–41 *passim*; criticized in Mesopotamia Commission's report on Kut disaster, 108; 'balance of power' policy of, 115–16; Khurma dispute and, 134–5; Turaba dispute and, 143–4; interdepartmental conferences with Foreign Office, 143–5; subsidies debate and, 162–3, 165; Colonial Office takes over responsibility for Middle East affairs from, 160, 165–6
India Office *see* India, British Government of
Iraq, 101, 104, 152, 167, 178, 190, 191, 192, 193, 195; Sa'udi invasion of, 14; blockade of supplies to, 102–3; rebellion in (1920), 128; Uqair Protocols define frontier between Najd and, 159; Faisal placed on throne of, 167; Najdi border dispute with, 174–6, 178–82; Kuwait Conference, 195, 196, 198–210; Ikhwani raids in, 174–5, 178, 209, 210; Najd-Hedjaz War and, 217–18, 219, 220; and Clayton-ibn Sa'ud negotiations on frontiers, 227, 229–30; and Bahra Agreement, 229–30; 'Ali exiled to, 231; Ikhwan Rebellion and, 237–9; and Bon Voisinage Agreement between Najd and, 230
Iraq Neutral Zone, 180, 208, 210, 238
Iraqi Desert Police, 174
Ireland, 128; Home Rule for, 35; Easter Rising, 91
Italy: invasion of Tripoli by, 34, 43, 118n

Jabal Shammar, 18, 104, 190, 200
Jabir, Shaikh of Kuwait, 93; attends Great Durbar at Kuwait,

Jabir, Shaikh of Kuwait—*contd.*
99, 100; awarded CIE by British, 99; agreement with ibn Sa'ud concerning the Ajman, 100; death of, 123n
Japan, British alliance with, 12
Jariya: ibn Sa'ud's and Salim's rival claims to, 170, 171, 172
Jarrab, battle of (1915), 81, 86, 91, 92
Jauf, 179; annexed by ibn Sa'ud, 159, 190; captured by Rashidi, 168; dispute over, 190–3, 211n, 212n; and Kuwait Conference, 205
Jedda, 38, 43, 80, 144, 149, 150, 176, 210–11, 223, 224, 230; siege of (1925), xx, 221; Husain-Philby talks in, 111–12; Sa'udi invasion of Hedjaz and, 219–20; ibn Sa'ud enters, 231
Jerusalem, 189; fall of, 108, 111; Sir Ronald Storrs appointed Governor of, 111
Jihad, 147; Sultan's proclamation of (1914), 76, 77
Jordan (Acting British Consul in Jedda), 230, 231
Jubail, 61, 181
Jutland, battle of, 91

Kapnist, Count Vladimir, railway scheme of, 5, 9
Karbela, sacking of (1801), 14
Katif, 48, 86
Kedourie, E., 79
Kemball, Colonel, Political Resident in Gulf, 22
Keyes, British Political Agent in Bahrain, 60
Khalid ibn Luwai, Sharif, Amir of Khurma, 130–1, 135, 136, 153n, 232n; attacks and destroys 'Abdullah's army, 142
Khaz'al, Shaikh of Mohammera, 79, 84, 87, 99, 104
Khilafat Committee, Indian, 217, 218, 219, 220, 221
Khurma dispute, xx, 111, 117, 127,
130–41, 142, 143, 145, 146, 151, 201, 207
Kinship group, Arabian, xvi–xvii
Kitchener, Field-Marshal, 77
Knox, Colonel: Kuwait Conference chaired by, 196, 198–9, 200–1, 203, 204, 205, 206, 207, 208–9, 210, 222, 225, 227
Kut al Amara, 124n; Turkish capture of, 79, 91; Mesopotamia Commission's report on, 108
Kuwait, 1, 2, 3, 5, 12, 25, 36, 39, 58, 109, 152, 163; joint Russo-French visit to (1903), 6; Anglo-Ottoman relations concerning, 7, 8–10, 12; Mubarak gains power in, 8; as terminus for Baghdad Railway, 8, 9; Britain obtains secret bond from, 9–10, 28–9n; ibn Sa'udis exile in, 19; Mubarak defeated by Rashidi at Sarif, 19; and Turkish threat to, 19–20; meeting between ibn Sa'ud and Turks in, 60–1; as ally of British during First World War, 79; Ajman tribe granted asylum in, 93; the Great Durbar at, 99–102; blockade enforcement by, 102–3, 111; Uqair Protocols define frontier between Najd and, 159, 179–82, 188n; friction between Sa'udis and, 159, 164; and border dispute between Najd and, 170–4; Ikhwan Rebellion and, 238
Kuwait Conference, 189–90, 194, 195, 196, 198–208, 222, 223, 225, 227, 229
Kuwait Neutral Zone, 180–1, 187n, 188n

Lansdowne, Lord, 11, 12
Lawrence, T. E., 81, 83, 109, 149, 167, 191, 211n, 243, 244
Leachman, Col. G. E., Political Agent of the Desert, 106, 107, 124n, 138
Lith, 220, 221
Lloyd George, David, 149

INDEX 281

Longrigg, Stephen, 240–1
Lowther, Sir G., 37, 44
Lupin, HMS: Faisal-ibn Sa'ud meeting aboard, 239

Ma'an: transferred to Transjordan, 221, 222–7, 229
McMahon, Sir Henry, 79, 96, 107, 122n
Mahmud II, Sultan of Turkey, 14
Mallet, Louis, 48, 51, 55–6, 57, 60, 62, 63, 70n
Mann, Dr: appointed as ibn Sa'ud's personal representative in London, 196–7
Maritime Truce, 15
Masterton-Smith, J., Report of, 196, 197
Maude, General Sir Stanley, 100, 107, 124n
Mecca, xix, 38, 131, 139, 142, 217; Sa'udis' capture of (1803), 14; disputes over ibn Sa'ud's pilgrimages to, 139, 142, 144, 145, 146, 148, 150–1, 176–8; Sa'udis advance on and capture of (1924), 219, 220
Medina, xix, 38, 116, 142, 199, 200, 204, 217, 220, 224; Sa'udis capture of (1804), 14; Turkish Hedjaz railway to, 40, 78; Turks besieged in, 102–3, 104, 106, 134; fall of (1919), 140; surrenders to ibn Sa'ud, 230
Mesopotamia, 155n, 157n, 163, 169; Turkish capture of Kut al Amara, 79; British campaign during First World War in, 73, 76, 79–80, 82, 86, 94, 95–6, 97, 136; rebellion in (1921), 166; *see also* Baghdad; Iraq
Mesopotamia Commission (1917), xviii, 108
Mesopotamian Expeditionary Force, 76, 81
Midhat Pasha, 7, 18
Mohammera, 79, 84, 87, 99, 173; *see also* Treaty of Mohammera
Montagu, Edwin, Secretary of State for India, 108, 143, 146, 148, 149, 162, 163
More, Major J. C., Political Agent in Kuwait, 173, 179
Morley, John, Secretary of State for India, 24
Morocco, 34
Moslems: Indian, 74, 76, 118n, 127, 143, 219, 220, 221; Sultan's proclamation of *jihad*, 76, 77; *see also* Pilgrimages
Mubarak al Sabah, Shaikh of Kuwait, 8, 9, 10, 12, 19–20, 22, 24, 25, 28n, 32n, 36, 58, 61–2, 72n; defeated by Rashidi (1901), 19; relations with Sa'udi exiles, 20; ibn Sa'ud's letters to, 39, 59–60; death of, 93
Muhammad 'Ali, 14, 15
Muhammad 'Ali (leader of Khilafat Committee), 217
Muhammad ibn 'Abd al-Wahhab *see* Ibn 'Abd al-Wahhab
Muhammad ibn 'Ali al Idrisi, Sayyid, 64, 182n
Muhammad ibn 'Aun, Sharif of Mecca, 16, 17
Muhammad ibn Rashid, 18, 19, 21, 22, 24, 32n, 81, 82, 83, 86, 87, 163, 165, 190, 200, 206; assassination of, 168
Muhammad ibn Sa'ud, 13–14
Muhammad Pasha Daghestani, General, 19
Muhammad al-Nama, 71n
Muhsin Pasha, Vali of Basra, 19–20
Mulla Hafiz, 206–7, 214n
Muntafiq tribe, 56, 174, 175, 178
al Murra tribe, 93
Muscat, 2, 3, 5, 9, 15, 17, 23, 28n, 40, 51
Mustafa Kemal (Ataturk), 183n
Mutair tribe, 170, 174, 180, 208, 238

Najd, 12, 13–14, 18, 19, 42, 43, 45–6; ibn Sa'ud appointed *quimaqam* of, 22; 'Blue Line' (eastern boundary) of, 52, 70n, 71–2n; ineffi-

Najd—*contd*.
cient enforcement of British blockade in, 102–3; frontiers defined by Uqair Protocols, 159, 179–82; border dispute with Kuwait, 170–4; and border dispute with Iraq, 174–6, 178–9; dispute over Wadi Sirhan, 189, 193–6; and Kuwait Conference, 196, 198–210; war between Hedjaz and, 216–31; Clayton's mission to ibn Sa'ud, 227–30; Ikhwan Rebellion, 237–9; Bon Voisinage Agreement between Iraq and, 239; Yemen War, 239–40; renamed Sa'udi Arabia (1934), 240; *see also* Ibn Sa'ud

Nationalism: Arab, 37, 66n, 74, 77–8, 82, 94, 146, 161, 183n; Turkish, 37, 77, 161; Indian, 74, 127, 128, 143, 217; post-war, in Middle East, 128

Nicolson, Sir Arthur, 48

Nivelle offensive, 108

Noel, Major, 152

Nuri al Sha'lan, Chief of the Ruwala, 64, 190–1, 206

Nuri Bey, Major, 43

O'Connor, Sir Nicholas, 22, 25, 32n

Oilfields, 76, 79, 80, 118n, 167, 181, 187, 240–2

Oman, 4, 15, 16, 17, 23, 51, 53, 147, 163

Omar Fauzi, Major, 71n

Ormsby-Gore, William, 154n, 226

Ottoman Empire *see* Turkey

Ottoman Public Debt Administration, 10, 42

Palestine, 79, 116, 119n, 136, 157n, 161, 163, 167, 178, 189, 192, 201, 206; *see also* Transjordan

Pan-Islamism: Abdul Hamid's support for, 37, 74

Parker, Alwyn, xix, 44, 45, 46, 51, 54, 68n

Passchendaele campaign, 108

Pearl trade: Bahrain as centre of, 28n

Pelly, Col. Lewis, Political Resident, 17, 47, 171

Permanent Mandates Commission, 226

Perseus, HMS, 10, 20

Persia, 5, 6, 80, 118n, 128, 149, 190

Persian Gulf: 19th-century British policy in, 1–25

Philby, H. St J. B., xv–xvi, xix, 23, 69n, 72n, 81, 90, 129, 130, 145, 179, 195, 241; 1917 mission to ibn Sa'ud, 108–12, 116–17; character of, 109, 244; Jedda talks with Husain, 111–12; his view of Khurma dispute, 131–2, 133, 134, 135, 137, 139–41; and British plan replacement of, 137, 138; leaves Riyadh, 138; 1919 mission to ibn Sa'ud cancelled, 143–4; 1922 mission to Jauf, 191–2, 211n; becomes adviser to ibn Sa'ud, 237; role of, 243–4

Pilgrimage(s) (*Hajj*) to Mecca and Medina, 139, 142, 144, 145, 146, 148, 150–1, 165, 176–8, 216–17, 218, 220, 221–2, 236

Piracy, 1, 8, 12–13, 14–15, 28n, 46, 55

Pirate Coast *see* Trucial Coast

Political Agents (British) in Persian Gulf, xix, 3; in Bahrain, 46–7, 197; *see also* Bray, Capt.; Dickson, H. R. P.; Keyes; Prideaux, Capt.; Trevor; in Kuwait *see* Grey, Col.; Hamilton, Col. R. E. A.; More, Major J. C.; Shakespear, Capt. W. H. I.

Political Resident(s) (British) in Persian Gulf, xix, xxn, 22; functions of, 2–3; *see also* Cox, Sir Percy; Kemball, Col.; Pelly, Lewis; Trevor

Potsdam Agreement (1910) on Baghdad railway, 42

Prideaux, Capt., Political Agent at Bahrain, 21

INDEX 283

Qaf, 201; Transjordan's occupation of, 192; Wahhabi attack on, 194; ceded to ibn Sa'ud, 223, 227-8

Qasim, 16, 38, 39, 94, 99, 101, 106, 178; ibn Rashid marches on, 93; as centre of overland trade, 103

Qasim ibn Thani, Shaikh of Qatar, 7, 23, 51, 52

Qatar, xix, 16, 23, 24, 52, 53, 55, 70n, 147, 187n; Anglo-Ottoman relations concerning, 7-8; ibn Sa'ud asks 'Abdullah to expel Turks from, 51; British policy of non-interference over, 51-5; British traders in, 53, 55

Qatif, 7, 39, 41, 53, 61, 181; ibn Sa'ud's capture of (1913), 44-5

Qawasim pirates, 15

Quraish tribe, 38, 76

Ras Tanura, 241

Rashidi dynasty, 18, 19-20, 190; post-war end of, 167-70; *see also* Muhammad ibn Rashid; Sa'ud ibn Rashid

Red Sea, 75, 78

Rihani, Amin, 130

Ritchie, Sir George, 185n

Riyadh, 17, 19, 36; captured by ibn Sa'ud (1902), 20-1; Storrs and Philby Missions to (1917), 107-12; congress of Ikhwani leaders convened at (1924), 216-17

Royal Air Force, 167, 238

Russia, 1; 1894 alliance with France, 4-5; threat to British in Persian Gulf of, 5-6; Kapnist railway scheme, 5-6, 9; joint Franco-Russian visit to Kuwait (1904), 6; Anglo-Russian Agreement (1907), 6, 12; ibn Sa'ud offered aid by, 22; Potsdam agreement with Germany on Baghdad Railway, 42, 67n

Russian Revolution, 108

Russo-Japanese War, 6

Ruwala tribe, 168, 191, 194, 195, 206, 229

Sa'd (ibn Sa'ud's brother), 38, 39, 92

Sakaka, 168, 205

Salim, Shaikh of Kuwait, 104, 107, 109, 111, 123n; inefficient enforcement of blockade by, 102-3; Nadj-Kuwait border dispute, 170-3; death of, 173

Salisbury, Lord, 6-7, 65

Samir Efendi, Mutasarrif of Hasa, 71n

Samuel, Sir Herbert, High Commissioner for Palestine, 189, 190-1, 192, 208, 224; denies Husain refuge at Amman, 220, 226

San Remo Conference, 128, 147

Sarif: Mubarak defeated at (1901), 19

Sa'ud ('Abdullah Abd al Rahman's brother), 18

Sa'ud ibn Faisal, 38

Sa'ud ibn Rashid, 56, 64, 82, 83, 87, 93, 97, 98, 101, 102, 106, 110, 113, 115, 117, 136, 145; ibn Sa'ud defeated at battle of Jarrab by, 81, 86, 91, 92; Ajman tribe join, 93; marches on Qasim, 93; ibn Subhan deserts him for British, 103-4; peace overtures to ibn Sa'ud from, 104-5, 106

Sa'ud ibn Salah Al Subhan (ibn Subhan): deserts ibn Rashid for British, 103-4; ibn Sa'ud's contempt for, 106

Sa'udi Arabia: discovery of oil in, 240-2; *see also* Hedjaz; Najd

Sa'udis, Sa'ud dynasty: British relations in 19th century with, 13-25; internecine strife among, 18, 37-8; and Turkish expansionism in Arabia, 18-19; in exile, 19-20; and relations with Mubarak, 19-20; victory at Bukariya of, 22; British policy towards (1910-14), 35-65; confrontations between ibn Sa'ud and Husain, 37-8, 39, 43; capture of Sa'd, 38, 39; Araif revolt

Sa'udis—*contd.*
against ibn Sa'ud, 38–9; Turkish relations with, 37, 38, 40, 43–65; ibn Sa'ud seizes Hasa and Qatif, 43–5; proposed talks between Turks and ibn Sa'ud, 58; Turkish Treaty with (1914), 60–2, 83, 248–9; British wartime relations with, 83, 84–5, 87; Anglo-Sa'udi Treaty (1915), 83–91, 128, 135, 250–6; wartime role of, 91–9; the Great Durbar at Kuwait, 99–102; blockade of enemy supplies by, 102–3, 111; Storrs and Philby Missions to ibn Sa'ud (1917), 107–12, 116; Ikhwan movement, 111, 112, 115, 116, 128–30; British 'balance of power' policy and, 114–16; Khurma and Turaba disputes, 117, 127–52; and dispute over pilgrimages to Holy cities, 144, 145, 146, 148, 150–1, 176–8; territorial expansionism of, 159, 169–70; British propose development of ports and trade, 162; friction between Kuwait and, 159, 164; agreement with Rashidi leaders of Hail, 168–9; Najdi-Kuwaiti border dispute, 170–4; and Najdi-Iraqi dispute, 174–6, 178–82; Jauf, Qaf and the Wadi Sirhan, 189, 190–6; and Kuwait Conference, 196, 198–210; invasion of Hedjaz by, 216–31; and capture of Mecca, 220; and siege of Jedda, 221; Ikhwan Rebellion, 237–9; ab-, breviated genealogy of (App. 1) 247; *see also* ibn Sa'ud

Sayyid Omar Bey, 71n
Sayyid Talib, 44, 56, 61–2, 68n, 71n, 83
Senussi tribe, 79
Sha'ib al 'Auja: ibn Sa'ud's victory at, 238
Shakespear, Capt. William Henry Irwine, Political Agent at Kuwait, 40, 41, 50, 59, 69n, 82, 171; his relations and meetings with ibn Sa'ud, 36, 39, 44–5, 46, 47–8, 49, 53, 61–2, 83, 84–6, 87; and report on developments in Arabia (1914), 64–5; death of, 81, 86–7, 119n, 120n

Shakir, Amir, 133–4, 135
Shammar, 103–4, 105, 135, 136, 138, 154n, 168, 169, 174, 175, 202
Sharif of Mecca *see* Husain ibn 'Ali; Muhammad ibn 'Aun
Shatt al-Arab, 8, 42, 80
Shawkat 'Ali, 217
Shuckburgh, 116–17, 141
Slavery, slave trade, 1, 5, 46
Smuggling, 102, 123n
Somme, battle of the, 91
Standard Oil Co. of California, 240, 241
Storrs, Sir Ronald, 112; Mission to ibn Sa'ud of, 107, 108, 109–10, 111; appointed Governor of Jerusalem, 111
Subaihiya: Turco-Sa'udi meeting at (1914), 60–2
Subsidies, British, 150, 151, 157–8n, 159–67, 183n, 193–4, 216
Sudan, British officials in, 76–7, 78
Suez Canal, 79; British wartime control of, 75, 76
Sulaiman Shafiq Pasha, Vali of Basra, 43
Sur: Wahhabi raid on (1865), 17, 18
Sykes, Sir Mark, 101, 106
Sykes-Picot Agreement, 73, 78, 91, 95, 190
Syria, 77, 99, 100, 147, 155n, 157n, 161, 164, 190; Arab nationalism in, 128, 146, 147, 151; Faisal proclaimed king of, 142, 222; and British support for Faisal, 147

Taif, 142, 144, 148, 177, 211; Wahhabi capture of (1924), 218, 219
Talaat Pasha, Turkish Grand Pasha, 56, 57
Taqi al-Din Ahmad ibn Taimiya, 13

INDEX 285

Thomas, J. H., Colonial Secretary, 210
Toynbee, Arnold, 191, 222, 231n
Trans-Arabian railway (Haifa-Baghdad), British interest in building, 190
Transjordan, 159, 179, 180, 182, 189; 'Abdullah proclaimed king of, 167; disputes over Jauf and Wadi Sirhan between Sa'udis and, 190–6, 211n, 212n; Wahhabi defeat at Umm (1922), 192; Kuwait Conference, 196, 198–201, 205–8; Najd-Hedjaz war and, 216, 217–18, 219, 220; Ikhwan raids in, 192, 194, 195, 231n; 'Aqaba and Ma'an incorporated into, 221, 222–7; Clayton's negotiations with ibn Sa'ud over frontiers, 227–8; and Hadda Agreement (1925), 228–9
Treaty of Jedda (1927), 236, 237
Treaty of Lausanne, 189
Treaty of Mohammera (1922), 169, 175–6, 199, 201, 207, 237; repudiated by ibn Sa'ud, 178–9
Treaty of Peace in Perpetuity (1853), 15
Treaty of Sèvres, 127
Treaty of Taif (1934), 239
Trenchard, Sir Hugh, 167
Trevor, Political Agent at Bahrain, 53–4, 56, 199, 200; appointed Political Resident in Persian Gulf (1923), 196
Triple Entente (England, France and Russia), 42
Tripoli (Libya): invaded by Italy (1911), 34, 42, 118n
Trucial Coast (Pirate Coast), xiv–xv, xix, 2, 7, 14–15, 55
Trucial Shaikhdoms, 2, 7, 9, 16, 17, 23, 28n, 82, 163, 236
Turaba dispute, xx, 117, 127, 142–3, 144, 145, 146, 147, 151, 201, 207
Turkey, Turks (Ottoman Empire), xiv, 1, 17, 19, 163, 164, 222; Baghdad Railway scheme, xix, 5, 6, 8, 9–11, 12, 42, 43; Russians seek concession to build railway from Tripoli to Kuwait, 5–6; rise of German influence in, 7; activities in Kuwait and Hasa-Qatar area, 7–8; Young Turk revolution, and counter-revolution, 12, 34, 37; Bulgaria declares independence from, 12, 34; and Bosnia-Herzegovina annexed by Austria, 12, 34; Hasa captured by, 18; Rashidi alliance with, 18, 19–20, 21, 22; expansionism in Arabia of, 18–19; Kuwait threatened by, 19–20; ibn Sa'ud appointed *qaimaqam* of Najd by, 22; German relations with, 25; decline of empire, 34–5; and Balkan Wars, 35, 42, 45; Arab relations with, 37, 38, 40, 43–65 *passim*; rail line to Medina of, 40; ibn Sa'ud seizes Hasa and Qatif, 43–5; British relations with (1910–14), 34, 35, 36–7, 40–1, 42, 44–65; Husain's relations with, 38, 76; Anglo-Turkish Convention (1914), 42–3, 45, 70n; ibn Sa'ud seeks expulsion from Qatar of, 51–2; 'Blue Line' as demarcation of territories in eastern Arabia of, 52, 70n, 71–2n; talks with ibn Sa'ud proposed by, 58; Treaty with ibn Sa'ud (1914), 60–2, 83, 248–9; war declared between Britain and, 65, 118n; partition of Empire, 73; British wartime relations with, 73, 75–6, 77, 78–80, 85, 116, 134; Indian sympathy for, 74; Sultan's proclamation of *jihad*, 76; wartime relations with Arabs, 78, 82, 102–3; Kut al Amara captured by, 79, 91; Sa'udi wartime relations with, 83, 84–5, 87, 94; and blockade of supplies to, 102–3, 111; garrison besieged in Medina, 102–3, 134; Treaty of Sèvres imposed upon, 127;

Turkey, Turks—*contd.*
  Anglo-French Declaration (1918), 138; Chanak crisis (1922), 179; Treaty of Lausanne, 189; Caliphate abolished by (1924), 209, 211, 216, 217
Turki (ibn Sa'ud's eldest son), 103
Twitchell, Karl S., 240

Umm, Transjordan: Ikhwani defeat at (1922), 192
Umm al Qurun: Clayton-ibn Sa'ud negotiations at (1924), 227–30
'Uqair, 44, 53, 61, 172, 181; meeting between ibn Sa'ud and Cox (1916), 99; Conference (1921), 130; Conference (1922: signing of Protocols at), 159, 179–82, 197, 202, 204, 230, 237, 240; Cox-ibn Sa'ud meeting (1920), 172–3

Van Der Meulen, D., 124n
Versailles Peace Conference, 127, 128, 140
Vickery, Col., 147, 150
Von Stemrich, German Consul-General in Constantinople, 9

Wadi Sirhan, 217, 223, 229; dispute over, 189, 193–6, 201; and Kuwait Conference, 205, 206, 208
Wahhabism, Wahhabis, xiv, xv, xix, xxn, 7; rise of, 13–14; and British relations in 19th century with, 14–25; Ikhwan movement, 111, 112, 115, 116, 128–30; and Khurma dispute, 111, 130–41, 142, 143, 145, 146, 151; and Turaba dispute, 142–4, 145, 146, 147, 151; defection of Husain supporters to, 143; defeated at Umm, 192; Qaf attacked by, 194; invasion of Hedjaz by, 216–31; and fall of Mecca, 220; and siege of Jedda by, 221; and fall of Medina to, 230; *see also* Sa'udis

Warner, Sir W. Lee, 40
William II, Kaiser of Germany, 4
Wilson, Sir A. T., xix, 23, 36, 100, 109, 117, 119n, 126n, 135, 136, 138, 139, 140–1, 147, 148, 150, 157n, 162, 163, 167, 168, 172, 184n
Wilson, Col. C. E., British Agent at Jedda, 106, 112–13, 124n, 132, 133, 145, 147
Wingate, Sir Reginald, 78, 106, 109–10, 112–13, 114, 116, 133, 134, 137, 138, 141
Witte, Count, Russian Finance Minister, 9
World War I, xv, xvi, xix, 6, 35, 243; war declared between Britain and Turkey, 65; Anglo-Sa'udi relations during, 73–126; Gallipoli Campaign, 73, 79, 91; Turkish capture of Kut al Amara, 79; Indian Expeditionary Force sent to Mesopotamia, 80; Sa'udi role in (1916–18), 91–9; Turkish garrison besieged in Medina, 102–3, 134; Baghdad captured by British, 104, 106, 108; and fall of 'Aqaba, 108; Jerusalem captured, 108, 111; blockade of enemy supplies, 91, 102–3, 111; Treaty of Sèvres imposed on Turkey, 127; Anglo-French Declaration (1918), 138; fall of Damascus, 138; and fall of Medina, 140; Versailles Peace Conference, 127, 128, 140; and Treaty of Lausanne, 189
Wratislaw, British Consul in Basra, 9

Yahya, Imam (of Yemen), 239
Yanbu', 220; surrenders to ibn Sa'ud, 230–1
Yemen: Imam declares for Turks in First World War, 79; war with Najd, 239–40; and Treaty of Taif, 239
Young, Hubert, 165, 184n

Young Turk Revolution (1908), 12, 34, 37, 74, 77
Ypres, battle of, 91
Yusif Yasin, Sa'udi Minister of State, 237

Zaid (Faisal's brother), 176, 207, 208
Zakat (arms tax), 16
Zionists, 73, 119n
Zuhaff (Turkish warship), 10, 20